# Corruption in Comme Enterprise

C000128908

This edited collection analyses, from multiple disciplinary perspectives, the issue of corruption in commercial enterprise across different sectors and jurisdictions. Corruption is commonly recognised as a major 'social bad', and is seriously harmful to society, in terms of the functioning and legitimacy of political-economic systems, and the day-to-day lives of individuals.

There is nothing novel about bribes in brown envelopes and dubious backroom deals, ostensibly to grease the wheels of business. Corrupt practices like these go to the very heart of illicit transacting in both legal markets – such as kickbacks to facilitate contracts in international commerce – and illegal markets – such as payoffs to public officials to turn a blind eye to cross-border smuggling. Aside from the apparent pervasiveness and longevity of corruption in commercial enterprise, there is now renewed policy and operational attention on the phenomenon, prompting and meriting deeper analysis.

Corruption in commercial enterprise, encompassing behaviours often associated with corporate and white-collar crime, and corruption in criminal commercial enterprise, where we see corruption central to organised crime activities, are major public policy issues. This collection gives us insight into their nature, organisation and governance, and how to respond most appropriately and effectively.

**Liz Campbell** is Professor of Criminal Law at Durham University. Her research is socio-legal, and currently is focused on responses to corruption, organised and organisational crime; and the presumption of innocence. She is interested in the interfaces between criminal law and regulation and between criminal and legal behaviour, and the politics of criminal law definitions. Her research has been funded by Research Council UK's Partnership for Conflict, Crime and Security; Arts and Humanities Research Council; Law Foundation of New Zealand; Fulbright Commission; Modern Law Review; and Carnegie Trust.

**Nicholas Lord** is a Reader in Criminology at the University of Manchester. Nicholas has research expertise in white-collar, financial and organised crimes, and their regulation and control. He is currently undertaking funded research into the misuse of corporate vehicles in the concealment of illicit finances (PaCCS), the nature and governance of domestic bribery (British Academy), the counterfeit alcohols (Alcohol Research UK), the finances of modern slavery (N8) and to undertake a Global White-Collar Crime Survey (White & Case LLP). His book *Regulating Corporate Bribery in International Business* (2014, Routledge) was the winner of the British Society of Criminology Book Prize 2015.

# Corruption in Commercial Enterprise

Law, Theory and Practice

**Edited by**
**Liz Campbell and Nicholas Lord**

Routledge
Taylor & Francis Group

LONDON AND NEW YORK

First published 2018
by Routledge

2 Park Square, Milton Park, Abingdon, Oxfordshire OX14 4RN
52 Vanderbilt Avenue, New York, NY 10017

*Routledge is an imprint of the Taylor & Francis Group, an informa business*

First issued in paperback 2019

*British Library Cataloguing in Publication Data*
A catalogue record for this book is available from the British Library

*Library of Congress Cataloging in Publication Data*
Names: Campbell, Liz, author. | Lord, Nicholas, author.
Title: Corruption in commercial enterprise: law, theory, and practice / Liz
    Campbell, Nicholas Lord.
Description: Abingdon, Oxon [UK]; New York, NY : Routledge, 2018. |
    Includes bibliographical references and index.
Identifiers: LCCN 2017054010| ISBN 9781138063341 (hbk) | ISBN
    9781351602228 (web pdf) | ISBN 9781351602211 (epub) | ISBN
    9781351602204 (mobipocket)
Subjects: LCSH: Business enterprises—Law and legislation—Corrupt
    practices. | Corporations—Corrupt practices. | Corporations—Corrupt
    practices—Prevention.
Classification: LCC K5216 .C36 2018 | DDC 345/.0268—dc23
LC record available at https://lccn.loc.gov/2017054010

ISBN: 978-1-138-06334-1 (hbk)
ISBN: 978-0-367-89390-3 (pbk)

Typeset in Galliard
by Swales & Willis Ltd, Exeter, Devon, UK

# Contents

# Notes on contributors

**Jay S. Albanese** is a Professor in the Wilder School of Government & Public Affairs at Virginia Commonwealth University (USA). He received his PhD from the School of Criminal Justice at Rutgers University, and served as Chief of the International Center at the National Institute of Justice. Dr. Albanese has conducted research and published work on organised crime, transnational crime, corruption, human trafficking, white collar crime and ethics. He is a past president and fellow of the Academy of Criminal Justice Sciences, and Executive Board member of the American Society of Criminology.

**David BaMaung**, Honorary Professor at Glasgow Caledonian University, has worked in law enforcement for 38 years, with 12 of these specifically relating to the area of counter terrorism protective security. During this time, one of his key interests has been the topic of insider threat and how it can be mitigated against, and he has been responsible for developing insider threat exercising programmes for law enforcement and other infrastructure areas. David has been involved in a number of academic research projects in relation to insider threat, including a project with CPNI to develop an educational programme for the HR community on insider threat awareness. Along with his co-author, he is currently engaged in research with Coventry University concerning organisational culture, corruption and its motivations.

**Maurizio Bellacosa** graduated in Law in 1989 at LUISS University in Rome, where he is now Professor of Criminal Law, European Criminal Law and Environmental Criminal Law. He is the author of two monographs – on crimes of unfaithful management of companies (2006) and on ministerial crime (2012) – of four encyclopedia entries and of other publications, in particular on issues regarding corporate criminal law. He has been a lawyer and partner since its inception of the law firm Severino-Penalisti Associati, founded by Prof. Paola Severino. He is a Judge on the Anti-Doping Tribunal of Nado Italia.

**Rose Broad** is a Lecturer in Criminology at the University of Manchester. Her doctoral research considered criminal justice constructions of people convicted for human trafficking offences. Rose has since undertaken further research in the area of human trafficking including work with law enforcement in relation to the prosecution pipeline and into the financial aspects of human trafficking. Rose is also involved in work that considers the wider policy frameworks for human trafficking and modern slavery and the widening of the criteria for those held responsible for these exploitative activities, including corporations.

**Liz Campbell** is Professor of Criminal Law at Durham University. Her research is socio-legal, and currently is focused on responses to corruption, organised and organisational crime; and the presumption of innocence. She is interested in the interfaces between criminal law and regulation and between criminal and legal behaviour, and the politics of criminal law definitions. Her research has been funded by Research Council UK's Partnership for Conflict, Crime and Security; Arts and Humanities Research Council; Law Foundation of New Zealand; Fulbright Commission; Modern Law Review; and Carnegie Trust.

**John Cuddihy**, as a former senior police officer responsible for managing and mitigating threats within high risk environments, considered 'insider threat' to be an enabler by those many threat actors who operated nationally and transnationally. Indeed, he was the strategic lead for insider threat within his then Force, Strathclyde Police and thereafter within Police Scotland, developing and implementing strategies, with a focus on organisational behaviour and how this could influence the security culture. His work in this area has continued as Visiting Professor, Coventry University, and as a consultant to public, private, academic and third sector organisations within the United Kingdom and overseas.

**Calum Darling** is a solicitor and former prosecutor, specialising in the investigation and prosecution of corruption, economic crime and terrorism offences. Previously a Procurator Fiscal Depute in the Crown Office in Scotland, he lives and works in London.

**Adriaan Denkers** operates as an independent scientific researcher and consultant for government agencies. Adriaan studied social psychology and received his PhD based on research on the psychological aftermath of crime victimisation. He worked as a scientific researcher for the Dutch government (Social and Cultural Planning Bureau, the Tax Administration, Customs and Excise, Fiscal Intelligence and Investigations agency) and as an Assistant and Associate Professor in the Departments of Social Psychology and Penal Law and Criminology at the Vrije Universiteit, Amsterdam. His research interests include positive and negative (organisational) deviance, individual differences, organisational culture and climate, law enforcement and regulation.

**Alan Doig** is currently Visiting Professor, Newcastle Business School, Northumbria University; previously he was Professor of Public Services Management at Liverpool and Teesside Business Schools where he devised and led the first MA in Fraud Management. He has led anti-corruption projects in a number of countries, from Egypt to Lithuania; he has also been the Council of Europe's full-time Resident Advisor in Turkey for the public ethics and prevention of corruption project and the UNODC UNCAC mentor to Thailand. He has published extensively on corruption, fraud and public ethics.

**Mark Findlay** is a Professor in the Law School, Singapore Management University. He has held chairs in Sydney, Leeds, Nottingham, the South Pacific, and Hong Kong. His current areas of research are law and regulation, and international and comparative criminal justice. In a research career that has seen the publication of 26 monographs and over 150 journal articles and book chapters, Mark has advised UN agencies and international organisations on corruption prevention and control. His work on crime and globalisation focuses on corruption in transitional cultures.

**Liliya Gelemerova** is an Honorary Senior Lecturer at the University of Manchester, a member of the Steering Committee of Finance against Trafficking and a Senior Financial Crime Advisor at an international bank in London. Formerly Head of International Contacts and Legal Coordination at Bulgaria's Financial Intelligence Unit, Liliya has a background in financial intelligence that includes many years of training in anti-money laundering practices. Having gained experience with Transparency International, Berlin, Liliya moved to London where she worked for several investigative consultancy firms, managing a wide range of due diligence and financial crime investigation projects for corporations, financial institutions and law firms. Liliya defended her PhD in global anti-money laundering policies at Tilburg University, the Netherlands, in 2011.

**Jackie Harvey** is Professor of Financial Management and Director of Business Research at Newcastle Business School. Her research is focused in the area of criminal financial management, in particular money laundering. Early outputs considered costs and benefits of regulatory compliance before moving on to evaluate the effectiveness of the Anti-Money Laundering Framework. Jackie has been invited to speak at a number of very high profile academic and practitioner conferences in both the UK and Europe. She is on the Editorial Board for the European Cross-Border Crime Colloquium that brings together researchers from across Europe. Her main teaching interests focus on risk and investment management together with financial market regulation. Prior to becoming an academic, Jackie, whose PhD is in Taxation Policy, spent ten years working for a major merchant bank, followed by a three-year posting as fiscal policy adviser (under the auspices of the British Government) to the Ministry of Finance in Belize.

**Aleksandra Jordanoska** is Lecturer at the School of Law, the University of Manchester. She has research expertise in regulatory enforcement and misconduct in financial markets, and broader interests in regulation theory and financial technology. Aleksandra has published papers on complex fraud, financial crime and arts in prisons, and is co-author, together with David Friedrichs and Isabel Schultz, of *Key Thinkers in Criminology: Edwin Sutherland* (Routledge, 2017). She completed her PhD in Law and Criminology at the School of Law, Queen Mary University of London, and her MPhil in Criminology at the Institute of Criminology, Cambridge University.

**Colin King** is Reader in Law at the University of Sussex and co-Founder of the Crime Research Centre. He was an Academic Fellow at the Honourable Society of the Inner Temple from 2014–2017. In March 2016 Colin gave oral evidence at the Home Affairs Select Committee Inquiry into the Proceeds of Crime Act. He is co-author of a forthcoming monograph on *Negotiated Justice and Corporate Crime* (King and Lord, Palgrave). Colin is co-editor of *The Handbook of Criminal and Terrorism Financing Law* (King, Walker, and Gurulé, Palgrave, 2018) and *Dirty Assets: Emerging Issues in the Regulation of Criminal and Terrorist Assets* (King and Walker, Ashgate, 2014). He is currently conducting empirical research on proceeds of crime legislation as part of an AHRC Leadership Fellowship.

**Nicholas Lord** is a Reader in Criminology at the University of Manchester. Nicholas has research expertise in white-collar, financial and organised crimes, and their regulation and control. He is currently undertaking funded research into the misuse of corporate vehicles in the concealment of illicit finances (PaCCS), the nature and governance of domestic bribery (British Academy), the counterfeit alcohols (Alcohol Research UK), the finances of modern slavery (N8) and to undertake a Global White-Collar Crime Survey (White & Case LLP). His book *Regulating Corporate Bribery in International Business* (Routledge, 2014) was the winner of the British Society of Criminology Book Prize 2015.

**Anna Markovska** is a Senior Lecturer in Criminology at the Department of Humanities and Social Sciences, Anglia Ruskin University. She has written and researched widely on issues of corruption, organised crime and prohibition in Ukraine, and completed a British Academy sponsored project on migrant workers and policing. She is currently undertaking research into the practicalities of policing modern day slavery.

**Kenneth Murray** is a Chartered Accountant and forensic accounting professional with extensive investigative and reporting experience. His expertise is underpinned by extensive professional experience in business and finance gained in his early career, which covered the areas of audit, capital markets, corporate finance and venture capital. He has extensive experience of the investigation of economic crime as well as the presentation of evidence in high profile cases as a professional witness to court. He has also provided strategic advice throughout his career and is the author of a number of papers on economic crime published in the academic press.

**Petrus C. van Duyne**, psychologist and jurist, carried out research at the Dutch Ministry of Justice and as Professor until 2011 at Tilburg University, the Netherlands. At present he is visiting Professor at Northumbria University and Utrecht University. He researched decision making by Public Prosecutors and judges after which he undertook research on fraud, economic and organised crime in the Netherlands and surrounding countries, and participated in organised crime projects in the Western Balkans. He has researched money laundering and corruption in Serbia. He followed the unfolding anti-laundering policy critically and published extensively on this subject. Since 1999 he has organised Cross-border Crime Colloquiums.

# Acknowledgements

This book is one of the major outputs of our research network on 'Corruption in (Non-)Criminal Commercial Enterprise', funded by the Arts and Humanities Research Council. We are very grateful to the Council for its support, as well as to the University of Edinburgh, the University of Manchester, and Durham University.

We have benefited greatly from the contributions and expertise of various colleagues in refining our thoughts on the issues and in creating and fostering the research network. Special thanks are due to Michael Levi, Karin van Wingerde, Colin King, Lindsey Miller, John Paterson, Daniel Carr, Rose Broad, David Gadd, Veronica Ruiz Abou-Nigm, Burkhard Schafer, Sharon Cowan, Gerry Maher, Chloë Kennedy, Andrew Cornford and Niamh Nic Shuibhne, who helped in the development of our initial funding application, and provided valuable insights, input and support throughout the network and beyond.

We would like to thank all those involved in the different events of the network: the speakers, chairs, discussants and participants in the workshops who shared their expertise and time so generously. The success of the final public roundtable in particular hinged on the contributions from Sue Hawley (Corruption Watch), Kristin Jones (Crown Prosecution Service) and Michael Levi (Cardiff University). We are grateful for the assistance of Sina Mühling, Lisa Kendall, Alison Stirling, Lesley Dobson, Georgia Salpingidou and Julie Platten in organising the events.

# Corruption in commercial enterprise
## An introduction

*Liz Campbell and Nicholas Lord*

## Corruption: a concept, conception and method

This edited collection analyses the issue of corruption in commercial enterprise across different sectors and jurisdictions, and from multiple disciplinary perspectives. Of course, there is nothing novel about bribes in brown envelopes and dubious backroom deals, ostensibly to grease the wheels of business. And corrupt practices like these, and more, go to the very heart of illicit transacting in both legal markets, such as kickbacks to facilitate contracts in international commerce, and in illegal markets, such as payoffs to public officials to turn a blind eye to cross-border smuggling. Aside from the apparent pervasiveness and longevity of corruption in commercial enterprise, now there is renewed policy and operational attention on the phenomenon, prompting and meriting deeper analysis here.

At the core of this collection is the elusory and contested concept of corruption. The term is used to denote a diverse array of behaviours, human characteristics, states of being and conditions, across varied social contexts, and sometimes is employed without sufficient care or reflection. Moreover, myriad legitimate and illegitimate actors can be implicated or involved in corruption, such as business people and public officials as well as criminal actors and organised crime networks, with varied motivations and intentionality. They may or may not recognise the harmful, unethical or immoral nature of their 'corrupt' behaviours and relations, depending on their historical/cultural traditions and mores. Though this illustrates that corruption is not a singular construct deployed for particular ends only, nevertheless 'it' is portrayed as a global and inherent 'bad' in the influential, mainstream discourse of anti-corruption non-governmental and intergovernmental organisations such as the United Nations or Transparency International.

The orthodox conceptualisation of corruption is 'the abuse of entrusted power for private gain' (Transparency International, 2017) or 'the abuse of public office for private gain' (World Bank, 1997: 8). Yet these narratives, while recognising central inherent characteristics such as an abuse of power or that function usually for some form of private gain, common across all 'corrupt' behaviours, are ill-defined. They incorporate a set of behaviours that are qualitatively different, and, as such, include bribery and embezzlement alongside nepotism and patronage. One could argue that there are benefits to a wider definition of corruption, insofar as it serves a useful rhetorical purpose by communicating to the public about dubious and harmful behaviours, whether in politics or business and beyond. We suggest that such an expansive approach is not useful for scientific and analytical purposes, where defined parameters are required. Though a broad definition can help to maximise the impact of the 'anti-corruption movement', for empirical (and other) types of analysis it is crucial to understand and define the core behaviours more precisely. Furthermore, the prevailing understandings of corruption often do not appreciate the complex 'situated production' of corrupt transactions. That is, the individualising and de-contextualising of these behaviours shifts attention away from organisational, structural and cultural conditions in which corruption occurs and is sustained, from the nature of the illicit relations between cooperating legitimate and illegitimate actors, and from the interdependencies of licit and illicit markets and systems. Therein lie the dangers of the conventional and dominant interpretations of corruption.

In addition, academics have sought to frame the narrative and their subsequent scholarly focus broadly to include a vast array of public and private behaviours (see Whyte, 2015) with corruption being defined as 'the distortion and subversion of the public realm in the service of private interests' (Beetham, 2015: 41). Consequently, corruption is used to represent an array of legally and socially unacceptable behaviours, such as multi-million-pound bribes in the context of legitimate international business, misconduct by politicians (e.g. the MP expenses scandal) or public officials (e.g. police cover ups such as Hillsborough) on the one hand, and varying forms of abuse of function, such as cronyism, and conflicts of interest on the other. Depending on one's theoretical leanings, what is corrupt in a given setting could centre on public opinion, public office or public interest. As a result, the term has become so inclusive that its logical consistency and scope diminishes, and in turn it loses analytical significance, with its ambiguity creating a nebulous framework covering an admixture of domestic and global 'social bads'. Thus, while there are defensible alternative conceptions of corruption, importantly each derives from and enables distinct analytical or moral ends. These differences need to be recognised and parsed.

Despite the diversity of meanings of corruption, it has been argued that bribery is the predominant form of corruption (Lord and Doig, 2013). If we 'de-moralise' the concept of bribery by moving away from judgments as to ethics or morality, and instead focus on the purpose, means and ends of improper payment, then we can see that in their most basic form such illicit transactions are a method of obtaining or inducing a desired outcome as part of a relationship of exchange. By focusing on exchange between actors rather than moral judgment or blame, we recognise that such transfers of power or money seek to sidestep legally prescribed procedures to regulate the relation (Deflem, 1995: 243), and in this inheres an abuse or misuse of otherwise 'normal' relationships (Doig, 2006: 116). With this in mind, many of the contributions in this collection focus on those behaviours that involve illicit (financial) transactions, particularly bribery, to obtain some form of influence or advantage. Indeed, we argue that those other behaviours that some people might call 'corrupt' are better conceptualised in other ways. For instance, police cover-ups are better conceptualised (and in fact pursued in the courts) as police misconduct, and appropriation of public funds through politicians' expense claims is better thought of as embezzlement or fraud (see Campbell, 2016b).

Beyond such theoretical and practical understandings, corruption is a legal conception also, with different meanings and manifestations in the national and international spheres. It is the eponymous and animating idea of the United Nations Convention against Corruption, and is alluded to in the Preamble to the United Nations Convention against Transnational Organised Crime. Crucially, however, what is corrupt is not necessarily a crime, and conceiving of crime of a certain gravity or sophistication as *de facto* corruption is mistaken. Indeed, in the domestic UK sense, corruption is narrow and ill-defined, and does not constitute a standalone criminal offence (Campbell, 2016a: 122).

## Corruption, organised crime and commercial enterprise

Corruption in commercial enterprise, whether in purportedly legal commerce or otherwise, can bring benefit to those involved through guaranteeing or expediting the resolution of business deals, and through unjustly preferring and rewarding certain parties. It involves and brings into sharp relief the critical interdependencies between organised crime and corruption, and the porous boundaries between legal and illegal markets. Corruption and organised crime have been identified as two priority issues by the UK government and also are high on the agenda of other sovereign states and intergovernmental bodies such as the European Union and United Nations. Consequently, we see convergence towards certain understandings of these problems and the accompanying harmonisation of legal frameworks and operational policy responses. However, as outlined earlier, the core concepts of 'corruption' and 'organised crime' remain problematic in their definitional ambiguities. The dominant popular interpretations of 'organised crime' justify a political and policy framing of 'it' as highly organised, Mafia-type external threats, rather than in terms of criminal networks and criminal cooperation produced under particular social and geohistorical conditions. This, thereby, provides opportunities and justifications for governments and law enforcement authorities to increase resources, improve international cooperation, and so on, to 'fight' such threats (which nevertheless remain elusive) (see Edwards and Levi, 2008). But such popular constructions are analytically weak. Moreover, their transposition into law has led to overly expansive and questionable provisions (Campbell, 2016a).

This collection attends to this issue in advocating the reframing of both 'organised crime' and 'corruption' in terms of the 'organisation of serious crimes' whereby analytical focus is placed on criminal (e.g. the 'routine/daily' activities and crime commission process) and social organisation (e.g. social/ criminal networks and relations) rather than the singular, abstract and discrete concepts of 'corruption' and 'organised crime' themselves (see Edwards and Levi, 2008). This provides a framework for analysing the interdependencies and intersections of both corruption and organised crime and shifts attention away from traditional policy approaches and the academic literature that has tended to treat the issues as distinct and discrete. More specifically, this collection shifts the focus to the organisation of serious crime activities in the context of licit commerce, aiming to explore how corruption is used as a tool of otherwise legitimate business; how organised criminal networks use corruption to permeate and maintain legitimate business interests; and the extent to which the two are interdependent and intersect.

Corrupt relations and practices are 'organised', but the extent to which this is so varies, as does the necessity of the interdependence between criminal and non-criminal enterprise. The level of organisation and interdependency reflects the ease with which willing offenders are able to find co-offenders to carry out offences (including the 'enablers' and 'facilitators' of these crimes such as lawyers, accountants, etc.) and the ease with which the necessary elements of the crime commission process can be carried out (e.g. identifying bribe receivers and paying them) (see Levi, 2008). With this in mind, many contributions to this collection examine the corrupt activities of legitimate businesses, controlled by legitimate actors, as well as the corrupt activities of ostensibly legitimate businesses that are controlled by illegitimate/criminal actors, as well as their intersection. They explore the nature of corrupt relations, practices and processes in particular situations and how these are shaped by various antecedent influences such as political and historical context and existing social networks. In doing so, this collection adopts a multi-disciplinary and jurisdictionally comparative approach, involving chapters from international academics and practitioners in the fields of law, criminology, sociology and political science.

## Research network on 'Corruption in (Non-)Criminal Commercial Enterprise'

This edited collection stems from our research network on 'Corruption in (Non-) Criminal Commercial Enterprise', funded by the Arts and Humanities Research Council (2015–17). The network activities involved a series of workshops and a public lecture, examining the organisation of corruption in commercial enterprise, vulnerabilities to this, and how to develop suitable legal and other responses. For the first time, this network facilitated discussion between key parties on detecting such criminality, appraising existing preventive and reactive measures, and developing rigorous and critical academic research that is informed by evidence, experience and practice.

Three workshops and a public roundtable brought into dialogue informed actors from the policy, practitioner and academic communities to explore corruption and bribery in a variety of contexts. The workshops on corruption in criminal commercial enterprise, corruption in non-criminal commercial enterprise and corruption at the intersections, respectively, were held in Edinburgh,

Manchester and Brussels so as to ensure cross-jurisdictional involvement. Participants included law enforcement (National Crime Agency, Police Scotland, Europol), prosecution agencies (Serious Fraud Office, Crown Office and Procurator Fiscal Service), the Scottish Government, non-governmental anti-corruption organisation Corruption Watch, private sector firms and institutions, and academics from various universities.

Common themes to emerge from the events included the contestability of definitions, growing and distinct vulnerabilities, and the need for novel and unorthodox responses. Throughout we noted the interweaving of criminal and non-criminal commercial enterprise, and the symbiotic relationship between licit and illicit enterprise. Debate centred around key questions: who are the offenders and how can we explain and better understand their behaviours? In what ways do organisational structures and cultures as well as third-party professional actors facilitate or encourage corruption in business? Do we need to reconsider what punishment 'looks like' or involves, and how should this be communicated to affected stakeholders to ensure 'justice'?

## Book outline

This edited collection is divided into three parts, looking at the *organisation* of corruption in commercial enterprise, *vulnerabilities* to this, and *responses*.

Part I explores the organisation of corruption in commercial enterprise, examining how, why and under which conditions corruption in commercial enterprise develops and occurs. These chapters contribute to the development of a more nuanced and grounded understanding of corruption, and elucidate the interplay between corruption and legitimate and illegitimate markets.

Mark Findlay draws on and develops his extensive corpus of academic research to posit that corruption is understood best as a business relationship, rather than as a matter of morality or governance. In so doing he explores the nexus between corruption and enterprise by examining corruption and transitional market cultures in particular. He considers the transparency 'paradigm' in corruption control and posits the market model as a more effective control foundation. The intersection of corruption and organised crime forms the core of Jay Albanese's analysis, exposing the relationship between these forms of criminality. He presents an empirical hierarchy of corrupt conduct, based on a large range of case files from the United States over a three-year period. He distinguishes tipping points where a legitimate entity such as a business or government agency shifts from exploiting a system through low-level bribery to operating like a criminal enterprise with organised schemes involving the solicitation of bribes. Kenneth Murray considers the corruptive influence of criminal money on legitimate markets, with particular reference to organised crime in Scotland. He draws on academic literature and case studies to ascertain the extent to which the supply processes and money management processes used by organised crime groups represent an efficient and resilient mechanism to enable the accumulation and distribution of significant amounts of criminal capital within the legitimate economy.

Rose Broad and Nicholas Lord shed light on how and why corruption facilitates the trafficking of humans into both licit and illicit markets in the UK. Though corruption is a potential facilitator of human trafficking and a necessary cost in traffickers' activities, UK policy and anti-trafficking initiatives have not examined this to any significant extent. The issue of transparency addressed by Mark Findlay is explored further by Liz Campbell, who suggests that corruption in commercial enterprise often is enabled and enhanced by the use of legal structures like companies, trusts and partnerships to conceal the 'beneficial ownership' of assets. Features of corporate opacity help to generate, conceal and maintain the resources necessary for many corrupt relations and actions. This has prompted various legislative responses which seek to improve transparency, but questions remain about these laws' likely effectiveness, as well as their implications for human rights.

Part II centres on vulnerabilities to corruption in commercial enterprise, be that personal, cultural, structural or systemic weaknesses and threats. The chapters explore how to detect and categorise such vulnerabilities, as well as isolating critical intervention points in the organisation of corruption.

David BaMaung and John Cuddihy investigate the exploitation of human vulnerabilities in corrupt practices, and examine how to expose and react to this. Their perspective, drawing on significant operational and strategic policing experience, centres on people and culture, and seeks to manage and mitigate the threat posed by those involved in corrupt practices. Adriaan Denkers adopts a distinctive methodology in his study of the causal influence of organisational anti-corruption measures and bonuses on corruption in the Netherlands. While it seems that prevention and detection measures and employee training do not substantially contribute to explaining corruption in organisations, his results show a robust impact of bonuses on corruption, implying that corruption in Dutch organisations might be, at least partly, a consequence of incentive schemes. The particular vulnerabilities of the energy sector are interrogated by Anna Markovska and Petrus van Duyne in their conceptualisation of corporate criminality. They examine the role of culture and political context and influence in corruption and corporate criminality with specific reference to the gas industry in Ukraine.

Part III surveys the various responses that are and could be deployed in respect of corruption in commercial enterprise. The chapters analyse the mixes of legal and extra-legal mechanisms and structures that can be developed to inform the responses of both state and non-state regulators and interveners. Some of these responses relate to policing through conventional public means, whereas other mechanisms necessitate a reliance on financial regulation and the responsibilisation of private actors.

Aleksandra Jordanoska studies how corruption in the City of London is policed through the regulatory regime of the Financial Conduct Authority, the UK's business financial regulator. She draws on regulatory scholarship to make sense of how public agencies carve out their supervisory remit with respect to the oversight of bribery in industries, as well as the role and resources employed by the regulated entities in this process. Liliya Gelemerova, Jackie Harvey and Petrus van Duyne focus on the assessment of corruption risk by banks. They critique legislation and regulators' deficient guidance, how banks approach risk and review the challenges banks face in the context of UK and US anti-corruption and related anti-money laundering legislation, purportedly introduced to help the finance industry fight corruption and other criminality. In terms of substantive legal responses, Calum Darling explores the trend towards requiring persons in certain positions or relationships to report knowledge or suspicions of crime. This duty to report crime is applicable to professionals who facilitate corruption; he suggests it is valuable in creating a hostile legal context for facilitators of corporate bribery or the laundering of the proceeds of corruption. A comparative approach is adopted by Maurizio Bellacosa in analysing the Italian legal framework on the fight against corruption. He considers the repressive and preventive dimensions of the Italian system, analysing substantive crimes of corruption in the public and private sectors as well as corporate criminal liability and the National Anti-Corruption Plan. Though policy transfer and international law are influential here, he also reminds us of the significance of national tradition and legal originality. Two chapters look especially at responses that are not predicated or contingent on criminal prosecution and conviction, namely the use of deferred prosecution agreements and mechanisms targeting assets such as civil recovery, financial sanctions and reparation. These legal responses can be adopted after charge and/or conviction for bribery and related offences. Nicholas Lord and Colin King identify a strategic preference on the part of the British state for negotiation, rather than contention, in responding to corruption and bribery. They explore this negotiation of non-contention, seeking to understand its nature and purpose, by detailing the use of two non-prosecution based approaches, civil recovery and deferred prosecution agreements (DPAs). They rightly question whether negotiated non-contention is emerging as the new accommodation of corporate bribery. Alan Doig picks up this theme in broader comparative context, noting the increasing use of pre-prosecution settlements and DPAs in various jurisdictions for corporate entities involved in bribery. Despite the financial aspects of many such settlements where overseas bribery is involved, only limited funds have been dedicated for anti-corruption purposes through a number of *ad hoc* arrangements. He analyses the possible development of an agreed process for the use of any recovered funds for anti-corruption work, considering how to ensure that the funds would be put to the best use.

## Bibliography

Beetham, D. (2015) 'Moving beyond a narrow definition of corruption', in Whyte, D. (ed.) *How Corrupt is Britain?* London: Pluto.

Campbell, L. (2016a) '"Corruption by organised crime": A matter of definition?' *Current Legal Problems*, 69(1): 115–141.

Campbell, L. (2016b) 'Organised crime and corruption in the UK: Responding through law', *Criminal Law Review* 1: 20–34.

Deflem, M. (1995) 'Corruption, law, and justice: A conceptual clarification', *Journal of Criminal Justice*, 23(3): 243–258.

Doig, A. (2006) *Fraud*. London: Routledge.

Edwards, A. and Levi, M. (2008) 'Researching the organization of serious crimes', *Criminology & Criminal Justice*, 8(4): 363–388.

Levi, M. (2010) 'Organized fraud and organizing frauds: Unpacking research on networks and organization', *Criminology and Criminal Justice*, 8(4): 389–419.

Transparency International (2017) *How Do You Define Corruption?* available at www.transparency.org/what-is-corruption/#define.

Whyte, D. (2015) *How Corrupt is Britain?* London: Pluto.

World Bank (1997) *Helping Countries Combat Corruption: The Role of the World Bank*, available at www1.worldbank.org/publicsector/anticorrupt/corruptn/coridx.htm.

# Part I
# The organisation of corruption in commercial enterprise

# 1 Corruption as business across market contexts

*Mark Findlay*

Commencing from the position that corruption is best understood as a business relationship, this chapter explores the nexus between corruption and enterprise by broadly examining corruption and transitional market cultures. It addresses the transparency 'paradigm' in corruption control and posits the market model (rather than one based on morality or governance) as a more effective control foundation. Particularly in transitional cultures with markets effected by complex relationships of obligation and dependency (which are mirrored in many illegitimate market arrangements), the chapter proposes transparency in the form of reflexive account-ability in specific market relationships and transactions of market power, as being crucial for control. The analytic purpose of the chapter is to postulate a busi-ness taxonomy of corruption which exposes its reliance on power imbalance, and thereby suggest that corruption is a force for market dis-embedding[1] (with all its negative impacts on social good).

## Corruption: a moral or market issue?

For the analysis to follow, corruption is delineated either as a breach of trust or as enrichment through some market advantage based on power imbalance.[2] In so constructing corruption, there is a conscious avoidance of moral para-digms when appreciating corruption as a market relationship. While adopting a business/market perspective, the analysis will flag important moral issues underpinning corrupt relationships, transactions and outcomes as abuses of power, particularly when more just and fair wealth or resource distribution is diverted through corrupt market arrangements, as in transitional economies.[3]

---

1 This is an analytical concept drawn from the work of Karl Polanyi, suggesting the trend in exchange economies for markets to move away from the social.
2 The limitations inherent in defining corruption in terms of generic offence types is well repre-sented in the working paper of the UNODOC research material summary on defining corruption at http://www.track.unodc.org/Academia/Documents/IBA%20Defining%20corruption.pdf.
3 For the purposes of this chapter I employ the term 'transitional economies' to refer to post-colonial economies transforming usually from protected subsistence markets to fragile free trade market environments experiencing the strains of North/South world global economic dominance.

Looking at corruption in market terms is not meant to either highlight or diminish the private/public divide. Viewing corruption as a relationship of power wherein advantage is transacted as any other market variable does not exclude breaches of trust in public administration simply because the authority and discretion being bartered rests in the public sector. The advantage offered by a corrupt public official is still a market advantage. By focusing on corruption as a relationship, as a market dynamic rather than as some criminal category like bribery or embezzlement, there is no reason not to recognise generic offences such as the misappropriation of funds or misrepresentation. These are market practices which produce unfair and unjust enrichment. The market is the frame in which corruption relationships become profitable business for some, and loss for others.

However conceived, corruption is about power and its distribution. Relationships which may be determined as corrupt rarely involve stakeholders with equal or balanced market standing. In the understanding of corruption as business, there need always be a market frame within which advantage is transacted, no matter how simple that frame might be. Not every transaction of advantage which expresses power imbalances in the market will be corrupt, neither is it realistic to brand all relationships of obligation and dependency potentially corrupt, particularly in clan cultures. The distinguishing feature of a corrupt relationship, transaction or outcome in my thinking is the nature and intention of the advantage, better understood in market terms than as questions of institutional and individual probity. Corruption is usually all about easy money and the commodification of trust.

Corrupt business, simply commercially conceived, may take the form of profitable enterprise decisions for those who benefit. Understood in these terms, it is not difficult to see how the classification of legitimate/illegitimate advantage,[4] appropriate or inappropriate inducements, or Guanxi can be relative and difficult to objectify due to their cultural and market embedding. Corruption is a market force, and because of its exclusionist and anti-competitive directions, I will later argue, influences market dis-embedding, with all the negative consequences this process entails for social good.[5]

Corruption is in essence a market arrangement, not quarantined to illegitimate markets or to criminal enterprise. The failure to understand the market momentums behind corruption and its prevalence in particular market settings, I argue, constitutes a major impediment to successful corruption control. The latter part of the chapter will specifically challenge the contention that transparency facilitates corruption. This view is conditional on the essential qualification of transparency as a precondition for accountability. Transparency, rather than highlighting opportunities for corrupt arrangements and relationships particularly

---

4  Prevention of Bribery Ordinance (HK) Cap.201.
5  For a more fulsome discussion of Polanyian thinking concerning dis-embedding, and the influences of corruption on the market/social, see Findlay, M. (2017) *Law's Regulatory Relevance; Property, Power and Market Economies*, Cheltenham: Edward Elgar, chap 5.

in transitional market economies, if focused on the giving and receiving of advantage, and the purposes behind these market connections, and their intended outcomes, will enable more effective market-based control strategies (Findlay, 2014: 236). In this transactional sense, transparency is seen as a tool for reflexive accountability where other market players can be informed of the nature and consequences of corrupt market relationships and be empowered to engage in control through market self-regulation. For this to happen, market stakeholders outside a corrupt relationship must see it for what it is, and the damage it can cause to more organic market power arrangements.

The search for what makes corruption uniquely deleterious (morally, socially and in governance terms) is not an easy analytical venture, and is fraught with normative prescriptions. Adding to this difficulty is the reality that many of the market consequences of corruption can also be found in legitimate market forms. For instance, in a 'free market' economic paradigm (confined as this is to economic modelling and neo-liberal abstraction), corruption is anti-competitive. As such, this negative impact of corruption on market competition is hardly a distinguishing feature of corrupt market arrangements. The oligopolistic consolidations which have fuelled multinational commerce in the current age of neoliberal economic globalisation are designed as anti-competitive, and despite their tendency to limit market access and sometimes to 'rig' freer market forces, they have become an inescapable institutional feature of global mega-capitalism (Findlay, 2013: 170).

In order to more convincingly determine corrupt from other commercial market constellations, it is useful first to examine more popular representations of the phenomenon which do not necessarily work out from market origins. For instance, Rose-Ackerman (1999) defines corruption as the abuse of public office for 'private economic gain' (Rose-Ackerman, 1999: 75). Kofi Annan in a message to the First Conference of the States Parties to the UN Convention against Corruption (UNCAC) articulated that:

> In ways large and small, corruption hurts us all. It impedes social and economic development. It erodes the public's trust, hurts investment and undermines democracy and the rule of law. It facilitates terrorism, conflict and organized crime.

Central to the critical contribution of this chapter is the proposition that interpretations of corruption which focus on compromising public trust, distorting market balance or fostering crime and violence, fail to appreciate corruption as a business choice. As such, they distract control initiatives towards concerns for institutional governance, public morality or criminal motivations, and away from the more problematic but more fertile fields of market arrangements, relationships and outcomes. Some might say that this preference is a natural consequence of the connections promoted by major anti-corruption NGOs between corrupt conduct, failed governance, suspect public probity and questionable cultural feudalism (De Sousa et al., 2009). A more critical, perhaps cynical, interpretation would focus on a conscious avoidance of interrogating market transactions at the margins, which would highlight just how fragile an absolutist, objectivised approach to corrupt/non-corrupt business dualities might be (Boubaker and Nguyen, 2014).

In terms of 'business choice', I am not proposing some process of preferencing divorced from other commercial rationalities (such as competitive advantage or tender facilitation), neither is this a consideration of amoral calculation. Rather, the idea of choice recognises that as with any other business calculation, entering into corrupt relationships is primarily motivated by financial profit (individual more than operational) weighed against market risk. Reputational disadvantage, supply chain exclusion, regulatory penalty and individual criminalisation are all factored in as the impediments to corrupt preferencing. Only when profit maximisation, market share, personal gain and operational expedience trump an anti-corruption consciousness in business practice will corrupt relationships and transactions get treated as any other market variable.

The analysis to follow prefers to recognise the compelling evidence that corruption fuels poverty by subverting the fair and just distribution of economic gains and impacting negatively on public spending programmes that benefit the poor, such as health and education (Brown, 2007: ix–xi, at x). In so doing it looks at the market motivations for corrupt relationships and the cultural determinants[6] which may enable these to flourish. I would challenge the prevalent implication that corruption is more likely in developing economies, more tolerated in clan societies and a feature of governance frames where liberal democracy and rule of law are less robust (Boubaker and Nguyen, 2014; Findlay, 1999: chap. 6).

Putting the argument at its definitional base, corruption is a market dynamic, a relationship of power and dependency, with clear and quantifiable economic consequences. Corruption means business, and corrupt business arrangements make money for some at the expense of others. The market frame enables corruption because of the fundamental failing of more competitive advantage, in situations where exchange arrangements are less transparent and socially embedded.[7] Were this not so then bribing public officials and greasing contractual advantage through facilitation payments would not make good business sense.

I appreciate but challenge the Machiavellian assertion that corruption is a natural, indeed inevitable, consequence of empowering individual human greed in a political sense:

> We are generally reluctant to cultivate the qualities that enable us to serve the common good. Rather we tend to be 'corrupt', a term of art the republican theorists habitually use to denote our natural tendency to ignore the claims

---

6  In this sense, I am using 'culture' as an epithet for the business body corporate (in that sense market cultures) as well as the social and community frames of bonding which explain relationships of obligation and dependency.

7  For an excellent elaboration of Polanyi's analysis of market disembedding, see Dale, G. (2010) *Karl Polanyi: The Limits of the Market*, London: John Wiley and Sons, chap. 5.

of our community as soon as they seem to conflict with the pursuit of our own immediate advantage . . . how can naturally self-interested citizens be persuaded to act virtuously, such that they can hope to maximise a freedom which, left to themselves, they will infallibly throw away?

(Skinner, 1999: 170)

Rather, the argument moves to the recognition that corruption as a mechanism for market advantage is often difficult to distinguish from ruthless but resilient business practice. In this vein, it is too naive to deride corruption as a major obstacle to economic development, good governance and social-wellbeing. Neither is it, I argue, realistic to blame corruption in isolation as a reason for poor economic performance (World Bank, 2000).

Building on a more market-oriented analysis of corrupt business relationships and arrangements, it is possible to explore the social contexts in which corruption is fostered. Particularly, it is useful to understand why in some social situations, an anti-corruption consciousness is less likely to emerge as a strong counter-narrative in business affairs and market practices. Aligned with considerations of why, or why not corrupt relationships are specifically socially located sits perceptions of corruption and the manner in which these tend to be 'negotiated' in market contexts. Such negotiation is possible because of the ambiguity surrounding considerations of fair competitive advantage. In a social sense, for instance, it might seem an overly-nice distinction to justify facilitation payments to an official in order to expedite the exercise of her duties, and not to focus on the value of such payments, or to allow their legitimacy to be cloaked in sometimes-questionable local laws. In any case, I argue, essential market characteristics, power hierarchies and the degree to which markets are socially located will influence corruption perception, ambiguous facilitation, dominant competitive advantage preferences and the failure of control counter-narratives.

## Corruption and social bonding

Polanyi employs social embeddedness as a technique for appreciating market economies (Dale, 2010). His argument is that the further markets move from their essential or organic social locations, the more likely it is that they resemble fictional (or fictitious) commodities and market arrangements, producing outcomes which are not essentially determined by or determinant of general social goods. Polanyi asserts that in order to maintain the viability of the market/social nexus, states engage in a countermovement to ameliorate the social disadvantages of disembedded markets. This adaptivity to the negative outcomes of constantly disembedding markets has non-state parallels, and corruption can, in certain settings, perform a similar *balancing* function.

It is not too far-fetched to direct a similar analytical lens towards the influence corruption exerts on market viability. If healthy competition, for instance, is essential for a healthy market then corruption as an anti-competitive influence will undermine what may be theorised as more natural market forces. In addition, healthy market economies are not the exclusive domain of the rich and powerful. The social obligations of market benefit come hand-in-hand with markets that remain close to social purpose and benefit from and complement strong social bonds. In such a context corruption can be determined as a force that, due to its discriminatory, exclusionist and clandestine character, complements market transitions which Polanyi would evaluate as fictional or fictitious (i.e. promote individual wealth creation at the cost of more dispersed and diversified economic development).

Another interpretation is possible in this vein. Especially so for developing economies, foreign investment (FDI) may not be as attractive in heavily bureaucratised domestic environments, and if corruption cuts to the business 'quick', then it may act as a positive investment facilitator in otherwise atrophied administrative frames. This is good for business if at the same time it is bad for state capacity building. From a market perspective, in recognition that markets are not free and openly competitive, corrupt arrangements can, if not usually, channel resource and revenue distribution away from self-interested state regulators. Unfortunately, it is more common that corruption is a political province and as such is more likely to divert resource and revenue distribution from its more just and deserving flow.

Using these reflections, it may be possible to propose a taxonomy of corruption that emphasises its negative, and even rarely positive, influence on social good, rather than more simply its negative governance or morality considerations. In attempting such an exercise, I work from the somewhat unusual perspective of corruption as a market regulator. Employing a definition of regulation which is essentially concerned with intentional behavioural change,[8] then corrupt market arrangements, relationships and outcomes, even if not authorised for the purpose, are essentially designed to regulate markets to produce selective business advantage. The determination of such advantage as illegitimate requires normative rather than commercial evaluations.

A fundamental feature of both normative and commercial consideration of corruption is as power frames in the market that primarily undermine social good. The negative potential of corruption to invade social good alone is not an indelible determinant of corruption because other legitimate market frames may also undervalue or diminish social good.[9] Perhaps this connection between corruption and social good then becomes a question of balance quantified by the extent to which a corrupt market frame disembeds the market from social good.

In order to prepare a taxonomy that explains the relationship between corruption and social good, we first need to identify some of my assumptions which

---

8  Julia Black's definition 'the intentional use of authority to effect the behaviour of a different party according to set standards, involving instruments of information gathering and behaviour modification' – Black J. (2001) 'Decentring regulation: Understanding the role of regulation and self-regulation in a post-regulatory world', *Current Legal Problems*, 54: 103–147.
9  See the discussion of migrant labour market dysfunctions in Findlay (2016).

underlie the assertion that corruption is best viewed as a market variable with significant regulatory potential:

1   Markets are to varying degrees socially determined and regulated in part for social benefit.
2   Corruption regulates market with no primary consideration of social good.
3   Corrupt relations promote the giving and receiving of advantage which would not otherwise flow in a market context.
4   Corruption facilitates anti-competitive market arrangements.
5   As a result, corruption positions market players and advantages enterprises in discriminatory ways.
6   Corruption perverts crucial trust connections which enable efficient and organic market compliance.
7   Giving and receiving advantage, which might form corrupt market exchange, is culturally determined.
8   The nature of corruption is dependent on the nature of enterprise within which it evolves.
9   The transparency of market frames disables corruption's market influence.
10  Corruption is good business for some, to the disadvantage of the many.

The dangers inherent in concealing corruption's regulatory influence over market relationships and arrangements not in the least diminish the capacity of corruption control initiatives to deal with the negative influences on social good as a practical market concern. Therefore, following on from these assumptions, the taxonomy I suggest is as follows:

•   Corruption regulates otherwise insufficiently regulated markets.
•   Corruption exploits and exacerbates already existing external and internal market power imbalance.
•   Through the differential transaction of advantages under market conditions which would be considered neither organic nor accountable, corruption enables market preferencing and gives discriminatory business benefit to the few usually at the wider social cost to the many.
•   As a perversion of otherwise legitimate trust relationships in the market, corruption is risk averse when operating in market conditions which are not transparent and accountable. Away from disclosure and the adverse inferences which could be drawn from corruption revelation, forces for deterrence evaporate when parties in corrupt relationships calculate as unlikely the risks of market exposure and excommunication.

If corruption can distort market balance such as in North to South World trading contexts, then trade as a consequence can disembed domestic markets through utilising and facilitating corruption. It is useful for a more market-centred analysis of the nexus between corruption and trade/development models such as foreign direct investment (FDI), that the more meta-factors which disembed markets through global trade are made clear. In the trade context, globalisation on its own is not the culprit in the trade/development disembedding phenomenon, but rather it provides a means for markets to more readily intersect and for hegemonic economic advantage to expand. If one accepts that market facilitation in the form of exploiting power imbalances and institutionalised dependency blurs the boundaries between the corrupt and the legitimate, then this ambiguity sets a tone for selective and conditional market regulation. Failed state administrations either give no protection to rapacious external investment incursions, or conspire to enable their disembedding influences. In such circumstances, effected communities often face disempowerment through biased or corrupted local legal resistance. Foreign investors, particularly through preferred partial political pathways, have the benefits of extended rights but rarely with consequent responsibilities (Vervest and Feodoroff, 2015).

## Corruption as relations of power

Power is at the heart of obligation and dependency connections when considering social bonding and market arrangements. As already identified, corruption relies on power imbalances, and the obligations these create and maintain. Particularly in developing economies with clan social structures, external power frames can latch onto organic structures of obligation and dependency, and transform these into more exploitative and mechanical[10] social bonds.

Corruption transacting power is recognised as illegitimate except in self-interested business terms. When it comes to evaluating the legitimacy of power relations in the market context, this cannot be convincingly externally evaluated, unless the power framework has been externally imposed. For instance, facilitation payments may be justified as not amounting to corruption if they externally advance what is seen as a legitimate market advantage, but at the same time are endorsed by sympathetic domestic legal provisions.

One of the most universal characteristics of corruption as a phenomenon of power imbalance in the market is its tendency to distance those who deserve the benefits of market arrangements from those who capture these benefits through corrupt relationships. According to Hofstede (1997: 28), power distance (which is the dynamic of power/powerlessness) refers to 'the extent to which the less powerful members of institutions and organizations within a country expect and accept that power is distributed unequally'. The social reality of power distance can help explain why corruption seems more prevalent in particular socio-political settings than others. For example, in high power-distance countries, there is considerable dependence of subordinates on their superiors in the form of paternalism. Paternalism in this context is a system by which superiors

---

10  For the purposes of this analysis, I draw the market distinction between organic and mechanical forces as relating to those that originate and operate within closer market social bonds (organic) and those which originate externally and are introduced into the market without purposes primarily directed to social good.

provide favours to subordinates in return for their loyalty. Decisions are not made on the basis of some objective form of merit, but rather on a balance of that which rewards loyalty. A paternalistic system such as this leaves considerable room for corruption in the form of favouritism and nepotism. However, it would be unduly simplistic to blame clan loyalty as criminogenic and to direct control strategies to the dismantling of traditions of obligation and dependency which in other circumstances may provide positive and sustainable frameworks of social bonding and market trust. In fact, it is often the external injection into societies with high power differentials of mechanical market imperatives (such as Westminster-style governance) which pervert the positive potentials of obligation and dependency leading to corrupt advantage giving. So the effort to reposition traditional market arrangements away from corrupt relationships and outcomes should focus on the nature of power difference and the manner in which it can be corruptly exploited through external commercial facilitation. Again, I return to the consideration of corruption as business practice rather than as a cultural predisposition. In so doing it is necessary to confront the prevailing world view that the South World is a more corruptible governance context because of failings in state probity, political morality and responsible civil society.

## Concealing corruption as a business? South World vulnerabilities

In *Empire* Hardt and Negri observe:

> The passage to Empire emerges from the twilight of modern sovereignty. In contrast to imperialism, Empire establishes no territorial centre of power and does not rely on fixed boundaries or barriers. It is a *decentred* and *deterritorialising* apparatus of rule that progressively incorporates the entire global realm within its open, expanding frontiers. Empire manages hybrid identities, flexible hierarchies and plural exchanges through modulating networks of command. The distinct nationalist colours of the imperialist map of the world have merged and blended in the imperial global rainbow.
>
> (Hardt and Negri, 2000: xii–xiii)

Against a discussion of the paradoxes inherent in the current epoch of globalisation and its emergence out of post-colonial economic dominion, a power analysis can chart how trade between the North and South Worlds represents a new colonial enslavement (Hardt and Negri, 2000: 21, 201). The pressure for tearing down trade barriers and opening up developing markets to the ravages of advanced market economies has the consequence of advancing a new economic imperialism. Under the guise of development assistance, regimes such as FDI too often cripple recipient economies for the advantage of absentee shareholders, consequently capitulating to externally sourced debt (De Sousa Santos and Rodriguez-Garavito, 2005). Ironically, with free trade up till recently touted as good for global economic growth, this form of market imperialism has further entrenched the North/South economic and social divide and compounded dis-embedded relationships of economic dependency.

Corruption in the form of commercial facilitation is epidemic in developing markets, and particularly where these markets are built on social frames where traditional networks of obligation are deeply rooted, the discriminatory conse-quences of corruption exacerbate the negative incursion of foreign trade. My interest in corruption here is restricted to the manner in which it further disem-beds market economies once, and up until only recently, designed to prioritise communitarian interests. In fragile exchange markets only recently transposed into cash economies, corruption becomes a force for disembedding away from the social when individual wealth creation is prioritised over collective benefit and sustainability.

Adopting the perspective that corruption selectively (and destructively) complements market access, we ask how communitarian resistance to the new imperialism and the corruption it spawns has the effect of dispersing power back to the local, facilitating the re-embedding of market economies. To expose this nexus, I focus on the relationship between power dispersal (or what Tarrow refers to as dispersal) and market re-embedding:

> Diffusion is mis-specified if it is seen only as the 'contagion' of collective action . . . a key characteristic of cycles (of contention) is the diffusion of a propensity for collective action from its initiators to unrelated groups and to antagonists. The former respond to the demonstration effect of a challenge that succeeds – or at least escapes repression – whereas the latter produce the counter-movements that are [a] frequent reaction to the onset of contention.
> (Tarrow, 1998: 145)

Absent a more detailed discussion of corrupting markets and the re-embedding counter-movement, it is necessary to locate global trade as the context in which North World imperialism disembeds domestic markets away from the social. Globalisation enables the insidious spread of North World trade imperatives far beyond anything which may have been envisaged in the mercantile and colonial eras of North World hegemony.

Post-colonial globalising neoliberalism is creating renewed opportunities for corruption (Brown and Cloke, 2005). The global economic model is pressuring for state de-centring in the rush to stimulate rather than regulate FDI in devel-oping economies (Moran, 1998). Civil service devolution and downsizing has reduced the capacity of often-already disaggregated states to bargain effectively, particularly in transnational resource exploitation (Cohen and Lipson, 1999: 93). The resultant *marketisation* of fragile and vulnerable emergent economies in a voracious world climate of 'free trade' has not seen a reduction in rent-seeking opportunities that neoclassical economic theory once promised (McCourt, 2000; Nunberg, 1994).

The contested meanings of corruption are as much a feature of post-colonial economic re-colonisation, as they are an expression of orientalist hegemonic superiority when it comes to legal and governance models (Findlay, 2014: chap. 10). Definitions which emphasise political vice, economic greed and governance dysfunction are strategically used by international financial institutions, rich 'donor states and multinational commercial predators in international development settings, to demonise the recipients of bribes while consciously concealing the complicity of offering parties' (World Bank, 1997: 8). This individualisation of responsibility and its amoral/imprudent characterisation that prevails in North/South governance discourse, is in fact echoed in the language of international conventions coming out of UNCAC and the OECD, and emerging domestic legislation, despite their recognition of offering parties. These instruments continue to focus on individualised participation in corrupt relationships and the guilt this demonstrates, without contextualising these relationships as power and domination grounded now in North/South economic and trade asymmetries, which can be traced back to colonial constellations in unequal commercial arrangements. In a deeper sense, models of Westminster parliamentary democracy, often deeply ill-suited to more tribal governance structures, have further individualised power in the recipient markets so that the corrupt politician is a bi-product of the mechanical administrative influence vested in him or her from hegemonies abroad.

In the sense of a global economic hegemony which sees facilitation payments as good business and bribe-taking as graft, corruption becomes understood in a neoliberal, economistic anti-state paradigm. As such, it emphasises political patronage as a source of rents, and therefore skews anti-corruption policy towards deregulation and state marginalisation to reduce opportunities for officials to collect bribes, along with rapid privatisation said to enliven market competition. With control policy operating in such an idealised free market economic frame that ignores, even overrules, power asymmetries, market corruption and its control are mystified, while at the same time deeply embedded within the wider constructions of global neoliberal governance (Bracking, 2007).

Andvig et al. (2001) argue that the narrowness of the rational-legal paradigm for defining corruption – as private abuse of the Weberian public space – is clearly utilitarian in concealing its economic dependencies when compared to the anthropological insights gained by examining these socio-cultural logics informing everyday practices in the market. Thus, while the rational-legal paradigm understands corruption as violating the distinction, clearly false, between public and private trust, the notion of public office located and deriving its purchase from the Weberian model of public administration fails both consciously and capriciously to understand corruption's real and negotiable market space (Bracking, 2007).

It is as unsatisfactory to restrict corruption to the public bureaucratic setting, as it is to award important distinctions of culture a potential to promote corruption as if some cultures are less prudential than others and as such more likely to direct frameworks of obligation and dependency to corrupt outcomes.

By disengaging corruption from the market, and by camouflaging its business essence with cultural ethnographies, it makes it more difficult to effectively control corruption through attacking the essential social/market bonds that encourage its market possibilities. Reiterating the consideration of power difference and obligation/dependency for these social arrangements to facilitate corruption, it is very often necessary for an external private business agent to funnel corrupt advantage. To direct the corruption control endeavour against the obligation and dependency frame rather than the external stimulus is like putting the cart before the horse. Operating unscathed, the external commercial stimulus will simply move to a safer domestic network of influence to channel corrupt advantage.

## Cultures of corruption?

Intrinsic cultural motivations such as structures of obligation originate from the internalisation of social norms existing within a society (Barr and Serra, 2010). Norms are *social* when their underlying values are shared, collectivised and consolidated so that deviation from the norm triggers social disapproval and with internalised norms generates feelings of shame and guilt (Elster, 1989; Posner and Rasmusen, 1999; Young, 2008). In this process of meaning confirmation, cultural values 'justify and guide the ways that social institutions function, and their goals and modes of operation. Social actors draw on them to select actions, evaluate people and events, and explain or justify their actions and evaluations' (Licht et al., 2007).

In societies with complex structures of obligation and dependency, the giving and receiving of advantage, rather than evidencing corruption (Findlay, 1999: chap. 5), may be the cement which binds a community in material trust (Hauk and Saez-Marti, 2002). As mentioned already, if we have carried out a sufficiently sophisticated evaluation of the active and failed social bonds that allow corruption to flourish, then the role of culture as a market facilitator, rather than as a corruption stimulus, becomes clear. It would, for example be as silly to suggest that the family is criminogenic when we look at Italian organised crime as it would be to ignore the reality that families are a crucial frame for Italian business whether the enterprise is legitimate or otherwise.

In order to interrogate bonds of obligation and dependency, Paldam (2002) used Huntington's (1996) study on the 'clash of civilizations' to cluster nation states into various geo-political and historical groupings. He developed three sub-models: one based on economic dynamics, the second on democracy variables and the third on cultural factors. Within this crude instrumentalist schema, Paldam found that a 'cultural determinist' view of corruption fared poorly as a tool for explaining market context and control potentials. He exposed no basis for the belief that corruption is embedded in the culture of the society such that it is immutable to that culture. Rather, corruption varied more within the same Huntingtonian cultural areas than across them, suggesting that culture does not necessarily have an impact on corruption greater than incipient economic or political factors.[11] There is a particular failing even in such a culturally sympathetic exercise. The definition of what makes a relationship of obligation and dependency corrupt may reveal more about the externalities at work on our understandings of these arrangements, than on their cultural immersion and utility.

Getz and Volkema (2001) developed a behavioural framework to explain corruption where national cultural aspects are related to fundamental attitudes about social relationships and structures in which people live and work. They generated four hypotheses taken from Hofstede's (1980) dimensions. First, the greater the power distance, the stronger the relationship between economic adversity and corruption; in other words, the more hierarchical a society is, the more likely poor economic performance is related to corruption. Second, the higher the level of uncertainty avoidance, the more likely poor economic outcomes are related to corruption. Third, the more collectivist a national culture is, the stronger the relationship between economic adversity and corruption. Last, higher measured masculinity leads to a stronger relationship between economic adversity and corruption.

Let's unpack these observations one at a time:

- As mentioned in the discussion of corruption and cultures, hierarchical social structures and power distance do not explain propensities to corruption on their own. I suggest that for such social arrangements and relationships to be corrupted, there is an essential requirement for mechanical (usually external) market influences to introduce advantage transaction of a corrupt form and purpose.
- Uncertainty avoidance is a feature of frail and transitional economies. These are also economies with low levels of formal, accountable and transparent market regulation. As such they offer market conditions for corruption.
- Collectivist national cultures will mean that the social and economic translation of external market influences will be more efficient and often less accountable and transparent. It is not the collectivist nature of a national culture which explains corruptibility, but the manner in which corrupt advantage transaction is received, communicated and concealed within the market.
- Masculinity in this analysis is code for paternalist social arrangements. These represent a particular exclusionist power framework where relationships of obligation and dependency are largely institutionalised within non-accountable power dispositions. It is the absence of accountability and transparency in the transaction of power within paternalist market arrangements which fosters corruption. Truly collectivist national cultures can work against this power distribution and its negative impacts on general social good.

---

11 These two approaches to analysis are summarised in Akbar, Y. and Vujić, V. (2014) 'Explaining corruption: The role of national culture and its implications for international management', *Cross Cultural Management*, 2(1/2): 191–218.

With these interpretations in mind, I return to the caution that before advancing some inextricable relationship between corruption and culture, ignoring the problems inherent in universalising or objectifying *culture*, it is necessary to give weight to the external influences of power which promote corrupt business relationships and the disempowered recipient market contexts within which the corrupt deals are struck. Only then can the vulnerability and indeed utility of strong frameworks of obligation be understood as open to external commercial manipulation.

## Transparency and legitimate market traction

Before proposing a transparency/accountability synergy for controlling corruption, I will return to some of the underlying assumptions which guide the preceding analysis. If corruption motivation and dynamics are viewed in business terms and contextualised as market variables, then prevention and control can be envisaged as any other process of market regulation. If corruption itself is understood as a perverse market regulator, unbalancing supply chains and dislocating natural competition, then responsibility for creating an anti-corruption consciousness as much rests with market players harmed by corrupt relationships. Particularly in transitional economies and post-colonial cultures where free trade and neo-liberal economic imperialism have manipulated indigenous frames of obligation and dependency, it is important to understand corruption as another feature of absentee commercial facilitation rather than some evidence of domestic political and cultural contingency.

One of the leading global anti-corruption NGOs, Transparency International, advocates a corruption control strategy that relies on making corrupt transactions more visible. Recently, there has developed a contrary view on the impact of corruption visibility particularly in transitional or developing economies (Coppier and Piga, 2006). The argument goes that if public officials are exposed as being corrupt in governance contexts where the anti-corruption consciousness is not widespread, a predisposition to the inevitability of corruption is embedded, and corruption is seen as a market norm, even as a preferred way of doing business, then transparency simply advertises who is for sale and at what price. The analysis is depressingly realistic in societies where corruption control is superficial, or itself problematic in its selective application and superficial benefit.

There is not time in this format to interrogate, and to do so in any convincingly empirical fashion, why transparency in certain social settings may do little to retard corrupt market transactions. Consistent with the chapter's theme that corruption is a market regulator, I suggest that even if this critical perspective on transparency is true and widespread, it can be met by a market approach. The approach advocated is qualifying transparency within the market to produce the information necessary to structure *reflexive accountability* among market stakeholders not caught up in these corrupt arrangements.

The first consideration is not to limit transparency to visibility. If there is no general supporting consensus to empower control strategies against corrupt market relationships or arrangements, then their revelation might do nothing more than confirm their impenetrability. Therefore, consistent with the understanding of corruption as an adverse market regulator, transparency must link account- ability with visibility. However, this assertion may seem little more than wishful thinking in an adverse market environment which either tolerates corruption or is fatalist as to whether any intervention can make a difference (Lindstedt and Naurinand, 2010).

Returning to the taxonomy offered earlier in this chapter, the risks associ- ated with corrupt market relationships and arrangements must, through contrary regulatory activity or alternative market consciousness, be increased by powerful requirements of accountability. But in transitional cultures with power distance, patriarchal hierarchies, predatory external market forces, compliant networks of obligation and dependency, and weak compromised states, from where will the regulatory initiative emerge? I say the market.

There are more market players (providers and consumers) who are disadvan- taged by the discriminatory business preferencing achieved through corruption, than those who enjoy its benefits. Market engagement requires the acquies- cence of many non-corrupt participants in the supply and demand chains. If, on revelation of corrupt relationships and arrangements in the market in which they share, non-corrupt players are made aware of the genuine dollars-and- cents business disadvantages they face as a consequence of corruption, then an active self-regulatory market backlash can be generated, and a process of market banishment can be promoted.

In a world without all-pervasive social media coverage, the essential exposure of corrupt market arrangements would not alternately be provided through com- promised state agencies and complicit law enforcement. Markets are becoming more digitised, and the commercial information on which they rely is more likely to accompany digitisation than to be produced by sources independent of market flows. There is no doubt that for the necessary market transparency to be more common place in vulnerable market settings, the non-corrupt market majority needs to identify and require basic information about the nature and strength of market relationships within the supply chains in particular, before these stake- holders will agree to service any market arrangement. In this way, corruption control becomes internalised and empowering. Corruption control becomes a business, rather than a moral consciousness, and as such the viability of corrupt enterprise is reduced through simple market displacement.

# Bibliography

Akbar, Y. and Vujić, V. (2014) 'Explaining corruption: The role of national culture and its implications for international management', *Cross Cultural Management*, 29(1/2): 191–218.

Andvig, J. and Odd-Helge, F. with Amundsen, I., Sissener, T. and Soreide, T. (2001) *Corruption: A Review of Contemporary Research*, Report R 2001: 7, Chr. Michelsen Institute, Bergen, Sweden. www.cmi.no/publications/861-corruption-a-review-of- contemporary-research (accessed 15/1/18).

Barr, A. and Serra, D. (2010) 'Corruption and culture: An experimental analysis', *Journal of Public Economics*, 94: 862–869.

Black, J. (2001) 'Decentring regulation: Understanding the role of regulation and self-regulation in a post-regulatory world', *Current Legal Problems*, 54: 103–147.

Boubaker, S. and Nguyen, D.K. (eds) (2014) *Corporate Governance in Emerging Markets: Theories, practices and case*. Berlin: Springer.

Bracking, S. (2007) 'Political development and corruption: Why "right here, right now!"?' in S. Bracking (ed.) *Corruption and Development: The Anti-Corruption Campaigns*. New York: Palgrave Macmillan, pp. 3–27.

Brown, B. (2007) 'Foreword', in S. Bracking (ed.) *Corruption and Development: The Anti-Corruption Campaigns*. New York: Palgrave Macmillan.

Brown, E. and Cloke, J. (2005) 'Neoliberal reform, governance and corruption in the south: Assessing the international anti-corruption crusade', *Antipode*, 36(2): 272–294.

Cohen, B. and Lipson, C. (1999) *Issues and Agents in International Political Economy*. Cambridge, MA: MIT Press.

Coppier, R. and Piga, G. (2006) 'Why do transparent public procurement and corruption go hand in hand?' *Rivista di Politica Economica*, 96(1): 185–206.

Dale, G. (2010) *Karl Polanyi: The Limits of the Market*. London: John Wiley and Sons.

De Sousa, L., Larmour, P. and Hindess, B. (eds) (2009) *Governments, NGOs and Anti-Corruption: The New Integrity Warriors*. Oxford, UK: Routledge.

De Sousa Santos, B. and Rodriguez-Garavito, C. (eds) (2005) *Law and Counter-hegemonic Globalization: Towards a Cosmopolitan legality*. Cambridge, UK: Cambridge University Press.

Elster, J. (1989) 'Social norms and economic theory', *Journal of Economic Perspectives*, 3(4): 99–117.

Findlay, M. (1999) *The Globalisation of Crime: Understanding Cultures in Transition*. Oxford, UK: Oxford University Press.

Findlay, M. (2013) *Contemporary Challenges in Regulating Global Crises*. Basingstoke, UK: Palgrave Macmillan.

Findlay, M. (2014) *International and Comparative Criminal Justice: A critical introduction*. Oxford, UK: Routledge.

Findlay, M. (2016) *Property, Labour and Legal Regulation: Dignity or Dependence?* Cheltenham, UK: Edward Elgar.

Findlay, M. (2017) *Law's Regulatory Relevance; Property, Power and Market Economies*. Cheltenham, UK: Edward Elgar.

Getz, K. and Volkema, R. (2001) 'Culture, perceived corruption, and economics: A model of predictors and outcomes', *Business and Society*, 40(1): 7–30.

Hardt, M. and Negri, A. (2000) *Empire*. Cambridge, MA: Harvard University Press.

Hauk, E. and Saez-Marti, M. (2002) 'On the cultural transmission of corruption', *Journal of Economic Theory*, 107(2): 311–335.

Hofstede, G. (1980) *Culture's Consequences: International Differences in Work-related Values*. Thousand Oaks, CA: Sage.

Hofstede, G. (1997) *Cultures and Organizations: Software of the Mind*. New York: McGraw Hill.

Huntington, S. P. (1996) *The Clash of Civilizations and the Remaking of World Order*. London: Simon & Schuster.

Licht, A., Goldschmidt, C. and Schwartz, S. (2007) 'Culture rules: The foundations of the rule of law and other norms of governance', *Journal of Comparative Economics*, 35: 659–688.

Lindstedt, C. and Naurin, D. (2010) 'Transparency is not enough: Making transparency effective in reducing corruption', *International Political Science Review*, 31(3): 301–322.

McCourt, W. (2000) *Public Appointments: From Patronage to Merit*, Working Paper No. 9, Human Resources in Development Group Working Paper, pp. 1–15. http://hummedia. manchester.ac.uk/institutes/gdi/publications/workingpapers/archive/hr/hr_wp09. pdf, accessed 11/1/2018.

Moran, T. (1998) *Foreign Direct Investment and Development: The New Policy Agenda for Developing Countries and Economies in Transition*. Washington, DC: Institute for Economic Investment.

Nunberg, B. (1994) *Managing the Civil Service: Reform Lessons from Advanced Industrialised Countries*. Washington, DC: World Bank.

Paldam, M. (2002) 'The cross-country pattern of corruption: Economics, culture and the seesaw dynamics', *European Journal of Political Economy*, 18: 215–240.

Posner, R. and Rasmusen, E. (1999) 'Creating and enforcing norms, with special reference to sanctions', *International Review of Law and Economics*, 19: 369–382.

Rose-Ackerman, S. (1999) *Corruption and Government: Causes, Consequences and Reform*. Cambridge, UK: Cambridge University Press.

Skinner, Q. (1999) 'The Republican ideal of civil liberty', in M. Rosen and J. Wolff (eds) *Political Thought*. Oxford, UK: Oxford University Press, pp. 161–171.

Tarrow, S. (1998) *Power in Movement: Social movements and contentious politics* Cambridge: Cambridge University Press.

Vervest, P. and Feodoroff, T. (2015) 'Licensed to grab: How international investment rules undermine agrarian justice', *Transnational Institute*, www.tni.org/sites/www. tni.org/files/download/licensed_to_grab.pdf.

World Bank. (1997) *World Development Report 1997: The State in a Changing World*. New York: Oxford University Press.

World Bank. (2000) *World Development Report 2000: Attacking Poverty*. New York: Oxford University Press.

Young, P. (2008) 'Social norms', in S. Durlauf and E. Lawrence (eds) *The New Palgrave of Economics*. London: Macmillan.

# 2 When corruption and organised crime overlap

## An empirical hierarchy of corrupt conduct

*Jay S. Albanese*

## Introduction

Public and commercial corruption, involving the illicit exchange of money or its equivalent for illicit benefits, dominates research and anti-corruption efforts, but the specific underlying behaviours are not always clearly identified. This study examines several hundred corruption cases occurring over a three-year period. These cases are grouped into five different types from the least to most organised forms of corruption. A tipping point is reached when a business or government agency turns from exploiting the system by pilfering or low-level bribery to operating like a criminal enterprise with organised schemes involving solicitation of bribes and extortion. Examples are provided from actual cases to illustrate a hierarchy of corrupt conduct and how organised forms of corruption are less common, but usually more serious, than individual or less organised graft. It is proposed that applying the principles of both enterprise theory and situational crime prevention might provide a path forward in anticipating and reducing the incidence of such corruption.

## Commercial corruption, public corruption, white collar crime, organised crime

Corruption, white collar crime, and organised crime are sometimes linked, but not always in a clear way. A focus on the underlying behaviours behind these different forms of misconduct offers useful insights into their nature, seriousness, and prevention avenues. Empirical data from court cases are applied in this chapter to illustrate a hierarchy of conduct that lies beneath corruption of various types.

Commercial corruption is distinguished from public corruption in that it involves efforts by private business or corporate interests to influence illicitly legitimate business or government activity. Public corruption involves self-dealing conduct on the part of government officials. Clearly, these two broad types of corruption overlap in many cases when bribes are offered by the private sector, or solicited by public officials to corrupt a lawful procurement, contracting, regulatory, or oversight procedure (Albanese, 2011; Lord, 2016; Rose-Ackerman and Palikfa, 2016; Wedman, 2013; White, 2013).

Both commercial and public corruption have in common conduct that is a *deviation from* legitimate business or government activity. Both can be considered forms of white collar crime, because these characteristics fulfil the prescribed or conventional definitional elements (Albanese, 1995; Holmes, 2015). Organised crime is distinguished from white collar crime (and from commercial and public corruption) because, rather than a deviation from lawful activity, it is a *continuing criminal* enterprise designed to *profit primarily* from crime (Albanese, 2015; Simpson, 2013).

There are, of course, similarities between white collar crime and organised crime in that they both require organisation and rationality in their commission. Organised crime is also not restricted to the activities of criminal syndicates. A study of a major banking scandal found that if we use the term organised crime to denote continuing conspiracies that include the corruption of government officials, 'then much of the savings and loan scandal involved organised crime' (Pontell and Calavita, 1993: 39). Similar to the financial crisis of 2008, a recurring theme of conspiracies between banking officials ('insiders') and accountants, lawyers, and real estate developers ('outsiders') operated as a continuing criminal enterprise far beyond a simple fraud (Gummesson, 2014; Kenny, 2014; Pontell and Calavita, 1993). If we compare these kinds of corrupt relationships with more traditional organised crime techniques such as no-show jobs at construction sites or payoffs for 'protection', we find that they are more similar than different, often involving some combination of bribery, fraud, and extortion. Examples like these illustrate that much of the crime committed by private corporations, politicians, and government agencies is as serious and harmful as the organised crimes of criminal enterprises (see Albanese, 1995; Cobin, 2009).

In addition, corruption is often equated with bribery, because bribery is commonly used as an indicator of corruption. Empirical research shows, however, that corruption occurs in forms beyond only bribery (Andersson, 2017; Vargas-Hernández, 2011). Therefore, greater precision is needed to understand the differences in the behaviours that underlie corrupt conduct of different types.

It is the purpose of the analysis in this chapter to examine the proposition that there is a continuum of conduct along which an entity moves from typical commercial or public corruption into organised crime. That is to say, there is a scale or progression of corrupt conduct when a business or government agency turns from pilfering or bribing others to operating like a criminal enterprise, using organised schemes involving fraud, solicitation, or extortion. This insight can be used to demonstrate that corrupt conduct moves along a continuum that might be better anticipated for purposes of prevention.

Figure 2.1 illustrates the distinctions between corruption in or by business (commercial corruption) and corruption in or by government officials (public corruption). They are similar in that they usually involve violation of both public and private interests, and some form of fraud in circumventing procurement procedures, regulations, or the permissible scope of conduct by government officials. The public interest is subverted when public officials (elected or appointed) engage in behaviour that advances private interests instead of the common good. Public interest is also subverted when decision-making by public officials occurs outside of the democratic process, thereby denying citizens

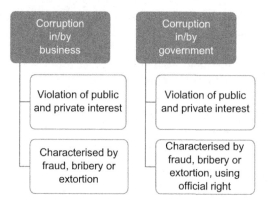

*Figure 2.1* Commercial versus public corruption

(i.e. taxpayers, voters) equal participation in that process. Common examples include public officials promoting the private interests of large donors instead of the public interest, or making procurement decisions that benefit one's own private interest versus the public interest. When these situations occur, public trust in the democratic process is undermined (Dawood, 2014; Rawls, 1971; Schulter, 2017; Thompson, 2005).

Corruption in and by business has important similarities and differences to public corruption. In business corruption, the private party seeks to influence a public authority or a private party to their advantage using money, favours, or intimidation. Business managers and corporate officers also hold authority and fiduciary responsibility on behalf of others (i.e. employees, shareholders, customers), which can be abused for private gain in transactions involving public officials or other private parties (DeMarco, 2016; Heffernan and Kleinig, 2004; Wedman, 2013).

## A five-part hierarchy of corruption

There are multiple forms of corrupt conduct which derive from the general definitions of corruption (noted in Figure 2.1) into specific substantive offenses found in many criminal codes. The most common examples of specific offenses involving corrupt conduct include:

- Embezzlement – misuse of one's authority to obtain funds or property from one's organisation; a violation of financial trust.
- Fraud – theft by deception, usually involving obtaining funds or property to which one is not entitled, when it involves the misuse of public or private authority.
- Bribery – a voluntary exchange of any benefit intended to influence an official or corporate act. These exchanges can result from either receiving or soliciting benefits.
- Extortion – obtaining property, using threats of future physical or reputational harm.

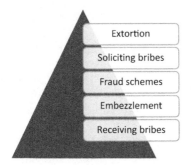

*Figure 2.2* Ranking seriousness of corruption offenses

These examples of corrupt conduct vary in their level of seriousness, as measured by the size, threat, and rationality of scheme, and the harm produced. Figure 2.2 illustrates this variation, rising from the least serious, least organised, and requiring the least effort, up to the most serious, and most organised forms. The level of organisation moves from individual, less sophisticated corruption (e.g. taking a bribe offer and embezzling funds with little oversight) to more organised forms involving more participants and more aggressive corrupt behaviour (e.g. soliciting bribes systematically or extortion of bidding contractors).

Looking at the ranking in Figure 2.2, receiving bribes is the most passive form of corruption, whereas soliciting bribes or kickbacks using threats is the most predatory and serious. Likewise, the misappropriation of funds (embezzlement) is less serious than larger fraudulent schemes, which often require more individuals and some level of organisation to execute. Extortion can be considered the most serious of these corruption offenses, because it involves soliciting money or property to which one is not entitled with the added threat of harm for noncompliance with the solicitation.

## Research approach

To test this proposed five-part typology of corruption offenses, 283 federal criminal cases in the US were reviewed over three years (2013–15). Federal cases in the US involve either violations of federal law or crimes involving multiple states. Nearly all corruption cases in the US are prosecuted at the federal level. An empirical study found 94% of all corruption cases in the US are prosecuted at the federal level with very few prosecuted in state courts (Cordis and Milyo, 2016).

These corruption cases were brought by U.S. Attorneys' Offices across the US in 94 separate judicial districts, which are geographically dispersed. Using keyword searches, each office's cases were reviewed to identify corruption cases. A total of 283 indictments and convictions were identified over the three-year period.

Analysis of these cases found that many different statutes were employed in the prosecutions, but a small number of charges accounted for the majority of all cases. It was discovered that eight different kinds of underlying corrupt conduct or behaviour accounted for all the cases. They are summarised below:

1   Receipt of bribe – a public official took a benefit to influence an official act.
2   Solicitation of a bribe – a public official solicited an unauthorised payment or benefit for an official act.
3   Extortion – a public official obtained property, using threats of future harm.
4   Contract fraud – a public official or private contractor received payment on a government contract through deception, misstatements, or false representations.
5   Embezzlement – a government employee or private contractor used their access to government funds or property without authorisation to benefit himself or herself.
6   Official misconduct – a public official performed an unauthorised act, or failed to perform a legal duty, in order to receive a benefit or harm another.
7   Obstruction of justice – a private or public official intentionally impaired a lawful government procedure (usually an audit or investigation).
8   Violation of regulatory laws – a private or public official did not abide by rules designed to ensure fairness in and safety in the conduct of business or politics. These were administrative, environmental, labour, manufacturing violations, or unfair trade practices.

## Analysis

For the purposes of this analysis, only the first five categories listed above were included (receipt of bribe, solicitation of bribe, extortion, contract fraud, embezzlement). There are two reasons for this selection. First, it was found that the first five forms of corruption were the largest categories of corruption cases in terms of prosecutions. The last three charges were focused on government cover-ups (#6 and #7), and corporate regulatory offences, which are less commonly resolved with criminal charges (#8).[1] The second reason is that the first five categories are also the most common primary charges in these corruption cases, whereas official misconduct, obstruction of justice, and regulatory offences were more often secondary charges in criminal cases. That is to say, the secondary charges were often related to attempts to conceal the primary offence (e.g. obstruction of justice most often occurred in an effort to cover up the original act of bribery). Of course, this analysis focuses only on known cases, so it is not possible to know how these categories correspond with corruption that is not detected, and these cases likely over-represent larger, more serious instances of corruption, as limited government prosecution resources often result in the screening out of less serious corrupt conduct cases than is detected.[2]

---

1   These corporate violations are usually charged as regulatory or administrative offences that result in civil fines, rather than criminal prosecution.
2   Interviews conducted as part of this project with multiple former federal investigators and prosecutors who handled public corruption cases confirm this observation regarding the screening out of less serious cases.

*Table 2.1* Summary of corruption cases

| Underlying conduct | Frequency | Percentage |
| --- | --- | --- |
| Receipt of bribe | 97 | 34.3 |
| Solicitation of bribe | 40 | 14.1 |
| Extortion | 19 | 6.7 |
| Contract fraud | 47 | 16.6 |
| Embezzlement | 80 | 28.3 |
| Totals | 283 cases | 100% |

Table 2.1 presents the results of the analysis of corruption cases. There were a total of 283 cases that resulted in indictment or conviction over three years (2013–2015) in these five categories.[3] Receiving bribes involving a government official and embezzlement of government funds were the largest categories of corrupt conduct, totalling 62.6% of all cases (i.e. 34.3% plus 28.3%, respectively). The least common charge was extortion at 6.7%.

If the charges are re-ordered in terms of their frequency of occurrence, an interesting pattern emerges, which is shown in Figure 2.3. The often less serious offences (i.e. receiving bribes and embezzlement) occur (are prosecuted) most frequently, whereas the more serious offences requiring more assertive conduct (i.e. extortion and soliciting bribes) are the least common.

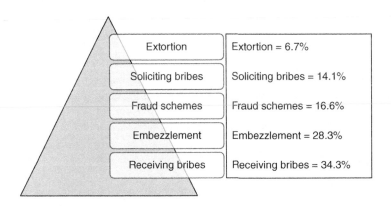

*Figure 2.3* Corruption charges by frequency

3 Because these cases often take multiple years to move from discovery to conviction, both indictments and convictions were counted, knowing that indictments (the vast majority of which result in guilty pleas) will be resolved in subsequent years. In a similar way, the convictions in our sample resulted from cases begun much earlier (outside our sampling frame from 2013–2015). It makes more sense to sample prosecutions by year (as a measure of anti-corruption activity) than to attempt to follow individual cases across time-periods of variable lengths.

The nature and relative seriousness of these cases are illustrated by reviewing fact patterns in the cases that underlie the numbers.[4] Below are brief summaries of the nature of the cases in each category. These fact patterns are summarised from the sample of 283 cases analysed.

> **Extortion** – A public official sells influence for decision or vote, police officers take cash to protect drug traffickers or protect gamblers or sex clubs, police solicit cash from criminals for non-arrest, sheriff demands campaign kickbacks from deputies, city officials pressure others for political donations in exchange for official action or jobs, or contractors threatened to hire union workers on public projects.

> **Soliciting bribes** – Public officials solicit kickbacks for services or contracts (motor vehicle and identity documents, passport, military procurement, city contracts, zoning), corrections officers solicit bribes to smuggle contraband into prison, bribes to police occur at border crossings, kickbacks are received for government loans or mortgages, or bribes from inmates are solicited or accepted to recommend release from prison.

> **Fraud schemes** – False documents for government loans or mortgages, identity theft tax fraud schemes, health care provider false billing frauds, false government claims schemes (BP oil spill, minority-owned businesses, military claims, marriage frauds), bid-rigging contracts, selling misbranded or counterfeit products to government, or overtime scams by government officials.

> **Embezzlement** – Public funds used for personal expenses, stealing funds from child welfare and school programs, tax collectors stealing tax funds, or public officials filing false expense reports.

> **Bribe receiving** – Bribery of officials for favouritism in government contracts, bribery of police officers for actions or inaction, building or zoning inspectors taking bribes, elected officials taking bribes for support or votes, bribes for government loans, or corrections officers accepting bribes to smuggle contraband into prison.

These fact-patterns show that corruption cases involving extortion and soliciting bribes are both organised criminal acts and predatory. These cases usually involve multiple defendants because they are carried out on a systematic, repeated basis. In this way, they resemble organised crime more than white collar crime, because they are developed to exploit a procedure or a subculture of an agency in order to profit *primarily* from crime (rather than carry out their government function as prescribed by law).

---

4 A fact pattern is a concise description of the events and circumstances of a particular case, without any discussion of their consequences under the law. The fact situation (also called fact pattern) is a summary of what took place in a case for which relief is sought or prosecution resulted.

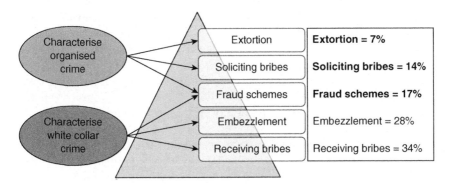

*Figure 2.4* The organisation of corruption

Fraud schemes were found in these cases to be more diverse in nature, straddling the line between white collar and organised crime. Some of these schemes are smaller, but were clear diversions from the legitimate business of the agency. On the other hand, some fraud schemes are more organised and ongoing, suggesting a subculture or ongoing conspiracy within the agency to engage in systematic criminal behaviour.

The corruption cases involving embezzlement and bribe receiving are dominated by misconduct at the individual level. Many fewer of these cases involve systematic misconduct by groups of individuals. These cases appear to involve individual exploitation of an available opportunity, rather than a continuing, organised, systematic effort to profit from crime. Therefore, embezzlement and bribe-receiving corruption cases in this sample are more clearly examples of white collar crime carried out at the individual level, rather than organised crime.

The differences in how these five types of corruption cases are organised are displayed in Figure 2.4. It is shown there how the facts of corruption cases involving extortion and soliciting bribes provide examples of organised crime due to their systematic, ongoing nature, whereas the corruption cases involving embezzlement and receiving bribes more closely resemble individual deviations from the otherwise legitimate business of the agency.

## Discussion

Given the data presented here, corruption as a form of white collar crime constitutes the majority of criminal cases prosecuted (i.e. cases involving embezzlement and receiving bribes together account for 62% of all cases). On the other hand, corruption cases manifesting as a form of organised crime constitute 21% of cases (i.e. extortion and soliciting bribes or kickbacks). The remaining category, corruption cases involving fraudulent schemes (17%), are quite diverse in their level of organisation and sophistication, so they cannot be placed clearly into a single category.

These findings might lead to the conclusion that a greater focus should be placed on the prevention of white collar corruption cases, given their larger number (at least in this sample of cases covering three years in a single country). However, there may be a tipping point when a business or government agency turns *from* pilfering *to* operating like a criminal enterprise. For example, what distinguishes a police agency that experiences a few corrupt officers, as opposed to one that experiences systematic corruption? What separates the corruption of a few individuals from the corruption of entire units within a corporation or government agency?

A case example helps to illustrate the point that there can be a progression in the nature of corrupt conduct. John Raphael was a consultant and lobbyist based in Columbus, Ohio, who was hired and paid by traffic control companies seeking to do business with government jurisdictions in Ohio. A red light camera enforcement company, based in Australia, hired Raphael to help obtain lucrative contracts to provide red light photo enforcement systems in the City of Columbus. (Red light camera enforcement involves the purchase and installation of cameras at busy intersections that capture drivers who run red lights. The system issues tickets, which are sent directly to violators using their licence plates to locate them. These systems have become popular among local governments in that they can generate large revenues for the jurisdiction, because a private company installs the cameras and sends the tickets to violators, in exchange for a percentage of the fines paid.)

Raphael repeatedly pressured and induced the red light camera enforcement company to make illegal campaign contributions to various elected officials. He said the company would lose its contracts if it did not make the payments. Karen Finley, the CEO of the red light camera company, together with another executive from the company, agreed to provide the campaign contributions through Raphael on the understanding that the elected public officials would assist the company in obtaining or retaining the red light contracts in their jurisdictions. They concealed the true nature and source of the payments using false invoices for 'consulting services', funds which Raphael covertly provided to the campaigns of the elected public officials. This scheme was ultimately discovered, and Finley was sentenced to 14 months in prison for the bribery and fraud scheme (U.S. Department of Justice, 2016b).

What makes this case especially interesting is that the red light camera company claimed it would not have made the political contributions without Raphael's repeated pressure to induce the company to make campaign contributions to the elected officials. The prosecution found that Raphael obtained the illicit campaign funds through the wrongful use of fear of economic harm. Raphael admitted that because of his actions, the company made over $70,000 in illicit campaign contributions, which were funnelled through Raphael in his own name and in the names of his family members, friends, and business associates in an effort to disguise their origin and remain under legal contribution limits. He pleaded guilty to extortion, and was sentenced to 15 months in prison (U.S. Department of Justice, 2015a, 2016a).

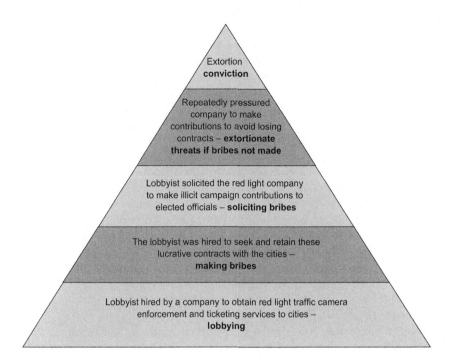

*Figure 2.5* Red light enforcement case progression

In addition, the red light enforcement company, Reflex Systems, cooperated with the U.S. government and entered into a non-prosecution agreement and the payment of significant restitution and civil compensation to the cities involved. (There was an analogous illicit payment scheme that occurred in Chicago with its own red light traffic enforcement, involving many of the same individuals.) (U.S. Department of Justice, 2016c).

Figure 2.5 illustrates the nature of the schemes that occurred in the two large cities. It is shown that a lawful lobbying arrangement transformed into a bribery scheme, and from there into an extortion scheme. The activity progressed from hiring a consultant to represent the firm, to bribery of customers (via illegal election contributions), to extortionate demands to the company to make illicit payments.

The red light traffic enforcement cases can be seen as an illustration of a tipping point when a business moves *from* lobbying and bribery *to* operating as an ongoing criminal enterprise. It is difficult to know from the available facts the intention of the contractor at the outset, but it is clear that progressively more serious criminal conduct occurred over the course of the red light scheme – moving from more passive bribery to more assertive bribe solicitation and extortion threats.

There are reasons why this situation might occur. Impediments created for the commission of organised crime, using more intensive legislation and more sophisticated law enforcement actions, make the commission of these crimes more difficult. This can result in those looking for criminal solutions to seek alternative means. For example, raising the difficulty of receiving bribes may result in more sophisticated or deceptive ways to offer or solicit bribes (e.g. corruption of public servants as a way to gather information or protect patterns of offending). The result is an inadvertent increase in the seriousness of corrupt conduct designed by offenders to evade the increased regulation or enforcement. Relying on several cases from Australia, one study concluded that enhanced legislative and law enforcement responses to crime may result in criminals increasingly making attempts to gain or shape 'insider knowledge' through the corruption of public officials in order to reduce the risk of apprehension as they commit crimes (Rowe et al., 2013). A descriptive study of EU countries examined a large number of corruption, crime, and social indicators in each country, and despite regional differences, it was found that the link between organised crime and corruption occurred most often when organised crime targeted low-ranking employees of police and public administration (Gounev and Bezlov, 2010; see also Tudzarovska-Gjorgjievska, 2015). These findings suggest that a relationship exists between the level of regulation and enforcement and how it impacts the nature of the criminal conduct it was designed to prevent (i.e. possibly making it more sophisticated, deceptive, and organised).

Additional research is needed on a larger number of cases to determine: (a) is there an inevitable progression from less to more serious corrupt conduct over time if it is not interrupted, and (b) what are the important factors that promote the existence and continuation and escalation of these corrupt schemes (in terms of changes in regulation or enforcement impacting the nature of corrupt conduct)? Regarding the second question, the facts of the cases analysed here suggest the possibilities for application of enterprise theory and situational crime prevention in many of the schemes that ended in criminal court. These two theories are selected given their successful application in multiple cases of organised and white collar crime (see Aromaa and Viljanen, 2006; Bullock et al., 2010; Felson, 2006; Huisman and Van Erp, 2013; Kleemans et al., 2012, Van der Schoot, 2006; Von Lampe, 2011). The possibilities for application of these theories to corruption-related crimes are discussed below.

## Potential application of enterprise and routine activities perspectives

Another case illustrates the potential for using theory to understand and prevent corruption schemes, in how they respond according to the changes in the nature of the available opportunities. George Wu was a U.S. Customs and Border Protection Officer who left his government position and started a private company, 'Great Eastern Immigration Services'. With associates (both inside and outside the government), Wu solicited money from immigrants in exchange for helping obtain benefits from the U.S. government, including permanent residence, and citizenship approvals and documentation. Wu used some of the money paid by the immigrants for bribes to public officials in exchange for granting immigration status.

In one instance, thousands of dollars in bribes were paid for an immigrant to pass an English proficiency exam even though she could not speak English. In another case, Wu paid an attorney $15,000 for assistance in securing legal permanent resident status for another immigrant. In still other cases, sham marriages were arranged to secure immigration permits for clients. The entire scheme was discovered when Wu unknowingly offered a bribe to an undercover agent investigating corruption in the immigration process. Wu and several associates were convicted of bribery and conspiracy, as were others including both government officials and private companies (U.S. Department of Justice, 2015b, 2016d).

Figure 2.6 illustrates the nature of Wu's illegal immigration scheme. His company, Great Eastern Immigration Services, engaged in an organised scheme to solicit bribes from the large pool (*available supply*) of immigrants in need of these services, which, in turn, spurred bribes to government officials authorised to approve immigration requests. The company exploited the large *demand* for immigration status approvals by manipulating both the immigrants and the

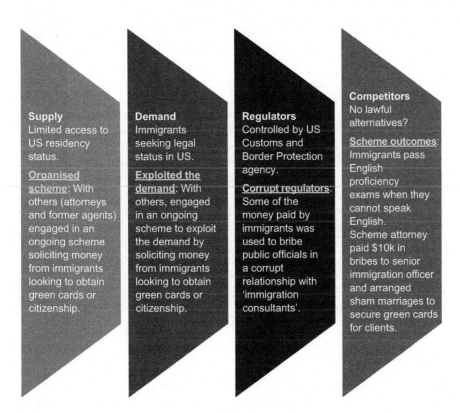

*Figure 2.6* Great Eastern Immigration Services: simple bribery v. ongoing criminal enterprise?

government agencies that deal with these requests. The scheme required corrupt *regulators* inside these government agencies. Finally, U.S. immigration agencies have monopoly control over the granting of immigration status, so there were fewer lawful alternatives available to immigrants (other than agencies that did not solicit bribes). What is not clear is the full extent to which corruption exists inside this marketplace of immigration review. Additional research on how that market works in the US would be required to make recommendations that are more specific.

The enterprise perspective sees organised crime and corruption as the product of market forces, similar to those that cause legitimate businesses to flourish or die in the legal sector of the economy. These market forces include the availability of supply, the nature and level of demand, the regulators who might thwart the illicit activity, and competitors which might reduce their profitability or even survival in the market (Albanese, 2012; Smith, 1980).

In an analogous way, the routine activities, or situational crime prevention, perspective concentrates on 'criminal settings' (environments conducive to organised crime activity, rather than on the motivations of individuals or groups of people). By focusing on the circumstances of crime, this perspective examines the availability of opportunities to commit specific crimes using the principles of routine activities: availability of attractive targets, a low level of supervision, and low risk of apprehension (Bullock et al., 2010; Eckblom, 2003). There is emerging evidence that the situational crime prevention approach can be useful in reducing more sophisticated crimes by limiting criminal opportunities and minimizing harm (Felson, 2006; Lord and Levi, 2017).

The enterprise and situational crime prevention perspectives might be applied in the case of corruption to develop crime prevention measures best suited to its entrepreneurial aspects. For example, the best methods for 'increasing the risks' for corruption of different types will be easier to develop, when information is known about how these risks are distributed among the suppliers, customers, regulators, and competitors from the enterprise perspective. Similarly, for situational crime prevention, 'increasing the effort' needed by offenders to carry out crimes (such as receiving or soliciting bribes), and reducing the rewards, provocation, and excuses requires more specific information on corruption of different kinds both within countries and transnationally. Therefore, the elements of enterprise theory can help to target the precise types of efforts likely to affect the incidence of different levels of corruption, and the principles of situational crime prevention may be accurately focused and comprehensive when applied through the lens of enterprise theory.

## Conclusion

This study provides insights into the variation in the nature of corruption in a large sample of criminal prosecutions for corruption-related offences. It was found that corruption ranges from more passive to more assertive forms, and that these forms may be responsive to changes in regulation or enforcement.

There are also limitations to this study, which lie in the data gathered; they are taken from three years' experience in a single country. More data from a broader array of jurisdictions would permit less descriptive and more generalisable results. In addition, this analysis relies on known, prosecuted cases. The advantage is that all the cases considered here have met a high burden of proof, but there are also undiscovered cases that are not included here. The measurement of corruption, and all other 'hidden' deviance, is difficult to measure by its covert nature (Albanese, 2011; Fisman and Golden, 2017; Simpson, 2013). Complainants rarely come forward, many governments do not aggressively investigate corruption cases, and some governments are implicated in corrupt conduct, making corruption convictions even less likely (Campbell, 2013; Chayes, 2015; Lord, 2016).

Nevertheless, this study provides insights from a single country's experience, and it provides points of departure for future work. For example, is the typology of corruption cases developed here generalisable in other nations? Would it hold up when looking at more cases over a longer period of time? Do the theoretical premises discussed have value for considering corruption prevention in general? These are issues that can be examined with additional data, but this study is a first step in that direction.

This analysis of several hundred U.S. corruption cases found their fact-patterns can be grouped into a typology of five different types from the least to most organised forms of corrupt conduct. There is suggestive evidence that a tipping point may be reached when a business or government agency turns from exploiting the system by pilfering, toward operating like a criminal enterprise with organised schemes involving fraud, solicitation, or extortion. The existence of a tipping point requires more research to move it from anecdotal case analysis to a more systematic review. That is to say, is there general movement from low effort crimes of opportunity (by and against business) to crimes involving organisation and the *creation* of corrupt opportunities? Intuitively, this is likely to occur in environments with a low risk of apprehension (a factor important in both the enterprise and routine activities perspectives), and when there is a monopoly or little competition for the product or service in question, and when supply and demand are both high and inelastic. Theoretically, both the enterprise and routine activities' perspectives address these concerns, although in different ways.

Future research needs to assess the risk factors for low effort corruption/ bribery *versus* creating corruption opportunities, and there might be important differences between opportunistic bribery versus more predatory rent-seeking behaviour. These differences may spur, in turn, a greater focus away from the more common crimes by and against business (e.g. embezzlement, bribe giving/ receiving) toward the less common, but far more serious, predatory crimes that seek to create corruption (extortion, bribery/kickback solicitations). This kind of analysis in the future will provide insight into the comparatively smaller numbers of serious organised crime-related corruption cases that may well have unseen impacts on less organised corrupt behaviour.

## Acknowledgement

This project was supported in part by Award No. 2015-IJ-CX-0007, awarded by the National Institute of Justice, Office of Justice Programs, U.S. Department of Justice. The opinions, findings, and conclusions or recommendations expressed in this publication are those of the author and do not necessarily reflect those of the Department of Justice.

## Bibliography

Albanese, Jay. (1995) *White-Collar Crime in America*. Upper Saddle River, NJ: Prentice Hall.

Albanese, Jay. (2011) *Transnational Crime and the 21st Century: Criminal Enterprise, Corruption, and Opportunity*. Oxford, UK: Oxford University Press.

Albanese, Jay. (2012) 'Deciphering the linkages between organized crime and transnational crime', *Journal of International Affairs*, 66: 1–16.

Albanese, Jay. (2015) *Organized Crime: From the Mob to Transnational Organized Crime*. Oxford, UK: Routledge.

Andersson, Saffan. (2017) 'Beyond unidimensional measurement of corruption', *Public Integrity*, 19: 58–76.

Aromaa, Kauko and T. Viljanen. (2006) *International Key Issues in Crime Prevention and Criminal Justice*. Helsinki: European Institute for Crime Prevention and Control [HEUNI].

Bullock, K., R.V. Clarke and N. Tilley. (2010) 'Introduction', in K. Bullock, R.V. Clarke, and N. Tilley (eds) *Situational Prevention of Organised Crimes*. Devon, UK: Willand Publishing.

Campbell, Liz. (2013) *Organised Crime and the Law: A Comparative Analysis*. Oxford, UK: Hart Publishing.

Chayes, Sarah. (2015) *Thieves of State: Why Corruption Threatens Global Security*. London: W.W. Norton.

Cobin, Seth Benjamin. (2009) 'Upperworld gangsters, underworld businessmen: Made men, corporate raiders and the discrepancies between the enforcement of organised and organisational crime. Or, why a last name that ends with a vowel still means hard time for a defendant', *Hamline Journal of Public Law & Policy*, 30(2): 627–682.

Cordis, Adriana S. and Jeffrey Milyo. (2016) 'Measuring public corruption in the United States: Evidence from administrative records from federal prosecutions', *Public Integrity*, 18: 127–148.

Dawood, Yasmin. (2014) 'Classifying corruption', *Duke Journal of Constitutional Law & Public Policy*, 9(1): 103–133.

DeMarco, Megan. (2016) 'Private actors and public corruption: Why courts should adopt a broad interpretation of the Hobbs Act', *Michigan Law Review*, 115(3): 413–438.

Eckblom, Paul. (2003) 'Organised crime and the conjunction of criminal opportunity framework', in A. Edwards and P. Gill (eds) *Transnational Organised Crime: Perspectives on Global Security*. Abingdon, UK: Routledge, pp. 242–263.

Felson, Marcus. (2006) *The Ecosystem for Organized Crime*. Helsinki: European Institute for Crime Prevention and Control.

Fisman, Ray and Miriam A. Golden. (2017) *Corruption: What Everyone Needs to Know*. Oxford, UK: Oxford University Press.

Gounev, Philip and and Tihomir Bezlov. (2010) *Examining the Links between Organized Crime and Corruption*. Sofia: Center for the Study of Democracy and European Commission.

Gummesson, Evert. (2014) 'Commentary on "The role of innovation in driving the economy": Lessons from the global financial crisis"', *Journal of Business Research*, 67: 2743–2750.

Heffernan, William C. and John Kleinig. (2004) *Private and Public Corruption*. London: Rowman & Littlefield Publishers.

Holmes, Leslie. (2015) *Corruption: A Very Short Introduction*. Oxford, UK: Oxford University Press.

Huisman, Wim and Van Erp, Judith. (2013) 'Opportunities for environmental crime', *British Journal of Criminology*, 53(6): 1178–1200.

Kenny, Kate. (2014) 'Banking compliance and dependence corruption: Towards an attachment perspective', *Law & Financial Markets Review*, 8: 165–177.

Kleemans, Edward, Soudijn, Melvin and Weenink, Anton. (2012) 'Organized crime, situational crime prevention and routine activity theory', *Trends in Organized Crime*, 15(2): 87–92.

Lord, Nicholas. (2016) 'Establishing enforcement legitimacy in the pursuit of rule-breaking "global elites": The case of transnational corporate bribery', *Theoretical Criminology*, 20: 376–399.

Lord, Nicholas and Michael Levi. (2017) 'Organising the finances for and the finances from transnational corporate bribery', *European Journal of Criminology*, 14: 365–389.

Pontell, Henry N. and Kitty Calavita. (1993) 'White-collar crime in the savings and loan scandal', *The Annals*, 525(1): 31–45.

Rawls, John. (1971) *A Theory of Justice*. Cambridge, MA: Harvard University Press, pp. 73–77.

Rose-Ackerman, Susan and Bonnie J. Palikfa. (2016) *Corruption and Government: Causes, Consequences, and Reform*. 2nd ed. Cambridge, UK: Cambridge University Press.

Rowe, Elizabeth, Tabor Akman, Russell G. Smith and Adam M. Tomison. (2013) 'Organised crime and public sector corruption: A crime scripts analysis of tactical displacement risks', *Trends & Issues in Crime and Criminal Justice*, 444, Australian Institute of Criminology.

Schulter, William E. (2017) *Soft Corruption: How Unethical Conduct Undermines Good Government and What to Do about It*. New Brunswick, NJ: Rutgers University Press.

Simpson, Sally S. (2013) 'White-collar crime: A review of recent developments and promising directions for future research', *Annual Review of Sociology*, 39: 309–331.

Smith, Jr., Dwight C. (1980) 'Paragons, pariahs, and pirates: A spectrum-based theory of enterprise', *Crime & Delinquency*, 26: 358–387.

Thompson, Dennis F. (2005) 'Two concepts of corruption: Making campaigns safe for democracy', *George Washington Law Review*, 73: 1036–1056.

Tudzarovska-Gjorgjievska, Emilija. (2015) *Corruption and Organized Crime Threat Monitoring Report*. Skopje: Macedonian Center for International Cooperation.

U.S. Department of Justice. (2015a) *Columbus Lobbyist Pleads Guilty to Extortion*. October 15. U.S. Attorney's Office Southern District of Ohio.

U.S. Department of Justice. (2015b) *Immigration Consultant and Former Federal Government Official Convicted in Scheme to Pay Bribes to Obtain Benefits for Immigrants*. August 14. U.S. Attorney's Office for the Central District of California.

U.S. Department of Justice. (2016a) *Ohio Lobbyist Sentenced to 15 Months for Extortionate Role in Conduit Campaign Contribution Scheme*. June 8. U.S. Attorney's Office Southern District of Ohio.

U.S. Department of Justice. (2016b) *Former CEO Sentenced for Bribery and Fraud Scheme Involving Red Light Camera Contracts in Ohio.* October 19. U.S. Attorney's Office Southern District of Ohio.

U.S. Department of Justice. (2016c) *Redflex Traffic Systems Enters into Non-Prosecution Agreement with United States.* December 27. U.S. Attorney's Office for the Northern District of Illinois.

U.S. Department of Justice. (2016d) *Former Federal Customs Official Sentenced to over 3 Years in Federal Prison in Scheme to Pay Bribes to Obtain Benefits for Immigrants.* May 13. U.S. Attorney's Office for the Central District of California.

Van der Schoot, C.R.A. (2006) *Organized Crime Prevention in the Netherlands.* The Hague: BJU Legal Publishers.

Vargas-Hernández, José G. (2011) 'The multiple faces of corruption: Typology, forms and levels', *Contemporary Legal & Economic Issues,* 3: 269–290.

Von Lampe, Klaus. (2011) 'The application of the framework of situational crime prevention to organized crime', *Criminology & Criminal Justice,* 11: 145–163.

Wedman, Andrew. (2013) 'The challenge of commercial bribery and organized crime in China', *Journal of Contemporary China,* 22: 18–34.

White, Richard. (2013). 'What counts as corruption?' *Social Research,* 80(4): 1033–1056.

# 3 Unfair advantage

## The corruptive influence of criminal money on legitimate markets

*Kenneth Murray*

The views expressed are those of the author alone and should not be taken as those of Police Scotland.

## Introduction

This chapter considers the corruptive influence exerted by criminal money in legitimate markets, with particular reference to experience in Scotland. Corruptive influence is defined for this purpose as the ability to obtain and abuse economic power; it may relate to relationships between parties as well as conduct in offices of authority. Corruption, or the ability to corrupt, is therefore an activity that involves abuse of influence as conferred by either money or authority. The continuum of corruptive practice that leads to abuse of markets or political power starts with the working capital necessary to exert influence. The availability of such capital can be presupposed to have a direct relationship to the availability of criminal money. But how does that happen? What are the mechanisms that enable criminal money to be made available for corruptive purposes?

## Cause and effect

The implied cause and effect relationship between criminal money and incidence of corruption within an economy can be represented in basic terms as follows in Figure 3.1.

Not all money used to corrupt is 'dirty' of course, but in Scotland, as in other countries,[1] where drug trafficking continues to deliver the bulk of criminal profits, and where there are mature illicit mechanisms for recycling this money so that it can be deployed in legitimate spheres, there is a need to improve understanding of how criminal money is transformed and deployed so that it can be used in 'legitimate' spheres, including for corruption.

There are, of course, well developed compliance mechanisms to ensure vigilance within banking systems (see Gelemerova et al., this volume), but

---

1 The European Monitoring Centre for Drug and Drug Addiction (EMCDDA) estimates that EU citizens spend $24 billion every year on illicit drugs (EMCDDA, 2016).

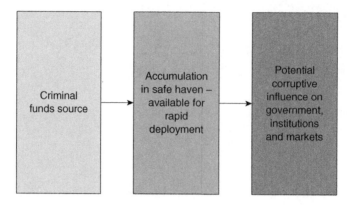

*Figure 3.1* Organised crime and corruption: the relationship between cause and effect

the processes that enable dirty cash from the streets to be transformed into legitimised assets on a property register or hedge fund investment account are still poorly understood and policed inadequately.

By the time the money is moved to a bank account it is often sufficiently well laundered to be indistinguishable from the legitimate money with which it has been mingled. Significant intelligence gaps persist, therefore, relating to the handling and management of criminal money before it is transferred to a bank account. Organised Crime Groups (OCGs) continue to harvest the rewards of their crimes despite the extensive compliance regimes set up to prevent that from happening. Another factor to consider is that money laundering prosecutions in all jurisdictions continue to be difficult to achieve, mainly due to challenges associated with proving knowledge on the criminality of the relevant funds. Money management mechanisms set up by criminal networks are, somewhat predictably, designed to exploit such difficulties. The objectives of mechanisms are to protect ill-gotten gains, but also to enable criminal funds to be redeployed in legitimate as well as illegitimate contexts.

## Exploiting the nature of money

'What is most vile and despicable about money is that it even confers talent. And will do so until the end of the world' (*The Idiot*, Dostoevsky, 1868), captured the quality of money to transform the abilities and powers of those who are able to acquire and deploy it. He also referred to money as 'coined freedom'. As a 'bearer' medium of exchange, money usually will be assumed to be legitimate, and of legitimate provenance, unless there are clear reasons that present and indicate otherwise. As a universal medium of exchange, its capacity to act as such around the world is seemingly unaffected by its provenance, despite the best efforts of the Financial Action Task Force (FATF).

Corrupt and criminal revenues therefore are capable of conferring 'talent', or influence, wherever it is deployed. The deployment of such funds in legitimate markets supports the establishment of business profiles that are capable of sustaining powerful market positions and exerting corruptive influence in the economies in which they are active. Their existence is often common 'street' knowledge in the localities and areas of business activity affected. Criminal money therefore represents an insidious influence on legitimate economies. It is known about but perhaps not very often spoken about – leading to an under-appreciation in wider circles of its true effect.

Improving collective response to this challenge therefore requires a significant improvement in overall awareness. Criminal money succeeds in making the jump from criminal to legitimate milieu, but understanding of criminal money flows prior to their being recorded on a bank account – or those which are not recorded on a bank account at all – is still generally poor. Partly this is due to the fact that the skill sets commonly deployed in this field are usually oriented around understanding commodity flows rather than money flows. The resultant lack of relevant 'money intelligence' thus tends to take operational activity down routes that generate little knowledge about the relevant criminal business processes. These intelligence gaps then become so large it seems an overwhelming task to think about filling them.

The result is a mismatch between the political rhetoric expressing the desire to tackle this problem and effectiveness on the ground. The desire to do something about 'high end money laundering', for instance, is often expressed (*Daily Telegraph*, 2015), without much insight offered as to how this might be achieved. The continuing incongruence between perception of the threat and ability to tackle it tends to undermine how seriously it is treated. Indeed, commentators critical of law enforcement's efforts in this area often accuse it of exaggerating the threat for its own purposes (Harvey, 2014; Sproat, 2009). The commentators can hardly be blamed for their conclusions where there is a lack of hard data to counter them. Repeating the 'absence of evidence is not the same as evidence of absence' maxim is not sufficient.

There is a need, therefore, for law enforcement to improve its understanding of how the relevant mechanisms work. It needs more effective strategies to tackle an attendant threat that is difficult to overstate. As Fiorentini and Peltzman (1997) put it:

> We feel that the economics of organised crime goes well beyond the realm of 'individual organisation'. The importance of this sector of human activity involves the economies of some countries and their international relations in such a deep and pervasive way that it may even affect the economic performance and constrain the macro-economic policies of their entire economies.

## Characteristics of criminal supply chains in Class A drug markets: the key role of the mid-level broker

So how does criminal money work its way into the legitimate economy? What are the processes? If we are able to start developing answers to these questions, the foundation blocks for an effective strategy against the corruptive effect of criminal money might start to be laid down.

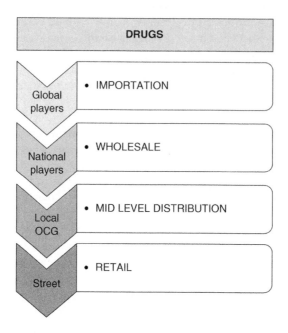

*Figure 3.2* The Class A drug supply chain in the UK

As indicated, the principal cash generator in most criminal markets is still Class A drug supply (although fraud and cybercrime are considered likely to become more prominent in the future). The way in which this 'industry' is organised in the UK is a function of some essential governing parameters. The most fundamental of these is the need to import the relevant commodity onto the UK's shores. The traditional Class A drug products – heroin, cocaine, cannabis (in large quantity) – are not cultivated or sourced locally. It follows that the obvious starting point for analysis of the supply chain (and its pricing structures) is the importation stage. From there, in general terms, the key processes can be characterised as wholesale, mid-level distribution and retail, as per Figure 3.2.

The supply chain is characterised by a relatively small number of high value transactions at the top end, tapering to a relatively large number of small value transactions at the retail end. The risk of being caught 'hands on' encourages the retail side of the chain to be diversified, characterised by loose associations and informal distribution networks; whereas the organisation of high value importations requires a high degree of financial substance and influence to be involved in them. At this end of the chain the transaction level often relates to multi-kilo quantities and multi-million-pound transactions. At the other end of the chain, individual retail transactions are settled in cash at prices of £10 and £20.

The cash dynamic of the process therefore can be characterised by stages of cash revenues settling supplier debt as illustrated in Figure 3.3.

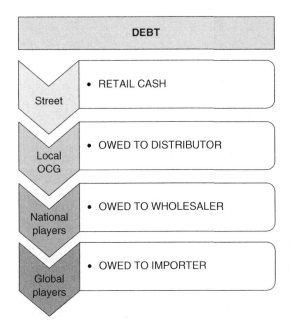

*Figure 3.3* The cash settlement chain associated with class A drug trafficking in the UK

This supply process is split, however, at the distribution stage, where the realm of large ticket credit-based transactions meets the realm of large volume, low denomination cash transactions. The key players at this level can be characterised as 'mid-level brokers'. These individuals have to have the trust of the big players above this level and be able to exercise the necessary discipline of the more divergent range of retail distributors below this level. Such mid-level brokers often deal in more than one product range and their pivotal role in the relevant supply process is illustrated in Figure 3.4.

The mid-level broker level can be seen from Figure 3.4, therefore, as occupying a key frontier in the process. In Scotland this frontier has a recognisable 'edge' determined by the measures traded. Under the mid-level, the commodity tends to be sold in imperial measures (typically ounces and fractions thereof), whereas above the mid-level metric measures are used (typically kilos and fractions thereof). The mid-level brokers therefore are charged with the realisation of kilo-denominated quantities into a revenue stream by managing a sales process (essentially a local retail distribution network) based on unit sales denominated in ounces.

The significance of the role in practice, however, relates to how cash revenues are handled as much as how the drugs are distributed. Intelligence suggests that mid-level brokers tend to distance themselves from direct contact with the commodity, whereas they are directly engaged in the task of collecting, storing and transmitting cash revenues.

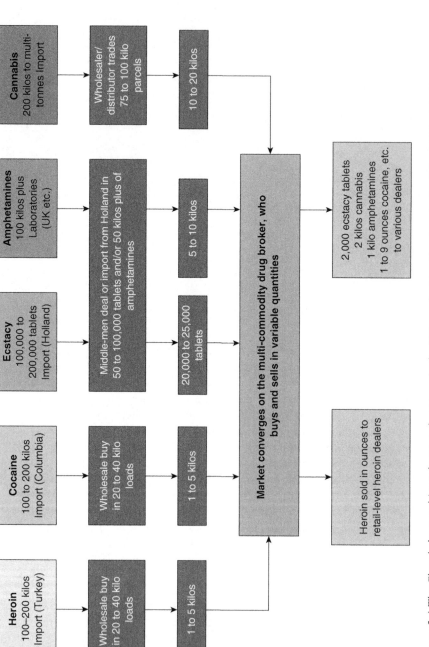

*Figure 3.4* The Class A drug multi-product supply process in the UK, emphasising the pivotal role of the mid-level broker

The pivotal position occupied by the mid-level broker with respect to criminal cash flows, derived from intelligence disseminations relating to prominent Scottish SOCGs, is illustrated in Figure 3.5 in respect of the supply of cocaine (the numbers vary in respect of the other commodities but the relationships between the various levels essentially remains the same).

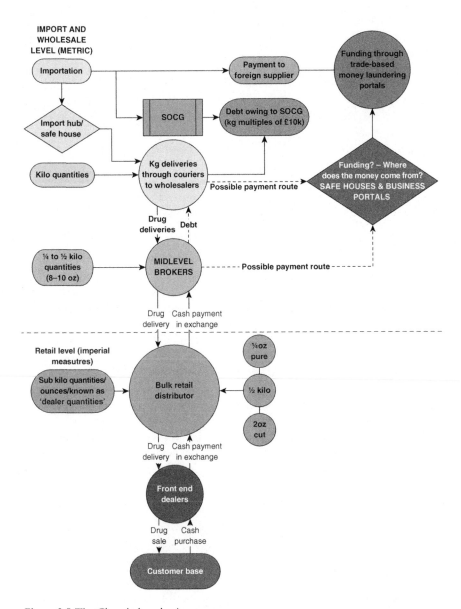

*Figure 3.5* The Class A drug business process

The mid-broker level represents the principal hinge between the cash generation, which is the revenue engine of the chain, and the accumulation of significant sums requiring to be laundered. It is the revenues collected and dispensed upwards from this level that provide the main SOCG players with their economic return. These can be in the form of monies dispensed through UK businesses, or foreign investments enabled by monies transferred through forex portals, or trade-based money laundering arrangements, or physical cash smuggling.

The revenues generated at the mid-level broker level are significant (i.e. c. £70k per kilo versus importation values of £10–20k per kilo) and are collected in cash. Prices tend to remain stable at street level because the quantities can be varied to ensure continuation of standard £10 or £20 street transactions. The key logistical challenge for the mid-level broker is to harvest the cash generated from dirty street sales and take it to a place where it can enter a process of transformation which enables it to be transformed into either a bank account or a business. This function is therefore at the heart of delivering the profitability associated with the entire enterprise.

It follows that the mid-level broker manages a key part of the process which enables its insertion into the legitimate economy. The key intelligence often missing is the means by which this process is achieved.

## Methods of transformation

Criminal cash from Class A drug supply will normally in the first instance be collected and stored in a safe house, or a business which acts as a safe house (e.g. a bar that acts as a 'drop bar', or simply a separate safe in a cash-generating business). It is the next stage that is critical – the stage that transfers it to a setting where it can hide amongst legitimate money. The uplift of the cash, its transfer, and then its insertion through some legitimate business portal, unsurprisingly, is the part of the process around which there is greatest secrecy on the part of the criminals. Historically, the general experience has been that these processes are resilient to effective intelligence penetration by law enforcement.

The cash collected will be absorbed locally under the carapace of 'onside' businesses, or otherwise moved abroad; either physically smuggled or wired under cover of legitimate trading. These processes suggest the existence of available expertise to execute them, and a requirement of that kind of expertise is that it is able to operate with one foot in the legitimate world and one foot in the criminal world.

A schematic picture of the necessary process, the basic business cycle, is presented in Figure 3.6.

The key cash transition process shown in Figure 3.6 is that from the safe house (which may be a cash shelter afforded by a business) to a place that will enable absorption of the criminal cash into some kind of safe haven. This is where the process of assimilation starts, which is key to the objective of turning this kind of money into 'normal money' capable of circulating in the legitimate economy. There is an implied need for some kind of 'portal' into a business, or a bank

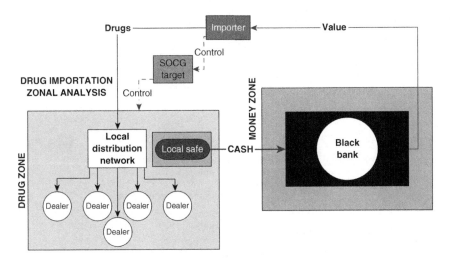

*Figure 3.6* The Class A drug basic business cycle

account attached to a business. The existence of companies with legitimate fronts and under the control of organised crime groups is therefore a necessary feature of successful drug trafficking – as necessary as the ability to source and import the commodity itself.

If money is held in trust, or on behalf of another party, there has to be a means of holding the custodian accountable to the beneficial owner. This is one of the essential properties of a bank, and intelligence in Scotland supports the notion that there are individuals and businesses operating essentially as unlicensed 'black banks' for criminal underground clients. These are trusted specialists in the handling and transporting of criminal money, and manage its transformation into money capable of being treated and used as legitimate money. In essence, this is where the criminal process of high-value money laundering starts to take place, using methods that require the cover of normal commerce to achieve its objectives.

## Money laundering methodologies under cover of commerce

The worldwide compliance mechanisms developed to prevent international banking systems being abused for money laundering have encouraged criminals to develop alternative methods to transfer large amounts of criminally generated wealth. Two of the most significant are *trade-based money laundering (TBML)* and *transaction laundering*.

In TBML, a legitimate company allows the paperwork attached to exported goods to be adjusted in such a way as to accommodate a criminal value to be exported. A simple example is shown in Figure 3.7.

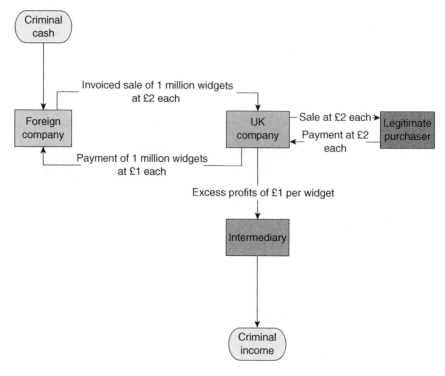

*Figure 3.7* Basic trade-based money laundering example

The criminal cash is paid to the foreign company, which then invoices the UK company for a value which is twice the money it actually receives. The criminal value is thus effectively transferred under the false passport of the invoice. The UK company has received the goods for half the invoiced value and is able to realise the profit on this by selling the goods for the invoiced value to a legitimate purchaser – essentially realising the criminal value through normal trading at normal prices. The realised criminal value can then be distributed by way of dividends or loans or other transfers to another vehicle in the UK, which in turn enables access for the intended recipients of the criminal value to the laundered funds – or more precisely funds *representing* the laundered funds – in the UK.

There are many variations on this theme. For example, it may be that the quantities of the commodity are falsified rather than the values relating to it. The key defining characteristic is the existence of some form of deceit in the invoicing – the 'passport' for the goods has been falsified to conceal the transfer of illicit value. Essentially, the complicit company has issued a false or fake passport to enable the transmission of value required. The success of the method is therefore dependent upon the criminal having access to the protection of legitimate businesses: the process is *enabled* by corruption (i.e. the bought willingness to falsify) as well as generating funds that can be used for corruptive purposes.

Another common method of laundering which is also dependent upon the existence of corrupt connections with legitimate business is *transaction laundering*. This method does not attempt to hide the criminal value to be transferred within a legitimate transaction. Instead the mechanisms for sending shipments and issuing invoices are essentially loaned out by the 'legitimate' company to the criminal enterprise in respect of whole transactions or series of transactions. It is particularly suited to companies who use merchant accounts to settle transactions. Legitimate websites are thus able to act as normal processing storefronts for criminal enterprises. Transactions may utilise shopping carts and payment pages on commercial websites, or virtual terminals. The payment methods used will vary from normal credit card payments to digital currency settlements using such e-wallets and bitcoin. The use of 'funnel accounts' also features with this form of laundering activity: a legitimate business may accept credit card charges from companies that do not have merchant processing accounts. It enters these charges as legitimate transactions in the card payment processing system.

The generic process involved is illustrated in Figure 3.8.

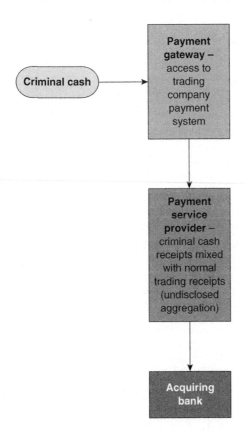

*Figure 3.8* Basic transaction laundering example

Another name for this practice, which perhaps more vividly captures its essence, is 'undisclosed aggregation'. Front companies are used to present a normal looking commercial portal to criminal trading. This might be achieved by the company taking on a 'silent partner' which it allows to use its account, or by allowing a rogue payment link to be embedded on its web page. In essence, these methods of 'undisclosed aggregation' represent a hijacking of the legitimate payment process – just as TBML represents a hijacking of the legitimate trading process. The end result is the absorption of criminal cash into the banking system (via the 'acquiring bank') under cover of legitimate trading payments. Again, it involves the use of a corrupt relationship between the criminal organisation and the commercial concern to transform the status of criminal profits, which can then be deployed for corruptive purpose in legitimate markets.

## Effects of corruptive influence: the kinds of things this money does

The two methods of laundering discussed are both dependent upon some kind of corrupt relationship being reached between the criminal enterprise and the legitimate enterprise. Some of these relationships may be coercive in nature, but Scottish experience indicates that the principal channels that enable drug profits to be either transported overseas (where the enforcement of money laundering due diligence may be less of a challenge than it is with UK based banks), or inserted into legitimate domestic 'homes' (which in any case usually implies the use of a bank account which will have passed the necessary due diligence checks), are controlled and orchestrated as part of complicit processes where there is a significant degree of trust evinced between the relevant parties.

These processes are sufficiently specialised and accomplished to endorse the notion of a 'black banking' system – capable of settling debts between criminal parties, providing storage of 'earned' wealth, and enabling transmission of settlement funds (either at home or overseas). Intelligence indicates that pension type arrangements are provided to criminal associates through these mechanisms funded by criminal monies deposited within the system.

The existence of such facilities has significant implications for assessing the extent to which commerce is susceptible to the influence of criminal funds and influence. If there are mature mechanisms for translating criminal funds so that they can be safely deployed in legitimate markets, this is bound to be a key driver for corruption in any market or economy absorbing those funds in their 'legitimised' state.

The impact of this kind of money on commercial markets, however, is not well documented. This is mainly because companies with access to criminal funds can exploit their unfair advantage under cover of legitimacy. The connection with organised criminality is often well known in the locale, but the overriding impression is that the principal influences have been rendered 'untouchable' behind a facade of apparently legitimate businesses. It is a phenomenon whose influence on legitimate markets, including those involving processes of public procurement, will continue to grow if unchecked. The reasons for this are not difficult to understand: these businesses are unfairly subsidised; they have access to cash cushions and unofficial financial safety nets; they have access to working capital and have no need to comply with bank conditions in order to gain access to it.

## Case studies

The following two anonymised cases illustrate the influence of this corruptive power in practice and are derived from operational experience in Scotland.

### 1) Abuse of subsidised home improvement schemes

'Green Deal' funding schemes designed to provide subsidised energy improvements for domestic homes formed a business sector in the UK which attracted criminal funds almost as soon as they were set up. The income stream available from the funding power company or government department was the key attraction. Companies were established to qualify as the 'Green Deal Providers' (GDP), which would earn this income by signing up households for energy saving improvements. On application by the relevant householder, the funding would be transmitted to the GDP from the relevant UK funding agency (the Green Deal Finance Company (GDFC)). In the case of 'Green Deals' the funding came from the major power companies; in the case of 'Eco' funding deals, targeted exclusively at households where the occupants were on benefits, it came from the government. The improvements themselves would be provided by sub-contractors, connected to and sourced by the organised crime groups, who commonly dealt in cash when it came to settling sales and paying wages.

The relevant business model therefore provided an ideal opportunity to insert criminal cash into a 'legitimate' business via the sub-contractors. Meanwhile that same 'legitimate' business, the GDP, could receive an income stream of impeccable provenance. The process is illustrated in Figure 3.9.

The 'Green Deal' schemes were set up with the intention of providing an incentive for householders to make their homes more energy efficient. The cost incurred would be met by a mechanism which essentially recouped the cost through the savings obtained on future energy bills. In addition to the environmental policy objective, the scheme also afforded opportunities for businesses to take advantage of the new business streams expected to materialise and provide economic benefits in the form of new jobs and profitable local businesses.

The schemes, however, were of a design which played straight into the hands of the distinctive capabilities of the local organised crime groups. They were able to assert control of the provision of this service in the territories in which they had influence – especially through their dominance of local council estates in respect of eco finance deals. In respect of the Green Deals at the higher end of the market, the organised crime groups – having access to sources of immediately available working capital not available to legitimate competitors – were able to deploy funds quickly to set up the van fleets and other infrastructure investments

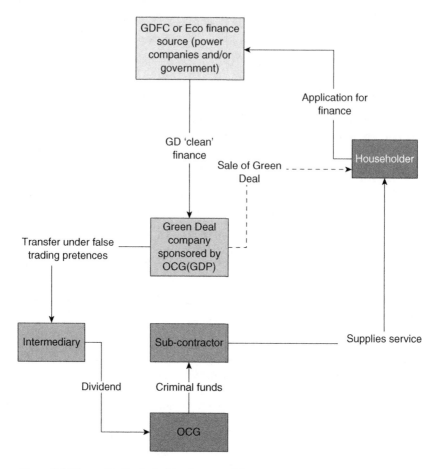

*Figure 3.9* 'Green Deal' criminal business model

necessary to claim the relevant business territory before other potential entrants to the market could get established.

Intelligence reports on a number of organised crime groups operating across the central belt of Scotland indicated the setting up of GDP companies as a copied business model. The mechanisms deployed usually involved the provision of the necessary start-up costs through a third-party non-bank loan provider. The owners and managers of the companies themselves were 'clean skins' with no personal record of serious criminal involvement.

There were a number of reasons which led to these schemes eventually being discontinued, but the standards of service and business behaviours of the principal companies are likely to have been a contributing factor. The Trading Standards Authority started to receive large numbers of complaints about work being contracted for and undertaken when not actually required. There were also complaints of poor workmanship. One of the largest of these companies in Scotland drew adverse public criticism for its disregard for rules relating to the making of cold calls to customers. In essence, the market had been corrupted to the detriment of consumers, potential entrants had been excluded, and local economies had been adversely affected as a result.

## 2) Distortion of public procurement process

Responding to the influence of organised crime in the context of public service provision can give rise to some difficult dilemmas. If the only providers of a necessary contracted service are firms known or thought to have connections to organised crime, the award of the contract to such parties in order to maintain continuity of service can, apart from anything else, give rise to embarrassing exposures in the press which reflect badly on the procuring authority.

In an attempt to manage such a situation, a major public procurement agency sought advice from the police in Scotland. The incumbent service provider had been exposed as having direct connection to individuals with media profiles as serious organised criminals. At that time, their personal and obvious business assets were the subject of an extended (ultimately successful) civil recovery process. The criminality that formed the basis of the civil recovery case arose from issues relating to the very same firm which had won the contract from the public procurement agency.

The initial issues arising in the procurement process were the extent to which under EU legislation it was possible to ask any of the kinds of probing questions that might be asked of tendering parties. Misleading perceptions about the extent such questions could be asked arose from a lack of appreciation as to what steps could be taken to 'screen' tendering parties before they were included on a short list. Once the short list had been drawn up, the general principle was that only economic factors could be used in the context of the award decision. A focus on this latter aspect of the process had tended to obscure the right of the procuring authority to ask any kind of probing question of a prospective tendering party *prior* to it being placed on the short list. The ability to ask such questions was, of course, directly in line with the overriding obligation of such authorities to protect the public.

In the particular procurement process referred to (the identity of the relevant authority is withheld to conform with confidentiality assurances given), the nature of the assistance provided by law enforcement was a review of the details of the relevant prospective tendering parties. This review was founded on relevant intelligence profiles and augmented by reference to open source information, especially Companies House filings.

The overall results of that exercise indicated a high degree of penetration by companies with known links, either current or historic, to organised crime. Of the ten applicants, two could be dismissed as non-credible applicants with no prospect of being able to deliver the service required. The eight remaining applicants could be split into two camps. One consisted of four tendering parties all with connections to the incumbent service provider. The incumbent had changed its disclosed directors and owners to break any ostensible connection with the tainted connections of its former owners. The way in which the company managed its dividend policy, however, together with funding issues arising from connected changes of ownership, provided indicators that the company was still under the influence of parties connected to organised crime. This interpretation was supported by the existence of the other three applicants from the same organised crime 'stable', all of which submitted bids that were less competitive than that of the incumbent.

The applicants from the other 'block' of tenders were all connected to individuals who also had a 'connected' reputation. These individuals owned firms providing the relevant service in an adjacent geographical area, where they were well known as being the local 'Mr Bigs' who had achieved their dominant position principally through intimidation of all potential rivals.

The procurement authority was in a difficult position. The available information did not provide sufficient grounds to exclude any of these applicant companies, despite what remaining suspicions existed. It was therefore suggested in these circumstances that each applicant be requested to sign a declaration that they had no connections either formal or informal with serious organised crime, or individuals or groups connected with serious organised crime. This recommendation was duly acted upon and all applicants, without exception, signed it.

On the face of it, that might be considered a somewhat cosmetic exercise. The practice of seeking such declarations is now established, however, in a number of public procurement processes in Scotland and it does confer significant benefits. It provides the procurement authority with leverage to seek civil action remedies, including cancellation of the contract, if subsequently it can be shown the declaration was not signed in good faith. There is also a measure of insurance against any adverse media coverage that might ensue from subsequent disclosures establishing links between the company winning the contract and serious organised crime.

Other benefits include improving the levels of risk awareness that can be deployed within procurement procedures. The fact that association with serious organised crime is acknowledged as a risk makes it likely it will be addressed more honestly and adequately. The kind of culture within which corruption thrives often demonstrates 'uncertainty aversion' (Selei and Bontis, 2009); a 'common knowledge' of wrong doing or inappropriate association is ignored and 'accepted', usually on the basis that it is perceived that trouble would come to those who sought to challenge it. By openly acknowledging the risk, the extent to which that culture can continue unabated is challenged by the fact that proactive steps have to be taken to demonstrate that this risk has been addressed.

A long-term benefit of this initiative is to encourage the establishment of a disciplining 'collar' around companies tendering for public contracts; a collar that can be tightened so that it squeezes corrupt behaviour from how such companies conduct themselves. The firm is forced to act, behave and appear in a manner consistent with that expected of any legitimate company serving the contract. If the criminal connections still exist – and pressures arising from those connections begin to impinge upon those standards – then the procurement authority has at least a basis for recognising and addressing the risk. More importantly, public procurement, and the culture around it, becomes more aware and pragmatic; becoming itself an influence for ensuring that all successful contractors are forced to act properly – as if they are legitimate, even if they are not. This could be regarded as a case of 'taking crime out of crime business', in line with the Findlay and Hanif (2012) view that the most effective approaches to dealing with organised crime in business are likely to be founded on market analysis, rather than traditional attitudes stuck on a rigid dichotomy between criminal and legitimate activity.

## Conclusion

Practitioner experience indicates that the corruptive influence of criminal funds deployed in legitimate markets will tend to create distortive and harmful effects that run deep into a nation's economy – affecting commerce and social structures in ways that are always likely to be for the worse than for the better. The essence of free enterprise, and the characteristic most often asserted to enable it to deliver economic growth, is fair competition; the objective of organised crime sponsored enterprise is usually to assert control and to distort and undermine fair competition, thus providing a drag effect on growth.

Tackling criminal cash as a cause of corruption therefore requires improved awareness of the financial and business engines that generate, and re-generate, the cycles of criminal money that perpetuate it. Law enforcement needs to continue to improve its expertise in this area so that it can offer better support to its partners, business and government through identification of high risk pressure points and thus provide a more secure platform for suitable risk assessment of corrupt practices.

The corruptive influence of organised crime can affect all aspects of commerce and public service provision, forming a drag on productivity and competitiveness and threatening the security of vital services to the public. It has a real, if not always adequately recognised, effect on people's lives. The very worst thing that can be done in relation to this problem is to look away and pretend it does not exist.

## Bibliography

*Daily Telegraph* (2015, 28 July) 'David Cameron vows to fight against 'dirty money' in UK property market'.

Dostoevsky, F. (1868) *The Idiot*, first published serially in *The Russian Messenger*.

*The Economist* (2015, 1 August) *Dirty Dens*, "'There is no place for dirty money in Britain . . . London is not a place to stash your dodgy cash"; thundered David Cameron in a speech this week'. www.gov.uk/government/uploads/system/uploads/attachment_data/file/246390/horr73.pdf.

EMCDDA (2016) *EU Drug Markets Report*, www.emcdda.europa.eu.

Findlay, M. (2014) 'Crime, development and corruption: Cultural dynamic-global challenge?' in S. Canneppele and F. Calderoni (eds) *Organised Crime, Corruption and Crime Prevention: Essays in Honour of Ernesto U. Savona*. Cham, Switzerland: Springer, pp. 179–186.

Findlay, M. and Hanif, H. (2012) 'Taking crime out of crime business,' *International Journal of Law, Crime and Justice*, 40: 338–368.

Fiorentini, G. and Peltzman, S. (eds) (1997) *The Economics of Organised Crime*. Cambridge, UK: Cambridge University Press, p. xiv.

Gounev, P. and Bezlov, T. (2010) *Examining the Links between Organised Crime and Corruption*. Sofia: Center for the Study of Democracy, European Commission.

Harvey, J. (2014) 'Asset Recovery Substantive or Symbolic', in C. King and C. Walker (eds) *Dirty Assets: Emerging Issues in the Regulation of Criminal and Terrorist Assets*. Abingdon, UK: Routledge, pp. 183–202.

H.M. Home Office (2009) *Extending our reach: A comprehensive approach to tackling serious organised crime*, www.gov.uk/government/publications/extending-our-reach-a-comprehensive-approach-to-tackling-serious-organised-crime.

Johnson, J. (2015) 'Corruption: New strategies', in N. Ryder (ed.) *Research Handbook on International Financial Crime*. London, Edward Elgar.

Klitgaard, R. (1998) 'International cooperation against corruption', *Finance and Development: A Quarterly Publication of the International Monetary Fund and the World Bank*, 35: 3–6.

Reuter, P. (2004) *The Organisation of Illegal Markets: An Economic Analysis*. New York: National Institute of Justice, and Honolulu, HI: University Press of the Pacific, reproduced from 1985 edition.

Selei, A and Bontis, N. (2009) 'The relationship between culture and corruption: A cross-national study', *Journal of Intellectual Capital*, 10(1): 165–184.

Sproat, P.A. (2009) 'To what extent is the UK's anti-money laundering and asset recovery regime used against organised crime?' *Journal of Money Laundering Control*, 12(2): 134–150.

# 4 Corruption as a facilitator of human trafficking

## Some key analytical issues

*Rose Broad and Nicholas Lord*

## Introduction

The aim of this chapter is to consider how and why 'corruption' facilitates the trafficking of humans into both licit (e.g. food supply networks) and illicit (e.g. prostitution) markets in the UK. Corruption has been identified as a potential facilitator of human trafficking and as a necessary cost in the operation of traffickers' activities (for example, see Bales, 2005; Zhang and Pineda, 2008). However, it is also suggested that corruption has been underestimated both as a method that enables traffickers to pursue their enterprise and in providing more permissive environments for human trafficking (OSCE, 2010). Despite evidence foregrounding the centrality of corrupt practices to the organisation of human trafficking, in terms of UK policy, corruption and associated behaviours have not formed a significant part of anti-trafficking initiatives, being notably absent in the Modern Slavery Strategy (HM Government, 2014).

In this chapter we review empirical evidence on the dynamics between corruption and the organisation of human trafficking. As corruption is an ill-defined concept (see Campbell and Lord, Introduction to this volume), we focus here on bribery and other forms of illicit exchange for gain that are used to facilitate the movement of people into the UK, though we use the concepts interchangeably. Thus, our analysis here focuses on illicit transactions that necessarily involve actors within government (e.g. politicians) and/or its decentralised units (e.g. public officials such as border officials, the police, military, transport and transit, education, healthcare, etc.) and that undermine the use of public funds during the provision of services, or private actors (e.g. logistics operators) whose common business practice provides scope for the facilitation and concealment of trafficking. While public and private officials might be more passive in these transactions (i.e. receivers of inducements), they may also be more active in extorting payments from would-be traffickers.

Our key argument is that by focusing on the potential interactions of traffickers, that is, those actors part of the criminal enterprise, with public and private officials (variously defined), across the 'recognised' sections of the trafficking process (i.e. recruitment, transportation, exploitation), we can begin to analyse (1) how and where opportunities for bribery emerge and the corresponding 'opportunity structures' (i.e. those conditions or elements that must be in place for the bribery to occur), (2) how these opportunities are realised by cooperating actors at the intersections of legitimate and illegitimate markets and relations, and (3) under which conditions critical points of vulnerability emerge in these interactions and processes and where potential points of intervention are most suitable.

Despite the lack of prosecuted cases in the UK (a status quo common across the globe) that involve bribery and human trafficking, we can nonetheless extrapolate associated facilitative conditions and an understanding of opportunity structures from analogous cases. For instance, in the case of Benizri,[1] the Israeli minister who was indicted on charges of taking and mediating bribes, fraud and breach of trust, we can see how his corrupt behaviours created opportunities in the recruitment processes of human trafficking. Benizri had leaked information regarding foreign worker quotas to a contractor in exchange for money, furniture and other personal gains. The information allowed the contractor to win tenders to bring foreign workers into the country, a practice that has been linked to increased risks of exploitation (Lewis et al., 2015). In another case from Bedford, Ohio,[2] legal officials were indicted for bribery, unlawful interest in a public contract and money laundering, among other charges, whilst also misleading investigations of a brothel. The opportunity for bribery arose in part due to vulnerabilities embedded in sexual relations that the men were having with women from the brothel. The engagement of sex workers and visits to brothels by public officials exemplifies one potential opportunity for the intersection of public officials with those involved in human trafficking.

This chapter explores these dynamics further and raises some key analytical issues for research in this area. The chapter is based on analysis of existing literature, publicly available information regarding cases, and policy and legislation, as well as drawing on our experience of researching related issues.[3] First, we consider the concepts of human trafficking and corruption and outline our conceptual parameters for the purposes of this chapter, followed by analysis of evidence supporting their intersection. Second, we organise the discussion around the three key processes of trafficking, as listed above, and discuss the dynamics of opportunities in terms of the structures, likely actors, scenes/situations, behaviours and conditions, that can and do emerge within each process. Third, we conclude by arguing that by contextualising corrupt interactions and transactions in this way, we can begin to elucidate common referents across cases that can in turn inform regulatory and intervention strategies.

1  *The Jerusalem Post*, 'Benizri indicted for fraud, bribes', 29 March 2006, www.jpost.com/Israel/Benizri-indicted-for-fraud-bribes-17500, last accessed: 31 October 2017.
2  *Cleveland 19 News*, 'Two Bedford city officials indicted on corruption and prostitution charges', www.cleveland19.com/story/24264366/two-bedford-city-officials-indicted-on-corruption-and-prostitution-charges, last accessed: 31 October 2017.
3  See, for example, Broad (2018; 2015) for empirical analysis of modern slavery cases in the UK and Levi and Lord (2011), and Lord and Levi (2017) on the relationships between corruption and organisation of serious crimes.

## The intersections of human trafficking and corruption

The issue of human trafficking[4] has been afforded increasing policy prominence in the UK (mirroring global trends in the development of human trafficking policy) since the late 1990s. The most consistently used definition of human trafficking stems from Article 3(a) of the Trafficking Protocol of the Palermo Convention (2000) which defines human trafficking to mean:

> [t]he recruitment, transportation, transfer, harbouring or receipt of persons, by means of the threat or use of force or other forms of coercion, of abduction, of fraud, of deception, of the abuse of power or of a position of vulnerability or of the giving or receiving of payments or benefits to achieve the consent of a person having control over another person, for the purpose of exploitation. Exploitation shall include, at a minimum, the exploitation of the prostitution of others or other forms of sexual exploitation, forced labour or services, slavery or practices similar to slavery, servitude or the removal of organs.

The development of this definition, which has underpinned the direction of much trafficking policy across the world, has been subject to criticism, particularly in relation to the inclusion of the term 'consent' and the implications of this for sex workers (for example, see Agustin, 2008 and Doezema, 2005). The initial framing of the problem in the UK was legislatively split into trafficking for sexual exploitation under the Sexual Offences Act 2003 and trafficking for labour exploitation under the Immigration and Asylum Act 2004 with anti-trafficking strategy largely focused on the problem of trafficking for sexual exploitation (Spencer and Broad, 2011). In 2013, recommendations were made for a single UK 'modern slavery' Act to deal with problems identified with the initial legislation including a lack of victim protection and the need for a more coordinated multi-agency approach (ATMG, 2013). This led to the advent of the UK Modern Slavery Act 2015, which has brought a very wide and diverse range of activities together in a process aptly termed 'exploitation creep' where all forced labour is defined as trafficking and all trafficking is viewed as slavery (Chuang, 2014). The inclusion of such diverse activities is conceptually difficult (for example, consider the complexities and differences between trafficking for sham marriage or for cannabis cultivation) and, for these reasons has led to criticism in the UK particularly in relation to the inclusion of forced labour in the modern slavery frame (see Balch, 2015).

One of the most significant changes facilitated by the Modern Slavery Act is the Section 54 Transparency in the Supply Chain (TISC) provisions which introduce obligations on corporations to consider their role in human trafficking.

---

4  The term 'human trafficking' is used throughout this discussion to refer to the range of activities which now come under this term. 'Human trafficking' is used more widely than modern slavery which largely applies in the UK, although at the time of writing is in the process of being adopted in other jurisdictions.

Under these provisions, corporations with an annual turnover of £36 million or more and who conduct their business (or part thereof) in the UK are required to publish a statement outlining whether they are taking steps to tackle 'modern slavery' and if so, the nature of these steps. However, despite this considerable policy development, the current framework for holding corporations responsible may not be sufficient to engender change (for example, see Lord and Broad, 2017; Phillips, 2015).

Corruption has long been recognised as a significant predictor of human trafficking in countries with a high incidence of trafficking and can act as a push factor from countries of origin and, conversely, anti-corruption strategy in both origin and destination countries has been identified as an activity that may reduce trafficking (Bales, 2007; Europol, 2013; Salt and Stein, 1997). However, little research has been conducted on the role of corruption and/or bribery in human trafficking, despite calls for such academic engagement (Bales, 2005). Bales (2007) identified the importance of governmental corruption[5] in the country of origin as a predictor of trafficking from that country as well as the role of corruption in the country of destination in relation to the permeability of borders, since corruption and particularly bribery of border officials have been found to facilitate border crossing in many countries (Transparency International, 2011). The OECD (2016) compared the categorisation of countries in the Trafficking in Persons report in 2014 with the Corruption Perception Index[6] of the same year, finding that those with the highest perception of corruption were also those countries whose governments did not fully comply with the minimum standards of anti-trafficking efforts set out in the Trafficking Victims Protection Act 2000. Furthermore, victims' experiences of corruption in the country of origin continue to act as a mechanism of control in the country of destination with traffickers using the perceptions of corruption to dissuade victims from reporting on the basis that authorities in the country of destination will be equally corrupt (Surtees, 2014; UNODC, 2011).

It has been suggested that trafficking would not be as prevalent without collusion between organised crime groups and corrupt officials (OECD, 2016; Tremblay, 2010). While there is research exploring the relationship between corruption and organised crime in the UK, and across Western Europe more generally, major research gaps remain (Levi and Lord, 2011; see Gounev and Ruggiero, 2012). However, we know that crime networks, whether hierarchically or more flexibly organised, that are seeking to transfer people across borders for illicit purposes or move and conceal them internally without raising suspicions, may view corruption, rather than violence and/or intimidation, as a more efficient or even necessary cost of business to maintain secrecy and the enterprise.

---

5  Using the International Corruption Index.
6  We should point out that we are critical of the underlying methodologies and conceptual framing of perceptions indices such as the CPI, and their politicisation, creating tensions between science and policy, but they continue to shape mainstream dialogue on (anti-)corruption. For an extensive analysis of these issues see Heywood and Rose (2014) and Andersson and Heywood (2009).

At key points in the trafficking process we see clear points of interaction and intersections between criminal enterprise and public/private sector officials, and it is here where corruption may be used to facilitate their activities. This raises questions over how criminal actors identify public officials that might be susceptible to bribery, how they establish and maintain relations with these actors, and how they transfer some form of advantage to them while keeping it concealed. In other words, how are corrupt relations engendered to induce public (or private) officials to circumvent the procedures that govern their official duties? For example, in some cases 'illegal businesses seek to operate securely by paying off the police, politicians, and judges or by permitting them to share in the profits of the illegal businesses' (Rose-Ackerman, 1999: 23); understanding the links between corruption and the organisation of serious crimes for gain in this way has been identified as a notable empirical gap (Levi and Lord, 2011).

Existing research has indicated different 'types' of trafficking organisation involved in the activity ranging from an individual working alone to more sophisticated, larger groups of people with a higher level of organisation (although the extent to which this can be regarded as 'organised crime' has been much debated – see, for example, Paoli, 2002). Models of trafficking involving larger groups of people and more organised operations have been most associated with corruption (Aronowitz, 2009). The OECD highlighted that trafficking is reliant on systemic corruption which facilitates parts of the trafficking process including non-conviction, re-trafficking of victims with behaviours ranging from 'active involvement, such as violating duties, accepting or transferring bribes, and facilitating transactions, to passive involvement, such as ignoring or failing to follow up on information that a crime may be taking place' (OECD, 2016: 5). Corruption and bribery have been identified as a cost taken into consideration by traffickers in economic models of trafficking (PACO, 2002; Salt and Stein, 1997; Webb and Burrows, 2009). In the UK context, it is likely that corruption at the intersections of organised criminal activities and the public sector are most commonly found at what is termed the 'petty' level, i.e. where local, regional and mid-level public officials abuse their entrusted power to undertake acts or omissions that contravene their public duties for personal financial gain (as opposed to what is termed 'grand', i.e. acts/omissions at a high level of government, or 'political', i.e. the manipulation of policies, institutions and rules of procedure by political decision-makers to sustain their power, status and wealth).[7] Private sector actors and officials can also be vulnerable to bribery as common business practices (e.g. logistics, transport) provide means for concealing the movement of trafficking victims, whether in a licit or illicit way.

Research by Spencer et al. (2010) focused on the role of corruption in the illegal movement of people across borders which, although problematic

---

7  For more on such classifications, see the website of Transparency International: www.transparency. org/whoweare/organisation/faqs_on_corruption#defineCorruption, last accessed 22 September 2017.

in combining trafficking and smuggling, identified no systemic corruption in the UK, but rather isolated instances of corruption within some key agencies. Similarly, in Home Office interviews (Webb and Burrows, 2009) with those convicted for 'organised immigration offences', cases of individual corruption and bribery were identified, particularly in relation to border crossing and the provision of false documentation. The role of corruption in the processes of human trafficking has been identified and explored elsewhere in the early stages of research in this area (Richards, 2004). Given the developments in knowledge and understanding of this intersection, revisiting what is now known about the processes of human trafficking and identifying those points at which corruption may intersect with human trafficking can provide a platform from which to consider law enforcement and/or regulation of this activity and for further research.

## Corruption and the trafficking process: recruitment, transportation and exploitation.

In this section we organise our discussion around the three processes of trafficking: recruitment, transportation and exploitation (explained and illustrated later). We then analyse each process in terms of the opportunity structures, likely actors, key scenes/situations, behaviours and conditions, and draw on known cases to contextualise these. For bribery to occur, an *opportunity* must be present. This is self-evident. However, it is not the mere presence of an opportunity that is important, but the particular characteristics of the opportunity; bribery in the context of human trafficking, like all forms of crime, has an 'opportunity structure' (see Benson et al., 2009). This is a set of conditions or elements that must be in place in order for the bribery to take place. Different settings and processes naturally create different opportunities that vary in accessibility and attractiveness to traffickers.

By understanding the opportunities that arise under the varying conditions of each trafficking process, we can begin to conceptualise how offenders discover and evaluate them. Understanding the dynamics of bribery opportunity in this way informs an understanding of the sequence of actions used by those traffickers who engage in bribery – that is, under which conditions do motivated traffickers, suitable bribery targets (i.e. public officials) and a lack of capable guardianship converge in time and space, and are there patterns of behaviour that may indicate likely areas of bribery? By thinking of bribery transactions as an 'event' at a particular time and space, which emerges under conducive settings and conditions, we can begin to extrapolate the characteristics of the occasion.

Criminological research informs us that criminals become aware of opportunities as they engage in their routine activities, finding 'targets' in familiar places, with opportunities most likely to be taken advantage of when they are closer to areas of familiarity (Brantingham and Brantingham, 1991). Furthermore, it might also be argued that bribery is most likely to take place at the *edges* (e.g. the less regulated and less transparent areas of officials' duties and behaviours

Table 4.1 Corruption, opportunity structures and the trafficking process

| Opportunity structure / process | Likely actors involved | Key scenes/situations for interaction/transaction | Key behaviours induced | Key facilitative conditions | Case examples |
|---|---|---|---|---|---|
| Recruitment | – Service providers (e.g. visas, marriage licences)<br>– Employment providers (recruitment agencies) | – Common socialising or professional venues of relevant officials (e.g. ministers, immigration and visas staff)<br>– Meetings in tendering processes between employment agencies and officials involved in immigration/visa processes | – Falsification of materials (e.g. work or marriage visas)<br>– imposition of unfair recruitment fees<br>– Theft of blank travel documents | – Incapable guardianship of individual officials (e.g. out-sourcing)<br>– Legal frameworks favouring the employer<br>– Lack of incentives for employers to report abuses | – Former Israeli Labour minister Benizri convicted for bribery in relation to obtaining fraudulent permits in the construction sector[1]<br>– Former chief of visa section in French embassy in Bulgaria convicted for issuing work visas to women trafficked from Bulgaria to work in prostitution[2] |
| Transportation | – Border officials (border control, immigration)<br>– Transport providers<br>– Logistics operators | – Known transport routes of logistics companies and their common stopping points (i.e. less regulated areas as part of routine behaviours)<br>– Commutes of border officials and transport providers (i.e. common paths)<br>– Socialising venues of border officials and transport providers (i.e. potential points of interaction) | – Neglect of duties in checking and reporting undocumented entry<br>– Bribery of individual officials<br>– Multiple use of travel documents | – Lack of adequate oversight of points of entry by supervising or additional officers<br>– Lack of adequate resources leaving certain points of entry understaffed and processes less scrutinised<br>– Lack of awareness of risk/ identification indicators | – Bribery of individual border officials in the UK (see Webb and Burrows, 2009)<br>– See UNODC (2011) for examples including bribery of border official en route from South Africa to Western Europe |

*(continued)*

Table 4.1 (continued)

| Opportunity structure / process | Likely actors involved | Key scenes/situations for interaction/transaction | Key behaviours induced | Key facilitative conditions | Case examples |
|---|---|---|---|---|---|
| Exploitation | – Law enforcement<br>– Criminal justice officials<br>– Regulatory organisations<br>– NGOs<br>– Employers | – Use of brothels by criminal justice professionals and resultant targeting of individual officers<br>– Manipulation of victims who have had contact with NGO/law enforcement and who are re-trafficked<br>– Audit visits to organisations by regulatory officials creating a potential point of interaction<br>– Business actors in markets and commerce where victims are trafficked (e.g. food supply networks) easily approached through legitimate channels or informally through social networks and social venues | – Advance warning of either law/enforcement or regulatory action (e.g. warning of planned brothel raid or audit visit)<br>– Obstruction of proper investigation and prosecution of cases<br>– Provision of victim location/information to traffickers<br>– Wilful blindness or active participation of business actors in using trafficked individuals | – Lack of adequate oversight of investigations by supervising/additional officer<br>– Lack of adequate resources leaving investigations led by single officer<br>– Poorly supervised business operations | – Public officials in Cleveland convicted for misleading the police investigation and bribery[3]<br>– Reports of public officials obstructing investigation of human trafficking activity in Romania and Bulgaria (US Department of State, 2016) |

Notes
1 See *The Jerusalem Post*, 'Benizri, Hirchson begin jail terms', 1 September 2009, www.jpost.com/Israel/Benizri-Hirchson-begin-jail-terms, last accessed: 31 October 2017.
2 U.S. Department of State, Country Reports on Human Rights Practices, Bureau of Democracy, Human Rights, and Labor 2001, 'France', 4 March 2002, www.state.gov/j/drl/rls/hrrpt/2001/eur/8253.htm, last accessed: 31 October 2017.
3 *Cleveland 19 News*, 'Two Bedford city officials indicted on corruption and prostitution charges' www.cleveland19.com/story/2424366/two-bedford-city-officials-indicted-on-corruption-and-prostitution-charges, last accessed: 31 October 2017.

where key actors interact – such as at border controls where much discretion is available at the individual level) of commonly trodden *paths* (e.g. the formal and informal procedures and networks that are common to the official, and that the trafficker can understand well) between key *nodes* (e.g. the cooperating or interacting actors in the bribery transaction such as the officials responsible for particular behaviours) in the offenders' network.

Table 4.1 outlines these key dimensions and we explore them further in the subsequent sections. Our discussion here is not comprehensive but indicative of the types of analytical questions that can be posed to better understand the corrupt transactions of traffickers and public and private officials. The content of Table 4.1 is based on our analysis of existing literature, documentation detailing known cases of modern slavery such as official information from enforcement and governmental authorities and media accounts, and our own expertise researching analogous phenomena. We applied a mode of analysis aligned with opportunity perspectives to extrapolate key features of the bribery-slavery dynamics across each of the trafficking processes. We elaborate these dynamics in the subsequent sections.

## Recruitment of potential victims or of public officials that are open to a bribe

The nature of recruitment varies widely including recruitment through a family member or acquaintance, through websites or local newspapers advertising work in a range of industries (for example, hotels and catering, agriculture, sex work) or through agencies or brokers acting as intermediaries between companies and potential recruits. Although recruitment most commonly occurs through family members, friends or acquaintances (Broad, 2015; O'Connell Davidson, 2015; Surtees, 2014), the role of public officials in the provision of necessary validation to support migration during the process of recruitment, for example, marriage licences or work visas, creates opportunities for corruption. These procedures establish paths which are routine to the public officials involved and which can be easily known and understood by a trafficker in order to identify where bribery of public officials involved could take place and individuals who may be vulnerable to such bribes (Tremblay, 2010). For instance, traffickers may gain insight into how and when formal meetings in tendering processes between employment agencies and officials involved in immigration/visa processes are structured, or they may target informal venues related to these such as common socialising or professional venues of relevant officials (e.g. ministers, immigration and visas staff).

Research with those convicted for 'organised immigration offences' in the UK found that illegally obtained passports may be acquired either through the theft of previously issued passports or blank passports obtained through corrupt relationships with passport authorities in countries of origin (Webb and Burrows, 2009). The theft of previously issued passports may not necessarily involve corruption although the use of such documents may create recourse for traffickers to target vulnerable officials and/or make use of less regulated routes. Once in traffickers' possession, either stolen or falsified passports can be used repeatedly to facilitate the movement of multiple people across borders (Spencer et al., 2010). Repeated use may not involve corruption of border officials although paths with lower levels of regulation would be more conducive to this type of activity occurring without attracting attention. The costs incurred through, for example, bribery of officials for the falsification of visas, create a greater burden for victims where the debt is passed onto the victim (UNODC, 2011).

The existing evidence suggests that in order for traffickers to facilitate their activities effectively, there are vulnerabilities to corruption that can be exploited: there is a 'a regulatory or socio-legal environment conducive to the trafficking trade' (Zhang and Pineda, 2008: 52). Understanding how common practices of official organisations, policy and mechanisms of recruitment and employment contribute to this environment is essential to developing knowledge of how traffickers may exploit, and how to address such practices. Recruitment processes in countries of origin and outsourcing of work by companies operating in the UK present different vulnerabilities to corruption. Although geographically distant, this may involve activity that an organisation outsourcing work may need to identify and set out steps for addressing under the TISC provisions (see HM Government, 2015). For example, large scale recruitment of workers has seen state officials in Israel convicted on bribery and corruption charges for assisting in obtaining work permits for workers in the construction sector (Kemp and Raijman, 2014). Guidance from HM Government and NGOs in the sector on issues for inclusion in TISC statements states that organisational recruitment policies as well as knowledge of other agencies' practices used in the recruitment process should be addressed (CORE, 2016; HM Government, 2015).

## Transportation

Transporting victims into the UK can be achieved in three ways with varying impact on the potential for corruption in the process:

(1) Where a victim has legitimate travel documents. In this instance, the vulnerability to corruption is low because there are fewer edges where key actors may interact.
(2) Where the victim travels with forged travel documents, which presents vulnerability to bribery and corruption at either the site issuing the forged documents (for example through officials involved in the provision of passports or work visas) or through interactions at the border.
(3) Where the victim travels with no travel documents, which presents vulnerability to bribery at the border crossing by creating the necessity for traffickers to secure the cooperation of a corrupt official in order to facilitate movement.

The opportunity for corruption during the transportation phase will be greater where international borders are crossed, facilitating greater interaction between public officials and traffickers. Although human trafficking need not entail trans-national travel, movement within the UK would entail a lower risk of corruption given the lack of official scrutiny and lack of interaction between traffickers and public officials in this context. The unintended impact of ostensibly unrelated policy changes can also exacerbate the situation: tighter border controls and more restrictive migration policies have been argued to increase the propensity of traf-fickers to approach corrupt officials to facilitate border crossings (Campana and Varese, 2016; Lee, 2011; Savona et al., 2014). Concerns have been raised regarding the impact of anti-trafficking strategy on the marginalisation of irregular migrants (see Agustin, 2008; Right to Remain, 2017). Anti-trafficking operations targeting brothels as well as a variety of licit markets including nail bars and construction can result in increased reliance on illegitimate forms of transport and work. In turn this can increase traffickers' recourse to corrupt officials to facilitate the processes due to the legal frameworks which exclude these groups from legitimate work.

Evidence suggests that many of the routes through which victims are transported into the UK involve the use of bribery and corruption to facilitate movement and border crossing, most commonly in relation to the individual bribery of border officials. Transport routes have been found to involve multiple stops and to travel through countries with a reputation for success in corrupting border officials; where traffickers have knowledge of less regulated points of entry, for example through Turkey (Savona et al., 2014); through Russia (Tverdova, 2011); through Albania, Lithuania and the former Yugoslavia (Holmes, 2009); and from Nigeria, through Southern Europe (Okogbule, 2013). Traffickers can seek to understand known transport routes and common stopping points (i.e. less regulated areas as part of routine behaviours) of logistics operators with a view to engaging and recruiting actors to collude in transporting victims. Allied with this, the commutes of border officials and transport providers (i.e. common paths), as well as their socialising venues, also present opportunities for traffickers to interact with suitable bribery targets.

## Exploitation

The exploitation phase can involve a wide range of licit and illicit markets through exploitative labour in sectors such as construction, catering, agriculture and food production, in the sex industry, through domestic servitude and through a range of criminal markets including begging, drug cultivation and selling, and shoplifting (UNODC, 2016). These markets provide different scenarios in which public and private officials may interact with traffickers and thereby provide opportunity for corruption to facilitate traffickers' activities. As stated earlier, the role of corruption in the exploitation phase of trafficking needs to be understood in the wider context of migration and employment to understand both the points of contact for individuals but also the wider legal and policy frameworks which may favour employers and marginalise migrant workers:

[t]he facilitation economy is constituted of a mix of illicit and semi-illicit activities that have to be placed within the broader field of other types of (illicit) businesses and crimes . . . through these dynamics, illicit migration facilitation and indentured sex work migration, defined as crimes by migration authorities and in international protocols, emerge as two among many business opportunities in a site of unemployment.

(Plembach, 2016: 13)

Increases in employment flexibility, including self-employment, sub-contracting, zero-hour contracts and increased use of agency work create more precarious circumstances for workers (particularly those who may not have legal status in the UK and therefore are willing to accept more exploitative conditions) but also create vulnerabilities for those organising and managing this work. Anecdotal evidence suggests that in the face of decreasing margins and tighter competition, there is increased temptation to take advantage of an offer of cheaper labour with a 'no questions asked' approach. Thus, business actors may be actively complicit in the exploitation and therefore be one side of an illicit exchange for gain, or may be wilfully blind to the potential use of trafficked individuals. In these terms, we may view those complicit employers as in some way 'corrupt', and this raises serious questions over the extent to which the business community can and should be held liable for failing to prevent exploitation within their business (see Lord and Broad, 2017) At best, business may be incompetent in the vetting and diligence of those they employ or easily deceived by competent traffickers. Audit visits to organisations by regulatory officials create potential points of interaction and opportunities for unscrupulous business actors to corrupt officials.

The Gangmasters and Labour Abuse Authority (GLAA) (previously the Gangmasters Licensing Authority (GLA)) is a UK non-departmental public body that was established in response to the deaths of cockle pickers in Morecambe Bay[8] and subsequent recognition for more effective regulatory structures for agriculture, horticulture and shellfish industries, including corrupt practices and bribery (Berket, 2015). Although the GLAA has recently undergone changes, including the change of title, a widening of its remit and additional powers,[9] the organisation remains relatively small when considering the tasks with which they are charged and the breadth of markets they are charged with investigating. As a result, the GLAA is not resourced to undertake extensive investigations of agencies or brokers operating further along the chain. The GLAA faced claims that they were negligent in approving the Gangmasters' licence in the case of DJ Houghton.[10] The case[11] involved six Lithuanian men who were trafficked to and

8   *BBC News*, 'Tide kills 18 cockle pickers', 6 February 2004, http://news.bbc.co.uk/1/hi/england/lancashire/3464203.stm, last accessed: 31 October 2017.

9   The Gangmasters and Labour Abuse Authority: www.gla.gov.uk/who-we-are/our-aims-and-objectives/the-gangmasters-and-labour-abuse-authority/, last accessed: 31 October 2017.

10  Atherton, M./*Food Manufacture*, 'Gangmasters Licensing Authority in "negligence" court case over "worst UK gangmaster ever"', 16 January 2017, www.foodmanufacture.co.uk/Regulation/Gangmasters-Licensing-Authority-accused-of-negligence-in-chicken-case, last accessed: 31 October 2017.

11  [2016] All ER (D) 84.

exploited in a chicken processing plant in the UK. The victims have successfully sued their exploiters and have received compensation for unpaid earnings, abuse and mistreatment representing a legal landmark in the UK. Lawyers for the victims claimed that the then GLA had knowledge of the mistreatment but gave the licence nonetheless. Although the GLA was not implicated in corruption or bribery in this case, it illustrates the opportunities for corruption or bribery of public officials in these roles by highlighting points of interaction between officials and those potentially involved in exploitation.

At the time of writing, the 'Independent Review of Employment Practices in the Modern Economy' is being undertaken, having been commissioned by Prime Minister Theresa May in October 2016. The GLAA is taking part as one of the three experts on a panel supporting the review, firmly identifying a link between more flexible labour structures and exploitative labour. In response to the Independent Review, the Law Society has addressed the balance of rights and responsibilities,[12] highlighting the current onus on the individual to assert that they are being exploited, rather than on the use of questionable working practices such as those employed by Sports Direct[13] where an investigation into a commercial transaction led to the exposure of poor working practices, rather than as a consequence of the workers using employment law to protect themselves (Law Society, 2016). The Law Society (2016) recommended that more onus be placed on companies to demonstrate that they are complying with employment legislation, for example the National Minimum Wage requirements, rather than the burden being borne by workers who may be in vulnerable positions. Making these processes more transparent can only reduce opportunities for potential corruption and create a more equal balance of power.

## Corruption and criminal justice processes

Beyond the regulation of the labour market, evidence also points to the potential for corruption during the criminal justice process. The Council of Europe has identified the opportunities for local police officers who have been targeted on the basis of individual vulnerability, for example as a result of financial difficulties or the use of brothels. These officers can perform various corrupt activities to facilitate exploitation or protection of businesses using trafficked victims in exchange for money or sexual services (PACO, 2002), for example by providing advance notice of raids or receiving bribes to neglect to conduct raids (Transparency International, 2011). Corrupt criminal justice professionals have also been found to facilitate ineffective investigations or prosecutions in exchange for bribes (UNODC, 2011). Given the low number of reports, investigations

12 See Department for Business, Energy and Industrial Strategy, 'The balance of rights and responsibilities' https://beis.dialogue-app.com/matthew-taylor-review/the-balance-of-rights-and-responsibilities, last accessed: 31 October 2017.

13 Davies, R./*The Guardian*, 'Brothers jailed for trafficking people from Poland to work at Sports Direct', 23 January 2017, www.theguardian.com/business/2017/jan/23/brothers-jailed-trafficking-poland-sports-direct-shirebrook?CMP=Share_iOSApp_Other, last accessed: 31 October 2017.

and convictions relating to trafficking related corruption, the risks associated with involvement by potentially corrupt officials are minimal (Transparency International, 2011) making the process of engagement by traffickers easier. Furthermore, there is also potential for the manipulation of victims who have had contact with NGO/law enforcement and who are re-trafficked.

Finally, not only 'human trafficking but also the deportation and rescue of trafficked victims present business opportunities' (Plembach, 2016). Programmes aimed at improving the situation in countries of origin are also open to corruption, for example where the corrupt diversion of resources through anti-trafficking NGOs benefits the elite in the context of development and inequality (PACO, 2002; Smith, 2010). Public officials charged with overseeing the distribution of funds' anti-trafficking strategy are thereby vulnerable to being approached for diversion of such funds in return for personal financial gain. Furthermore, evidence suggests that the impact of corruption is compounded for women, particularly those facing additional barriers to empowerment, for example throughout Africa (see Schimmel and Pech, 2004).

## Discussion and conclusion

By considering the opportunities for interaction between public and private officials and traffickers (and their 'structures'), this chapter has begun to identify opportunities for interaction which may lead to corruption during the processes of human trafficking to the UK. We provide insight into some key analytical issues for investigating the dynamics of corruption and human trafficking, and, in so doing, we can see how by understanding opportunities and their structures, possibilities for intervention can be identified. Despite there being only relatively few such opportunities, it is important that these situations be anticipated and attention focused on how these activities intersect, particularly given the absence of consideration of bribery and corruption from UK policy.

Data remains scarce on the role of corruption in human trafficking (UNODC, 2011). Barriers to the collection of reliable data in this area include the reluctance of corrupt officials to talk about their activities, undercover operations are ethically problematic due to the exploitative nature of the activity and victims are often unable or unwilling to discuss the role of corrupt officials in their victimisation (Holmes, 2009; Smith, 2016). Even in the absence of subsequent corruption in the UK, victims' experiences of corrupt officials and their relationships with traffickers can then be used by traffickers to coerce victims, adding to their fear of authority and lowering the likelihood of reporting (ATMG, 2013). On the basis of existing evidence, the OECD (2016) has developed 'Guideline Principles on Combatting Corruption related to Trafficking in Persons', which aims to provide a reference for countries establishing a framework to address this corruption with emphasis on both awareness raising and preventative measures. More specifically, this may include measures to increase the difficulty of forging travel documents (for example, biometric technologies), improving document storage and control (Van de Bunt and Van der Schoot, 2003). However, focusing on countries in the nascent stages of policy development in this area indirectly assumes a level of capability on the part of countries with established frameworks which may lead to vulnerabilities remaining unaddressed.

In addition to the potential for corruption within the trafficking process, the anti-corruption regulatory and legal frameworks can also inform the development of anti-trafficking policy and strategy (Ramasastry, 2013). The way in which organisations (or individuals acting on behalf of organisations) are held accountable for direct or indirect involvement in human trafficking is currently less robust than for other forms of corporate deviance, although there is capacity for these regulatory frameworks to move in similar directions (see Lord and Broad, 2017). At national and international levels, recommendations have been made for greater cooperation and coordination between anti-trafficking and anti-corruption practitioners and professionals (OECD, 2016). There is potential for greater integration of anti-corruption practice in human trafficking strategy and vice versa.

# Bibliography

Agustin, L. (2008) *Sex at the Margins: Migration, Labour Markets and the Rescue Industry*. London: Zed Books.

Andersson, S. and Heywood, P. (2009) 'The politics of perception: Use and abuse of transparency international's approach to measuring corruption', *Political Studies*, 57: 746–767.

Aronowitz (2009) *Human Trafficking, Human Misery: The Global Trade in Human Beings*. London: Greenwood Publishing Group.

ATMG. (2013) *In the Dock: Examining the UK's Criminal Justice Response to Trafficking*. London: Anti-Trafficking Monitoring Group.

Balch, A. (2015) *Understanding and Evaluating UK Efforts to Tackle Forced Labour Vulnerability, Exploitation and Migrants*. Basingstoke, UK: Palgrave Macmillan UK, pp. 86–98.

Bales, K. (2005) *Understanding Global Slavery: A Reader*. Berkeley, CA: University of California Press.

Bales, K. (2007) 'What predicts human trafficking?' *International Journal of Comparative and Applied Criminal Justice*, 31(2): 269–279.

Benson, M., Madensen, T. and Eck, J. (2009) 'White-collar crime from an opportunity perspective', in S. Simpson and D. Weisburd (eds) *The Criminology of White-Collar Crime*. Berlin: Springer.

Benson, M. and Simpson, S. (2015) *Understanding White-Collar Crime*. London: Routledge.

Berket, M.R. (2015) 'Labour exploitation and trafficking for labour exploitation: Trends and challenges for policy-making', in *ERA Forum* 16(3): 359–377.

Brantingham, P.J. and Brantingham, P.L. (1991) *Environmental Criminology*. Prospect Heights, IL: Waveland Press.

Broad, R. (2015) 'A vile and violent thing: Female traffickers and the criminal justice response', *British Journal of Criminology*, 55(6): 1058–1075.

Broad, R. (2018) 'Assessing convicted traffickers' needs: Negotiating migration, employment and opportunity through restricted networks', *Howard Journal of Criminal Justice*.

Campana, P. and Varese, F. (2016) 'Exploitation in human trafficking and smuggling', *European Journal on Criminal Policy and Research*, 22(1): 89–105.

Chuang, J.A. (2014) 'Exploitation creep and the unmaking of human trafficking law', *American Journal of International Law*, 108(4): 609–649.

CORE. (2016) *Beyond Compliance: Effective Reporting under the Modern Slavery Act*. London: CORE Coalition, available at http://corporate-responsibility.org/wp-content/uploads/2016/03/CSO_TISC_guidance_final_digitalversion_16.03.16.pdf. Accessed 8 January 2018.

Danailova-Trainor, G. and Laczko, F. (2010) 'Trafficking in persons and development: Towards greater policy coherence', *International Migration*, 48(4): 38–83.

Deflem, M. (1995) 'Corruption, law, and justice: A conceptual clarification', *Journal of Criminal Justice*, 23(3): 243–258.

Doezema, J. (2005) 'Now you see her, now you don't': Sex workers at the UN Trafficking Protocol Negotiations', *Social and Legal Studies*, 14(1): 61–89.

Doig, A. (2006) *Fraud*. London: Routledge.

Europol. (2013) *Serious and Organised Crime Threat Assessment 2013*. Europol Public Information, available at www.statewatch.org/news/2013/apr/eu-europol-socta-2013.pdf. Accessed 8 January 2018.

Farrior, S. (1997) 'The international law on trafficking in women and children for prostitution: Making it live up to its potential', *Harvard Human Rights Journal*, 10: 213–256.

Goodey, J. (2003) 'Migration, crime and victimhood', *Punishment and Society*, 5(4): 415–431.

Gounev, P. and Ruggiero, V. (2012) *Corruption and Organized Crime in Europe: Illegal Partnerships*. London: Routledge.

Heywood, P. and Rose, J. (2014) '"Close but no Cigar": The measurement of corruption', *Journal of Public Policy*, 34(3): 507–529.

HM Government. (2014) *Modern Slavery Strategy*. London: HM Government.

HM Government. (2015) Transparency in Supply Chains etc. *A practical guide Guidance issued under section 54 Modern Slavery Act* 2015. *London: HM Government*. Available at www.gov.uk/government/uploads/system/uploads/attachment_data/file/649906/Transparency_in_Supply_Chains_A_Practical_Guide_2017.pdf. Accessed 8 January 2018.

Holmes, L. (2009) 'Human trafficking and corruption: Triple victimisation', in C. Friesendorf (ed.) *Strategies against Human Trafficking: The Role of the Security Sector*. Vienna: National Defence Academy.

Home Office. (2012) An evidence assessment of the routes of human trafficking into the UK, available at www.gov.uk/government/uploads/system/uploads/attachment_data/file/115923/occ103.pdf. Accessed 8 January 2018.

Hyland, K. (2017) 'Letter to Sarah Newton, MP dated 10/01/17', available at www.antislaverycommissioner.co.uk/media/1126/letter-to-sarah-newton-mp-on-the-national-referral-mechanism.pdf. Accessed 8 January 2018.

Kemp, A. and Raijman, R. (2014) 'Bringing in state regulations, private brokers, and local employers: A meso-level analysis of labor trafficking in Israel', *International Migration Review*, 48(3): 604–642.

Law Society. (2016) *Response to the BEI Committee Inquiry into the Future World of Work and Rights of Workers*, available at www.lawsociety.org.uk/policy-campaigns/consultation-responses/beis-committee-inquiry-future-rights-of-workers/. Accessed 8 January 2018.

Lee, M. (2011) *Trafficking and Global Crime Control*. London and Thousand Oaks, CA: Sage.

Levi, M. and Lord, N. (2011) 'Links between corruption and organised crime, and research gaps', in D. Thelesklaf and P. Gomes Pereira (eds) *Non-State Actors in Asset Recovery*. Bern: Peter Lang.

Lewis, H., Dwyer, P., Hodkinson, S. and Waite, L. (2015) 'Hyper-precarious lives: Migrants, work and forced labour in the Global North', *Progress in Human Geography*, 39(5): 580–600.

Lord, N. and Levi, M. (2017) 'Organizing the finances for and the finances from transnational corporate bribery', *European Journal of Criminology*, 14(3): 365–389.

Lord, N. and Broad, R. (2017) 'Corporate failures to prevent serious and organised crimes: Foregrounding the "organisational" component', *The European Review of Organised Crime*, 4(2): 27–52.

National Crime Agency. (2017) *National Referral Mechanism Statistics – End of Year Summary 2016 National Crime* Agency report, available at www.nationalcrimeagency. gov.uk/publications/national-referral-mechanism-statistics/2016-nrm-statistics/788-national-referral-mechanism-statistics-end-of-year-summary-2016/file. Accessed 8 January 2018.

O'Connell Davidson, J. (2015) *Modern Slavery: The Margins of Freedom*. Basingstoke, UK: Palgrave Macmillan.

OECD. (2016) *Trafficking in Persons and Corruption: Breaking the Chain OECD Public Governance Reviews*. Paris: OECD Publishing.

Okogbule, N. (2013) 'Combating the "new slavery" in Nigeria: An appraisal of legal and policy responses to human trafficking', *Journal of African Law*, 57(1): 57–80.

OSCE. (2010) *Combatting Trafficking as Modern Day Slavery: A Matter of Rights, Freedoms and Security*. Vienna: OSCE.

PACO. (2002) *Trafficking in Human Beings and Corruption, Council of Europe, Report on the Regional Seminar, Portoroz, Slovenia, 19–22 June*', available at http://lastrada international.org/lsidocs/297%20Trafficking%20and%20Corruption%20(PACO).pdf. Accessed 8 January 2018.

Paoli, L. (2002) 'The paradoxes of organized crime', *Crime, Law and Social Change*, 37(1): 51–97.

Phillips, N. (2015) 'Private governance and the problem of trafficking and slavery in global supply chains', in L. Waite, G. Craig, H. Lewis and K. Skrivankova (eds) *Vulnerability, Exploitation and Migrants*. Basingstoke, UK: Palgrave Macmillan, pp. 15–27.

Plembach, S. (2016) 'Sex, deportation and rescue: economies of migration among Nigerian sex workers', *Feminist Economics*, 23(3): 1–26.

Ramasastry, A. (2013) 'Closing the governance gap in the business and human rights arena: Lessons from the anti-corruption movement', in S. Deva and D. Bilchitz (eds) *Human Rights Obligations of Business*. Cambridge, UK: Cambridge University Press, pp. 162–190.

Richards, K. (2004) 'The trafficking of migrant workers: What are the links between labour trafficking and corruption?' *International Migration*, 42(5): 147–168.

Right to Remain. (2017) *Blurring the Line between Slavery and Migration*, available at www. righttoremain.org.uk/blog/blurring-the-line-between-slavery-migration-operation-magnify-goes-public-with-97-workers-arrested/. Accessed 8 January 2018.

Rose-Ackerman, S. (1999) *Corruption and Governance*. Cambridge, UK: Cambridge University Press.

Salt, J. (2000) 'Trafficking and smuggling: A European perspective', *International Migration* Special Issue, 1: 31–56.

Salt, J. and Stein, J. (1997) 'Migration as a business: The case of trafficking', *International Migration*, 35(4): 467–494.

Savona, E.U., Giommoni, L. and Mancuso, M. (2014) 'Human trafficking for sexual exploitation in Italy', in B. Leclerc and R. Wortley (eds) *Cognition and Crime. Offender Decision Making and Script Analyses*. London: Routledge, pp. 140–163.

Schimmel, B. and Pech, B. (2004) *Corruption and Gender: Approaches and Recommendations for Technical Assistance – Focal Theme: Corruption and Trafficking in Women*. Eschborn, Germany: Deutsche Gesellschaft für Technische Zusammenarbeit.

Smith, C. (2016) *Report on Human Trafficking Issues to the 2016 Annual Session of the OSCE Parliamentary Assembly*, available at www.oscepa.org/documents/all-documents/special-representatives/human-trafficking-issues/report-20/3379-2016-annual-session-report-by-the-special-representative-on-human-trafficking-issues/file. Accessed 8 January 2018.

Smith, D.J. (2010) 'Corruption, NGOs, and development in Nigeria', *Third World Quarterly*, 31(2): 243–258.

Spencer, J. and Broad, R. (2012) 'The Groundhog Day of the human trafficking for sexual exploitation debate: New directions in criminological understanding', *European Journal on Criminal Policy and Research*, 18(3): 269–281.

Spencer, J., Broad, R., Aromaa, K., Junninen, M., Markina, A., Saar, J. and Viljanen, T. (2010) *Organised Crime, Corruption and the Movement of People Across Borders in the New Enlarged EU: A Case Study of Estonia, Finland and the UK. HEUNI Programme Funded Paper for the EU*, available at http://heuni.fi/material/attachments/heuni/reports/6KGTExkjH/HEUNI_report_69_Final.pdf. Accessed 8 January 2018.

Surtees, R. (2014) *Traffickers and Trafficking: Challenges in Researching Human Trafficking and Trafficking Operations*. Geneva: International Organisation for Migration, available at http://publications.iom.int/system/files/pdf/nexus_traffickers_and_trafficking_final_web.pdf. Accessed 8 January 2018.

Transparency International. (2011) *Corruption and Human Trafficking*. Working Paper 03/2011. Berlin: Transparency International.

Transparency International. (2017) *How Do You Define Corruption?* available at www.transparency.org/what-is-corruption/#define. Accessed 8 January 2018.

Tremblay, M. (2010) *Corruption and Human Trafficking: Unravelling the Undistinguishable for a Better Fight International Anti-Corruption Conference Workshop Report, Bangkok, Thailand, 10–13 November*, 2010, available at http://14iacc.org.s3-website.eu-central-1.amazonaws.com/wp-content/uploads/ws1.2CamilleKarbassi_LR.pdf. Accessed 8 January 2018.

Tverdova, Y.V. (2011) 'Human trafficking in Russia and other post-Soviet states', *Human Rights Review*, 12(3): 329–344.

UNODC. (2011) *The Role of Corruption in Trafficking in Persons*, available at https://issuu.com/transparencyinternational/docs/ti-working_paper_human_trafficking_28_jun_2011?mode=window&backgroundColor=%23222222. Accessed 8 January 2018.

UNODC. (2016) *Global Report on Trafficking in Persons*, available at http://reliefweb.int/sites/reliefweb.int/files/resources/2016_Global_Report_on_Trafficking_in_Persons.pdf. Accessed 8 January 2018.

US Department of State. (2016) *Trafficking in Persons Report 2016*, available at www.state.gov/documents/organization/258876.pdf. Accessed 8 January 2018.

Van de Bunt, H. and Van der Schoot, C. (2003) *Prevention of Organized Crime: A Situational Approach*. Amsterdam: Research and Documentation Centre of the Ministry of Justice in the Netherlands (WODC).

Webb, S. and Burrows, J. (2009) *Organised Immigration Crime: A Post-Conviction Study.* Research Report 15, available at http://webarchive.nationalarchives.gov.uk/20110314171826/http://rds.homeoffice.gov.uk/rds/pdfs09/horr15c.pdf. Accessed 8 January 2018.

World Bank. (1997) *Helping Countries Combat Corruption: The Role of the World Bank,* available at www1.worldbank.org/publicsector/anticorrupt/corruptn/coridx.htm. Accessed 8 January 2018.

Zhang, S.X. and Pineda, S.L. (2008) 'Corruption as a causal factor in human trafficking', in D. Siegel and H. Nelen (eds) *Organized Crime: Culture, Markets and Policies.* New York: Springer, pp. 41–55.

# 5 The organisation of corruption in commercial enterprise

## Concealing (and revealing) the beneficial ownership of assets

*Liz Campbell*[1]

## Introduction

This chapter examines how corruption in commercial enterprise, both in ostensibly legitimate businesses and also organised crime-controlled entities, is enabled and enhanced by the deployment of legal structures so as to conceal the "beneficial ownership" of assets. The opacity provided by different instruments can be exploited to generate, conceal and maintain the resources necessary for many corrupt relations and actions in commercial enterprise. Recognition of this phenomenon is stimulating various legal amendments at the domestic and transnational level, relating to the registration of ownership and the directorship of companies, in an effort to improve transparency and oversight and thus prevent and deter corruption. Critical issues remain under-explored regarding the laws' likely effectiveness, as well as their implications for human rights. This chapter brings together insights from criminal law, company law and regulatory studies to provide a novel doctrinal and theoretical analysis of the key legal measures that seek to improve transparency and thereby reveal the beneficial ownership of assets implicated in corrupt practices.

The assets that are necessary for and derive from corruption are often held in or transmitted through legal business structures and mechanisms, in what are termed generically "corporate vehicles". These are "legal entities through which a wide variety of commercial activities are conducted and assets are held", including corporations, trusts, and partnerships with limited liability characteristics (OECD, 2001: 12–13; FATF, 2006: 3). Corporate vehicles represent a critical component of contemporary economies, and are used to create and structure businesses, as well as being used for personal wealth management and investment purposes. They share features like separate legal personality by constituting legal entities separate from members or shareholders, and they often have limited liability characteristics in that partners or shareholders are liable only for their investment and their personal assets will not be reachable by the entity's creditors. In most instances, corporate vehicles are used legally, but they can also be

1 Thanks to Andrew Mohamdee for research assistance, and to Radha Ivory, Aleksandra Jordanoska, Nicholas Lord and John Paterson for their comments on previous drafts. Any errors are my own.

relied on to prevent the seizure or taxation of assets, to launder money and to conceal the proceeds or payments from bribery, due to the very qualities that make them valuable in legitimate contexts.

The crux of the issue in relation to corporate vehicles is their capacity to hide the true or ultimate "beneficial owner" of property, namely as the person that pays for or profits from corruption. As noted in a World Bank study of 150 cases of large-scale corruption (Van der Does de Willebois et al., 2011: 39), two arrangements are especially common in respect of monetary bribes:

> In one case, the giver of the bribe either creates or contracts with a consulting company to receive and pass on funds to the bribe receiver, thereby obscuring the chain of payment and creating a plausible explanation for the payments. In the second case, the recipient of the bribe creates a corporate vehicle to hide the assets and any connection that he may have to them. In cases in which the official is given a concealed stake in the venture or the company offering the bribe, these corporate vehicles become the opaque link between the corrupted party and the wealth acquired.

So a corporate vehicle is either created or used for the purposes of obfuscation. Though in some instances, the entity might actually be a consulting firm, say, that pays bribes, rather than a corporate vehicle with a sole criminal purpose, the key point being that corporate structures are used to conceal bribes, even if the third party has an otherwise legitimate function.

The term "beneficial owner", familiar to those in the common law world as referring to the beneficiary of a trust, is now used more broadly than its original usage to denote the person who will benefit from or can use particular assets. Issues of definition and scope of "beneficial owner" arise; there is a lack of clarity in and inconsistency between jurisdictions as to the term's meaning (FATF, 2010: 28; United Nations Economic and Social Council, 2010: 17). An extensive literature explores the meaning of beneficial ownership (Becker et al., 2015; Collier, 2011). Rather than rehearsing or resolving these debates, I take a functionalist approach, centring on the control over assets and the benefit accrued. I endorse the view that beneficial ownership should not be interpreted in a narrow, formally legal sense (OECD, 2014), but rather should be understood "as a material, substantive concept – referring to the de facto control over a corporate vehicle" (Van der Does de Willebois et al., 2011: 3).

Indeed, this is the approach of the European Union Fourth Anti-Money Laundering Directive (4AMLD), which came into force across the EU on 26 June 2017. Article 3(6)) describes "beneficial owner" as "the natural person(s) who ultimately owns or controls the customer and/or the natural person on whose behalf a transaction or activity is being conducted". Notably, there is no definition of "customer" in the Directive, and so it can encompass both natural and legal persons. The term "beneficial owner" also is referred to expressly, though not defined, in a number of international conventions and standards.

Article 14(1)(a) of the United Nations Convention against Corruption stipulates that each State Party shall "institute a comprehensive domestic regulatory and supervisory regime . . . [with] requirements for customer and, where appropriate, beneficial owner identification". In addition, the non-binding but highly influential Financial Action Task Force (FATF) Recommendations[2] refer directly to transparency and beneficial ownership of legal persons and arrangements (FATF, 2012). Recommendation 24 refers to need for "adequate, accurate and timely information on the beneficial ownership and control of legal persons" in preventing their misuse for money laundering or terrorist financing. Recommendation 25 requires such information on express trusts and provides that countries should consider "measures to facilitate access to beneficial ownership and control information by financial institutions". As is elaborated upon later, these standards are motivated by the perception that access to information is key in identifying and addressing the concealment of the beneficial ownership of assets.

This chapter brings together insights from criminal law, company law and regulatory studies to provide a novel doctrinal and theoretical analysis of the key legal measures that seek to improve transparency and thereby reveal the beneficial ownership of assets implicated in corrupt practices. I map three different structures that can be used to hide beneficial ownership and thus to facilitate corrupt practices in commercial enterprise: companies, trusts, and partnerships.[3] I consider why and how they are employed, examining their key characteristics. I critique the legal responses to their apparent misuse in the UK in particular, with reference to their different constituent jurisdictions, as well as commenting on the legal stimuli emanating from the European Union and other international organisations. Though much of the focus is domestic, the chapter's insights are widely relevant, as they speak to global policy and legal trends. Then I engage with some objections that might be raised to these legal changes, centring on normative, rights-based and empirical concerns. Finally, I place the legal developments in a conceptual framework, drawing on insights from criminal law, criminology and regulatory scholarship.

This chapter's analysis generates three major claims about the concealment of beneficial ownership in the organisation of corruption in commercial enterprise. The first is that the introduction of registers and other measures will not always reveal beneficial ownership, and, second, that even a strong and proportionate regime would only ever provide a partial response to corruption. Finally, further empirical work is needed to determine where scholarly and operational priorities should lie, in terms of legal structures, jurisdictions and criminal actors: our focus on certain mechanisms and structures could well be misplaced.

---

2 The FATF Recommendations were issued first in 1990, and then revised in 1996, 2001, 2003 and 2012. In addition, FATF monitors its members' implementation and operation of AML measures, as well as vulnerabilities to money laundering.

3 While other mechanisms (like hedge funds) potentially are relevant also, they are beyond the scope of this chapter.

# The context

Concerns about the misuse of different legal entities for corrupt purposes and their ability to conceal the identity of the ultimate beneficiaries of assets have been on the policy and policing agenda for a number of decades (T.M.C. Asser Instituut, 2000: 11). The Organisation for Economic Co-operation and Development observed in 2001 that

> Almost every economic crime involves the misuse of corporate entities – money launderers exploit cash-based businesses and other legal vehicles to disguise the source of their illicit gains, bribe-givers and recipients conduct their illicit transactions through bank accounts opened under the names of corporations and foundations, and individuals hide or shield their wealth from tax authorities and other creditors through trusts and partnerships, to name but a few examples.
>
> (OECD, 2001: 3)

In the domestic UK operational sense, the National Crime Agency (NCA; 2016: paras. 90–93) remarked that "high end money laundering" relies on corporate structures set up specifically with obscured beneficial ownership, in order to hide the nature and ownership of the funds. The NCA (2016, para. 111) further stressed that: "Bribe payers and recipients, intermediaries and professional enablers create and use corporate structures such as shell, subsidiary and subcontracting companies to channel bribe payments and the proceeds of corruption, as well as to obscure their criminal activity" (also National Crime Agency (2017: para. 55)).

In the political setting, notions of transparency are to the fore more and more, and momentum appears to be gathering in respect of the disclosure of beneficial ownership. The theme of the G8 Summit at Lough Erne in June 2013 was tax evasion and transparency of corporate ownership, and the "Beneficial Ownership Principles" were endorsed under David Cameron's leadership (Prime Minister's Office, 2013). Then in 2014 the G20 leaders adopted High Level Principles on Beneficial Ownership Transparency in Brisbane, declaring "financial transparency, in particular the transparency of beneficial ownership of legal persons and arrangements a 'high priority'" (G20, 2014). These concerns and the operationalising of the principles were given added impetus by the revelations in the Panama Papers in April 2016, followed closely by the political commitments made at the Anti-Corruption Summit in London, May 2016. That said, the associated legislative action has not been consistent.

This rhetoric and heightened political attention exemplify the perception that legal structures are deployed by individuals and enterprises involved in corrupt practices to create, conceal and contain illegally obtained assets. What remains less clear is what types of structures are used, to what extent, and why; and what difference, if any, the intensified policy focus and rapidly changing legal terrain make.

# Corruption and "corporate vehicles": responding through law

Three different corporate vehicles – companies, trusts and partnerships – and their use in corruption in commercial enterprise are now explored. Their perceived misuse is prompting legal changes in the domestic and transnational spheres. I analyse these legal responses, and consider some underexplored normative, rights-based and empirical objections. Notably, some of these structures are "on-shore", that is, located in the current jurisdiction, whereas others are off-shore, in being incorporated or registered in another jurisdiction, usually one with preferable rates of tax or simpler systems of incorporation. This cross-border dimension has implications for the responses to such abuse, and will be alluded to throughout the chapter. I also examine the use of "chains" of corporate vehicles, and the role played by professional intermediaries and service providers.

## Companies

The use of companies to facilitate and perpetuate criminality has long been recognised in both the academic and policy spheres (Malm and Bichler, 2013; Matrix Knowledge Group, 2007: 39; Petrunov, 2011; Schneider, 2004; Tombs and Whyte, 2015). This can involve otherwise legal firms as fronts for criminal purposes, such as the use of a pre-existing company with a legitimate business to launder or conceal assets. High-cash businesses, such as construction and taxi companies through to bars and strip clubs, provide a useful façade for the cleaning or safeguarding of assets. Shell companies with a sole or distinct criminal objective can also be created, with no significant assets or operations at the time of incorporation.

Such insights are not new. A UK Cabinet Office study in 2000 suggested that almost all complex UK money laundering schemes involved UK shell companies (Performance and Innovation Unit, 2000: 85). Once a company is formed, "nominee directors" may be installed while the identity of the actual beneficial owner(s) of the company is hidden (Performance and Innovation Unit, 2000: 86). This is of critical use in the context of corruption in commercial enterprise. Shell companies benefit from the reputation of the UK (Performance and Innovation Unit, 2000: 86), insofar as there may be a presumption or veneer of legitimacy. There is of course a tension between market imperatives and the need to prevent potential criminality, in that the ease of incorporation is seen as one of the strengths of the UK's competitive regulatory environment (Performance and Innovation Unit, 2000: 86).

In terms of the organisation of corruption in commercial enterprise in particular, the company itself could be the location or perpetrator of the criminal behaviour, or it could be used as the means by which the assets are hidden and the link to the corrupt individual is obscured. So, the company may be the payer or recipient of what look like legitimate payments, but are in fact bribes. Existing directors of the company may be the active or passive bribers. A bribed individual could also be made a director of a company, or given a concealed stake, as a way of hiding the nature of the bribes.

Undoubtedly, companies are used to hide and maintain the finances for corruption. The World Bank carried out research into 150 cases of large-scale corruption, finding that in the vast majority of them, a corporate vehicle was misused to hide the money trail and the corporate vehicle in question was a company or corporation (Van der Does de Willebois et al., 2011: 2). As yet, there are no comparable data on the UK.[4]

In an effort to respond to perceived exploitation of the corporate veil and its attendant secrecy, some recent legislative changes were made in the UK which may impact on the financing of corruption. Two of these will now be examined. In the first instance, Part 7 of the Small Business, Enterprise and Employment Act 2015 imposes requirements on companies to update more detailed information annually at Companies House. This has been amended subsequently to adhere to the requirements of the European Union's Fourth Anti-Money Laundering Directive (see Campbell, 2018). Second, the Small Business, Enterprise and Employment Act 2015 limits who or indeed what can be a company director.

Under Part 7 and Schedule 3 of the 2015 Act, UK companies must maintain a register of "people with significant control" (PSC), which is a means to identify the beneficial owner or controller of the entity. Each register must be available to the public and the details provided to Companies House annually, whereby it will be included in the central public register. Chapter 2 imposes duties on companies to gather information about PSC, and on others to supply such information, to enable them to keep such a register. The majority of companies and LLPs in the UK need to comply with these provisions or risk being convicted of a criminal offence; listed companies are broadly exempt as they are already subject to transparency obligations under the Financial Conduct Authority's Disclosure and Transparency Rules (Financial Conduct Authority, 2017). The rationale for the creation of such registers is to determine and record who controls certain entities in the UK.

"Significant control" (as defined in Schedule 1A of the Companies Act 2006) includes holding directly or indirectly more than 25% of company's shares or voting rights, or having the right to appoint or remove a majority of the directors. It also includes an individual who exercises significant influence or control over a trust or firm which does not have separate legal personality and has significant influence or control over the company. Non-compliance with the reporting and recording requirements is criminal. Failure to provide accurate information on a PSC register or to comply with notices requiring PSCs to provide information is a criminal offence for both the company and its officers, punishable by up to

---

4 This is being examined currently by Lord, N., Campbell, L. and Van Wingerde, K. in *The (Mis) Use of Corporate Vehicles by Transnational Organised Crime Groups in the Concealment, Conversion and Control of Illicit Finance*, available at http://gtr.rcuk.ac.uk/projects?ref=ES%2FP001386 %2F1.

two years' imprisonment (Companies Act 2006, s.790F). There is no statutory defence available to a company for breach of the provisions.

Article 30 of 4AMLD, to which the UK must adhere, requires EU member states to hold adequate, accurate and current information on the beneficial ownership of corporate and other legal entities incorporated within their territory in a central register, and provides that such information should be made available to specific authorities, organisations and those with a legitimate interest across the EU. Annual updating as provided for originally in the 2015 Act was not sufficient to meet 4AMLD's requirement for information to be "current", and so the Information about People with Significant Control (Amendment) Regulations 2017 introduced a requirement to notify changes in beneficial ownership within a shorter time frame. Entities must record changes to information on their PSC register within 14 days of obtaining the information and file that information within a further 14 days (Regulations 7 and 8). It is likely that in future EU Member States will need to put in place mechanisms to ensure the information in the register is also verified on a regular basis (European Commission, 2016).

Furthermore, Article 30(9) of 4AMLD provides for an exemption from access to beneficial ownership information in exceptional circumstances, such as where access would expose the beneficial owner to the risk of fraud, kidnapping, blackmail, violence or intimidation, or where s/he is a minor or otherwise incapable. There is no equivalent protection or qualification in the current UK scheme, indicating a more expansive reach. It remains to be seen both how or if this is enacted in the UK, and, if so, the extent to which it is used.

Though this registration initiative has laudable intentions, I suggest that its value is questionable, both in doctrine and implementation. In terms of the technical content, the threshold of 25% is arbitrary and easily circumvented. When the European Union Third Anti-Money Laundering Directive (3AMLD) was agreed in 2005, a 25% baseline was deemed to be sufficient, following the example in the FATF Guidance on Transparency and Beneficial Ownership (which, however, was careful to note that its Recommendations do not specify the appropriate threshold) (FATF, 2014: 15). Article 43 of 3AMLD required the Commission to present a report to the European Parliament and the Council on the "possible expediency and consequences of a reduction . . . from 25% to 20%" (European Commission, 2012). Though the Commission contemplated whether such modification was appropriate, it was not changed in AMLD4. It is likely that this will be lowered to 10% for certain entities which present a specific risk of being used for money laundering and tax evasion (European Commission, 2016). This threshold, as indeed would be the case for any, can be circumvented by dividing the ownership into smaller elements by those who seek to hide ownership and control. That said, total removal of a threshold would pose challenges in terms of implementation and locating who are the actual beneficial owners (and controllers). This would mean that, potentially, anyone with some stake could be a beneficial owner, which would dilute the scheme and render it more complicated in practical terms.

The next concern is that the register hinges to a large extent on self-reporting, and maintenance and monitoring of veracity will be onerous for Companies

House. Unless resource for Companies House is augmented, this scheme is not likely to be successful in its transparency aims.

In terms of implementation, registers provide a valuable starting point in identifying, monitoring and addressing criminal behaviour, but they need to be complemented and corroborated by other data sources. As observed in the World Bank study (Van der Does de Willebois et al., 2011: 5), they "are almost invariably archival in nature; they rarely conduct independent verification; and in many cases, they are already stretched for resources". They present a static outline of information that is likely to be partial and could possibly be false. Moreover, it is difficult, time-consuming and expensive to verify the data within them. As for enforcement, it appears that even if the data are available and verified, revealing problematic behaviour or questionable ownership, little is being done. Given the global nature of the issue, where responsibility for enforcement lies is questionable, and formal breach of the rules does not necessarily result in state action (Global Witness, 2016).

Fenwick and Vermeulen (2016: 18–19) have questioned rightly the "ratcheting up" of disclosure requirements in this way, on the basis that forcing more information into the public domain is unlikely to be useful and merely encourages new and more imaginative means of circumvention. They propose, on grounds of effectiveness, reputation and profitability, the "nudging" of firms to "embrace open communication" (Fenwick and Vermeulen, 2016: 41; also Thaler and Sunstein, 2008). While this is persuasive in respect of otherwise legitimate entities that sometimes may be engaged for illicit means, if the primary purpose of establishing the company is to provide a front for illegal activity, this aim is not feasible. No amount of nudging will offset or deter those with criminal and corrupt intentions.

The second significant legal change in UK company law, at least doctrinally, seeks to limit who or what can be a company director. At present, companies may appoint a corporate director as long as at least one of the other directors is an individual (Companies Act 2006, s.155 (though, as is explored in more detail later, introduction of this provision seems to have influenced the use of Scottish Limited Partnerships as an alternative vehicle, underlining the unintended consequences of legal changes in this sphere)). Section 87 of the Small Business, Enterprise and Employment Act 2015 introduced a requirement for all company directors to be natural persons (unless the appointment falls within one of the exceptions provided for by regulations made under s. 156B [Companies Act 2006, s.156A]) as part of the drive to ensure corporate transparency and facilitate more readily the identification of the true controllers/beneficial owners of the company. Though October 2016 was mooted as the date of enactment, this has been deferred, and the provision is not yet in force. The Department for Business, Energy and Industrial Strategy held a consultation about this in early 2017; further action to be taken has yet to be announced. The inverted order of the consultation process is curious to say the least. So, what was heralded as a key measure to offset potential abuse has been postponed, and it is unclear when it will be introduced. Political rhetoric has not been matched by any action regarding the natural person requirement, thus rendering it no more than a paper exercise to date.

*Trusts*

The next structure to be considered is the trust, whose role and value in relation to money laundering and corruption has been emphasised in many studies (Blum et al., 1998: 95; European Commission, 2000: 46; FATF, 2006: 61). Essentially, a trust is a common law construct that provides for the separation of legal ownership from beneficial ownership. It is a legitimate mechanism for transferring and managing assets, and is very useful in relation to minors, incapacitated individuals and for charitable purposes. It comprises an agreement between two private parties, and "enjoy[s] a greater degree of privacy and autonomy than other corporate vehicles" (OECD, 2001: 25). It should be added that when we talk of "trusts", there are a variety of sorts, with different features and characteristics, and they vary within and between jurisdictions. Nonetheless, the common dimensions of salience here are their private nature and limited regulation.

In addition to legitimate personal and financial planning purposes, the perception is that trusts can be employed for illicit ends, due to their autonomy and relative lack of oversight, and their ability and purpose to conceal the identity of the beneficiaries (OECD, 2001: 25). In relation to corruption in criminal enterprise, an individual could set up a trust as a repository for the profits from a bribe, or as a way of transferring the assets that will be used as a bribe. Holding assets in trust also is a way of concealing them from the authorities, as well as from other interested or involved parties in the criminal scheme.

Notwithstanding the potential value of trusts in this context, the World Bank review of 150 grand corruption investigations found that trusts were used infrequently (Van der Does de Willebois et al., 2011: 44), comprising 5 per cent of the corporate vehicles identified and appearing in about 15 per cent of the investigations, mostly in Latin America, the Caribbean and high-income nations. These findings may challenge the presumption about misuse of trusts. It is unclear whether this pattern would be replicated in the UK and in respect of "smaller" corruption schemes, that is, whether there is a connection between the scale of the corruption and the vehicle used. Nonetheless, one must be mindful that the cases explored in the World Bank review are unlikely to be representative, given that they comprise cases under investigation and that the "successful" misuse of trusts may never come to light.

There is increased impetus from the EU to address the use of trusts for illegitimate purposes by means of transparency conditions, with strong support from NGOs like Global Witness (Global Witness, 2017). Article 31 of 4AMLD, as transposed into domestic UK law by Regulation 45 of the Money Laundering, Terrorist Financing and Transfer of Funds (Information on the Payer) Regulations 2017, mandates the trustees of any express trust with tax consequences to hold adequate, accurate and up-to-date information on the beneficial ownership of the trust. HM Treasury explains that an "express trust" is one "that was deliberately created by a settlor expressly transferring property to a trustee for a valid purpose, as opposed to a statutory, resulting or constructive trust" (HM Treasury, 2017: 9.2). The original EU proposal was a public register for all trusts, but this faced resistance from the UK government, purportedly based on the grounds of protection of privacy, and of course the desire to protect a significant element of its wealth management industry (see Society of Trust and Estate Practitioners, 2014). The UK negotiated so that the register must contain trusts with a tax consequence only (though admittedly this comprises most trusts) and access is limited to appropriate authorities. In contrast to the companies' beneficial owner register, the information is not publicly available but can be accessed by law enforcement and the UK Financial Intelligence Unit only. This register is administered by Her Majesty's Revenue and Customs, and was launched in July 2017 as an online service.[5]

Of course, the same concerns about effectiveness of registers are pertinent here. The inherent nature of trusts is that they are private, autonomous and difficult to monitor. Indeed, these characteristics provide major advantages over other structures in terms of profit maximisation and capital mobility, leading commentators to view them as embedding and maintaining wealth inequality (Harrington, 2017). Regardless, trusts will not be replaced or displaced, and thus the registers can only be partial in their impact. Those who wish to use trusts to hide assets and their origins will use ever more complex structures or front-persons to conceal the true beneficial owner.

### *Partnerships*

The third corporate vehicle to be considered in respect of corruption in commercial enterprise is the partnership. Although partnerships are cited in OECD and FATF documentation as potentially problematic, in general it is perceived that they are not misused to the same extent as other corporate vehicles (OECD, 2001: 28). Like trusts, there may be a mismatch between their perceived vulnerability to corrupt use and the actual threat posed. There is special concern about a form of partnership that is distinct to Scotland only, which appears to be employed with increasing regularity to conceal corrupt and illegal practices and assets. The Scottish Limited Partnership (SLP) has particular characteristics that makes it appealing to those with assets to conceal or transfer.

The Organized Crime and Corruption Reporting Project, a non-governmental consortium of investigative media and journalists, reported in 2017 on *The Russian Laundromat*, an extensive financial fraud and laundering scheme that enabled vast sums to be moved from Russia, through Moldova and Latvia into Europe (Organized Crime and Corruption Reporting Project, 2017). Between 2010 and 2014, Russian officials and other individuals moved billions of dollars from Russia into Europe and the US. This involved the use of numerous corporate vehicles, including fictitious companies registered in London at Companies House. Furthermore, and crucially for the present discussion, more than 100 entities named in the Laundromat were Scottish Limited Partnerships (see Organized Crime and Corruption Reporting Project, 2017; BBC, 2015).

5 www.gov.uk/government/publications/trusts-and-estates-trust-details-41g-trust.

The SLP is like a general partnership in that it comprises two or more partners who carry on business with a view to profit. In a general partnership each partner is jointly and severally liable for partnership debts, whereas in a limited partnership liability differs depending on the type of partner. In an SLP there are two types of partner (general and limited), and there must be at least one of each. The general partner is liable for debts and obligations of the partnership, whereas the limited partner has liability limited to the extent of capital contributions. One major advantage of the SLP is that it has a separate legal personality, unlike limited partnerships constituted elsewhere in the UK. This means that the SLP itself can own assets, enter into contracts, sue or be sued, own property, borrow money and grant certain types of security. Thus, SLPs are used in investment fund structures, in tax structuring and oftentimes in relation to agricultural holdings. The SLP's principal place of business must be in Scotland in order to become registered, but it is possible to migrate this to another jurisdiction following registration and for the SLP's activities to be managed offshore.

Furthermore, although an SLP has a separate legal personality, it retains "tax transparency" in that it is taxed as though it did not have a separate legal personality, and no tax is payable by the SLP itself. Instead, partners are taxed on their share of partnership income and gains arrived at in accordance with their profit-sharing ratios. This "hybrid" status explains some of its appeal, in both legitimate and illegitimate contexts.

This popularity is represented in the trebling of the numbers of SLPs created since 2011, while there was a rise of less than 50 per cent for partnerships south of the border (Department of Business, Energy and Industrial Strategy, 2017: 8). It is likely that this is due to the tightening of company law in s.155 of the Companies Act 2006 which required all UK private and limited companies to have at least one director that is a natural person (see Transparency International UK, 2017: 9). This spike and the use of SLPs in the Russian Laundromat are intensifying calls for their radical reform (see Department of Business, Energy and Industrial Strategy, 2017).

Though originally SLPs were not covered by the PSC register and the associated requirements, the Scottish Partnerships (Register of People with Significant Control) Regulations 2017 modifies the regime to include them. Now SLPs and any general partnership constituted under the law of Scotland that is a "qualifying partnership", namely one with solely corporate partners, must deliver PSC information to Companies House. While this will serve to improve transparency to a degree, the same concerns about circumvention apply. Moreover, SLPs may be dissolved prior to the coming into force of the new regulation, and so will not be covered. Again, the economic attractiveness of such partnerships means that their abolition or substantial amendment is highly unlikely.

### Chains and intermediaries

Having analysed these structures as discrete forms, it is now vital to consider their use together, as this obscures further the origin and detail of illicit assets. Corrupt actors benefit in using all forms in a complex web of wealth management.

The outline provided of the distinctive features of certain corporate vehicles and their ability to hide assets linked to corruption indicates that the vehicles per se are not the (only) problem, rather it is their use in certain ways by certain people. Besides, the extent to which recent and forthcoming legal changes will impact on corrupt behaviour and assets is questionable. This concern is brought into sharp relief by the use of "chains" or "ladders" (Shaxson, 2011: 25) of corporate vehicles, spanning numerous different jurisdictions. This exploits the anonymity of these structures, and confounds attempts to locate and confirm beneficial ownership. So, a rudimentary scheme might involve an international business company in Russia owned by another company in Ireland, which in turn is owned by a third partnership in Scotland, which has assets in a trust established in England. In reality, the schemes are much more complex: as the OECD (2001: 32) said, "The possible permutations are virtually limitless". All of this serves to complicate and preclude successful investigations and actions such as asset recovery. Moreover, it underlines the weakness of some of the transparency provisions that have been introduced.

Of course, a critical dimension in hiding beneficial ownership through complex chains of corporate vehicles lies in the reliance on professional intermediaries, such as company formation agents, lawyers, and trust and company service providers (TCSPs) (FATF, 2006). Though the service of TCSPs is not required to establish a company in the UK, legal, accounting and financial advice will be useful in respect of all corporate vehicles used to store and move illicit assets. This professional expertise is particularly desirable in respect of the construction of offshore entities. There will be a spectrum of knowledge, motivation and intention in respect of TCSPs whose services are connected with the organisation of corruption, ranging from fully lawful yet unethical behaviour; lack of awareness as to the aims of their clients; careless or negligence in failing to carry out due diligence; through to deliberate enabling and facilitation (see Rostain and Regan, 2014).

In terms of legal responses, registered UK TCSPs need to be compliant with the Money Laundering Regulations 2017 regarding customer due diligence and suspicious activity reporting (see Campbell, 2018). When a TCSP is forming a company for a client, it must carry out due diligence, even if this is the only transaction being carried out for that customer (Regulation 4(2)). Moreover, HM Revenue and Customs has issued TCSPs with notice under Paragraph 1, schedule 23 of the Finance Act 2011 to provide information regarding the ultimate beneficial ownership of offshore companies and beneficial interest in offshore partnerships and trusts (HM Revenue & Customs, 2017). This is in an effort to ascertain who should be paying tax and to what level. However, measures like the PSC register will not capture all the entities created and handled by UK TCSPs, underlining how the legal landscape is patchy in its reach and application.

Overall, there is intensifying practitioner and academic consideration of professional facilitators of serious crime (Europol, 2013: 14; Home Office, 2013: 14; Middleton, 2005, 2008; Middleton & Levi, 2015). That said, and more specifically, the evidence base regarding TCSPs and the organisation of corruption in the UK is very limited. The World Bank review found inconsistency in terms of implementation by TCSPs of AML requirements, and differences between the form of structure: professional trustees tend to be more inquisitive about the source of funds to be vested in a trust than they would be if establishing a company (Van der Does de Willebois et al., 2011: 47). Whether this holds for the UK and a broader range of corrupt practices remains to be seen.

## Objections to legal changes

There is political unanimity as to the need to respond robustly to these ways of organising corruption in commercial enterprise, though the extent to which the rhetoric is matched by political, legal or operational action is not constant. Notwithstanding this political support, one can contemplate some objections, both principled and pragmatic, to the current and proposed legal responses, which have gained little traction in the debate to date. I now turn to consider these, focusing on human rights, effectiveness and unintended consequences.

In the first instance, these measures have potentially serious implications for civil liberties, whether we see that as limited to the "human rights of bad guys" (Ivory, 2014) or more broadly. Registers of personal data engage and potentially breach the right to privacy, as protected by Art 8 ECHR. The level of detail, the accessibility and the purpose for which the data are stored are all relevant here.

In addition to a successful challenge in the French courts to a public trust register on the grounds of manifest disproportionality,[6] concerns have been raised by European Data Protection Supervisor (2017), and in scholarly commentary (Noseda, 2017) about the implications these registers pose for privacy. The European Data Protection Supervisor expressed concern about breach of the data protection principle of "purpose limitation", on the basis that proposed amendments from the EU will introduce policy purposes other than countering anti-money laundering and terrorism financing. Regardless, it is unlikely that any comparable legal challenge could be raised to the current corporate PSC register in the UK, on the basis that this is a proportionate response to a legitimate aim. Moreover, the trust register, by virtue of its limited accessibility, is also likely not to fall foul of a challenge on human rights' grounds.

It is debatable how effective these legal responses will be. There is a lack of uniformity in legal doctrine in the UK. Beyond this, there are issues of statutory implementation, wherein the rhetoric around counter-corruption and transparency is not matched by application of the law. Moreover, the degree to which legal measures will be effective unless matched by sufficient resources is dubious. Beyond this, there are evident legal and operational disparities between jurisdictions, leading to "criminogenic asymmetries" (Passas, 1999) which are likely to steer decisions about the placement and use of assets implicated in corrupt practices.

On that point, significant questions remain about the degree to which the UK is serious about addressing the situation in its Overseas Territories and Crown

---

6 Décision n 2016-591 QPC du 21 Octobre 2016.

Dependencies. As outlined, the UK is perceived to have a strong legal framework in respect of transparency, though its implementation and application is inconsistent. Beyond this, there is valid concern about UK Overseas Territories and Crown Dependencies, such as the British Virgin Islands and the Cayman Islands, though there is little solid political action (Martini and Murphy, 2015). Notably, Jason Sharman found that there is a mismatch between perception and empirical data, in that high-income OECD countries are more problematic than so-called offshore centres:

> Not only do the world's major financial centers offer tighter secrecy, but corporate entities formed therein enjoy a status, standing, and legitimacy that are far less likely to arouse suspicion than those from stigmatized offshore locales.
>
> (Sharman, 2010: 139)

This is notable, as these common stereotypes have considerable traction and so detract from actual problematic issues and regions.

Furthermore, there are potential issues relating to the unintended and unpredictable consequences of such legal changes. As noted, legal and operational asymmetries between and within jurisdictions lead to crime displacement in terms of the location of assets and formation of structures. Indeed, this resembles the process of regulatory arbitrage by legitimate companies. For instance, the growth in use of SLPs is linked to previous alterations in company law. Moreover, it is conceivable that enhanced legislative and law enforcement responses will lead a "tactical displacement effect" (Rowe et al., 2013: 6), insofar as corrupt actors will rely on alternative means to reduce the risk of apprehension, perhaps through the increased use of intermediaries.

## Making sense of these changes

Theoretical insights from criminal law, criminology and regulatory scholarship shed light on the unarticulated rationales for these provisions. I suggest that the introduction of measures to improve transparency and reveal beneficial ownership exemplifies a move from a punitive to preventive and regulatory logic in addressing crime, and a co-existing adaptation and acting out in respect of crime control.

### *The preventive turn*

What is occurring in this context is the addressing of the criminal problem of corruption through mostly non-criminal law means. Such a way of dealing with corruption and other forms of serious financial crime was once unorthodox but is now commonplace – rather than the traditional criminal law mechanism of investigation and prosecution, here we have a "follow the money" (King, 2013) or at least a "target the money" approach. It is significant that this is not necessarily a precursor to prosecution, but rather can be a way of both preventing and disrupting corrupt practices, and of ascertaining the connections and nodes between criminal actors and/or politically exposed persons.

In essence, the response has shifted from punitive to preventive, both by moving from and limiting the use of criminal law, with the deployment of private law and regulatory measures. There is an eschewing of the orthodoxy for a more preventive logic, yet with the criminal law retained as the tool of last resort. This trend has considerable traction in respect of serious crime more widely, as is exemplified by the expansive criminal assets regime which in fact operates in the civil realm (Campbell, 2007; Hendry and King, 2015), and in the use of deferred prosecution agreements, which circumvents the conventional criminal trial and involves conditions and compliance requirements for corporate entities (Bronitt, 2017: 215; Lord and King, this volume). The use of registers is further evidence of this preventive turn.

Tightening the rules around beneficial ownership aims to act as a deterrent to potentially criminal actors as well as otherwise professional facilitators. Ultimately it makes monies less secure if they cannot be disguised and hidden effectively. Then, if identified, such assets can be recouped through civil forfeiture and confiscation, as contemplated by Article 31 UNCAC. Having said that, all of this is predicated upon the notion that there is money or property to recoup, which overlooks the "spend and go" habits of many criminals (Naylor, 2002; Steinko, 2012). Thus, this approach is likely to be relevant for a certain set and level of corrupt actors only, and will exclude those insulated by virtue of status, political position or connection.

### Regulating corruption

As well as denoting a preventive move, these legal measures outlined in this chapter involve the *regulation* of crime. They are both driven and implemented by a mix of state and non-state actors, relying on a combination of criminal and civil measures. This way of addressing problematic behaviour may be regarded as holistic and inventive, though runs the risk of being uneven in coverage and unprincipled in purpose. It is instructive to recall the observations of Julia Black (2001: 105) in relation to "command and control" regulation, where the State is "centred" and is envisaged as having the sole capacity to command and control, with a linear progression from policy formation through to implementation. The legal responses to the hiding of beneficial ownership in relation to corruption retain what Black reminds us is often denoted negatively by the term "command and control": poorly targeted, rigid, ossified, under-enforced rules, involving unintended consequences (Black, 2001: 105).

That aside, in structure and purpose the drive to reveal beneficial ownership seems to denote a move away from command and control regulation to a more diversified and participatory style, through the involvement of and reliance on private entities. A perhaps more charitable understanding is that this is a sort of "self-regulation" initiative. The creation of PSC registers and the associated annual reporting are predicated on the cooperation of private entities, yet as this is reinforced by the oversight of Companies House and ultimately the criminal law, it does not represent self-regulation or regulatory "decentring" (Black, 2001: 106). However, in respect of the creation of law relating to company directorship, a degree of regulatory "de-centring" is evident insofar as the UK Government now is deferring to the views of informed, regulated stakeholders. After HMG realised that it had insufficient knowledge to be able to identify the form and cause of the problem and to design an appropriate solution, it reopened the consultation through the Department for Business, Energy and Industrial Strategy. A less optimistic interpretation might view this as an official volte face after pushback from the business community, rather than a principled approach to the decentring of the regulatory response.

### Adapting to crime

We can also view these legal measures as embodying both practical and symbolic dimensions, in apparently adapting to the hiding of beneficial ownership as well as exemplifying political concern about the misuse of corporate vehicles. In the words of David Garland (2001: 105), the state more and more sees itself as faced with a "criminological predicament" and so must adjust its responses to the "new reality" of crime control. Responsibilising companies and other third parties in the context of counter-corruption and money laundering depicts this changing notion of governmentality, whereby the state is developing a form of rule which involves "the enlistment of others . . . and the creation of new forms of co-operative action" (Garland, 2001: 125). This observation should not be taken to denote support for these neo-liberal shifts away from state intervention, rather to explain how such a move is rationalised. One could claim that increased investment in criminal law responses, as well as enhanced regulation, auditing and inspections, would imply there would be no need to move away from the state. While this is arguable, and even if the political climate were such as to support more public expenditure, there would remain a need to involve private entities in their regulation and the monitoring of behaviour and transactions, for pragmatic reasons of access and resource.

Simultaneous to these practical objectives, the legislative activity embodies the notion that "something must be done" (Garland, 2001: 164), regardless of its likely or possible effect. Commitments to address corruption are made on the back of events like the Anti-Corruption Summit in London, in a fanfare of media coverage, with limited reflection on the evidence base for such promises and the likelihood of implementation.

## Concluding remarks

This chapter has assessed the value of a number of corporate vehicles in respect of corruption in commercial enterprise, through their enabling of the transfer of assets and the concealment of beneficial ownership. Inherent characteristics of companies, trusts and partnerships ensure their commercial significance in a capitalist economy, but also help to generate, conceal and maintain the resources necessary for corrupt practices. As the analysis exposes, the introduction of registers may go some way to addressing corruption in commercial enterprise, though this will only be partial. Serious questions about human rights, effectiveness and unintended consequences of these measures remain unanswered.

## Bibliography

BBC. (2015) *The Billion-Dollar Ex-Council Flat.* Available at: www.bbc.com/news/magazine-34445201, accessed 19 July 2017.

Becker, J. et al. (2015) *Klaus Vogel on Double Taxation Conventions.* Edited by E. Reimer and A. Rust. 4th edn. London: Kluwer Law International.

Black, J. (2001) 'Decentring regulation: Understanding the role of regulation and self-regulation in a "post-regulatory" world', *Current Legal Problems*, 54(1): 103–146.

Blum, J.A., Levi, M., Taylor, R.T. and Williams, P. (1998) *Financial Havens, Banking Secrecy and Money-Laundering.* New York: United Nations.

Bronitt, S. 'Regulatory bargaining in the shadows of preventive justice: Deferred prosecution agreements', in T. Tulich, R. Ananian-Welsh, S. Bronitt and S. Murray (eds) *Regulating Preventive Justice: Principle, Policy and Paradox.* Abingdon, UK: Routledge, pp. 211–226.

Campbell, L. (2007) 'Theorising asset forfeiture in Ireland', *Journal of Criminal Law*, 71: 441–460.

Campbell, L. (2018) 'Dirty Cash (Money Talks): 4AMLD and the Money Laundering Regulations 2017', Criminal Law Review 102–122.

Collier, R. (2011). 'Clarity, opacity and beneficial ownership', *British Tax Review*, 6: 684–704.

*Companies Act 2006.*

Department of Business, Energy and Industrial Strategy. (2017) *Review of Limited Partnership Law: A Call for Evidence.* Available at: www.gov.uk/government/uploads/system/uploads/attachment_data/file/583800/review-of-limited-partnerships-law-call-for-evidence.pdf, accessed 19 July 2017.

European Commission. (2012) *Report from the Commission to the European Parliament and the Council on the Application of Directive 2005/60/EC on the Prevention of the Use of the Financial System for the Purpose of Money Laundering and Terrorist Financing.* Luxembourg: Publications Office of the European Union.

European Commission. (2016) *Proposal for a Directive of the European Parliament and of the Council amending Directive (EU) 2015/849 on the prevention of the use of the financial system for the purposes of money laundering or terrorist financing and amending Directive 2009/101/EC*, COM(2016) 450 final 2016/0208 (COD), 5 July 2016.

European Commission and Transcrime, University of Trento. (2000) *Euroshore: Protecting the EU Financial System from the Exploitation of Financial Centres and Off-Shore Facilities by Organized Crime.* Available at: http://eprints.biblio.unitn.it/191/1/Euroshore.pdf, accessed 19 July 2017.

European Data Protection Supervisor. (2017) *Opinion 1/2017 of the European Data Protection Supervisor on a Commission Proposal amending Directive (EU) 2015/849 and Directive 2009/101/EC, Access to beneficial ownership information and data protection implications.* Available at https://edps.europa.eu/sites/edp/files/publication/17-02-02_opinion_aml_en.pdf, accessed 19 July 2017.

'European Parliament and Council directive (EU) 2015/849 on the prevention of the use of the financial system for the purposes of money laundering or terrorist financing' (2015) *Official Journal* L141, p. 86.

Europol. (2013) *EU Serious and Organised Crime Threat Assessment.* Deventer, Netherlands: European Police Office.

FATF. (2006) *The Misuse of Corporate Vehicles, Including Trust and Company Service Providers.* Paris: FATF.

FATF. (2010) *Money Laundering Using Trust and Company Service Providers.* Paris: FATF.

FATF. (2012) *International Standards on Combating Money Laundering and the Financing of Terrorism & Proliferation.* Paris: FATF.

FATF. (2014) *Transparency and Beneficial Ownership.* Paris: FATF.

Fenwick, M. and Vermeulen, E.P.M. (2016) *Disclosure of Beneficial Ownership after the Panama Papers.* Washington, DC: International Finance Corporation.

Financial Conduct Authority. (2017) *Disclosure Guidance and Transparency Rules sourcebook* (release 20, September 2017). Available at www.handbook.fca.org.uk/handbook/DTR.pdf, accessed 25 September 2017.

G20. (2014) *High-Level Principles on Beneficial Ownership Transparency.* Available at: www.ag.gov.au/CrimeAndCorruption/AntiCorruption/Documents/G20High-Level PrinciplesOnBeneficialOwnershipTransparency.pdf, accessed 19 July 2017.

Garland, D. (2001) *The Culture of Control: Crime and Social Order in Contemporary Society.* Oxford, UK: Oxford University Press.

Global Witness. (2016) *What Does the UK Beneficial Ownership Data Show Us?* Available at: www.globalwitness.org/en/blog/what-does-uk-beneficial-ownership-data-show-us/, accessed 22 September 2017.

Global Witness. (2017) *Don't Take It on Trust: The Case for Public Access to Trusts' Beneficial Ownership Information in the EU Anti-Money Laundering Directive.* London: Global Witness.

Halliday, T.C., Levi, M. and Reuter, P. (2014) *Global Surveillance of Dirty Money: Assessing Assessments of Regimes to Control Money-Laundering and Combat the Financing of Terrorism.* Chicago, IL: American Bar Foundation.

Harrington, B. (2017) 'Trusts and financialization', *Socio-economic Review*, 15: 31–63.

Hendry, J. and King, C. (2015) 'How far is too far? Theorising non conviction based asset forfeiture', *International Journal of Law in Context*, 11(4): 398–411.

HM Revenue & Customs. (2017) *Statutory Guidance: Trust and Company Service Provider (TCSP) Returns–Information Sheet.* Available at: www.gov.uk/government/publications/statutory-return-trust-and-company-service-provider-tcsp-records-of-beneficial-ownershipinterest-in-offshore-entities/trust-and-company-service-provider-tcsp-returns-information-sheet, accessed 19 July 2017).

HM Treasury. (2017) *Money Laundering Regulations 2017: Consultation.* Available at: www.gov.uk/government/consultations/money-laundering-regulations-2017/money-laundering-regulations-2017, accessed 19 July 2017.

Home Office. (2013) *Serious and Organised Crime Strategy* (Cm 8715). Available at: www.gov.uk/government/uploads/system/uploads/attachment_data/file/248645/Serious_and_Organised_Crime_Strategy.pdf, accessed 19 July 2017.

Ivory, R. (2014) *Corruption, Asset Recovery, and the Protection of Property in Public International Law: The Human Rights of Bad Guys.* Cambridge, UK: Cambridge University Press.

King, C. (2013) 'Follow the Money Trail: "Civil" forfeiture of "criminal" assets in Ireland', in P.C. van Duyne, (ed.) *Human Dimensions in Organised Crime, Money Laundering and Corruption.* Nijmegen, Netherlands: Wolf Legal Publishers, pp. 265–291.

Malm, A. and Bichler, G. (2013) 'Using friends for money: The positional importance of money-launderers in organized crime', *Trends in Organized Crime*, 16(4): 365–381.

Martini, M. and Murphy, M. (2015) *Just for Show? Reviewing G20 Promises on Beneficial Ownership*. (Transparency International) Available at: https://transparency.eu/wp-content/uploads/2016/11/TI_G20-Beneficial-Ownership-Promises_2015.pdf, accessed 19 July 2017.

Matrix Knowledge Group. (2007) *The Illicit Drug Trade in the United Kingdom*. London: Home Office.

Middleton, D. (2005) 'The legal and regulatory response to solicitors involved in serious fraud: Is regulatory action more effective than criminal prosecution?' *British Journal of Criminology*, 45(6): 810–836.

Middleton, D. (2008) 'Lawyers and client accounts: Sand through a colander', *Journal of Money Laundering Control*, 11(1): 34–46.

Middleton, D. and Levi, M. (2015) 'Let sleeping lawyers lie: Organized crime, lawyers and the regulation of legal services', *British Journal of Criminology*, 55(1): 647–668.

National Crime Agency. (2016) *National Strategic Assessment of Serious and Organised Crime 2016*. Available at: www.nationalcrimeagency.gov.uk/publications/731-national-strategic-assessment-of-serious-and-organised-crime-2016/file, accessed 19 July 2017.

National Crime Agency. (2017) *National Strategic Assessment of Serious and Organised Crime 2017*. Available at: www.nationalcrimeagency.gov.uk/publications/807-national-strategic-assessment-of-serious-and-organised-crime-2017/file, accessed 19 July 2017.

Naylor, R.T. (2002) *Wages of Crime: Black Markets, Illegal Finance, and the Underworld Economy*. Montreal: McGill-Queen's University Press.

Noseda, F. (2017) 'Trusts and privacy: A new battle front', *Trusts & Trustees*, 23(3): 301–310.

OECD. (2001) *Behind the Corporate Veil: Using Corporate Entities for Illicit Purposes*. Paris: OECD.

OECD. (2014) *2014 Update to the OECD Model Tax Convention*. Paris: OECD.

Organized Crime and Corruption Reporting Project. (2017) *The Russian Laundromat*. Available at: www.reportingproject.net/therussianlaundromat/, accessed 19 July 2017.

Passas, N. (1999) 'Globalization, criminogenic asymmetries and economic crime', *European Journal of Law Reform*, 1(4): 399–424.

Performance and Innovation Unit. (2000) *Recovering the Proceeds of Crime*. London: Cabinet Office.

Petrunov, G. (2011) 'Managing money acquired from human trafficking: Case study of sex trafficking from Bulgaria to Western Europe', *Trends in Organized Crime*, 14(2–3): 165–183.

Prime Minister's Office. (2013) *G8 Action Plan Principles to Prevent the Misuse of Companies and Legal Arrangements*. Available at: www.gov.uk/government/publications/g8-action-plan-principles-to-prevent-the-misuse-of-companies-and-legal-arrangements, accessed 19 July 2017.

Rostain, T. and Regan, M. (2014) *Confidence Games: Lawyers, Accountants, and the Tax Shelter Industry*. Cambridge, MA: MIT Press.

Rowe, E., Akman, T., Smith, R.G. and Tomison, A. (2013) *Organised Crime and Public Sector Corruption: A Crime Scripts Analysis of Tactical Displacement Risks*. Canberra: Australian Institute of Criminology.

Schneider, S. (2004) *Money Laundering in Canada: An Analysis of RCMP Cases*. Toronto: Nathanson Centre for the Study of Organized Crime and Corruption.

Sharman, J.C. (2010) 'Shopping for anonymous shell companies: An audit study of anonymity and crime in the international financial system', *The Journal of Economic Perspectives*, 24(4): 127–140.

Shaxson, N. (2011) *Treasure Islands: Tax Havens and the Men Who Stole the World*. London: The Bodley Head.

Society of Trust and Estate Practitioners. (2014), 'UK demands exemption from EU trust registry plan', Monday, 7 April, 2014. Available at: www.step.org/uk-demands-exemption-eu-trust-registry-plan, accessed 19 July 17.

Steinko, A.F. (2012) 'Financial channels of money laundering in Spain', *British Journal of Criminology*, 52(5): 908–931.

Thaler, R. and Sunstein, C. (2008) *Nudge: Improving Decisions about Health, Wealth, and Happiness. Front Cover*. New Haven, CT: Yale University Press.

T.M.C. Asser Instituut. (2000) *Prevention of organised crime: The registration of legal persons and their directors and the international exchange of information*. Available at: www.asser.nl/upload/eurlaw-webroot/documents/cms_eurlaw_id49_1_rapport.pdf, accessed 19 July 2017.

Tombs, S. and Whyte, D. (2015). *The Corporate Criminal: Why Corporations Must Be Abolished*. Abingdon, UK: Routledge.

Transparency International UK. (2017) *Offshore in the UK: Analysing the Use of Scottish Limited Partnerships in Corruption and Money Laundering*. London: TI UK.

United Nations Economic and Social Council. (2010) *Committee of Experts on International Cooperation in Tax Matters: Report on the Sixth Session*. Report E/C.18/2010/7. New York: United Nations.

Van der Does de Willebois, E., Halter, E.M., Harrison, R.A., Park, J.W. and Sharman, J.C. (2011) *The Puppet Masters: How the Corrupt Use Legal Structures to Hide Stolen Assets and What to Do About It*. Washington, DC: The World Bank.

Vermeulen, E.P.M. (2013) *Beneficial Ownership and Control: A Comparative Study – Disclosure, Information and Enforcement*. Paris: OECD.

# Part II

# Vulnerabilities to corruption in commercial enterprise

# 6 Corruption

## The exposure and exploitation of human vulnerabilities

*David BaMaung and John Cuddihy*

Corruption is an endemic problem which is transnational, and exists within business, critical infrastructure organisations, and wider society in general. Its causes can range from an individual's greed, to societal inequalities and the need to survive. Attempts to mitigate and manage corruption have focused around enforcement of criminal legislation, the application of effective corporate governance measures, and other deterrence strategies. However, irrespective of the causes, it is believed there are two common issues which apply across corruption in general. First, the corruption involves active participation by a member of the organisation, body, or government, etc. – the 'Insider'. This involves direct or indirect activity by the individual. The second issue relates to the culture of the organisation, and its potential acceptance of corrupt practices within its normal operational activities. In order to address corruption and its causes in a 'holistic' manner, as well as using traditional approaches, it is necessary to adopt a 'non-traditional' perspective to the problem by examining the role played by the individual 'Insider', and the wider impact of culture in facilitation and support of corrupt activities. By understanding these issues, there is an opportunity to 'treat' corruption through an innovative approach. The aim of this chapter is to look at corruption from a people and cultural perspective, and by developing an understanding of this, to manage and mitigate the threat, risk and harm posed by those who engage, or attempt to engage, directly, or indirectly in corrupt practices.

## Introduction

The traditional approach to managing and mitigating against corruption has been to attempt to introduce strong governance structures to detect and deter instances of individual, and more widespread, corruption. The Anti-Corruption Commission identify four methods of corruption control, namely:

- An effective anti-corruption agency
- Effective Acts/laws
- Effective adjudication
- Effective administration

(Anti-Corruption Commission, 2017)

The fight against corruption has primarily been led through the introduction and enforcement of anti-corruption legislation such as the UK Bribery Act 2010, the US Foreign Corrupt Practices Act (FCPA) of 1977, Russia's Federal Anti-Corruption Law No. 273, Brazil's Clean Company Act 2014 (Law No. 12,846), and the Canadian Corruption of Foreign Public Officials Act (CFPOA) 1998.

Additionally, a number of internationally agreed conventions have been created to identify acceptable business or working practices and clarify what would fall under the auspices of corrupt practices. Conventions can range from global in their outreach, to more regional purviews. Examples of recognised conventions include the United Nations Convention against Corruption (UNCAC) of 2005, The OECD Convention on Combating Bribery of Foreign Public Officials in International Business Transactions (OECD Convention) adopted in 1997,[1] the Council of Europe Criminal Law Convention on Corruption introduced in 2002; the Inter-American Convention Against Corruption adopted in 1996, and the African Union Convention on Preventing and Combating Corruption introduced in 2003. Corruption may manifest itself at a variety of levels. These can range from individual organisations (Aguilera and Vadera, 2008; Pinto et al., 2008), infrastructure sectors (Global Infrastructure Anti-Corruption Centre, 2016), and wider national and international bodies, organisations and countries.

In order to provide a truly 'holistic' response to the management and mitigation of corruption, the authors advocate a non-traditional approach to corruption, where attention is focused on the individual(s) involved in the corrupt activity, and the impact of insider threat on the wider 'culture' surrounding corruption, including the impact this has on the acceptance of corrupt practices by members of an organisation. Understanding the person participating in corrupt practices within their organisation, and what their motivations and drivers are, will allow a unique opportunity to identify and target specific behaviours and motivations of the corrupt insider.

To understand the issues involved, it is necessary to define what is meant by the following terms: 'corruption', 'insider threat', and 'culture'. Through understanding the widespread perception relating to these terms, it will be easier to relate them to each other and identify opportunities to understand and mitigate against corruption and corrupt activities.

## What is corruption?

At its most basic level, corruption can be defined as 'breaking the rules pertaining to a certain office, it can be defined economically, and it can be defined as acting against general interest' (Wagenaar, 2007). This definition does not refer to the breach of trust that is normally associated with the perception of corruption. However, a

---

1  Accepting that bribery is one of the main pillars of corruption, the OECD has developed a convention which considers that bribery is a widespread phenomenon in international business transactions, including trade and investment, which raises serious moral and political concerns, undermines good governance and economic development, and distorts international competitive conditions.

widely accepted definition of corruption is provided by Transparency International as being 'The abuse of entrusted power for private gain. Corruption can be classified as grand, petty and political, depending on the amounts of money lost and the sector where it occurs' (Transparency International, 2016a). This is very similar to the definition provided by the World Bank Group, namely 'the abuse of public office for private gain. Public office is abused for private gain when an official accepts, solicits, or extorts a bribe' (The World Bank Group, 2016). The key issues which traverse these and other definitions (Katz, 2011; Williams, 1987) include the abuse of public office or power which has been entrusted to an individual within an organisation, and the fact that such activity has been carried out for private gain.

Viewed from a wider societal perspective, corruption has been described as:

> A symptom of more deeply rooted problems in the society's structure related in particular to the means of attaining power and the weak or non-existent safeguards against its abuse.
>
> (Shihata, 1997: 257)

The general principles identified in the definition (such as corruption being related to problems within society's structure, and insufficient safeguards to prevent abuse), are supported by other informed commentators and reports (Department for International Development, 2015; Mishra, 2009).

On 11 July 2003, the signing of the African Union Convention on Preventing and Combating Corruption was a political statement of intent as the Convention criminalised corruption in the public and private sector, obligating state parties to adopt legislative, administrative, and other measures to tackle corruption. However, while such measures are to be welcome, the authors, during recent research in West, Central, and East Africa (Cuddihy, 2017), found that corruption was endemic across many countries within those regions.

Many of those interviewed considered that corruption was 'accepted' and in certain countries it was encouraged actively as opposed to discouraged. This in turn impacts on the society, promoting inequality, poverty, distrust, and significant distress. Such political corruption can lead to civil unrest and can fuel the propaganda of terrorists within the region, acting as an enabler to radicalisation, and leading to violent extremism. Indeed, it was reported by locals who openly discussed 'passive' acceptance, reflecting that 'there was no point in reporting the theft of a chicken to Police, as it would cost you a pig!'

During this research, the authors were faced with the question of whether there is such a concept as acceptable corruption, and if so what does 'acceptable' corruption mean? The authors are in no doubt that 'acceptable'[2] corruption is widespread across such regions and requires considerable international, national

---

2  The authors identify the term 'acceptable' corruption as that which could be applied to government, law enforcement, or other officials who perceive such behaviour as being part of what is expected in their environment, and is not necessarily perceived as indicating that they are 'corrupt' by undertaking such behaviour.

and local influence to stem its tide. Indeed, the socio-economic factors of poverty, inequality, education, and health are inextricably linked to corruption (Johnston, 2009). It is considered that 'passive' acceptance, (i.e. an overt submission of acceptance without any resistance), should not be seen as an option and individuals and organisations should demonstrate 'active' compliance of the African Unions Convention on Preventing and Combating Corruption. Such 'active' compliance demonstrates a responsibility on the part of the individual or organisation that they are willing to adapt to the environment and seek to change it for the better.

Kofi Annan, when UN Secretary General, stated that corruption is a key element in economic underperformance and a major obstacle to poverty alleviation and development (Annan, 2004). If we are to engage in 'acceptable corruption', we are accepting the continuation of poverty, leading to widespread disease and social inequality, which affords criminals and others the opportunity to flourish within the created vacuum, enabling the spread of extremism, terrorism, and transnational organised crime.

## What constitutes an 'insider threat'?

While the actual individuals carrying out corrupt activity within an organisation can vary from school educators (Brown, 2015), to dentists (BBC News, 2014), to charity workers (Smyth, 2013), to bank employees (Campbell, 2013), to doctors (Boseley, 2013), to policemen (Alexander, 2012; Brown, 2012; Leask and Swain, 2011; Milligan, 2013; Townsend, 2013), the one thing these individuals have in common is that they represent an 'insider' threat, enabling the impact of corruption within their respective organisations, whether this threat relates to reputational damage, financial loss, or the theft of intellectual property.

The focus of much research and mitigation effort in this area has been on the activity related to corruption, e.g. a breach of trust, the taking advantage of processes, access, and procedures to obtain advantage, or to disadvantage another. However, understanding the individual(s) participating in corrupt practices, their primary motivation and complex combination of other drivers, is critical if one wishes to look at targeting specific behaviours and identified motivators of a corrupt insider.

The current understanding of what constitutes an 'insider' and the threat they pose to an organisation can vary, with no commonly agreed definition. Einwechter (2002), defines an insider as 'someone who is entrusted with authorized access, who instead of fulfilling assigned responsibilities, manipulates access to a system to exploit it'. Knowledge of internal systems is also critical in Probst et al.'s (2007) definition, which argues that an insider posing a threat to an organisation will have developed a strong knowledge about internal procedures, potential high-value critical internal targets, and points of vulnerability. Greitzer et al. (2012) go further by stating that insider threat relates to 'harmful acts that trusted individuals might carry out' and that 'the insider threat is manifested when human behaviours depart from established policies, regardless of whether it results from malice or disregard for security policies'. Brackney and Anderson (2004) refer to an insider threat as consisting of malevolent actions carried out by an employee who is already trusted by the organisation, and who has access to sensitive information and information systems.

From a government perspective, while there are no agreed definitions of insider threat, numerous examples exist, and the government definitions are usually more explicit in the actions and content which identify insider activity, than the definitions found within the academic literature base. The National Insider Threat Task Force (2011) in the United States describe insider threat as 'a threat posed to U.S. national security by someone who misuses or betrays, wittingly or unwittingly, his or her authorized access to any U.S. government resource'. In the UK, the Centre for the Protection of National Infrastructure (2013) describes an Insider as 'a person who exploits, or has the intention to exploit, their legitimate access to an organisation's assets for unauthorised purposes'. Despite the lack of agreement over a precise definition of insider threat, there is a strong emergence of key themes emanating from the literature of what defines an insider. BaMaung et al. developed a model which identifies five of these key themes (Figure 6.1).

There is a general consensus that *trust*[3] is a core element exploited by those who are engaged or may engage in insider activity (Bishop, 2005; Einwechter, 2002; Greitzer et al. 2012; Probst et al., 2007; RAND, 2004). Second is the notion of *accessibility*. Most of the definitions that exist reference access to premises (real or virtual), security critical areas, or systems within their narrative (Greitzer et al., 2012; Loffi and Wallace, 2014; Probst et al., 2007; Punithavathani et al., 2015; RAND, 2004). Third is the element of *knowledge*. In many definitions, the threat is posed when an insider uses knowledge of the organisation and its systems and/or security procedures to cause harm (Loffi and Wallace, 2014; Mitnick and Simon, 2002; Punithavathani et al., 2015; Schneier, 2000). However, the authors would posit that in the event of collusion with a hostile third party, the insider may conduct their activity without necessarily having full knowledge of the intentions of this third party. The next theme that is evident is that of the *exploitation* of vulnerabilities (Loffi and Wallace, 2014). The fifth theme is that of *intent*. In many instances, there is a requirement that the insider must be exploiting vulnerabilities and security protocols for commercial, criminal, and/or terrorist gain and/or to cause harm (Einwechter, 2002; Loffi and Wallace, 2014; Mitnick and Simon, 2002; Probst et al., 2007). Another way of viewing this may be that a vulnerability may not initially exist, but one is created through the actions of the insider, which can thereafter be exploited.

Understanding the key motivations underpinning insider attacks can in many cases be difficult to ascertain. Indeed, there may not be one single motivation attributable to such incidents, and in many cases, the motivating drivers may be both multiple and highly dynamic, as well as intentional or unintentional.

---

3  It may be interesting to note that there is an element of 'trust' between the insider and the driver of corruption. There is an element of irony in this!

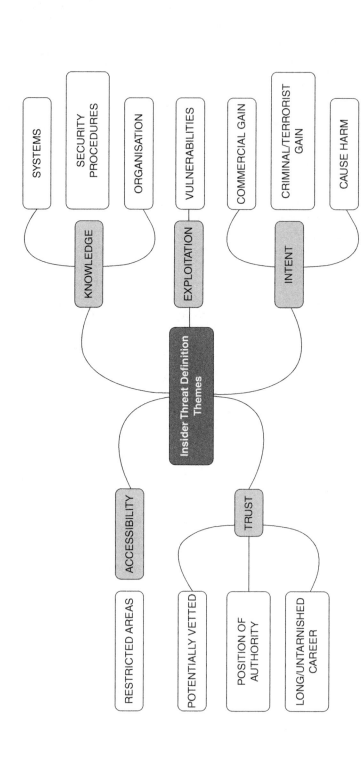

*Figure 6.1* Key insider threat themes
(BaMaung et al, 2016)

In turn, this adds considerably to the complexity of countering the threat, risk, and harm associated with actual insider events. In understanding insider motivations at such a micro level, we can best identify relevant ways to counter any activity which may potentially harm to the organisation. Relevant to corruption, common motivations may include disgruntlement (on the part of employees), criminal intent (individual and organised criminal gain), and, in certain circumstances may lead to acts of espionage.

A fundamental motivation of an insider attack is often aligned with an individual's disaffection with their organisation or work and is, in many instances, a result of that organisation's failure to recognise an individual's job-related achievements (Keeney et al., 2005; Kowalski et al., 2008). Despite this, research by the NIAC (2008) found that there was no direct correlation between disgruntlement and insider threat, with their findings concluding that the vast majority of disgruntled staff do not engage in actual attacks. Nevertheless, research conducted by Shaw and Fischer (2005) found that nine out of ten cases of insider attack studied illustrated significant issues within their employment, and that in nearly all cases, those employees demonstrated signs of disgruntlement and personal problems 1 to 48 months prior to an attack. These findings are furthered by Greitzer et al. (2012) whose research highlights through a survey of professionals that disgruntlement can be identified through understanding the behaviour of employees in their workplace.

Attacks which are inherently concerned with financial gain and sabotage are undoubtedly the most commonly researched areas in academic and practitioner discourses, with many studies not isolating single motivating factors, but instead illustrating the linkages between motivating factors. Randazzo et al. (2004), through joint research between the US Secret Service National Threat Assessment Center and the CERT Coordination Centre, examined known insider incidents within the banking and financial sectors (2003–2004) and established that financial gain was the primary motivation of most attackers. In 2006, research conducted by Lynch (2006) highlighted numerous examples of criminal intent by insider attackers. In one example, data broker Acxiom Corporation, were victims to significant data theft that resulted in losses of $5.8 million. The perpetrator was identified as a contract employee who was subsequently sentenced to 45 months in prison.

The impact of criminal activity by staff on organisations is significant. On the related issue of fraud, if we use employee fraud as an example of 'insider attack', the ACFE[4] (2016) estimated that the typical organisation loses 5% of revenues each year to fraud. While the median loss caused by the frauds was $150,000, 23.2% of cases involved losses of $1,000,000 or more. The total loss caused by the cases in the ACFE study exceeded $6.3 billion. No sector is immune from the threat of fraud, and many of the sectors that suffer from fraud are also ones that can be targeted by corruption. These can include banking and financial services,

---

4  Association of Certified Fraud Examiners.

government and public administration, and manufacturing industries, while the mining, real estate, and oil and gas industries are also victim to this type of crime.

The ACFE (2016) study also provided further insight into the type and roles of employees involved in fraud, which it is suggested could help organisations develop appropriate people security risk assessment policies.[5] A particularly interesting finding was the exponential impact of collusion on the level of fraud. The more individuals who are involved in a fraud, the more it allows greater opportunities to overcome mitigation measures, and through such a process could significantly increase the potential sums of money which are capable of being defrauded.

Collusion helps employees evade independent checks and other anti-fraud controls, enabling them to steal larger amounts. The median loss in a single person fraud was $85,000, rising to $633,000 when five or more persons are involved. Potentially, checks and balances which can be employed to mitigate against such actions, e.g. increasing the number and rank of signatories for different levels of financial authority, may help reduce the impact of such events. This evidences a 'layered approach' to security and access.

Furthermore, the ACFE study found that employee frauds were more likely to be committed by employees working in certain areas, clearly where there are more opportunities. The ACFE found that 75% of frauds were committed by employees working in accounting, operations, sales, executive/upper management, customer service, purchasing, and finance. However, more positive findings from the ACFE study show that where there were anti-fraud controls, fraud losses were reduced and were of shorter duration.

With regards to the wider issue of corruption and the role played by an insider, if we engage in passive acceptance of corruption through the culture that exists in many developing nations, we are creating a void for 'insiders' to expand the threat of corruption and undermine a Government's ability to provide basic services, which in turn feeds inequality and injustice and discourages foreign aid and investment. It is the authors' belief that a holistic approach is required to the international scourge that is corruption. Moreover, the enabler of 'people' is required in order to fulfil the requirements of bribery, and specifically, the role of the 'insider' is critical in such behaviour.

As can be seen, for corruption to flourish, it is necessary to have an active insider who is aware of the threat actor initiating the corruption within an organisation. If we start to think of this individual as an insider threat to the organisation, we allow their behaviour to be seen in a wider context than simply an isolated event by a corrupt individual. There is the potential to better understand motivations and behaviours, and from this, the potential to develop targeted mitigation measures.

---

5  Refers to the risk assessing of certain roles within organisations, which are organisational or asset critical. Policies for such roles/individuals may have greater control and monitoring measures put in place for them than for other less critical roles/members of staff.

## Corruption and culture: a close fit?

What factors can encourage and support corruption and corrupt practices? Possibly the most important factor is how widespread and accepted corrupt behaviour is amongst an individual and their peers. If corrupt behaviour is seen as 'accepted' practice, there is a lesser likelihood of reporting by peers and truly addressing the issue. The influence of 'group norms' and the surrounding culture on an individual's behaviour is seen as paramount (Taylor, 2015a). Evidence shows that 'organizational culture, structures and incentives' are highly influential in causing individuals to engage in systematic corrupt practices (Taylor, 2015b; Taylor and Torsello, 2015). Culture can impact on the acceptance of corruption and corrupt practices on a number of levels. At a micro level, the acceptance of bribery and corrupt practices within an organisation can affect how the organisation conducts its business and defines what is acceptable and what is not. This may be further complicated by the fact that many businesses operate internationally, and in those countries where they operate, there are differences in the type of acceptance to corruption, with some countries adopting a passive stance, while others pursue a more active one. At a national level, corruption may occur to a greater or lesser degree within a country, and indeed it may be so ingrained within society and societal norms that it is seen as part of normal life. Although not all may 'accept' such a culture, they may feel powerless to act against it, hence a perception of passive acceptance. Poverty and social inequality are a breeding ground for corrupt practices, and corruption may be seen as a way of progressing within the relevant cultures and societies. Corruption can be endemic and its relationship with culture crosses national boundaries (Seleim and Bontis, 2009).

Not every country accepts or encourages a culture of corruption within its government and businesses, and indeed, organisations such as Corruption Watch monitor corruption levels within different countries and encourage tackling corruption at all levels. The Corruption Perceptions Index 2016 (Transparency International, 2016b) assessed 176 countries regarding the level of corruption within them. No country achieved a perfect score (100) and two-thirds of countries surveyed scored less than 50.[6] The global average score was 43. Countries such as Denmark, New Zealand, and Finland proved to be virtually corruption free, while North Korea, South Sudan, and Somalia were found to be highly corrupt. Taylor (2016) describes the difficulties of operating in such environments as the challenges of operating ethically in environments with a culture of corruption. In addition to corruption being present within countries, it can also be present in infrastructure sectors which traverse national boundaries.

Organisational culture can also have a positive or negative influence, and can play a key role in mitigating the acceptance and opportunities for corruption and corrupt practices within an organisation (Campbell and Goritz, 2014). If it is of the correct type, corporate culture can influence organisational productivity

---

6 Where 0 relates to a highly corrupt country and 100 represents a country free from corruption.

and the climate in which it exists (Wong, 2007). As well as having an impact on organisations and their practices, national culture can also shape and influence economic prosperity (Harrison and Huntington, 2000) Although a country may have an overarching national culture, within that country different organisations may exist, each with a variety of different organisational cultures.

Cuddihy (2017) found that during a number of Anti-Money Laundering/ Countering Terrorist Financing (AML/CTF) and Countering Violent Extremism (CVE) workshops he ran in Africa on behalf of the United Nations, the view of in-country participants was that culture must be influenced from a variety of quarters, not least of all, government. If the policymakers operate within a culture of corruption, then those organisations that seek to do business with such administrations are more likely to 'accept' the culture of corruption in order to succeed. Acceptance of a culture of corruption can be passive or active. Active acceptance would indicate an acceptance that corruption occurs, while taking appropriate measures to manage the risk. Passive acceptance is simply accepting that corruption is prevalent without making any attempt to manage or mitigate the issue.

Wong (2007) defines corporate culture as referring to:

> The prevailing implicit values, attitudes and ways of doing things in a company. It often reflects the personality, philosophy and the ethnic-cultural background of the founder or the leader. Corporate culture dictates how the company is run and how people are promoted.

He identifies what he describes as 'toxic corporate cultures'[7] which lead to dysfunctional organisational relationships and adaptability to change. Wong identifies five different 'types' of toxic culture, all of which impact negatively on an organisation. These are:

- Authoritarian-hierarchical culture
- Competing-conflictive culture
- Laissez-faire culture
- Dishonest-corrupt culture
- Rigid-traditional culture

While each of these cultures creates dysfunctionality within organisations, corruption in itself may be a by-product but not necessarily the core ethos within four of the five cultural types. This is not the case in the organisations with dishonest-corrupt cultures – where greed and corrupt practices are ingrained in the organisational DNA. The authors will now focus on this type of organisational culture to better understand the negative and corrosive impact this form of culture has on the acceptance of corruption and corrupt practices.

---

7 An organisation can have all of these cultures and leadership styles at some point; however, it is how, when and where used that will determine the extent to which they are either functional or dysfunctional.

Such a culture focuses on greed, power, and profit, with scant regard paid to legal issues or ethics. In such organisations, the acceptance of corruption in all its forms – cheating, fraudulent practices, and bribery – is pervasive at all levels. Enron is a clear example of this type of organisation, where creative accounting and misleading profit reports were seen as completely acceptable. Eichenwald (2005) identifies Enron as an organisation which had lost its moral compass. The lack of oversight of behaviours and practices, and poor regulation led to a culture of self-interest and profit seeking, where even shareholders' interests were secondary (Free et al., 2007). Improper transactions and decisions were approved at all levels. While the main cultural influence according to Wong's definition was a clear culture of dishonesty and corruption, a secondary factor was an authoritative/hierarchical culture where the practices of management were not questioned, and a laissez faire approach prevailed where excuses were allowed to flourish. Ethical considerations were ignored by the organisation as a whole, in pursuit of profit.

Corruption can also be endemic and ingrained within certain sports and sporting associations. This is made all the more complex when the sport is encompassed within countries and regions where corruption is tolerated and indeed incorporated within the societal framework. If we look at FIFA as an example of an organisation mired in allegations of corruption, in 2015, nine FIFA officials and four executives from sport management companies were arrested on suspicion of taking an estimated $150m in bribes over the previous two decades (Humm, 2015).

Using Wong's definition of toxic organisational culture, FIFA would arguably meet this criterion. The then-president of FIFA, Sepp Blatter, has been seen by many as instrumental in such a corrupt culture flourishing in FIFA, and James Marsh, head of Consultancy at Symposium, believes that FIFA represents a systemic failure rather than individual failings. He sees defective leadership as creating the culture where corrupt individuals were allowed to behave in the manner they did (Humm, 2015). Geggel (2015) also supports this viewpoint and posited that many officials at FIFA engaged in a 24-year self-enrichment scheme through the corruption of international soccer. Dyke and Whittingdale (2015) also described a culture of kickbacks and corruption within FIFA.

Another important factor influencing corruption is that of governance, which can be very much shaped by the culture of a country and the acceptance of practices which could be seen as potentially 'questionable'. Governance can potentially be either good or weak. Good governance is about the processes for making and implementing decisions, rather than about simply making the right decision (Grindle, 2010). If the process is sound, the decision may not always be the right one, as history has so often told us. However, one person's view of 'good governance' may not be the same as another's. The importance of good governance was highlighted by Kofi Annan when he declared in the United Nations Millennium Declaration that good governance is perhaps the single most important factor in eradicating poverty and promoting development (Annan, 1998). Others have opined that 'good governance' is an extremely elusive objective and it can mean different things to different organisations, not to mention to different actors within these organisations (Gisselquist, 2012).

On the other hand, 'weak' governance does not necessarily result in corrupt practices borne out of a lack of integrity. It may simply be because of not knowing or understanding the best or most effective process to utilise in any given set of circumstances. Governments may be honest but inefficient because no one has an incentive to work productively, and narrow elites may capture the state and exert excess influence on policy (Rose-Ackerman, 2005). As such, it is considered that 'effective governance' is required to manage and mitigate the potential for vulnerabilities being exposed and exploited by those who would seek to engage in corrupt practices. There are many important facets to effective governance, including accountability, transparency, responsiveness, adherence to the rule of law, and inclusiveness.

## How do we address corruption?

In order for an organisation, infrastructure sector, or country to combat corruption, it is essential that it creates a clear vision statement which articulates the intention to operate to high ethical standards, and to combat and mitigate the opportunities for corruption. For example, Transparency International has 'Our Vision is a world in which government, politics, business, civil society and the daily lives of people are free of corruption' (Transparency International, 2017). In addition to attacking corruption, the Anti-Corruption Commission also identifies a role for culture in their Vision – 'To create a strong anti-corruption culture that permeates throughout the whole society' (Anti-Corruption Commission, 2017).

This organisational vision must be led from the top down and be reinforced at every level within the organisation. The vision will tend to drive the strategic intent and direction of the organisation. From this, the strategies to counter corruption can be developed and employed in furtherance of its business. Key functions within an organisation such as HR, finance, marketing, sales, legal, procurement, etc. must be engaged in this process in order to provide a holistic approach to identify areas where such vulnerability may be more prevalent. It may then be possible to develop a risk mitigation system relating to high risk and vulnerable posts, and increase vetting requirements, support, and education available to these post holders, in a way that manages and mitigates the potential threat.

Based on this risk and vulnerability assessment process, it should be possible to develop insider threat/corruption led exercises to raise awareness and assist in the development of an 'acceptable practices' culture within the organisation. A potentially innovative approach could be for an organisation to acknowledge and incorporate staff engagement with anti-corruption policies and practices into staff appraisals. However, the issue of rewarding staff financially for reporting irregularities and criminal behaviour by colleagues is seen as contentious by many (Miceli et al., 2008).

## A strategic way forward: using an IMPACT framework to understand and combat corruption

In order to understand and combat the wider issues surrounding corruption, its drivers, enablers, and impact, the authors developed a conceptual framework to assist in this purpose (the IMPACT Framework).

The IMPACT framework has been used within law enforcement and other agencies, in an operational environment. It assists in the development of an organisational vision and agreed strategies, while at the same time identifying the 'enablers' that exist which propagate criminality or other hostile activity. These enablers are located within an 'activity corridor', which leads from the vision, to the final outcomes. This concept has been illustrated graphically by the authors in Figure 6.2.

The agreed anti-crime strategies are applied within the 'activity corridor'. This in turn changes the identified *enablers* to crime, into *inhibitors*. The resultant outcomes from such activity demonstrate the positive impact that such a change in approach can have. This impact can be measured against the vision and strategies used to manage and mitigate the threat, risk, and harm posed by those engaged in criminality.

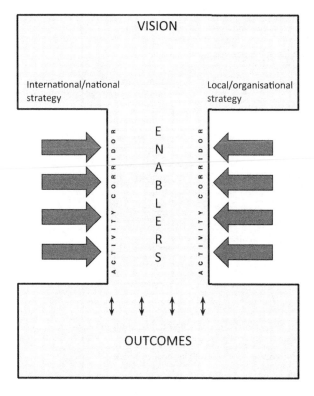

*Figure 6.2* IMPACT MAP (IMAP)

It is worthy of note that the operational experience of the authors has highlighted that the enablers to *organised crime* and *terrorism* are shared, demonstrating the nexus that exists between both threats. It is suggested by the authors that terrorists have simply appropriated criminal enablers for extremist and terrorist purposes. Indeed, one such enabler is corruption, which if tackled, can impact on a wide variety of threat actors, and can have considerable socio-economic impact.

By applying this framework to the enablers of corruption, the authors have identified a vision, namely to 'Manage and mitigate the threat, risk and harm posed by those who engage, or attempt to engage, directly, or indirectly in corrupt practices'. They also reflect on those national and international strategies that when fused together with a bespoke insider threat strategy, will impact on the identified enablers within the activity corridor.

This coordinated and focused approach utilises a SMART process (Strategic Multi Agency Response Teams), which is a fusion of multiple organisations' experience, expertise, and legislation. Through collaboration and coordination,

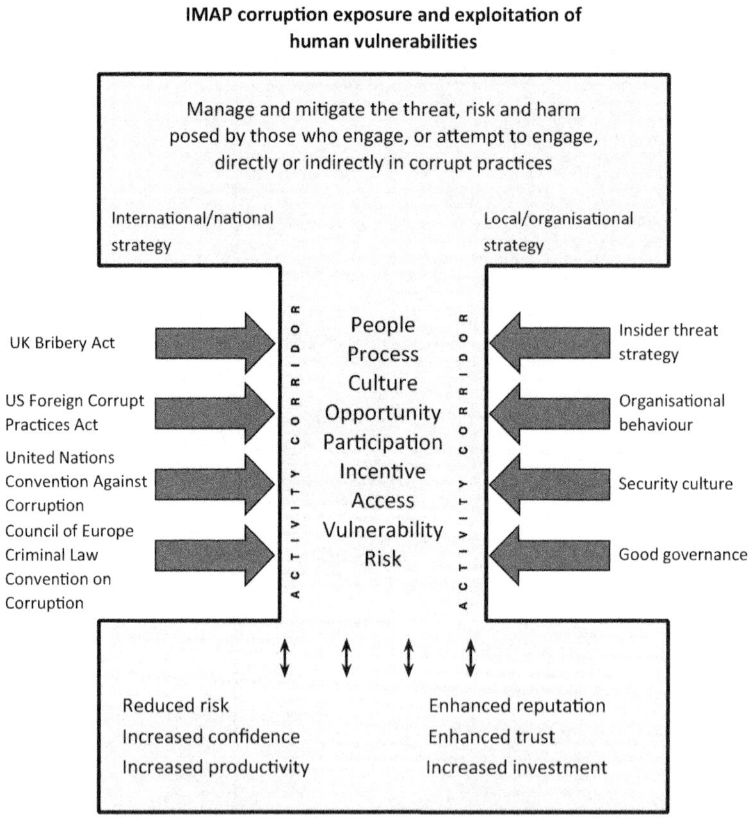

*Figure 6.3* IMAP corruption exposure and exploitation of human vulnerabilities

this approach led to an integrated response, which is developed through enhanced social relations and trust. This coordinated fusion allows for organisations within the public, private, academic, and third sectors to work unhindered towards their common goal, which in this context is managing and mitigating the threat of corruption. It is a visible demonstration of positive impact delivering achievable, realistic, and measurable outcomes, which together will create a hostile environment to prevent corruption from flourishing. In so doing, it will manage and mitigate the threat of exposure and exploitation of human vulnerabilities (Figure 6.3).

## Conclusion

As can be seen, corruption is a complex problem which exists within organisational, national, and international contexts. The causes are many, and range from an individual employee's greed, through to societal and cultural acceptance of corrupt behaviour and widespread corruption. In the event of corruption within an organisation or other entity, at a micro level the participants can best be described as 'insiders' who threaten the reputation or financial standing of their organisation through their corrupt behaviour, which negatively impacts on the behaviour of the wider organisation and staff members. At a macro level, the organisation may lend itself to corrupt activity based on its organisational culture and appetite/acceptance for corruption. It is therefore necessary to adopt a 'non-traditional' approach to the problem by addressing the micro issues and the role played by the individual 'insider', as well as the macro issues involving organisational culture and its role in facilitation and support of corrupt activities. Only by adopting this 'holistic' approach, in combination with traditional responses of punitive legislation and international conventions, can we hope to effectively combat corruption and all of its consequences.

## Bibliography

ACFE. (2016) *Report to the Nations on Occupational Fraud and Abuse: 2016 Global Fraud Study*. Austin, TX: Association of Certified Fraud Examiners.

Aguilera, R. and Vadera, A. (2008) 'The dark side of authority: Antecedents, mechanisms, and outcomes of organizational corruption', *Journal of Business Ethics*, 77: 431–449.

Alexander, D. (2012) 'Police officer jailed after helping gangland assassins hunting murdered Kevin "Gerbil" Carroll', *Daily Record* online 3 July 2012. Available at: www.dailyrecord.co.uk/news/uk-world-news/police-officer-jailed-after-helping-895262, accessed 5 March 2016.

Annan, K. (1998) *Press Release SG/2048 GA/9443 – 21 September 1998*. United Nations Millennium Declaration. New York: United Nations.

Annan, K (2004) *Foreword, United Nations Convention Against Corruption*. New York: United Nations Office on Drugs and Crime.

Anti-Corruption Commission. (2017) *Vision, Mission and Strategic Objectives*. Available at: http://www.acc.org.bd/about-acc/vision-mission-strategic-objectives, accessed 14 April 2017.

BaMaung, D., McIlhatton, M., MacDonald, M. and Beattie, R. (2018) 'The enemy within? The connection between insider threat and terrorism', *Conflict and Terrorism*, 41(2): 133–150.

BBC News. (2014) *Sutton Coldfield fraud dentist Joyce Trail told to pay back £1.4m*. BBC News Birmingham and Black Country, 6 March 2014. Available at: http://www.bbc.co.uk/news/uk-england-birmingham-26476882, accessed 15 February 2015.

Bishop, M. (2005) 'Position: Insider is relative', in *Proceedings of the 2005 Workshop on New Security Paradigms*. New York: Association for Computing Machinery, pp. 77–78.

Boseley, S. (2013) 'Drugs companies pay doctors £40m for travel and expenses', *The Guardian*, 5 April 2013. Available at: https://www.theguardian.com/society/2013/apr/05/drug-companies-pay-doctors-40m, accessed 15 February 2015.

Brackney, R.C. and Anderson, R.H. (2004) 'Understanding the insider threat', *proceedings of a March 2004 Workshop*. Santa Monica, CA: Rand Corporation.

Brown, C. (2012) 'Corrupt policeman "had links to collapsed Kevin Carroll murder trial"', *The Scotsman*, 7 May 2012. Available at: http://www.scotsman.com/news/scotland/top-stories/corrupt-policeman-had-links-to-collapsed-kevin-carroll-murder-trial-1-2279131, accessed 12 July 2014.

Brown, E. (2015) 'Nine Atlanta educators in test-cheating case are sentenced to prison', *The Washington Post*, 14 April 2015. Available at: https://www.washingtonpost.com/local/education/eight-atlanta-educators-in-test-cheating-case-sentenced-to-prison/2015/04/14/08a9d26e-e2bc-11e4-b510–962fcfabc310_story.html, accessed 19 June 2015.

Campbell, J. (2013) 'Ulster Bank employee "may have stolen 500k", tribunal reveals', *BBC News Northern Ireland*, 19 December 2013. Available at: http://www.bbc.co.uk/news/uk-northern-ireland-25451447, accessed 14 January 2014.

Campbell, J. and Goritz, A.S. (2014) 'Culture corrupts! A qualitative study of organizational culture in corrupt organizations', *Journal of Business Ethics* 120(3): 291–311.

Centre for the Protection of National Infrastructure. (2013) 'CPNI insider data collection study, 2013'. Available at: https://www.cpni.gov.uk/system/files/documents/63/29/insider-data-collection-study-report-of-main-findings.pdf, accessed 5 April 2017.

Cuddihy, J. (2017) UNODC Anti-Money Laundering/Countering Terrorist Financing (AML/CTF) and Countering Violent Extremism (CVE) Workshops. Dakar, Senegal 7–9 February 2017.

Department for International Development. (2015) 'Why corruption matters: understanding causes, effects and how to address them'. *Evidence paper on corruption* January 2015. Whitehall, London: The Department for International Development.

Dyke, G. and Whittingdale, J. (2015) 'Fifa "culture of kickbacks and corruption" targeted by FA and culture secretary', *The Guardian*, 9 July 2016. Available at: https://www.theguardian.com/football/2015/jun/01/fifa-football-association-culture-secretary-john-whittingdale, accessed 15 July 2016.

Eichenwald, K. (2005) *Conspiracy of Fools: A True Story*. New York: Broadway Books.

Einwechter, N. (2002) *Preventing and Detecting Insider Attacks Using IDS*. SecurityFocus, March 2002. Available at: https://www.symantec.com/connect/articles/preventing-and-detecting-insider-attacks-using-ids?page=1, accessed 17 December 2017.

Free, C., Macintosh, N. and Stein, M. (2007) 'Management controls: The organizational fraud triangle of leadership, culture and control in Enron', *Ivey Business Journal*. July/Aug issue.

Geggel, L. (2015) 'FIFA scandal: The complicated science of corruption', *Live Science*. Available at: http://www.livescience.com/51010-fifa-how-corruption-develops-science.html, accessed 6 June 2016.

Gisselquist, R.M. (2012) *Good Governance as a Concept, and Why This Matters for Development Policy.* Working Paper No. 2012/30. Helsinki: UNU-WIDER.

Global Infrastructure Anti-Corruption Centre. (2016) *About GIACC* – GIACC Resource Centre. Available at: http://www.giaccentre.org/index.php, accessed 2 February 2017.

Greitzer, F.L., Kangas, L.J., Noonan, C.F., Dalton, A.C. and Hohimer, R.E. (2012) January. 'Identifying at-risk employees: Modeling psychosocial precursors of potential insider threats', in *System Science (HICSS), 2012 45th Hawaii International Conference.* New York: IEEE, pp. 2392–2401.

Grindle, M.S. (2010) *Good Governance: The Inflation of an Idea.* HKS Faculty Research Working Paper Series, RWP10–023. Cambridge, MA: John F. Kennedy School of Government, Harvard University.

Harrison, L.E. and Huntington, S.P. (eds) (2000) *Culture Matters: How Values Shape Human Progress.* New York: Basic Books.

Humm, S. (2015) 'Was Fifa's corrupt organisational culture developed by its leaders?' *HR Review*, 28 May 2015. Available at: http://www.hrreview.co.uk/hr-news/strategy-news/fifas-corrupt-organisational-culture-developed-leaders/57124, accessed 8 August 2016.

Johnston, M. (2009) 'Poverty and corruption', *Forbes* online. Posted 22 January 2009. Available at: http://www.forbes.com/2009/01/22/corruption-poverty-development-biz-corruption09-cx_mj_0122johnston.html, accessed 20 April 2010.

Katz, K. (2011) 'Here comes the bribe: Canada's efforts to combat corruption in international business', 69 *The Advocate* (Canada) 501.

Keeney, M. and Kowalski, E. (USSS) and Cappelli, D., Moore, A., Shimeall, T. and Rogers, S. (CERT/SEI) (2005) *Insider Threat Study: Computer System Sabotage in Critical Infrastructure Sectors.* Pittsburgh, PA: Carnegie Mellon University Software Engineering Institute/U.S. Secret Service. Available at: www.cert.org/archive/pdf/insidercross051105.pdf, accessed 17 December 2017.

Kowalski, E.T., Randazzo, M.R., Keeney, M. (USSS) and Cappelli, D. and Moore, A. (CERT/SEI) (2008) *Insider Threat Study: Illicit Cyber Activity in the Government Sector.* U.S. Secret Service and CERT/SEI.

Leask, D. and Swain, S. (2011) 'Security fears after gangs target police', *Herald Scotland*, 14 February 2011.

Loffi, J.M. and Wallace, R.J. (2014) 'The unmitigated insider threat to aviation (Part 1): A qualitative analysis of risks', *Journal of Transportation Security*, 7: 289–305.

Lynch, D.M. (2006) 'Securing against insider attacks', *Information Security and Risk Management*, 15(5): 39–47.

Miceli, M.P., Near, J.P. and Morehead Dworkin, T. (2008) 'A word to the wise: How managers and policy-makers can encourage employees to report wrongdoing', *Journal of Business Ethics*, 86: 379–386.

Milligan, L. (2013) 'Victoria Police reveals "gravest breach of security"'. *Australian Broadcasting Corporation.* Broadcast 7 May 2013. Available at: http://www.abc.net.au/7.30/content/2013/s3754078.htm, accessed 5 September 2013.

Mishra, A. (2009) 'The cancer of corruption', *Forbes* online, posted 22 January 2009. Available at: http://www.forbes.com/2009/01/22/bribes-poverty-corruption-biz-corruption09-cx_am_0122mishra.html, accessed 20 April 2010.

Mitnick, K. and Simon, W. (2002) *The Art of Deception.* Hoboken, NJ: Wiley.

National Insider Threat Task Force. (2011) *National Insider Threat Task Force – Mission Fact Sheet.* Available at www.dni.gov/files/NCSC/documents/products/National_Insider_Threat_Task_Force_Fact_Sheet.pdf, accessed 3 January 2018.

NIAC. (2008) *The National Infrastructure Advisory Council's Final Report and Recommendations on the Insider Threat to Critical Infrastructures*. Washington, DC: DHS/NIAC.

Pinto, J., Leana, C.R. and Pil, F.K. (2008) 'Corrupt organizations or organizations of corrupt individuals? Two types of organizational-level corruption', *Academy of Management Review*, 33(3): 685–709

Probst, C.W., Hansen, R.R. and Nielson, F. (2007) 'Where can an insider attack?' In T. Dimitrakos, F. Martinelli, P.Y.A. Ryan and S. Schneider (eds) *Formal Aspects in Security and Trust*. Berlin: Springer, pp. 127–142.

Punithavathani, D.S., Sujatha, K. and Jain, J.M. (2015) 'Surveillance of anomaly and misuse in critical networks to counter insider threats using computational intelligence', *Cluster Computing*, 18(1): 435–451.

RAND. (2004) *Understanding the Insider Threat*. Santa Monica, CA: RAND Corporation.

Randazzo, M.R., Keeney, M., Kowalski, E. (USSS) and Capelli, D. and Moore, A. (CERT/SEI) (2004) *Insider Threat Study: Illicit Cyber Activity in the Banking and Finance Sector*. Pittsburgh, PA: U.S. Secret Service and CERT Coordination Center/ Software Engineering Institute, p. 25.

Rose-Ackerman, S. (2005) *The Challenge of Poor Governance and Corruption*. Especial 1 DIREITO GV L. Rev., pp. 207–266.

Schneier, B. (2000) *Secrets and Lies: Digital Security in a Networked World*. New York: John Wiley & Sons Inc., pp. 100–115.

Seleim, A. and Bontis, N. (2009) 'The relationship between culture and corruption: A cross-national study', *Journal of Intellectual Capital*, 10(1): 165–184.

Shaw, E.D. and Fischer, L.F. (2005) *Ten Tales of Betrayal: The Threat to Corporate Infrastructure by Information Technology – Insiders Analysis and Observations*. (No. PERS-TR-05-13). Monterey, CA: Defense Personnel Security Research Center.

Shihata, I. (1997) 'Corruption: A general review with an emphasis on the role of the world bank', in B. Rider (ed.) *Corruption: The Enemy Within*. The Hague: Kluwer Law International, p. 257.

Smyth, S. (2013) 'Treasurer told police she stole £220,000 for luxury cruises from her employers because she wanted to "live a little better"'. *Daily Mail* online 12 August 2013. Available at: http://www.dailymail.co.uk/news/article-2390291/Treasurer-told-police-stole-220-000-luxury-cruises-employers-wanted-live-little-better.html, accessed 9 December 2013.

Taylor, A. (2015a) 'What impact does organizational culture have on corruption?' *Ethics Intelligence Experts Corner*. Available at: www.ethic-intelligence.com/experts/8879-relationship-organisational-culture-corruption/, accessed 7 February 2017.

Taylor, A. (2015b) 'Organizational culture in corrupt companies'. *Corporate Compliance Insights 9/7/2016* Available at: http://corporatecomplianceinsights.com/organizational-culture-corrupt-companies/, accessed 7 February 2017.

Taylor, A. (2016) *What Do Corrupt Firms Have in Common?* Centre for the Advancement of Public Integrity. *Integrity in Brief Series* – April 2016. Available at: http://web.law.columbia.edu/sites/default/files/microsites/public-integrity/files/what_do_corrupt_firms_have_in_common_-_capi_issue_brief_-_april_2016.pdf, accessed 7 February 2017.

Taylor, A. and Torsello, D. (2015) *Exploring the Link Between Organizational Culture and Corruption*. CEU Business School Working Paper Series 2015: 14. Available at: http://business.ceu.edu/projectSetup/files/workingpapers/workingpaper4dt.pdf, accessed 12 January 2016.

The World Bank Group. (2016) *Helping Countries Combat Corruption: The Role of the World Bank*. Available at: www1.worldbank.org/publicsector/anticorrupt/corruptn/cor02.htm, accessed 3 September 2016.

Townsend, M. (2013) 'Undercover police "gave drugs to dealers in return for information"'. *The Guardian* online 6 April 2013. Available at: www.theguardian.com/uk/2013/apr/06/undercover-police-drugs-dealers-information, accessed 9 February 2017.

Transparency International. (2016a) *Anti-Corruption Glossary*. Transparency International web site. Available at: www.transparency.org/glossary/term/corruption, accessed 3 September 2016.

Transparency International. (2016b) *Corruption Perceptions Index 2016*. 25 January 2017. Available at: www.transparency.org/news/feature/corruption_perceptions_index_2016, accessed 14 April 2017.

Transparency International. (2017) *Our Organisation: Mission, Vision and Values*. Transparency International. Available at: https://www.transparency.org/whoweare/organisation/mission_vision_and_values/, accessed 14 April 2017.

Wagenaar, P. (2007) Review of 'Corrupt histories. Studies in comparative history' by Emmanuel Kreike and William Chester Jordan (eds). *Crime, History & Societies*, 1(2): 151–153.

Williams, R. (1987) *Political Corruption in Africa*. Aldershot, UK: Gower.

Wong, P. (2007) *Lessons from the Enron Debacle: Corporate Culture Matters!* International Network on Personal Meaning (INPM). Available at: www.meaning.ca/archives/archive/art_lessons-from-enron_P_Wong.htm, accessed 30 June 2011.

# 7 Mickey-Mouse-money and gingerbread cookies

## Bonuses and organizational measures as predictors of corruption in organizations

*Adriaan Denkers*

## Introduction

The great financial turmoil that started a decade ago in 2008 shook the world and intensified the societal discussions about unethical behaviour in organizations. Excessive corporate incentive schemes, particularly within the banking sector, caused outrage, were publicly scrutinized and were seen as one of the central causes of the economic crisis, as well as of inequality, greed, unethical conduct and corruption (Luyendijk, 2015; Shrivastava and Ivanova, 2015). Public authorities around the world reacted. Central banks and enforcement agencies intensified their efforts, and governments installed new legislation to (further) criminalize organizational unethical behaviour. An example of such legislation is the Dodd-Frank Wall Street Reform and Consumer Protection Act in the United States. Further to that, political opposition to market constraints appeared to temporarily subside, leading to the installation of stricter laws; after more than a decade of heated debate, the UK parliament approved the United Kingdom Bribery Act 2010. As a consequence of public outrage and of subsequent government interventions, corporations around the world increased investments in risk and compliance departments and in managing employees' ethical standards. Nevertheless, one of the presumed principal causes of the crisis and of organizational unethical behaviour, that is incentive schemes consisting of targets and bonuses, still remains relatively untouched. In the direct aftermath of the economic crisis, some initiatives were undertaken to limit the size of bonuses. These measures appear to have been ineffective. For instance, in 2016 the average bonus on Wall Street ($138,210) was equivalent to the 2010 average, the year the Dodd-Frank Act came into effect. Although the economic crises evoked an extremely critical public and scientific debate about excessive bonuses and their detrimental consequences (Braithwaite, 2009; Joutsenvirta, 2013), authorities and companies both seem unable or unwilling to seriously address this topic. This is especially true with respect to the general bonus culture within organizations. A bonus culture refers to the importance that is placed within an organization on reaching targets and receiving the related bonuses, regardless of the absolute value of the bonus (Braithwaite, 2009). Scientific evidence about the influence of incentive schemes on corruption within the organizational context is sparse. There has been no research investigating the influence of bonus culture on corruption.

This chapter takes the typical form of a scientific paper based on an empirical study: Introduction, Method, Results and Discussion. The chapter aims to contribute in several ways to the growing body of knowledge on organizational corruption. The core purpose is to assess the plausibility of a causal relationship between organizational anti-corruption measures, bonus culture and corruption within the context of organizations. To my knowledge, this is the first study to make an attempt at determining if there might be a causal relationship between these variables within an organizational context. Knowledge about the degree to which organizational measures and a bonus culture are responsible for the level of organizational corruption is not only important from a scientific point of view but also has the potential to aid the development of more effective anti-corruption interventions.

This chapter also contributes to the literature on organizational corruption by introducing a research method to the field.[1] In order to establish if a causal relationship between organizational measures, bonus culture and corruption may exist, a cross-lagged correlational study was conducted among economic-crime experts in Dutch organizations. Of course, correlational data can never provide absolute certainty about causation. However, with the aid of a cross-lagged design, one can provide an indication of causality. This indication is also known as "Granger causality" (Granger, 1969). Although most social scientists would argue that an experimental design is the gold standard for establishing causality, in certain circumstances experimental research may be too precarious. For instance, in neurosciences, human participants may risk serious physical injury as a result of experimental intervention in the brain. Because knowledge about the causality is often essential for the development of interventions, the Granger causality approach is a popular method in neuroscientific research (e.g. Bressler and Seth, 2011). In other areas of research, manipulation of situations is practically unfeasible, rendering the conduct of proper experimental research an illusion. This holds true for the present study. Companies would probably be unwilling to participate in an experiment in which they are randomly and double blindly assigned to implement one or another incentive scheme (for information on field experiments in organizations, see Eden, 2017). Not surprisingly, the Granger's causality approach is a popular method among organizational scientists (e.g. Lev et al., 2010; Makni et al., 2009; Schuurman et al., 2016). For reasons unknown, Granger's causality approach seems virtually absent from scientific research on criminal or unethical behaviour, and, more specifically, in research on corruption.

## Corruption

Only relatively recently have society and science focused their attention on corruption within organizations. Until the mid-1990s, the focus was predominantly on corruption in other countries – generally so-called "developing" countries

---

1 The author developed the questionnaires for PWC-Netherlands, to be used for the production of the PWC's Dutch Economic Crime Survey (Denkers and Huisman, 2015).

(Wedel, 2012). Within that line of research, anthropologists, economists and political scientists found that corruption was prevalent and embedded in the governments of those "other" countries (Olken and Pande, 2012).

During the past decades, the realization that corruption also exists within the boundaries of "our own" borders came as a shock. This realization was often caused by big scandals. For instance, in 2001, the Netherlands was appalled by the evidence that price fixing, prior consulting, duplicate accounts, fictitious invoices and active bribery of civil servants had been flourishing within the Dutch construction industry (Graafland, 2011). A parliamentary inquiry committee was instigated. There was public consternation following the remarks of the director of one of the building corporations who downplayed bribery as dropping "Mickey-Mouse-money" or "pepernoten" (gingerbread cookies traditionally handed out to children in The Netherlands at the celebration of the feast of Saint Nicolas). The investigations brought home that within the Dutch building industry corruption was common practice and that many Dutch civil servants had been taking bribes (Van Den Heuvel, 2005). Similar scandals around the world led to an intensified public and scientific focus on companies' involvement in corruption.

Although the wealth of scientific work on corruption still focuses on (explaining) differences between countries, during the past decades, the science of organizational corruption has been rapidly developing (Aguilera and Vadera, 2008; Ashforth and Anand, 2003; Collins et al., 2009; Den Nieuwenboer and Kaptein, 2008; Lord, 2013; Pinto et al., 2008; Rabl and Kuehlmann, 2008; Zyglidopoulos et al., 2017). The science of organizational corruption is dedicated to explaining corruption committed within or by organizations.

The literature provides many definitions of organizational corruption, and the field of organizational corruption is extremely multidisciplinary. Scientists from accountancy, anthropology, economics, criminology, law, management and organizational sciences, psychology and sociology all contribute to the field. Although this does highlight a broad consensus among scientists that corruption is an important societal issue, this multitude of disciplines also contributes to conceptual and methodological confusion. As a consequence, under the title of "organizational corruption", various unethical or undesirable organizational behaviours have been studied. Most scientists agree that a definition of organizational corruption should at least entail "the abuse of authority or entrusted power" (see Campbell and Lord, Introduction to this volume). In the Netherlands, anti-corruption laws relevant to businesses are laid down in the Dutch Criminal Code. These laws predominantly relate to bribery and describe infringements involving the private sector (when no public official is involved) and public sector,[2] criminalizing both the offeror and the recipient. Related crimes, which are regarded by some scholars as forms of corruption, like

---

2 Dutch Penal Code: for public sector, Art. 127 and 363; for judges, Art. 178 and 364; for private sector, Art. 126, 328ter and 328quater.

anti-trust infringements, fraud and theft are described in other articles of Dutch Law and are therefore not considered to be corruption. Because the participants in the present study are economic crime experts within Dutch organizations, they are most likely to perceive corruption from a Dutch legal point of view.

### Organizational anti-corruption measures

During the past decades companies have increasingly invested in detecting and reducing unethical and illegal behaviour within their organization (Graycar and Sidebottom, 2012; Luo, 2005; Pinto et al., 2008). Examples of such organizational measures are (the enforcement of) codes of conduct (Anand et al., 2004; Ashforth et al., 2008; Trevino et al., 1999), adequate systems of internal controls (Adams, 1994), segregation of duties and job rotation (Wells and Gill, 2007), and training for employees' ethics and integrity (Armstrong, 2005; Trevino et al., 1999).

Research on the effects of these measures on corruption is scarce, but the results generally suggest beneficial outcomes. A correlational study suggests that having a code of ethics is related to reduced instances of bribery (Goel et al., 2015). However, because of the correlational design, a reverse relationship – the absence of bribery stimulates or enables companies to implement a code of ethics – or a spurious relationship – both low bribery rates and installation of a code of ethics are caused by a third variable, for instance ethical leadership – cannot be ruled out. Experimental research suggests that an adequate system of internal controls may reduce corruption, although such a system may also undermine employees' intrinsic motivation to act ethically (Armantier and Boly, 2011; Schulze and Frank, 2003). One study points to inadequate internal control procedures and lack of attention to integrity as indicative of corruption (De Graaf and Huberts, 2008). The results from both a case study and an experimental study suggest that rotation of staff may reduce the risk of bribery (Abbink, 2004; De Graaf and Huberts, 2008).

This leads to the following hypothesis:

> Hypothesis 1. Organizational measures – prevention, detection and training – cause (Granger) a reduction in corruption.

### Bonuses and corruption

Bonuses, known under different names in the literature, like pay-for-performance or incentive schemes, have received much scientific attention (e.g. Frydman and Jenter, 2010). A wealth of research suggests that bonuses are capable of promoting all kinds of unwanted and illegal behaviour, varying from executives' excessive risk-taking and financial misrepresentation (Harris and Bromiley, 2007; Minhat and Abdullah, 2016), teachers' cheating (Jacob and Levitt, 2003) and participants' deceitful behaviour or non-cooperative choices in experiments (Balliet et al., 2011;

Cohn et al., 2014; Gill et al., 2013). Explanations for such findings are mostly given from a rational economic perspective: if the rewards of unethical behaviour outweigh the costs, people tend to behave in an unethical manner. Many corruption scientists follow the same line of reasoning with regards to corruption: corruption prevails where it is profitable (Misangyi et al., 2008; Rose-Ackerman, 2001). Rational economic reasoning suggests that bonuses, especially when the related targets are difficult to be met by legal means, are most likely to promote corruption in organizations.

Up until now, remarkably little of the literature focuses specifically on the relationship between bonuses and corruption. Some economists suggest that bonuses could be constructed in such a way that they would counter corruption, by aligning targets with anti-corruption (Cracau and Franz, 2013). The feasibility of that plan seems highly doubtful for two reasons. First, businesses generally give bonuses to employees for reaching tangible targets, for instance for bringing in new clients or contracts. Abstaining from corrupt behaviour does not seem tangible. How does one operationalize a target for "not paying a bribe", or for "behaving ethically"? Second, and more importantly, having a system of targets and bonuses installed might not only stimulate corruption through rational economic reasoning, but might also influence the ethical climate within an organization. A bonus culture that stresses the importance of reaching targets and attaining financial rewards within an organization is most likely to stimulate the notion that everyone within the company is predominantly looking out for "number one", and that gains and losses are what are considered to be important within the company. A bonus culture may thereby promote a more egoistic climate within the organization. Simultaneously, a bonus culture may undermine the notion that principles or benevolence are driving forces within the company. A growing body of literature suggests that the ethical climate is a dominant predictor of unethical behaviour in organizations, such as corruption (Kish-Gephart et al., 2010; Martin and Cullen, 2006; Peterson, 2002; Stachowicz-Stanusch and Simha, 2013; Treviño et al., 2014; Victor and Cullen, 1988). This line of research suggests that an egoistic climate, which logically seems to be in line with a bonus culture, is most likely to cause corruption. This leads to the next hypothesis:

Hypothesis 2: A strong bonus culture causes (Granger) corruption.

People and organizations differ in the degree to which they are aware of the possibility that crime may occur. Some may consider it highly likely, while others will have never even thought about the option. The degree to which organizations are aware of the risk of crime may strongly influence their decisions about installing measures against crime. This awareness may also influence the degree to which one is capable of detecting crime. Crime awareness may therefore influence the relationship that emerges in research concerning corruption. The results of the analyses in the present study will therefore be controlled for crime awareness.

# Method

## Procedure

In 2014 and 2016 a questionnaire was completed by members of the Flycatcher panel who were experts in economic crime within their companies. The questionnaire studies were performed for the PwC Nederland Economic Crime Survey. Flycatcher is a private firm that specializes in online research (www.flycatcher.eu[3]). Experts in economic crimes were selected for this study because they are expected to be more informed about incidences of economic crime and about organizational measures than other employees. In order to select experts in economic crimes, the questionnaires were preceded by a selection questionnaire. This selection questionnaire was administered to all working respondents within the panel. Prospective participants had to be functionally responsible within the organization for monitoring, preventing or dealing with at least one of the following economic crimes: theft of goods or money, fraud, corruption, information theft, anti-trust infringements and/or cybercrime. As noted earlier, theft, fraud and anti-trust infringements, and certain forms of cybercrime, can be regarded as specific types of corruption. In this study only corruption, as laid down in Dutch law, is considered. Experts in these other related types of economic crimes are, however, presumed to also be knowledgeable about corruption. In 2014, 3,865 panel members (48% response rate) completed the selection questionnaire. In 2016 the same procedure was followed. However, in 2016, the questionnaire was first distributed among the members of the panel who had completed a questionnaire in 2014. In both years, the number of participants was limited to 875. In total, 344 (39%) of the original participants also completed the questionnaire in 2016. In 2016, as well as the original members, other members who met the criteria were invited to participate. Participation was voluntary and anonymous. The questions were presented in a randomized order. The final sample of participants who completed the questionnaire, after the data quality check (e.g. for flat-liners), in both 2014 and 2016, consisted of 875 experts in economic crime.

## Participants

Over half of the participants were male (53% in 2014 and 59% in 2016). The participants' ages ranged from 18 to 65. Compared to the general Dutch population, participants with a higher education and income level were overrepresented in both years.

---

3 The Flycatcher panel has approximately 16,000 members who agreed to participate regularly in online surveys. On average, panel members receive eight surveys a year. In exchange for the completion of questionnaires, respondents receive a small reward in the form of points, which can be converted into gift vouchers. The Flycatcher panel meets the ISO quality standards for social science research and is used exclusively for research and not for any other purposes, such as sales or direct marketing. Panel members may terminate their panel membership at any time. Panel members cannot select the type of surveys for which they wish to be invited.

The participants' expertise in economic crimes involving corruption was 41% in 2014 and 57% in 2016. In 2014, 17% of participants' organizations had fewer than ten employees within the Netherlands; this was 15% in 2016. In 2014, 61% of the participants reported working for an organization with more than 100 employees in the Netherlands, of which 31% reported working for an organization with more than 1,000 employees in the Netherlands; in 2016, this was 59% and 28%. In 2014 and 2016 48% and 55% of the participants, respectively, reported working for an organization with employees outside of the Netherlands, of which 33% and 23% respectively reported more than 1,000 employees abroad. In 2014 and 2016, 16% and 21%, respectively, noted that they worked for an organization that was listed at a stock exchange.

### *Measures*[4]

The questionnaires consisted of questions about the degree to which the organization had been confronted with economic crimes, bonuses, organizational measures against economic crime, employee training and crime awareness.

## Dependent variable

*Corruption.* Participants were asked: "During the past two years, how often has your organization been confronted with the following types of economic crime:", followed by five types of economic crime: corruption, theft of goods or money or fraud, information theft, anti-trust infringements and cybercrime. The answer options were: "never", "at least once", "more than 5 times", "more than 10 times" and "Don't know". The "Don't know" answers were recoded as "No".[5] Table 7.1 shows the frequencies of participants' answers to these questions in 2014 and 2016.

*Table 7.1* Economic crimes in 2014 and 2016

|  | 2014 | | | | 2016 | | | |
|---|---|---|---|---|---|---|---|---|
|  | *Never* | *>= Once* | *>= 5* | *>= 10* | *Never* | *>= Once* | *>= 5* | *>= 10* |
| Corruption | 79.4% | 13.9% | 3.7% | 3.0% | 73.6% | 16.9% | 7.2% | 2.3% |
| Theft/fraud | 35.8% | 30.2% | 16.6% | 17.5% | 36.5% | 33.3% | 17.4% | 12.9% |
| Information theft | 72.8% | 17.9% | 6.2% | 3.1% | 62.5% | 24.5% | 9.0% | 4.0% |
| Anti-trust | 82.3% | 12.9% | 2.9% | 1.9% | 77.8% | 15.5% | 5.0% | 1.6% |
| Cybercrime | 77.8% | 13.5% | 4.2% | 4.5% | 66.3% | 20.1% | 8.5% | 5.1% |

4  Only measures that are relevant for the current study are elaborated on.
5  The reason for regarding "Don't know" answers as "No" was that during the pre-tests of the questionnaires, participants mentioned that they had selected "Don't know", because, although they had no knowledge that the crime had occurred during the past two years, they couldn't rule out that it had occurred. Other participants during the pre-tests mentioned selecting "No", because as far as they were aware the crime had not taken place during the past two years.

Table 7.1 suggests that in 2016 more Dutch organizations were subject to corruption, information theft, anti-trust infringements and cybercrime than in 2014. The frequencies also suggest a skewed distribution of responses on these items in both years; most participants report that their organization was not confronted with corruption, information theft, anti-trust infringements or cyber-crime. In an attempt to somewhat normalize the distributions, the inverse scores were computed for use in the analysis.[6]

Participants who had indicated that their organization was subject to corruption were asked, "Did the corruption involve . . .", followed by three non-exclusive answering options, indicating passive corruption ("asking, accepting, or expecting money, goods or services"), active corruption ("offering, granting or promising money, goods or services"), or "other". In both 2014 and 2016, the majority of participants indicated the corruption to be either passive (respectively, 51.1% and 59.7%) or active (respectively, 60.6% and 60.2%). In both 2014 and 2016, only a small minority indicated the corruption to be neither active nor passive (respectively, 2.8% and 3.9%). This suggests that the participants pre-dominantly perceived corruption in line with Dutch anti-corruption legislation. In this study, the question of the prevalence of corruption in the organization was the dependent variable.

## Independent variables

*Bonus culture.* Participants were asked: "To what extent do targets and perfor-mance rewards (e.g. bonuses) play an important role within your organization?" followed by two items: "Our organization connects critical benefits for employees to reaching their targets" and "An important part of the salaries in our organization consist of performance rewards (e.g. bonuses)". Participants could answer these items on a five-point rating scale, ranging from "completely disagree" to "com-pletely agree". In both years, the crime awareness scales were reliable ($\alpha_{2014}$ = .77 and $\alpha_{2016}$ = .81). For both years, scales were constructed by taking the means of these items. Correlation of these scales in 2014 and 2016 among participants who filled out both questionnaires is high (r = .54, p < .001), suggesting that bonus structures in companies were pretty stable over the years.

*Organizational measures against corruption.* Participants answered questions about three types of organizational measures: prevention, detection and training. These questions were linked to economic crime in general, not specifically to cor-ruption. With regards to prevention and detection measures, participants were asked: "Which measures did your organization take, or will your organization

---

6  Inverse score = 1 − 1 / (1 + score). This manipulation results in a shorter distance between scores in the less prevalently scored tails of the variable; the distance between "No" and "At least once" reduces from 1 when uncorrected to $((1 − 1(1 + "0")) − (1 − 1(1 + "1"))) = 0.5$ after the manipula-tion; between "at least 5 times" and "at least 10 times" the distance reduces more, from 1, when uncorrected, to $((1 − 1(1 + "2")) − (1 − 1(1 + "3"))) = 0.08$. This manipulation results in less weight of the "extreme" scores in the emptier tail.

be taking in order to counter economic crime?" This question was followed by a list of measures. Five of these measures are aimed predominantly at preventing economic crimes: "Job rotation for vulnerable positions", "Transparent organizational rules", "Confidant (or trust-person)", "Whistle blowers' hotline" and "Code of conduct concerning corruption for external parties". Four of these measures are aimed predominantly at detecting economic crimes: "Systematic internal audits", "Active monitoring of internal and external electronic traffic", "Systematic risk analyses of markets, industries, business partners and transactions" and "Due diligence audits of corporate transactions". Four answering options were presented for each item: "No", "Planned for next year", "Yes" and "Don't know". The "Don't know" answers were recoded as "No", because if an organization's expert on economic crimes doesn't know if measures are or will be installed, the measures are most likely not (to be) installed. Table 7.2 shows the frequencies of responses on these in 2014 and 2016.

The frequencies depicted in Table 7.2 suggest that in 2016 somewhat more organizational measures were installed or planned than in 2014. A scale for organizational prevention measures and detection measures was constructed by adding the "Yes" answers on the related items. As might be expected, correlations between 2014 and 2016 are reasonably high for both prevention and detection measures ($r_{prevention} = .41, p < .001; r_{detection} = .47, p < .001$).

With regards to employee training, the participants were asked: "In which of the following areas does your organization offer training to employees?", followed by eight topics: "Ethics", "Integrity", "Anti-corruption", "Cyber security",

*Table 7.2* Organizational measures against economic crimes (prevention and detection) in 2014 and 2016

|  | 2014 | | | 2016 | | |
|---|---|---|---|---|---|---|
|  | *No* | *Planned* | *Yes* | *No* | *Planned* | *Yes* |
| Prevention |  |  |  |  |  |  |
| Job rotation | 75.2% | 9.4% | 15.4% | 71.3% | 11.8% | 16.9% |
| Transparent rules | 36.5% | 10.3% | 53.1% | 35.4% | 12.6% | 52.1% |
| Confidant | 50.8% | 7.8% | 41.4% | 44.5% | 10.5% | 44.9% |
| Whistle blowing | 69.3% | 7.3% | 22.4% | 60.8% | 11.4% | 27.8% |
| Corruption code | 67.2% | 7.5% | 25.3% | 60.0% | 12.0% | 28.0% |
| Detection |  |  |  |  |  |  |
| Internal audits | 40.6% | 11.7% | 47.8% | 37.0% | 12.2% | 50.7% |
| Active monitoring | 54.5% | 9.6% | 35.9% | 48.5% | 11.2% | 40.3% |
| Risk analyses | 67.4% | 9.0% | 23.5% | 61.6% | 12.5% | 25.9% |
| Due diligence | 66.8% | 8.2% | 25.0% | 62.5% | 11.9% | 25.6% |

*Table 7.3* Frequencies of training for employees in 2014 and 2016

|  | 2014 | 2016 |
| --- | --- | --- |
| Ethics | 27.5% | 25.7% |
| Integrity | 36.0% | 36.7% |
| Anti-corruption | 10.7% | 11.4% |
| Cyber security | 18.6% | 28.0% |
| Anti-trust | 8.0% | 9.3% |
| Risk management | 25.4% | 28.1% |
| Security and control | 22.9% | 25.1% |
| IT infrastructure | 18.3% | 23.0% |
| At least one of the above | 63.2% | 70.5% |

"Anti-trust infringements", "Risk management", "Security and control" and "IT infrastructure". The participants could answer by clicking on a box next to each item. A scale was constructed by adding the number of boxes ticked. Table 7.3 shows the frequencies of participants' answers in 2014 and 2016.

Table 7.3 suggests that the majority of companies offer training to their employees and more so in 2016 than in 2014. Training employees in the field of cyber security has gained particular popularity. However, the most popular training in both 2014 and 2016 seems to be on integrity. The employee training scale is strongly related over years ($r = .50$, $p < .001$).

## Control variable

*Crime awareness* was measured with the question: "To what extent do you believe the next factors are relevant with regards to economic crime within your organization?", followed by three items, derived from the classical and popular criminological Routine Activity Theory (Cohen and Felson, 1979): "Lack of supervision", "Suitable target" and "Employee morality". Participants could answer on a five-point rating scale, ranging from "not at all relevant" to "completely relevant". A higher score on these items is supposed to signify more awareness of the fundamental factors that explain crime. Participants with low scores state that supervision, being a possible target and employee morality are unrelated to economic crime and are therefore believed to be unaware of crime. In both years the crime awareness scales seemed to be reasonably reliable ($\alpha_{2014} = .72$ and $\alpha_{2016} = .66$). Scales were constructed by taking the means of these three items. The auto-correlation of crime awareness, between 2014 and 2016 is reasonable ($r = .37$, $p < .001$).

### Statistical analyses

In order to establish the degree to which organizational measures and bonuses are related to corruption, first, regression analyses were conducted separately on the samples of 2014 and 2016. In these analyses crime awareness was also entered into the equation.

Next, the link between organizational measures and bonuses and corruption was addressed in the context of "Granger causality" (Granger, 1969). The Granger causality analyses were conducted on the data of the participants who had completed both questionnaires (2014 and 2016). This approach, applied to two years of data, involved two regression models (Makni et al., 2009). In the first model, corruption in 2016 is the dependent variable and the bonus culture and organizational measures in 2014 the independent variables. In the next four models, bonus culture or one of the organizational measures in 2016 is the dependent variable. All other variables from 2014 are entered as independent variables in these models. In both the first and the second models, the influence of crime awareness is added as a control variable in order to rule out a spurious relationship caused by this variable. If in the first model organizational measures or bonuses in 2014 significantly influence corruption in 2016, this can be taken as an indication that bonuses "Granger cause" corruption. Similarly, if in the second model corruption significantly influences organizational measures or bonuses, this result indicates that corruption in 2014 may cause the concerning variable in 2016. Bootstrapped confidence intervals[7] (CI) were also provided to give a more robust estimate of the effect (n = 1000; 95%). All bootstrapped confidence intervals confirmed robustness of significant findings.

## Results

The results of the cross-sectional regression analyses on the samples in 2014 and 2016 include corruption as the dependent variable; and bonuses, prevention and detection measures, and employee training as independent variables. Crime awareness was also included in the analyses as a control variable. The results of these analyses are summarized in Table 7.4. Besides the correlations and regression statistics ($\beta$, t and significance), Table 7.4 also presents the CIs of bootstrap analyses.

The results depicted in column 2 of Table 7.4 show that all independent variables in 2014 are correlated positively to corruption. In 2016 the same pattern of correlations is depicted (see column 5), with the exception of detection measures. These correlations suggest organizational measures are (almost) all consistently positively related to corruption. Also, crime awareness is related positively to corruption. In line with hypothesis 1, organizational measures (prevention, detection and employee training) are positively related to corruption. The results

---

7  Bootstrapping is a statistical technique involving resampling the original data many times with replacement, resulting in a large number of new samples (here 1,000). The statistical analyses are performed on each of these samples, resulting in confidence intervals for the estimated parameters. Bootstrapping is especially useful when distribution assumptions have been violated, as is the case in this study and most studies involving crime.

*Table 7.4* Cross-sectional regression analyses in 2014 and 2016 with corruption as dependent variable and bonus culture, prevention and detection measures and employee training and crime awareness as independent variables

| | 2014 | | | | 2016 | | | |
|---|---|---|---|---|---|---|---|---|
| | $r$ | $\beta$ | $t$ | CI | $r$ | $\beta$ | $t$ | CI |
| Bonus culture | .17 *** | .12 | 3.42 ** | .011; .042 | .23 *** | .18 | 5.19 *** | .028; .059 |
| Prevention measures | .11 ** | .01 | .20 | −.012; .014 | .07 * | .04 | .79 | −.010; .021 |
| Detection measures | 13 *** | .04 | .95 | −.009; .022 | .04 | −.05 | −1.02 | −.025; .008 |
| Employee training | .18 *** | .12 | 3.02 ** | .004; .027 | .11 ** | .04 | .92 | −.006; .016 |
| Crime awareness | .11 ** | .07 | 2.13 * | .003; .038 | .23 *** | .17 | 4.89 *** | .035; .074 |

* p < .05; ** p < .01; *** p < .001
$F_{2014}(5, 869) = 9.83^{***}$; $R^2_{Adj.\ 2014} = 4.8\%$; $F_{2016}(5, 869) = 15.16^{***}$; $R^2_{Adj.\ 2016} = 47.5\%$

of the regression analyses suggest that bonuses and crime awareness uniquely contribute to explaining corruption in both 2014 and 2016. This suggests that the amount of observed corruption by economic-crime experts within organizations can be explained consistently by the importance of bonuses and the degree of crime awareness. This is in line with hypothesis 1. Prevention and detection measures do not appear to add to the explained variance. This result is not in line with hypothesis 1. In 2014, employee training does add to the explained variance. However, counter to hypothesis 1, employee training and corruption are positively related.

Table 7.5 presents the results of the regression models testing both hypotheses: the suggested "Granger causal" relation between corruption and bonus culture and organizational measures. Table 7.5 shows correlations, regression statistics and bootstrap confidence intervals. The crucial statistics for the test of "Granger causality" are presented in italics.

The first model in Table 7.5 shows that bonuses in 2014 significantly contribute to explaining corruption in 2016, over and above the influence of corruption in 2014. This is in line with the second hypothesis: bonuses "Granger cause" corruption. Contrary to the first hypothesis, none of the other variables is significant in the first model. Organizational measures do not appear to have a causal influence on corruption. The second model shows that corruption in 2014 does not influence bonuses in 2016, indicating that the relationship between bonuses and corruption is unidirectional. In none of the other models is the dependent variable in 2016 influenced by corruption in 2014. This suggests that there are no causal relationships between organizational measures and corruption. The three organizational measures in 2014 do seem to explain each other in 2016. Employee training in 2014 explains both organizational prevention and

*Table 7.5* Test of "Granger causality" between corruption and bonuses, corrected for the influence of crime awareness, prevention and detection measures and employee training

| 2014 | Corruption 2016 | | | | Bonuses 2016 | | | |
|---|---|---|---|---|---|---|---|---|
| | r | β | t | CI | r | β | t | CI |
| Corruption | .35 *** | .30 | 5.85 *** | .153; .396 | .21 *** | .09 | 1.82 | −.028; .839 |
| Bonuses | .25 *** | .17 | 3.20 *** | .013; .057 | .54 *** | .50 | 10.13 *** | .397; .624 |
| Employee training | .14 ** | .07 | 1.14 | −.006; .024 | .17 ** | .05 | .97 | −.038; .102 |
| Prevention measures | .07 | .01 | .12 | −.019; .020 | .04 | −.04 | −.75 | −.120; .056 |
| Detection measures | .09 | .01 | .17 | −.023; .024 | .07 | .01 | .14 | −.092; .107 |
| Crime awareness | .03 | −.05 | −.95 | −.034; .012 | .19 *** | .07 | 1.40 | −.041; .203 |

| 2014 | Employee training 2016 | | | | Prevention measures 2016 | | | |
|---|---|---|---|---|---|---|---|---|
| | r | β | t | CI | r | β | t | CI |
| Corruption | .09 | .01 | .88 | −.517; .851 | .06 | −.01 | −.27 | −.388; .740 |
| Bonuses | .20 *** | .07 | 1.40 | −.699; .889 | .19 *** | .09 | 1.72 | −.034; .280 |
| Employee training | .50 *** | .37 | 7.10 *** | .272; .526 | .37 *** | .20 | 3.60 *** | .055; .299 |
| Prevention measures | .38 *** | .13 | 2.27 * | .015; .326 | .41 *** | .25 | 3.99 *** | .114; .391 |
| Detection measures | .37 *** | .14 | 2.49 * | .027; .376 | 34 *** | .11 | 1.79 | −.008; .270 |
| Crime awareness | .11 * | .03 | .63 | −.066; .310 | .13 ** | .07 | 1.36 | −.057; .308 |

| 2014 | Detection measures 2016 | | | | Crime awareness 2016 | | | |
|---|---|---|---|---|---|---|---|---|
| | r | β | t | CI | r | β | t | CI |
| Corruption | .05 | −.04 | −.73 | −.809; .400 | .08 | .00 | .00 | −.309; .305 |
| Bonuses | .21 *** | .13 | 2.50 * | .044; .294 | .26 *** | .16 | 3.02 ** | .043; .207 |
| Employee training | .34 *** | .15 | 2.81 ** | .017; .216 | .15 ** | .02 | .27 | −.044; .059 |
| Prevention measures | .34 *** | .03 | .53 | −.086; .139 | .16 ** | .08 | 1.22 | −.037; .115 |
| Detection measures | .47 *** | .38 | 6.47 *** | .277; .538 | .16 ** | .07 | 1.09 | −.038; .123 |
| Crime Awareness | .09 | .02 | .47 | −.113; .189 | .37 *** | .32 | 6.32 *** | −.200; .407 |

* p < .05; ** p < .01; *** p < .001

$F_{Corruption}$ (6, 337) = 10.37***; $R^2_{adj. Corruption}$ = 14.1%; $F_{Bonuses}$ (6, 337) = 26.60***; $R^2_{adj. Bonuses}$ = 29.2%; $F_{Awareness}$ (6, 337) = 12.73***; $R^2_{adj. Awareness}$ = 17.0%; $F_{Training}$ (6, 337) = 24.87***; $R^2_{adj. Training}$ = 29.5%; $F_{Prevention}$ (6, 337) = 17.18***; $R^2_{adj. Prevention}$ = 23.4%; $F_{Detection}$ (6, 337) = 20.25***; $R^2_{adj. Detection}$ = 26.7%

detection measures in 2016; and both organizational prevention and detection measures in 2014 explain employee training in 2016. This suggests that one type of organizational measure leads to organizations installing other measures. The last model shows that crime awareness in 2016 is not explained by corruption in 2014, or by any of the organizational measures in 2014. However, crime awareness in 2016 is explained by bonuses in 2014. This suggests that incentive schemes lead to organizations being more aware of crime. This result was not foreseen and seems difficult to explain. Possibly, the notion that incentives schemes can lead to economic crimes raises the awareness of crime among those responsible for tackling it.

## Discussion

This study is, to my knowledge, the first to examine bonus culture and organizational measures as "Granger causal predictors" of organizational corruption. The results of the study offer no evidence for the hypothesis that organizational measures mitigate corruption. Organizational anti-corruption measures do not consistently explain corruption within organizations. Organizational measures are found to be positively correlated to corruption in the same year, but do not explain any variance of corruption above bonuses and crime awareness. The cross-lagged analyses revealed that organizational measures do not predict corruption, nor does corruption predict the installation of organizational measures. In short, the results of this study suggest corruption and organizational measures are unrelated. This might be considered a startling finding, because organizations do appear to invest heavily in installing and maintaining such measures. A possible reason for this finding is that the psychological mechanisms targeted by these measures are not core to employees' choices about engaging in corruption. The organizational measures generally rely on the notion that criminal opportunities and lack of deterrence cause corruption. However, recent research shows that, with respect to explanations for corruption, the influence of normative beliefs and perceived opportunities to comply by far outweigh the influence of perceived opportunities and the perceived costs and benefits of engaging in corruption (Gorsira et al., 2016). Therefore, the organizational measures may have been designed to influence individual motives that are not central to corrupt decisions. If so, one cannot expect such measures to be effective in curbing corruption.

In contrast, the results of this study depict bonus culture to be a robust predictor of corruption. Both the cross-sectional and the cross-lagged analyses show a strong and consistent relationship between bonuses and corruption. Participants who report a strong bonus culture also report more corruption. Bonuses explain corruption in both 2014 and 2016, and bonuses in 2014 explain corruption in 2016, while corruption does not appear to predict bonuses. This suggests that bonus culture "Granger causes" corruption, or to put it differently, that corruption is more likely to emerge in companies in which incentive schemes play a prominent role.

This study contributes to the literature on organizational corruption in several ways. First, this is the first study that provides knowledge about organizational measures and incentive schemes as possible causes of corruption in real organizations. Many experimental studies have proven causality, but even if conducted among professionals – most experimental studies' participants are students – the experimental situation generally does not look like the organizational setting, and the choices that the participants are asked to make generally, at best, vaguely resemble those that employees and directors face with respect to corruption (Abbink, 2006). In the present study, corruption was operationalized by asking experts of economic crimes in organizations about the amount of corruption they had observed. Second, this study introduces a research method to the field. The present study suggests that the "Granger causality approach" may be suitable for the field of organizational corruption. It seems to bridge adequately the gap between studies that do describe real corruption but do not provide information about causality, and laboratory experiments that are capable of proving proof of causality but are distant from corruption as it factually takes place within organizations. Third, the study casts doubt on the current organizational measures' effectiveness in curbing corruption. Organizations invest time and money in their fight against corruption. In order to keep or get organizations on board in the battle against corruption, it seems important that these organizational anti-corruption measures do what they are supposed to do: prevent corruption. Fourth, the results of the current study suggest that the bonus culture, in which incentive schemes are perceived to be important, might be of utmost importance for understanding corruption in organizations.

These results must be interpreted with some limitations in mind. First, this study is conducted with the aid of self-reports. Self-reports are subject to many biases. Although the participants are experts within the field of economic crimes, which is likely to diminish the influence of some such biases, it cannot be ruled out that, for instance, self-serving biases have influenced the responses. Second, the measurements of the concepts in this study are "rudimentary": the questionnaires merely established if a concept was present or not and did not go into the differences within the concepts. For instance, there are many different incentive schemes. This study asked participants about the importance of targets and bonuses in the organization. The general robust finding that a bonus culture appears to evoke corruption, might not hold equally strong for every type of incentive scheme and in every situation. More knowledge is needed about the characteristics of targets and bonuses in relation to corruption. Third, the current study only takes the years 2014 and 2016 into account. Organizational anti-corruption measures may take a longer time to become effective. Future studies should therefore consider an extended period of evaluation of the relationship between corruption and organizational concepts, in order to assess the long-term "Granger causal" relationships. Fourth, although the Granger causality approach does firmly indicate the plausibility of a causal relationship, it does not prove such a relationship between variables.

For organizations and the compliance industry, these results suggest that, with respect to corruption, a focus on the organization's bonus culture, instead of "blindly" investing in organizational measures, may prove a fruitful route. For new start-ups, the implications of the results of the present study are clear: do not introduce an incentive scheme if you don't want corruption. For existing companies with an operational incentive scheme, the implications are less straightforward. Although the results of the present study clearly suggest that a strong bonus culture promotes corruption, the study does not imply that removing an incentive scheme reduces the chances of corruption – the impact of removing incentive schemes was not the focus of this study. The same applies to anti-corruption measures: this study does not hold any information on the consequences of removing organizational anti-corruption measures. Also, incentive schemes may produce other advantages or disadvantages beyond the reach of the present study. Future practical research on bonus culture and corruption could focus on one of two directions. First, it could focus on finding a way of abolishing incentive schemes and their negative side-effects, such as corruption, without diminishing their positive effects. Second, research could focus on how to maintain an incentive scheme whilst simultaneously eliminating its negative consequences. The results of these lines of research seem of particular importance to organizations currently operating under a strong bonus culture, but who are simultaneously determined to be free from corruption: the companies that stress the importance of reaching targets and earning bonuses, but do not want their managers and employees dropping or picking up Mickey-Mouse-money or gingerbread cookies.

### Acknowledgements

This work was based on data from the Economic Crime Survey (PwC, 2017).

# Bibliography

Abbink, K. (2004). Staff rotation as an anti-corruption policy: An experimental study. *European Journal of Political Economy*, 20(4), 887–906.

Abbink, K. (2006). 14 Laboratory experiments on corruption. In S.-R. Akkerman, ed., *International handbook on the economics of corruption*, 418–440. Northampton, MA: Edward Elgar Publishing.

Adams, M. B. (1994). Agency theory and the internal audit. *Managerial Auditing Journal*, 9(8), 8–12.

Aguilera, R.V., & Vadera, A. K. (2008). The dark side of authority: Antecedents, mechanisms, and outcomes of organizational corruption. *Journal of Business Ethics*, 77(4), 431–449.

Anand, V., Ashforth, B. E., & Joshi, M. (2004). Business as usual: The acceptance and perpetuation of corruption in organizations. *The Academy of Management Executive*, 18(2), 39–53.

Armantier, O., & Boly, A. (2011). A controlled field experiment on corruption. *European Economic Review*, 55(8), 1072–1082.

Armstrong, E. (2005). Integrity, transparency and accountability in public administration: Recent trends, regional and international developments and emerging issues. *Economics & Social Affairs*. United Nations.

Ashforth, B. E., & Anand, V. (2003). The normalization of corruption in organizations. *Research in Organizational Behavior*, 25, 1–52.

Ashforth, B. E., Gioia, D. A., Robinson, S. L., & Treviño, L. K. (2008). Introduction to special topic forum: Re-viewing organizational corruption. *Academy of Management Review*, 33(3), 670–694.

Balliet, D., Mulder, L. B., & Van Lange, P. A. M. (2011). Reward, punishment and cooperation: A meta analysis. *Psychological Bulletin*, 137(4), 594–615.

Braithwaite, J. (2009). Restorative justice for banks through negative licensing. *British Journal of Criminology*, 49, 439–450.

Bressler, S. L., & Seth, A. K. (2011). Wiener-Granger causality: A well established methodology. *Neuroimage*, 58(2), 323–329.

Bryan, C. J., Adams, G. S., & Monin, B. (2013). When cheating would make you a cheater: Implicating the self prevents unethical behavior. *Journal of Experimental Psychology: General*, 142(4), 1001–1005.

Cohen, L. E., & Felson, M. (1979). Social change and crime rate trends: A routine activity approach. *American Sociological Review*, 44(4), 588–608.

Cohn, A., Fehr, E., & Maréchal, M. A. (2014). Business culture and dishonesty in the banking industry. *Nature*, 516(7529), 86–89.

Collins, J. D., Uhlenbruck, K., & Rodriguez, P. (2009). Why firms engage in corruption: A top management perspective. *Journal of Business Ethics*, 87(1), 89–108.

Cracau, D., & Franz, B. (2013). Bonus payments as an anti-corruption instrument: A theoretical approach. *Economic Letters*, 120(1), 1–4.

de Graaf, G., & Huberts, L. W. J. C. (2008). Portraying the nature of corruption using an explorative case study design. *Public Administration Review*, 68(4), 640–653.

Denkers, A. J. M., & Huisman, W. (2015). *Economic Crime Survey Nederland 2014.* Amsterdam: PwC. Available at www.pwc.nl/nl/assets/documents/pwc-economic-crime-survey-nederland-2014-2015-deel-3.pdf.

Den Nieuwenboer, N. A., & Kaptein, M. (2008). Spiraling down into corruption: A dynamic analysis of the social identity processes that cause corruption in organizations to grow. *Journal of Business Ethics*, 83(2), 133–146.

Eden, D. (2017). Field experiments in organizations. *Annual Review of Organisational Psychology and Organizational Behavior*, 4, 91–122.

Frydman, C., & Jenter, D. (2010). CEO compensation. *Annual Review of Financial Economics*, 2, 75–102.

Gill, D., Prowse, V., & Vlassopoulos, M. (2013). Cheating in the workplace: An experimental study of the impact of bonuses and productivity. *Journal of Economic Behavior & Organization*, 96, 120–134.

Goel, R. K., Budak, J., & Rajh, E. (2015). Private sector bribery and effectiveness of anti-corruption policies. *Applied Economics Letters*, 22(10), 759–766.

Gorsira, M., Denkers, A. J. M., & Huisman, W. (2016). Both sides of the coin: Motives for corruption among public officials and business employees. *Journal of Business Ethics*. https://doi.org/10.1007/s10551-016-3219-2.

Graafland, J. (2011). Construction fraud. In W. Dubbink, L. van Liederkerke & H. van Luijk, eds, *European Business Ethics Casebook; The Morality of Corporate Decision Making. Issues in Business Ethics*, 159–177. e-book, Springer.

Granger, C. (1969). Investigating causal relations by econometric models and cross-spectral methods. *Econometrica*, 37, 424–438.

Graycar, A., & Sidebottom, A. (2012). Corruption and control: a corruption reduction approach. *Journal of Financial Crime*, 19(4), 384–399.

Harris, J., & Bromiley, P. (2007). Incentives to cheat: The influence of executive compensation and firm performance on financial misrepresentation. *Organizational Science*, 18(3), 350–367.

Heuvel, van den, G. (2005). The parliamentary enquiry on fraud in the Dutch construction industry collusion as concept between corruption and state-corporate crime. *Crime, Law & Social Change*, 44(2), 133–151.

Jacob, B. A., & Levitt, S. D. (2003). Rotten apples: An investigation of the prevalence and predictors of teacher cheating. *The Quarterly Journal of Economics*, 118(3), 843–877.

Joutsenvirta, M. (2013). Executive pay and legitimacy: Changing discursive battles over the morality of excessive manager compensation. *Journal of Business Ethics*, 116, 459–477.

Kish-Gephart, J. J., Harrison, D. A., & Treviño, L. K. (2010). Bad apples, bad cases, and bad barrels: Meta-analytic evidence about sources of unethical decisions at work. *Journal of Applied Psychology*, 95(1), 1–31.

Lev, B., Petrovits, C., & Radhakrishnan, S. (2010). Is doing good good for you? How corporate charitable contributions enhance revenue growth. *Strategic Management Journal*, 31(2), 182–200.

Lord, N. (2013). Responding to transnational corporate bribery using international frameworks for enforcement: Anti-bribery and corruption in the UK and Germany. *Criminology and Criminal Justice*, 14(1), 100–120.

Luo, Y. (2005). An organizational perspective of corruption. *Management and Organization Review*, 1(1), 119–154.

Luyendijk, J. (2015). *Swimming with Sharks: My Journey into the World of the Bankers*. Norwich, UK: Guardian Faber Publishing.

Makni, R., Francoeur, C., & Bellavance, F. (2009). Causality between corporate social performance and financial performance: Evidence from Canadian firms. *Journal of Business Ethics*, 89, 409–422.

Martin, K. D., & Cullen, J. B. (2006). Continuities and extensions of ethical climate theory: A meta-analytic review. *Journal of Business Ethics*, 69(2), 175–194.

Minhat, M., & Abdullah, M. (2016). Bankers' stock options, risk-taking and the financial crisis. *Journal of Financial Stability*, 22, 121–128.

Misangyi, V. F., Weaver, G. R., & Elms, H. (2008). Ending corruption: The interplay among institutional logics, resources, and institutional entrepreneurs. *Academy of Management Review*, 33(3), 750–770.

Olken, B. A. & Pande, R. (2012). Corruption in developing countries. *Annual Review of Economics*, 4, 479–509.

Peterson, D. K. (2002). Deviant workplace behavior and the organization's ethical climate. *Journal of Business and Psychology*, 17(1), 47–61.

Pinto, J., Leana, C. R., & Pil, F. K. (2008). Corrupt organizations or organizations of corrupt individuals? Two types of organization-level corruption. *Academy of Management Review*, 33(3), 685–709.

PwC Nederland. (2017). *Economic Crime Survey Nederland 2017*. Amsterdam. Available at www.pwc.nl/nl/publicaties/economic-crime-survey-2017.html.

Rabl, T., & Kuehlmann, T. M. (2008). Understanding corruption in organizations: Development and empirical assessment of an action model. *Journal of Business Ethics*, 82(2), 477–495.

Rose-Ackerman, S. (2001). A civil economy: Transforming the market in the twenty-first century. *Journal of Economic Literature*, 39(3), 950–952.

Schulze, G. G., & Frank, B. (2003). Deterrence versus intrinsic motivation: Experimental evidence on the determinants of corruptibility. *Economics of Governance*, 4(2), 143–160.

Schuurman, N. K., de Boer-Sonnenschein, M., Ferrer, E., & Hamaker, E. L. (2016). How to compare cross-lagged associations in a multilevel autoregressive model. *Psychological Methods*, 21(2), 206–221.

Shrivastava, P., & Ivanova, O. (2015). Inequality, corporate legitimacy and the Occupy Wall Street movement. *Human Relations*, 68(7), 1209–1231.

Stachowicz-Stanusch, A., & Simha, A (2013). An empirical investigation of the effects of ethical climates on organizational corruption. *Journal of Business Economics and Management*, 14(1), S433–S446.

Treviño, L. K., den Nieuwenboer, N. A., & Kish-Gephart, J. J. (2014). (Un)ethical behavior in organizations. *Annual Review of Psychology*, 65, 635–660.

Trevino, L. K., Weaver, G. R., Gibson, D. G., & Toffler, B. L. (1999). Managing ethics and legal compliance: What works and what hurts. *California Management Review*, 41(2), 131–151.

Victor, B., & Cullen, J. B. (1988). The organizational bases of ethical work climates. *Administrative Science Quarterly*, 33(1), 101–125.

Wedel, J. R. (2012). Rethinking corruption in an age of ambiguity. *Annual Review of Law and Social Science*, 8, 453–498.

Wells, J. T., & Gill, J. D. (2007). Assessing fraud risk. *Journal of Accountancy*, 204(4), 63.

Zyglidopoulos, S., Hirsch, P., De Holan, P. M., & Phillips, N. (2017). Expanding research on corporate corruption, management, and organizations. *Journal of Management Inquiry*, 26(3), 247–253.

# 8 Contextualising corporate criminality in different cultural settings

## The case of the gas industry in Ukraine

*Anna Markovska and Petrus C. van Duyne*

## Introduction

Many Europeans will be familiar with the Russian-Ukrainian energy crises since 2008. In December 2008, both countries negotiated over the renewal of gas supply contracts (BBC, 2009). On New Year's Day 2009, Russia cut the gas supply to Ukraine, saying it would "pump only enough for customers further down the pipeline" (BBC, 2009). The gas crises have usually been analysed under a political agenda, and as such discussed in terms of Russian foreign policy. While political aspects remain acutely important, on its own they do not present the full picture.

The lack of political and economic strategy to reform energy dependency has been visible in Ukraine ever since 1991 (Balmaceda, 2008). Paradoxically, Ukraine is an energy-poor country, but it has provided rich opportunities for significant profit generation from energy related activities. Also, it is the country's political and business elite who have benefited from the deals while preventing a restructuring of the energy dependency. This paradox may be solved if we look at the corruption which is rampant at all levels in Ukraine, most seriously at the level of the political and industrial elite.

Anti-corruption sentiments have dominated the international agenda since the late 1990s. Also, since that time, some of the notorious corruption scams have dominated the life of Ukrainian society, as criminal groups within the government have misappropriated the natural resources of Ukraine. One recent example of this occurred in April 2017, when the National Anti-Corruption Bureau of Ukraine (NABU) alleged that a former Member of Parliament (MP) was involved in the creation of a criminal organisation. The former MP in question was also known as the former Head of the Verkhovna Rada Committee on Fuel and Energy. The investigation by NABU uncovered "public funds embezzlement of State Enterprise (SE) Eastern Mining and Processing Plant (EMPP) during the procurement of the uranium concentrate" (NABU, 2017b). The former MP "signed a contract with an intermediary company, controlled by him, for supply of uranium concentrate at higher prices. As a result, in 2014–2016 the SE suffered losses in the amount of $17.28 million" (NABU, 2017b). This case is representative of many economic crime cases under investigation by NABU since its formation in 2015.

These crimes by the political elite entail not only financial harm. From the new political elite of an independent Ukraine, corruption spread to the police and judiciary (Hellman and Kaufmann, 2001; Varese, 2000). It also significantly undermined the attitude of ordinary people towards the establishment (Markovska and Serdyuk, 2015). Lack of transparency, accountability and effective enforcement have created a fertile soil for the abuse of public funds by state officials.

These developments were hardly new or surprising. Almost a century ago, the author of *Dog's Heart*, Michail Bulgakov, noted that honest people live a boring life, but thieves can live sumptuously anytime (Bulgakov, 2007). During the Russian empire, the luxurious life at the expense of the state had been the accepted norm for royals and those close to them. Konstantinov (2006) writes, that during the reign of Catherine II, in the second part of the 18th century, bribery was officially denounced, but the great emperor of Russia was spending money from the state budget to pay her favourites. The luxurious life of those favourites was breathtaking to ordinary people. Similarly, in 2016, ordinary Ukrainians were shocked when politicians declared their vast wealth in the first official online wealth declaration exercise (Prentice, 2016).

The definitions of serious corporate crimes usually involve corporations that deliberately deceive officials and the public. Braithwaite (1984: 6) defined corporate crimes as the "conduct of a corporation, or of employees acting on behalf of a corporation, which is proscribed and punishable by law". This concept examines more closely the ways crimes are committed, and the nature of corporate offending. Simpson (2002: 8) argues that corporate crimes are "undertaken in the pursuit of organisational goals", it is how "managers experience and express the moral imperatives of their work environment and how organisational needs are formulated and inculcated into managerial decisions" (Jackall, 1988, as quoted in Simpson, 2002: 9). Tombs (2008: 18–19) discusses corporate crime as a wide-ranging term, and defines it as "illegal act or omissions, punishable by the state under administrative, civil or common law, which are the result of deliberate-making or culpable negligence within a legitimate formal organisation". Discussing the ambiguity of the state crime concept, Green and Ward (2017: 446) note that state crime can also involve "the illegitimate use of state agencies' powers over the allocation of resources". In extreme situations, we can discuss the criminalisation of the state or the development of the "shadow state". Green and Ward (2017: 447) use an example of some African states where "theft of public resources by a ruling elite appears to be the ruling principle of the state". How to best combine the debate about corporate, state and organised crimes remains an issue in criminology.

Levi and Lord (2017: 731) note "the importance of the organisational context, structure, culture and opportunity" in understanding white-collar and corporate crimes. The authors point to the less studied area of non-business contexts, for example state institutions and their organisational cultures.

The subject of fraud within the non-business context is especially relevant in Ukraine. It can be argued that in Ukraine, most of the popularly discussed corporate crimes start with the state officials deliberately undermining the integrity of the state and the economic development of the country (NABU, 2017a). How unique is the Ukrainian experience? Berger (2011) catalogues the abuse of corporate and government powers in the USA. The infamous Watergate scandal, allegations during the Clinton presidency, and profiting from war and disaster are just a few examples from the list discussed. It underlines the need to protect public ethical conduct. Promoting ethical conduct within private and public sector is obviously as important in Ukraine as elsewhere. This is all the more so as Ukrainian corporate criminality is often directly linked to state institutions. This is because in the Ukrainian context, state institutions provide opportunities for deliberate abuse of state resources (both natural and financial), and at the same time offer protection from prosecution (parliamentary immunity or corrupt payments to law enforcers).

This chapter aims to address critically the structure, culture and opportunities of white-collar and corporate crimes within the gas industry in Ukraine in order to scrutinise the "who and how" questions of corporate criminality. We begin with a very brief overview of the gas dependency issue, and proceed to discuss corporate criminality within the gas industry.

## The main question of dependency

During Soviet times, all that mattered was the fulfilment of (five-year) production plans for the whole of the Soviet Union. From this perspective, very little attention was paid to the individual needs of the republics. The bigger picture included the abundance of resources of the USSR as the dominant ideological tenet. Interdependence between republics was encouraged, while little thought was given to the sustainability of the economic development of the individual republics within the whole. The Soviet Ukraine was a good illustration of this situation. Being the main gas supplier for the other republics during the 1950–1970s, the gas production volumes of Ukraine were significantly reduced "for the sake of all-Soviet development" (Wolczuk, 2016). By the 1980s, the Ukrainian Soviet Socialist Republic was left dependent on gas supplies from Russia. This did not matter to the Soviet Union's leadership as long as production plans were fulfilled. In the 21st century this resulted in Ukraine becoming an energy-poor country that could no longer fulfil its energy needs. According to the International Energy Agency[1] (IEA, 2012), in 2011 Ukraine was a net gas importer, while domestic gas production could meet only 33% of its demand. Since the 2010s, the structure of Ukrainian gas imports has changed dramatically, from the monopoly of Russian gas, to the gas supplied from Central Asia and beyond. IEA (2012) also states that Ukraine is beginning to make some progress in the way its gas dependency is managed, stating that there are some early indications of the diversification of the energy sources.

1 The International Energy Agency (IEA) is a Paris-based autonomous intergovernmental organization established in the framework of the Organisation for Economic Co-operation and Development in 1974. The IEA acts as a policy adviser.

IEA (2012: 109) comments that Ukraine has inherited an impressive gas transmission system (GTS) "with unique characteristics, such as a dense network of multiple primary and secondary pipelines coupled with major storage facilities". By volume, Ukraine was the largest gas transit country in the world in 2006 (IEA, 2006). Pirani et al. (2012) estimate the gas transit revenue to be around $2.34 billion in 2008. Balmaceda (2015: 95) argues that Ukraine stands out from the rest of the former Soviet Union countries in that it has the largest variety of domestic profit-related opportunities in the energy trade area. These profits can be considered as external and internal. Balmaceda (2015: 18) notes the following external potentials: "energy price differentials between domestic and market prices"; hidden subsidies, transit revenue, payments by external parties for use of gas storage facilities, profits from advantageous barter arrangement (2015: 18). The internal factors include profits made by intermediary companies (2015: 18).

This position should have given Ukraine a comfortable financial base for stable economic development. However, nothing could be further from the truth. As a matter of fact, these opportunities have been grasped by a small group of politically influential people, who have abused their business, legal and political powers for their own profit (Kupatadze, 2012). Was this a matter of political failure or should this be qualified as an act of organised crime? The latter is the usual angle to describe or explain the economic and political problems of Ukraine. But is it correct? We will add another interpretation and discuss these crimes committed by Ukrainian officials from the perspective of corporate criminality in order to advance our understanding of state corporate criminality.

## Getting power under the "roof": the role of Business-Administrative Groups (BAGs)

After obtaining independence, most of the slogans about natural resources and the way they would work for the benefit of the population were silently abandoned. It is unclear whether it was too difficult to develop a long-term strategy to improve the country's economy. All we know is that the politicians in the newly independent Ukraine in the early 1990s did not think about the "implications of being an energy-poor state burdened with highly energy-intensive economic structures" (Wolczuk, 2016). Instead, people in power explored short-term, profit-seeking opportunities (for example, see "Onyshchenko's gas scheme", NABU, 2017c). Whilst Ukraine was at the top of the world's energy inefficient economies, selected politicians accumulated wealth, and the price was a failure to formulate and implement a coherent strategy to change the situation.

In order to understand the political failure in developing a sound energy strategy, we need to understand the management of energy dependency and the role of the political and business elite in Ukraine. Balmaceda (2015: 97) analysed the management of energy dependent post-Soviet countries, arguing that three of the most important elements of the analysis in Ukraine are: (a) the system of interest demarcation, (b) the role of the executive, (c) and the role of Parliament. From 1991, the interaction of these three elements has shaped and directed not only the policy developments but also the level of state corporate criminality in Ukraine.

Post-1991 development of Ukraine is usually framed in the context of powerful oligarchs and "clans" (Glenny, 2008; Kupatadze, 2012). Balmaceda (2015) employs the definition of *Business-Administrative Groups* (BAGs). These groups bring together "economic resource and administrative decision-making powers" (Balmaceda, 2008: 17). The composition of these groups has developed over time, but by the late 1990s three major groups had emerged that represented the different regions of Ukraine: Dnipropetrovsk, Donetsk and Kyiv (Kupatadze, 2012). These groups represented their interests through a number of channels: political parties, media sources and the Verkhovna Rada (Ukrainian Parliament). Ordinary Ukrainians recognised these groups by their adherence to the main political oligarchs.

- The *Dnipropetrovsk group* was represented by the Working Ukraine Party (Andrii Derkach and Serhii Tyhypko).
- The *Donetsk group* was represented by the party of the Regions (Victor Yanukovych and Rinat Akhmetov).
- The *Kyiv group* was represented by the Social Democratic Party of Ukraine (Viktor Medvedchuk, Hryhorii Surkis, Leonid Kravchuk) (Balmaceda, 2008; Kupatadze, 2012).

It is interesting to note that media sources gave each group a nickname and reported widely on their activities, from lavish celebrity like life-style to the crimes involved.

Balmaceda (2008: 39) notes that while the BAGs competed for controls, they also had to maintain a general system of division of interest, "implying a mutual demarcation, and presidential balancing between them". Division of interest and mutual respect were essential features of peaceful coexistence. This implies a specific role of the President which consists of offering the oligarchs "the roof", or the protection against each other. There was a need for strong presidential powers, and the 1996 Constitution strengthened the position of the President, thus allowing President Kuchma a better regulatory approach between the BAGs (2008: 39).

Balmaceda (2008: 39–40) employs the example of Kuchma's presidency to show that the President "played a complex role . . . moving between his role as arbiter within various interest groups and as representative of his own interests". From the late 1990s, the system was in place where the Verkhovna Rada translated the interests of BAGs into laws and regulations. As such, the old party ideology was replaced by specific short-term financial aspirations of the groups. We can effectively call it the elite Ukrainian dream, the desires of the Ukrainian political elite to enrich themselves at the expense of the state. Rushenko (2014) extended this thesis, and argued that the system of criminal management was much improved by 2010, enforcing among the other elements, the system of parallel illegal taxation in the country (as discussed in

Markovska and Serdyuk, 2015). This system covered each region that had to fulfil not only official obligations to the state, but also unofficial. The unofficial duties included the collection of bribes and extortion money from businesses to be deposited into the "common accounts". This practice has created "obshak" or common funds of a criminal community, the sort of savings account to be used for common purposes (be it for political objectives, e.g. during the election campaigns or business (Rushenko, 2014).

To understand the power interaction, it is important to acknowledge that Members of Parliament in Ukraine have effectively worked as the lobbying groups for the economic interests of the BAGs (Balmaceda, 2008).

## Criminality in gas production and distribution

In the early 1990s, politicians in Ukraine had a choice to either develop a long-term energy strategy that would take the whole country to a less energy dependent future, or to explore short-term opportunities within the sector. The short-term financial promise of the latter was significant enough to ignore long-term developments. What followed was a creation of a multitude of commercial enterprises and simple schemes with one objective: to collect and move financial assets out of the country as quickly as possible. In this regard, the gas sector represents an interesting but by no means unique example where commercial enterprises created with the help of government officials covered a number of illegal and corrupt activities.

## The legal context of gas production and distribution in Ukraine

Ukraine has an established institutional framework to control natural resources. The IEA (2012) comments that energy is considered to be a political issue, with the Ukrainian parliament and the President involved in the decision-making process. The Cabinet of Ministers is the institutional body responsible for policy co-ordination and oversight of state energy companies (IEA, 2012). A number of institutions at the national level have energy policy responsibilities, among them the IEA (2012: 23–24) that lists the following bodies:

- The Ministry of Energy and Coal Industry is responsible for most energy supply policies and for co-ordinating energy policies across government and providing advice to parliament.
- The Ministry of Ecology and Natural Resources is responsible for licensing and production sharing agreements for hydrocarbon development and for climate change policy.
- The Ministry of Finance is responsible for taxation relevant to the energy sector.
- The Ministry of Economy and Trade Development is leading the strategy for the energy efficiency policies.

- The State Agency on Energy Efficiency and Energy Saving is tasked with advancing energy efficiency and promoting the deployment of renewable energy sources.
- The National Commission for State Energy Regulation (NERC) has a role as supervisor of the natural gas and electricity markets.
- The Anti-Monopoly Committee is responsible for preventing excessive concentration of market power.

Politicians ensured that the institutional framework developed to regulate the gas production and distribution was under their control. This control was exercised with little accountability and transparency, so very quickly it turned into abuse of power rather than control (NABU, 2017c). In 2014, following the transparency slogans of the Maidan revolution, the Ukrainian State Geological fund published the list of companies that have been issued with licences to develop and extract natural resources in Ukraine. The list identified the owners of the private companies that received permits to extract gas. It was obvious that most businessmen involved in the gas and oil extraction were at some point in their career directly or indirectly related to the work of the state agencies listed earlier. As of August 2014, the list included 108 companies that received governmental permits in the gas industry (Golovnev and Vinnichuk, 2014). Of the companies that obtained the permits, 20 have shared ownership with the government. The permits issued by the state allowed the private companies to use gas extraction facilities for free. The largest gas company is "Ukrgasvudobutok" (owned by Naftogas Ukraine), which has obtained 145 permits. Gas produced by this company is by law directed for domestic use, at the prices regulated by the state. The biggest oil company "Ukrneft" holds about 90 special permits for extraction of hydrocarbon, and most of them are to extract the oil. The list includes a number of companies either jointly owned with foreign companies or with foreigners on the Board of Directors. For example, the geographical participation spreads from Canada to Italy, Austria and the UK. While represented in small numbers, the foreign individuals are believed to bring in some sense of legitimacy and transparency, providing business with new foreign names on the websites. However, Risen (2015) and Bullough (2017) question the real intentions of the foreign actors involved.

The Ukrainian gas market consists of imports and domestic production. In terms of imports, from 1991–2015 it used to obtain gas from Russia and Central Asia. In terms of domestic production, there are two important separations: NAK Naftohaz (state controlled company) and independent producers. NAK Naftohaz is responsible for the export, technical pipeline operations and maintenance, domestic distribution and part of the gas trading from independent producers. Balmaceda (2015: 115) notes that NAK Naftohaz was given a special status to be accountable not to the Ministry of Energy and Coal Industry, but directly to the Cabinet of Ministers. This move made it easier for the company to be "misused for rent-seeking purposes by interested actors within and outside the company".

In the late 1990s, the illegality of the sector came to be understood as operating through the "privatization of energy dependency rents and profits", often by politicians, and "while shifting the costs to the state and the society as a whole" (Balmaceda, 2015: 115). In a nutshell, BAGs earned the money at the expense of the state budget, as it was ensured legally that all the losses of the companies would be offset with the help of the state budget.

Wolczuk (2016: 119) argues that the state policy allowed monopolisation of the import and domestic gas structures:

> Naftogaz of Ukraine was in fact created as a vertically integrated oil and gas company engaged in the full cycle of operations in gas and oil field exploration and development, production and exploratory drilling, gas and oil transport and storage, and supply of natural gas and LPG to consumers . . . Naftogaz developed into a fronting institution controlled by and benefiting the governing elites – it was set up to socialise the costs of energy and the privatisation of the rent . . . The governing elites managed to conduct their business with no public scrutiny and accountability.

In simple terms, the costs of the energy management were for the state (the society at large) and the profits were for the private person as beneficiaries.

## Permits to steal: the opportunities for abuse of power

Chornovil (2015) discusses mechanisms of gas distribution in Ukraine and explains how the private companies abuse the arrangement (see Table 8.1).

According to Ukrainian regulations, gas produced within the territory should be prioritised for domestic or household users only. However, if state shares in the company are below 50%, gas produced domestically can be sold to industrial users. Domestic users receive the so-called agreed "social price", and the industrial users pay the full price. Table 8.1 shows that in 2013 around 15m cubic metres of gas was produced for the purpose of domestic consumption and the state received through NAK Naftogas Ukraine 5,587.6 billion UAH. In the same year around 6m cubic metres of gas was produced for the purpose of the industrial consumption and the private owners received nearly 28,757 billion UAH.

*Table 8.1* Ukrainian gas production and distribution for industrial and domestic use in 2013 (in million cubic metres) (based on Chornovil's data, 2015)

| Gas for industrial users | Gas for domestic users (household) |
|---|---|
| Produced: 6,087.4 million m³ (28.3%) | Produced: 15,423.4 million m³ (71.7%) |
| Average price: 4,724.00 UAH per m³ | Average price: 362.28 UAH per m³ |
| Difference in price = 4,361.72 UAH | |
| Gas sold to the industry: total sum of **28,756.9 million UAH** | NAK Naftogas Ukraine: total sum of **5,587.6 million UAH** |

Companies producing gas for industrial consumption usually operate under a joint venture agreement with the state. Chornovil (2015) explains that the private owner is allowed to exploit the gas extraction equipment built by the state, and sells gas for industrial purposes. The state company "Ukrgazdobucha" created a joint venture with private companies in order to issue permits to use the wells for gas production. The private owners invest money into the work and service the well. This is now more regulated. If private companies show that their investment in the joint company exceeds 50% and the state owns less than 50% of the company, this creates the opportunity to sell gas for industrial needs. Profits should be shared proportionally with the state; however, the official profits of these companies are usually minimalised to avoid paying the state and to transfer money to the "grey" sector of the economy. The way it works can be shown in the example of the "Nadra Geocentr" company in the next paragraph.

In 2007, the private company "Nadra Geocentr" signed a joint venture agreement with the state company "Ukrgazdobucha" to extract gas. The registered address of the "Nadra Geocentr" company was the address of a Ukrainian MP who was a business partner of the Minister of Ecology, which points to a conflict of interest. By 2013, 36 permits to extract gas had been issued to the company. Official data suggest that by 2014, Nadra Geocentr had produced 118m cubic metres of gas (Chornovil, 2015). In the first quarter of 2015, the company produced 69m cubic metres of gas. This is what is officially known. However, only 10% of the wells have equipment in place to register the production volume. Lack of a transparent system of production control had already been identified as a serious issue by the International Energy Agency in its reports in 2006, and again in 2012. The problem is where the company shows an official growth in its production of gas, but at the same time declares a minimal profit. The loser in this case is the "Ukrgazdobucha", the state company that let out the wells. It has received very little income from these arrangements as the rent was in proportion to the profits made, providing a reason to keep profits low. This inconsistency has never been investigated and Nadra Geocentr is probably a phantom company.

Chornovil (2015) also notes the use of fictitious companies to siphon off money from official channels. For example, in 2014 Nadra Geocentr sold 23m cubic metres of gas at the price of 4700 UAH per thousand cubic meters (including VAT) to the Morisel Group. Morisel Group sold this gas to another company at the new price of 9,600 UAH per thousand cubic metres. According to Chornovil (2015), the address of the Morisel Group was fictitious. In 2014 the Morisel Group sold 33m cubic meters of gas; however, according to the official record, they paid only 1,673 UAH (less than £100) in taxes (Chornovil, 2015). This was explained by "significant expenses" the company had sustained. However, the company transferred about 184m UAH to at least five other fictitious companies during the year (Chornovil, 2015). Overall, the "permit to steal" includes the minimisation of official profits and the use of fictitious companies to buy and supply services, a trusted trick to create "intangible" expenses.

It is also important to acknowledge the role of the corrupt lawyers. Bonner (2017) notes that the legal community of Ukraine is often viewed as intermediaries in corruption, "bribing judges and officials". The financial reporting of the legal firms resembles that of the businesses just discussed, "complicated offshore entities designed to minimise or evade taxes" (Bonner, 2017) According to Chornovil (2015), such practice peaked during the presidency of Yanukovych.

To stop this abuse, in 2014 the new government increased rent payments for the gas wells under joint venture schemes. New rules stipulate that the rent of 20% is to be increased in three stages, reaching 70% by the end of the 2015. So, under this proposal, if the state company "Ukrgazdobucha" sells the gas produced on its wells at the price of 1,600 UAH per cubic metre, it should pay 70% of this amount to the state (Ledenev, 2015). The government calculated that the new rental agreements should bring 21 billion UAH to the state budget in 2015, 11 billion UAH more than in 2014. About 5 billion UAH is supposed to be earned directly from the new rent on the joint venture. However, according to Chornovil (2015), the new rules only work in 50% of cases, as some producers use the money due to the government to bribe state officials to avoid payments. The rent increase was supported by international organisations such as the International Monetary Fund, seen as a practical step to fight corruption and a pre-condition for monetary help (Ledenev, 2015).

## Enforcement challenges: chasing $23m corruption money and foreign interests

This is a difficult and embarrassing case. On 28 April 2014, the UK Serious Fraud Office (SFO) announced the opening of a criminal investigation into possible money laundering arising from suspicions of corruption in Ukraine. "The SFO has obtained a restraint order freezing approximately $23m of assets in the UK in connection with this case" (SFO, 2014). This case was popularly known in Ukraine as the Zlochevsky case or the Burisma Oil case (Argument, 2017). Bullough (2017) notes that the case and the "pleasingly specific" number of $23m dominated the discussion at the Anti-Corruption Summit in London in 2014.

The $23m belonged to the accounts of two companies that were effectively controlled by Mykola Zlochevsky, a Ukrainian politician. In 2016, he was Ukraine's 48th richest man, worth $97m (Forbes Ukraine, 2016). Mr Zlochevsky has years of experience of working within the government structure, holding positions as the Head of State Committee for Natural Resources from 2003–2005, and the Minister of Ecology from 2010–2014. Parallel to his political life, Zlochevsky opened a business venture. Zlochevsky's company obtained 25 special permits for the extraction of hydrocarbons. In 2002, Zlochevsky opened one of the largest independent gas company, Burisma Oil, registered in Cyprus. Bullough (2017) details his correspondence with the lawyers of Zlochevsky, who argued that "Mr Zlochevsky's wealth is not a result of corruption or criminal conduct. He made his wealth before entering the office". However, it is interesting to see that the best performing times for the company are the times when Zlochevskyy occupied his official positions (Bullough, 2017).

Bullough (2017) explains that "according to a court judgment from January 2015, the $23m in the account that had been frozen in London was the proceeds of the sale of an oil storage facility, which Zlochevsky owned via a shell company in the British Virgin Islands". Bullough (2017) also notes that "the $23m arrived in London from Latvia". The case wasn't properly investigated by the Ukrainian authorities, and in January 2015 Mr Justice Nicholas Blake rejected the SFO argument and released the money (Bullough, 2017). An investigation conducted by Bullough (2017) suggests that Mr Justice Blake in his judgment about the assets made reference to the letter from 2 December 2014, "signed by someone in the Ukrainian prosecutor's office, which stated baldly that Zlochevsky was not suspected of any crime". This was unknown to the Kyiv prosecutor who initiated the case and had collected all the evidence. Lawyers for Mr Zlochevsky used the letter to reject any suspicions regarding their client. However, in March 2015, in an interview on TV channel 112, Ukraine's first deputy general prosecutor, David Sakvarelidze, suggested that one of the detectives working on the case received a $7m bribe for the letter addressed to the Old Bailey (Politrada, 2015).

To many observers the mysterious letter from the Ukrainian prosecutorial office meant incompetence and corruption (Bullough, 2017). However, Ukraine is only part of the story. In 2015 *New York Times* reported the speech of the US Ambassador to Ukraine, Mr Pyatt, in Odessa. He expressed his irritation about the slow progress being made in the fight against corruption and referred to this case saying that "those responsible for subverting the case by authorising those letters should – at a minimum – be summarily terminated" (Risen, 2015).

The story of Burisma Oil doesn't end here. What the US Ambassador didn't say was that starting from 2014, to improve the image and to avoid further allegations of corruption, the company appointed a number of well-known foreigners (see Burisma Oil, 2017). The strategy that is beginning to take pace in Ukraine seems to be to hire respectability from abroad. That is no guarantee for respectability inside the country.

## New legal context and old prosecution realities

Over the last 20 years, Ukrainian efforts to fight corruption were predominantly on the legislative front (Markovska and Pridemore, 2003). In the absence of effective control over legislative drafting and in the presence of a corrupt judiciary, these legal developments were often high-jacked by BAGs. Anti-corruption efforts "on paper" have always been driven by the international community, and from 2014 a new wave of legal and institutional developments could be observed. Since 2014, Ukraine has improved its institutional framework dealing with corruption: it adopted an Anti-Corruption Strategy for 2014–2017; set up the new Supreme Court; the Public Integrity Council; the Asset Recovery and Management Agency; the National Agency on the Prevention of Corruption; the National Anti-Corruption Bureau (NABU); and the Specialised Anti-Corruption Prosecutor's Office (SAPO) (Kheda, 2016). The most recent achievement is the introduction of the e-declaration system on wealth for politicians and senior civil servants.

The Law of Ukraine No.1700-VII "On preventing Corruption" dated 14 October 2014, is the main legislative act that defines legal and organisational principles for the anti-corruption system in Ukraine (Verhovna Rada, 2014). The law became fully effective from 26 April 2015.

Kheda (2016) notes that although legislation to fight corruption is constantly under development, it was only in 2014 that Ukraine introduced specific legislation providing for criminal liability for companies, but only private companies, that are not in state or municipal ownership. A corrupt payment to a private company officer, a corrupt payment to a public services official, offering, promising or providing unjustified benefits to an official, or improper influence are considered to be corruption crimes committed by the company's authorised representative on behalf of and in the interests of this company (Kheda, 2016). If the company is found guilty of committing a corruption offence, "it may be ordered to pay a fine ranging from 5,000–75,000 Hrv tax-exempted incomes" (Kheda, 2016). As of 2016, this amount varies between €3,600 and €54,000). The new legislation also requires companies to "develop . . . and implement . . . adequate measures for preventing corruption in their activities", and introduces the requirement for a new "anti-corruption compliance programme of the legal entity and an anti-corruption compliance officer of a company" (Kheda, 2016).

The "Law on Introduction of Amendments to Some Legislative Acts of Ukraine Concerning the Identification of Ultimate Beneficial Owners of Legal Entities and Public Figures" was adopted by the Verkhovna Rada of Ukraine on 21 May 2015 and took effect from 26 May 2015. The law allowed for a six-month transitional period during which companies had to submit the information about the "Controller" (ultimate beneficial owner) to the State registrar. For the first time, the law obliged legal entities "to disclose information about the ownership structure of their founders and members, as well as the information about ultimate beneficial owners of the legal entity" (Davydenko, 2014).

The most important issue of any legislation is enforcement. The new Anti-Corruption legislation is about two years old, making it difficult to judge its effectiveness. However, getting tough on corruption is not an easy task. Even after the Maidan protest of 2013–2014, no significant corruption case has been brought to trial during 2015–2016. This seems to be consistent with previous years (Kheda, 2016; Markovska and Serdyuk, 2015). Kheda (2016) argues that prosecution remains a highly subjective business: "mainly prosecution and conviction have been carried out with respect . . . (to). mid- or low-level officials, judges and public entity officers, as well as related to so-called 'social corruption' (for example against doctors and teachers)".

Bullough (2017) discusses the real problems facing investigators and quotes the Head of the Prosecutor's Special Investigations Department, who said that the problem is that the assets of the elite criminals are often held or registered in countries such as Monaco, Cyprus, Belize or British Virgin Islands. It is not unusual to wait for a reply to a request for three or four years. In one case it is alleged that the authorities in Monaco forwarded "4,000 pages of documentation relating to one oligarch in French, Arabic and English" (Bullough, 2017). The papers remain untranslated because of various bureaucratic issues.

Kostanyan (2017) notes that the commitment of the Specialised Anti-Corruption Prosecutor's Office to prosecute has been extremely low. "Out of 63 indictments sent to the courts, only four people received a prison sentence, and no high-level official has been convicted to date" (Kostanyan, 2017: 2). The EU Decision 2014/119/CFSP "provides for freezing of funds and economic resources of certain persons identified as responsible for the misappropriation of Ukrainian State funds"(EU Council Regulation, 2014: 1). The list includes 14 individuals, among them are: the former president of Ukraine, the former Minister of Internal Affairs, the former Prosecutor general to Ukraine, the former Head of Security Services of Ukraine, the former Minister of Justice, the former Head of Administration of President of Ukraine, etc. The reasons for listing most of them is embezzlement of Ukrainian state funds and their illegal transfer outside of Ukraine (EU Council Regulation, 2014). It is unknown what has happened to these persons or their assets on this list.

Pavlo Lazarenko remains the most significant anti-corruption case in the history of Ukraine after 1991. Lazarenko was Prime Minister of Ukraine from June 1996 until the summer of 1997. In his positions as Minister of Energy and then Prime Minister, he "was able to provide contracts, permits, licenses, or government guarantees. The transactions . . . allegedly netted Lazarenko approximately $114m over 2 years, although his overall profits may have been considerably larger" (OCO, 2015: 57). Lazarenko had strong political ambitions, and was focusing on the Ukrainian presidency when a criminal investigation was opened against him. Afraid of imprisonment in Ukraine, Lazarenko fled to the USA in 1999 to seek political asylum. However, the US authorities indicted him on 53 counts of money laundering, conspiracy to commit money laundering, wire fraud and interstate transportation of stolen property (OCO, 2015). In June 2009 Lasarenko was tried and sentenced to "97 months in prison, ordered to pay a $9m fine and forfeited $22,851,000 and various specified assets resulting from his money laundering convictions" (FBI, 2009). He served his sentence between 2009–2012 in the federal prison at Terminal Island, USA, and as of 2016 has been fighting for an asylum status in the USA (Wayne, 2016).

This was just one old case, not even tried in Ukraine itself. The meagre law enforcement performance elaborated earlier is certainly not trust-inspiring. Indeed, in a 2016 public opinion survey in Ukraine (Centre for Insights in Survey Research, 2016) it appeared that 71% of Ukrainians believe the country is going in the wrong direction. Interestingly, 46% of respondents believe that the abolition of immunity for MPs and judges would be a move in the right direction for the country. This is followed by 38% of respondents suggesting that the right direction would be the introduction of a clear mechanism to make civil servants accountable; and 34% believing that the right measure would be the arrest and prosecution of well-known current office holders who are allegedly involved in corrupt activities (Centre for Insights in Survey Research, 2016). It is clear that a proportion of the public understands the severity of the crimes committed by the elite, and is frustrated about the lack of successful prosecutions.

## Conclusion: corporate, state or organised criminality?

This chapter has critically addressed corporate criminality in Ukraine by focusing on aspects of structure, culture and opportunities for white-collar and corporate criminal activities. Each aspect discussed features of the systematic and organised abuse of state power by civil servants and higher office holders. Therefore, we propose to subsume such law-breaking under the concept of corporate criminality. This is supported by Lord et al. (2017) who suggest that given the similarities in techniques used by organised criminal groups and corporate criminals, the most effective way to analyse such serious crimes is at the convergence zone of the three concepts: corporate, white-collar and organisational crimes.

Serious corporate criminality within the gas sector in Ukraine has been organised by the BAGs with the support of office holders as government representatives. This deliberate deception of business and abuse of public office by both business and government representatives highlights an important dimension of the discussion on the definition of corporate crime. Corporate criminality in this cultural context includes corruptive negotiations between ruling political and business elites.

We have identified the following set of three markers of state organised criminal conduct within the gas sector in Ukraine. First, the abuse of state power and neglect of transparency. More specifically, abuse of authority in the state licensing of natural resources. In this connection we observe the politicisation of business in the following ways: (a) the establishment of institutional frameworks designed to expressly pretend to "negotiate" with the industry, for example the practice of using state funds to cover a variety of premeditated losses or expenses; (b) the close association of Members of Parliament with the business world; and (c) the failure to disclose and halt *mala fide* business activities by key persons while serving in the public sector.

The second set of markers revolve around methods used to defraud the state. These include: (a) falsifying accounts to show low levels of tax return; and (b) the use of fictitious companies to create a web of non-existing activities or services (see Campbell, this volume, Chapter 5).

Third, the weak enforcement and prosecution mechanisms that result in the absence of successful prosecution of corruption-related cases. On paper, Ukraine has established a sound institutional framework to fight corruption. However, the practicalities of day-to-day law enforcement remain deeply problematic. Weak enforcement is found in insufficient investigative skills; an (in)ability to co-operate with other jurisdictions; the unwillingness of courts to imprison corrupt officials; and the prevalence of lenient sanctions (for example, fines).

One of the requirements is to identify offenders in corporations and public administration. To this end we need a precise delineation of the concept of corporate criminality, taking account of the Ukrainian political and socio-economic context: the interactions and thin lines between corporate and public stakeholders. Indeed, in many cases known to NABU (2017a), the initiators of corporate criminality are Members of Parliament and civil servants. Developing the framework of state-organised corporate crime will improve theoretical and practical understanding of how it happens, who are the main perpetrators, and why anti-corruption campaigns fail to stop serious financial criminality within business and government. There is much money at stake. In 2016, the Financial Monitoring Center in Ukraine reported that the total amount of money that elite criminals had misappropriated over the previous three years was about 200 billion UAH (approx. €6.6 billion; Argumanet.ua, 2017). This is in glaring contrast to law enforcement: in the first three months of 2017, only a trifling amount – 5,000 UAH (€160) – of corrupt proceeds were confiscated following court orders (Argumanet.ua, 2017). It is clear that "the system" consists of little more than a paper reality, a rebirth of the proverbial Potemkin village. This needs to be broken down and replaced with a new method of thinking about organised corporate crime.

## Bibliography

Argument. (2017) *The Return of the State Funds*. Available at: http://argumentua.com/novosti/v-2017-godu-v-byudzhet-vernuli-5100-griven-ukradennykh-korruptsionerami-v-2015-m-1649-tys (accessed 4 May 2017).

Balmaceda, M. M. (2008) *Energy Dependency, Politics and Corruption in the Former Soviet Union. Russia's Power, Oligarchs' Profits and Ukraine's Missing Energy Policy, 1995–2006*. BASEES/Routledge Series on Russia and East European Studies. London: Routledge.

Balmaceda, M. M. (2015) *The Politics of Energy Dependency: Ukraine, Belarus and Lithuania between Domestic Oligarchs and Russian Pressure*. Toronto, ON: Toronto University Press.

BBC. (2009) *Q&A: Russia-Ukraine Gas Row*. Available at: http://news.bbc.co.uk/1/hi/world/europe/7240462.stm (accessed 4 May 2017).

Berger, R. J. (2011) *White-Collar Crime: The Abuse of Corporate and Government Power*. Boulder, CO: Lynne Rienner Publishers.

Bonner, B. (2017) *Stelmashchuk: Ukraine's Legal Profession Party to Blame for Corruption*. Available at: www.lexology.com (accessed 4 May 2017).

Braithwaite, J. (1984) *Corporate Crime in the Pharmaceutical Industry*. London: Routledge and Kegan Paul.

Bulgakov, M. (2007) *A Dog's Heart*. Harmondsworth, UK: Penguin.

Bullough, O. (2017) *The Money Machine: How a High-Profile Corruption Investigation Fell Apart*. Available at: www.theguardian.com/world/2017/apr/12/the-money-machine-how-a-high-profile-corruption-investigation-fell-apart (accessed 4 October 2017).

Burisma Oil. (2017) *Board of Directors*. Available at: http://burisma.com/en/board-of-directors (accessed 4 May 2017).

Centre for Insights in Survey Research. (2016) *Public Opinion Survey Residents of Ukraine: May 28–June 14, 2016*. Available at: www.iri.org/sites/default/files/wysiwyg/2016–07–08_ ukraine_poll_shows_skepticism_glimmer_of_hope.pdf (accessed 4 April 2017).

Chornovil, T. (2015) *"Ukrgasdobucha": Systemic Criminality*. Available at: http://argumentua. com (accessed 5 March 2017).

Davydenko, I. (2014) *Adoption of a Number of Anticorruption and Anti-Money Laundering Laws in Ukraine*. Available at: www.lexology.com (accessed 4 May 2017).

EU Council Regulation. (2014) Council Regulation (EU) No. 208/2014 of 5 March 2014. *Official Journal of the European Union*. Available at: www.ukpandi.com/ fileadmin/uploads/uk-pi/Documents/Legal_sources/2014_Sanctions/EU_COUNCIL_ REGULATION_208_2014_Ukraine_5Mar2014.pdf (accessed 4 March 2017).

FBI. (2009) *Press Release: Former Ukrainian Prime Minister Sentenced to 97 Months in Prison Fined $9 Million for Role in Laundering $30 Million of Extortion Proceed*. Available at: https://archives.fbi.gov/archives/sanfrancisco/press-releases/2009/ sfl11909a.htm (accessed 4 May 2017).

Forbes Ukraine. (2016) *100 Richest List*. Available at: www.forbes.net.ua/ratings/4 (accessed 4 May 2017).

Glenny, M. (2008) *McMafia: Crime without Frontiers*. London: The Bodley Head.

Golovnev, S. and Vinnichuk, Y. (2014) *The Natural Resources of Ukraine and Who Do They Feed*. (Kogo kormyat nedra Ukrainu?). Available at: http://argumentua.com (accessed 5 March 2017).

Goncharuk, A. G. and Storto, C. I. (2017) Challenges and policy implications of gas reform in Italy and Ukraine. *Energy Policy*, 101, 456–466.

Green, P. and Ward, T. (2017) Understanding state crime, in A. Liebling, S. Maruna, & L. McAra (eds.), *Oxford Handbook of Criminology*, 6th ed. Oxford, UK: Oxford University Press.

Hellman, J. and Kaufmann, D (2001) Controlling the challenge of state capture in transition economies. *Finance and Development*, 38(3). Available at: www.imf.org.

IEA. (2006) *Ukraine Energy Policy Review 2006, OECD/IEA, Paris*. Available at: www. iea.org/publications/freepublications/publication/ukraine2006–1.pdf (accessed 4 October 2017).

IEA. (2012) *Ukraine2012. Energy Policies beyond IEA countries. International Energy Agency*. Available at: www.iea.org/publications/freepublications/publication/ Ukraine2012_free.pdf (accessed 4 October 2017).

Kheda, S. (2016) *Ukraine: Bribery & Corruption*. Available at: www.globallegalinsights. com/practice-areas/bribery-and-corruption-laws-and-regulations/ukraine. Accessed 4 April 2017.

Konstantinov, A. (2006) *Corrupted Russia*. (In Russian). Moscow: OLMA-Press.

Kostanyan, H. (2017) *Ukraine's Unimplemented Anti-Corruption Reform*. Available at: www.ceps.eu/publications/ukraine%E2%80%99s-unimplemented-anti-corruption- reform (accessed 5 April 2017).

Kupatadze, A. (2012) *Organised Crime, Political Transitions and State Formation in Post- Soviet Eurasia*. Basingstoke, UK: Palgrave Macmillan

Ledenev, A. (2015) *Where Is Our Gas?* Available at: www.forbes.net ua (accessed 4 April 2017).

Levi, M. and Lord, N. (2017) White-collar and corporate crimes, in A. Liebling, S. Maruna, & L. McAra (eds.), *Oxford Handbook of Criminology*, 6th Ed. Oxford, UK: Oxford University Press.

Lord, N., van Wingerde, K. and Campbell, L. (2017) Organising the 'monies' of corporate crimes. Unpublished presentation. EUROC workshop, 'Understanding corporate crime: theory and methods', 29–31 August Utrecht. *For information see* http://escnewsletter.org/newsletter/2015-2/european-working-group-organisational-crime-euroc-working-group-report (accessed 30 August 2017).

Markovska, A. and Pridemore, W. A. (2003) Laws without teeth: An overview of the problems associated with corruption in Ukraine. *Crime Law and Social Change* 39(2), 193–213.

Markovska, A. and Serdyuk, A. (2015) Black, grey or white? Finding the new shade of corruption in Ukraine, in van Duyen, et al. (eds.), *The Relativity of Wrongdoing: Corruption, Organised Crime, Fraud and Money Laundering in Perspectives.* Oisterwijk, The Netherlands: Wolf Legal Publishers.

NABU. (2017a) *NABU Completed Pre-Trial Investigation of the Case of the Head of State Fiscal Service of Ukraine.* Available at: https://nabu.gov.ua/en/novyny/nabu-completed-pre-trial-investigation-case-head-state-fiscal-service-ukraine (accessed 4 October 2017).

NABU. (2017b) *NABU Detectives Detained a Former Member of Parliament.* Available at: https://nabu.gov.ua/en/novyny/nabu-detectives-detained-former-member-parliament-updated (accessed 4 October 2017).

NABU. (2017c) *Indictment Of 8 Suspects Involved in So-Called "Onyshchenko's Gas Scheme" Was Sent To Court.* Available at: https://nabu.gov.ua/en/novyny/indictment-8-suspects-involved-so-called-onyshchenkos-gas-scheme-was-sent-court (accessed 4 October 2017).

OCO. (2015) *Ukraine and the EU: Overcoming Criminal Exploitation Toward a Modern Democracy?* Available at: www.o-c-o.net/wp-content/uploads/2013/11/Ukraine-and-the-EU-Overcoming-criminal-exploitation-toward-a-modern-democracy.pdf (accessed 4 April 2017).

Prentice, A. (2016) *Ukrainians Shocked as Politicians Declare Vast Wealth.* Available at: www.reuters.com/article/us-ukraine-crisis-corruption-idUSKBN12V1EN (accessed 4 April 2017).

Politrada. (2015) *Sanctions From the Ex-Minister of Ecology Were Removed Because of the $7m Bribe.* Available at: http://politrada.com/news/sanktsii-s-eks-ministra-ekologii-nikolaya-zlochevskogo-snyali-iz-za-vzyatki-v-7-millionov-dollarov/ (accessed 5 May 2017).

SFO. (2014) *Money Laundering Investigation Opened.* Available at: www.sfo.gov.uk/2014/04/28/money-laundering-investigation-opened/ (accessed 5 May 2017).

Pirani, S., Stern, J. and Yafimava, K. (2012) *The April 2010 Russo-Ukrainian Gas Agreement and Its Implications for Europe.* Oxford Institute for Energy Studies, NG42. Available at: www.oxfordenergy.org/wpcms/wp-content/uploads/2011/05/NG_42.pdf (accessed 5 May 2017).

Risen, J. (2015) Joe Biden, his son and the case against a Ukrainian oligarch. *New York Times.* Available at: www.nytimes.com/2015/12/09/world/europe/corruption-ukraine-joe-biden-son-hunter-biden-ties.html?_r=0 (accessed 4 August 2017).

Rushenko, I. (2014) From 'criminal revolution' to 'criminal society'. (In Ukrainian). *Sociology: Theory, Methods and Marketing,* 2, 3–23.

Simpson, S. S., (2002) *Corporate Crime, Law, and Social Control.* Cambridge, UK: Cambridge University Press.

Tombs, S. (2008) Corporations and health safety, in J. Minkes & L. Minkes (eds.), *Corporate and White-Collar Crime.* London: Sage.

Varese, F. (2000) Pervasive corruption, in A. Ledeneva & M. Kurkchiyan (eds.), *Economic Crime in Russia.* London: Kluwer Law International, pp. 99–111.

Verhovna Rada (2014) Про засади державної антикорупційної політики в Україні (Антикорупційна стратегія) на 2014–2017 роки, Відомості Верховної Ради (ВВР), 2014, № 46, ст.2047. In Ukrainian. (The Law of Ukraine on Preventing Corruption). Available at http://zakon3.rada.gov.ua/laws/show/1699-18, (accessed 5 April 5 2017).

Wayne, L. (2016) *A Ukrainian Kleptocrat Wants His Money and U.S. Asylum.* Available at: www.nytimes.com/2016/07/07/business/international/a-ukrainian-kleptocrat-wants-his-money-and-us-asylum.html (accessed 4 October 2017).

Wolczuk, K. (2016) Managing the flows of gas and rules: Ukraine between the EU and Russia. *Eurasian Geography and Economics,* 57(1), 113–137.

YouTube (2006) *Russian-Ukrainian Gas Trade.* Available at: www.youtube.com/watch?v=iXuzSx-QbeM (accessed 5 September 2017).

# Part III

# Responding to corruption in commercial enterprise

# 9 The dark side of finance

## Policing corruption through regulatory means

*Aleksandra Jordanoska*[1]

This chapter addresses the important but understudied topic of the policing of bribery and corruption through the supervisory and enforcement techniques of financial regulators. The specific focus is on the UK financial markets and the regulatory regime of the conduct of the business financial regulator, the Financial Conduct Authority (FCA).[2] The UK houses a significant part of the global financial services industry, and London has cemented its position as a crucial world financial centre. Nationally, finance is one of the most important sectors for the UK economy, contributing in 2016 with £124.2 billion in gross value added (GVA), 7.2% of the UK's total GVA (House of Commons, 2017). In international terms, the size of the market and the range of participants mean that London has the largest capital flow in the world, though it is still uncertain how Brexit will impact its prestige and the robustness of UK financial regulation if there is an exodus by financial institutions towards alternative European centres.

The provision of services whose essence is the cross-border intermediation of capital, the high level of industry competition, and the remuneration structures organised around commission-based incentives to win new business domestically and abroad expose the industry to corruption vulnerabilities. Despite the global reach and significance of financial markets, and despite the post-crisis regulatory activism towards establishing global governance frameworks, financial markets are still predominately regulated locally, through national financial regulators. The localism of regulatory oversight makes surveillance activities by national regulators crucial for establishing the boundaries of appropriate behaviour. National financial regulators also provide the most important mechanism in the social control of corporate crime in financial markets, as evidenced by comparing the regulatory and criminal justice responses to the crisis (Pontell et al., 2014).

This chapter is an initial attempt to use theoretical and analytical tools from regulation theory scholarship to make sense of how public agencies carve out

---

1 My grateful thanks to Liz Campbell and Nicholas Lord for their insightful comments on a previous draft.
2 The FCA was originally established as the Financial Services Authority (FSA). Reference will be made to the FCA when discussing current practices; to both the FSA/FCA when discussing a common organisational trend, and to the FSA only when discussing historic developments.

their supervisory remit with respect to the oversight of bribery and corruption in industries; what are the role and resources employed by the regulatees in this process, as well as to chart developing trends and new modes of governance within the regulatory state in general. The chapter first proceeds to offer a typology of the roles of financial regulators in policing the interaction between corrupt activities and financial markets, narrowing down the present focus on corruption *by* financial institutions. The chapter then charts how risk-based thinking, priorities and activities permeate the control of bribery and corruption on both sides of the regulatory relationship. On the regulator's side, I examine the demarcation of the anti-bribery and corruption (ABC) regulatory mandate, rules and enforcement, and the risk-based and hybrid meta-regulation supervisory practices. On the regulatees' side, I examine the (flaws of) internal ABC risk-based frameworks and the role of senior management. The chapter uncovers certain innovative modes of governance, and provides a critical discussion of regulatory shortcomings and ABC regime implementation challenges.

## 1 The role of financial regulators in policing corruption: a typology

Financial regulators are key stakeholders in the policing of corruption interactions associated with, or perpetrated through, financial markets in three distinct areas: corruption *by* financial institutions, corruption *in* financial institutions, and corruption *through* financial institutions. Though, as will be seen later, these activities vary qualitatively in terms of the modes and aims of the illicit behaviour. I suggest that this typology is useful for capturing the extent and complexity of the role of financial regulators in overseeing the interaction between corrupt activities and financial markets. Also, similar regulatory designs, techniques and regulatees' responses through compliance systems and control commonly address all three areas of interaction.

First, financial regulators oversee corruption *by* financial institutions, understood as 'an abuse of an entrusted power for private gain' (Transparency International, 2017; also Rose-Ackerman and Palifka, 2016). This concerns the involvement of financial institutions in paying illicit transactions to domestic or foreign public officials to win beneficial contracts or entrance into a market (bribery), and, in the regulatory regime, this also extends to the risk of financial institutions engaging in such behaviour (FCA, 2016). Corruption *by* financial institutions commonly is governed by a dual criminal justice and regulatory regime. In the UK, the criminal justice response tackles bribery through the Bribery Act 2010, and the Serious Fraud Office (SFO) leads on bribery considered serious and complex.[3] The regulatory oversight is through the FCA and the Financial Services and Markets Act (FSMA) 2000, and the present chapter unpacks the remit and practicalities of this regime.

---

3  See e.g. the first UK Deferred Prosecution Agreement in *SFO v Standard Bank* (see further chapters by Lord and King; and Doig, this volume).

Second, financial regulators have the task of policing corruption *in* financial institutions; this concerns what political scientists have termed 'institutional corruption' (Lessig, 2013; Thompson, 1995). The concept was originally developed to designate the institutional behaviour of public bodies that damages that institution's legitimate procedures, and the confidence of the relevant publics in that institution (Lessig, 2013; Thompson, 1995). Recently, 'institutional corruption' has been used to designate the involvement of investment banks in various harmful activities such as: short-termism thinking (Salter, 2013); 'the rule-making game' in which the industry successfully lobbied for the loosening of the Volcker-rule during the implementation of the Dodd-Frank Act 2010 through technical exemptions (Salter, 2010); and the collusive and systemic noncompliance with the reporting process in the LIBOR rigging scandals (O'Brien, 2013). Though such activities can also commonly encompass abuse of an entrusted power, corruption *in* financial institutions is more harmful and damaging to the legitimacy of the industry than corruption *by* financial institutions, since it has reduced public confidence in private industry participants and, by extension, in the public institutions that regulate them. Corruption *in* financial institutions is therefore a central problem to the governance of finance, and a range of regulatory provisions aim to mitigate it. For example, in the wake of the financial crisis, the FCA enacted the Remuneration Codes,[4] aimed at discouraging risk-taking and short-termism.

Third, financial regulators play a key role in policing corruption *through* financial institutions. This concerns the involvement of financial institutions in the facilitation of bribery payments through their services. Financial markets are entrusted with the all-important task of intermediating capital from those who have it to those who need it, and some of this intermediation might also consist of facilitating the flow of tainted credit. Comparatively, financial institutions have a significant role to play in enabling the flow of bribery money through opening accounts for the payment of bribes to foreign officials or third parties connected to them (Lord and Levi, 2017). Corruption *through* UK financial institutions is monitored through the FCA's extensive anti-money laundering (AML) regime (see FCA, 2016).

The subsequent discussion primarily focuses on the FCA's approach towards supervising corruption *by* financial institutions, yet the discussion on the Authority's regulatory behaviour and modes of governance, as well as the firm-level organisational compliance frameworks that develop in response, are also pertinent to the operation of the FCA's policing of corruption *in* and *through* financial institutions.

## 2 The carving of the regulatory mandate: bribery and corruption as regulatory risks

The FCA's ABC regime was constructed upon the previous section 6 of FSMA. Section 6 defined the reduction of financial crime as one of the FSA's regulatory

---

4 SYSC 19A-19DR. SYSC stands for the 'Senior Management Arrangements, Systems and Controls' chapter of the FCA Handbook.

objectives, giving it a mandate to make rules and supervise the markets to the effect that the regulated firms are aware of the risks of, and have adequate procedures to prevent and detect, financial crime. The FCA inherited the FSA's market conduct regulatory functions, yet its objectives are slightly different. It now has a single strategic objective of ensuring that the supervised markets function well,[5] with further operational objectives of: protecting consumers; protecting the integrity of the UK financial system; and promoting effective competition.[6] In the legislative ordering, the 'minimising financial crime' objective has been downgraded to examples of what protecting 'integrity' means. Though this might mean that financial crime is now being given a less prominent place in regulatory considerations, reducing financial crime still features in the Act as a statutory duty as opposed to, for example, being relegated to the FCA's administrative rulemaking powers. The FCA therefore remains an important agent, with significant powers, in the network of social control organisations with some remit in policing financial crime (Levi, 2010).

However, while FSMA specifically defined financial crime 'to include any offence involving' fraud or dishonesty, market abuse and market manipulation, and money laundering,[7] the remit over bribery and corruption has been derived by the FSA from a wider interpretation of the use of the term 'to include' any offence involving such behaviour. Though FSMA did not, and still does not, impose a specifically defined prerogative upon the FSA/FCA to tackle ABC-related issues, the Authority appropriated these due to its overarching risk-based regulatory approach. The FSA/FCA's risk-based regulation relies on distributing resources on the basis of assessing the degree of risk to its statutory objectives by a regulatory issue (Black, 2005; FCA, 2017a). The possibility that regulated firms may be involved in facilitating bribery was prioritised as a particular risk to both the financial crime prevention and market confidence objectives. The first FSA actions in the ABC area started only in 2007, after its probe into the payments that Aon, a wholesale insurance broker, had made to overseas third parties to win business without adequate procedures to assess and mitigate bribery and corruption risks. Aon was ultimately fined,[8] but importantly, the probe instigated a re-cast of bribery and corruption involvement by regulated firms into an important 'worry' or 'risk to the objectives' within the risk-assessment framework. This prompted a tailored communication to the CEOs of wholesale insurance broker firms in 2007 (the 'Dear CEO' letter by then-director Thomas Huertas), setting out the FSA's expectations and calling them to review 'their business practices to ensure that they are not involved in, or associated with, illicit payments'.[9]

The FSA therefore pursued a formal jurisdiction over ABC compliance that would minimise the likelihood of attracting, what Hood (2007) terms, regulatory

5　S. 1B(2) FSMA.
6　Ss. 1C(1)-1E(1) FSMA.
7　Now the statutory definition also includes terrorist finance (section 1H(s) FSMA).
8　Aon FN 06/01/09.
9　www.fsa.gov.uk/static/pubs/ceo/ttp_letter.pdf.

blame for ABC supervisory failures, particularly in view of the heightened political debates over the reform of the UK anti-bribery legislation that would ultimately result in the Bribery Act 2010 (on the legislative history, see Alldridge, 2012). The regulation of finance is crucially underpinned by 'domestic politics' (Helleiner and Pagliari, 2010), which also drive domestic regulators in drafting their governance foci. The blame was also diffused through carving up a specific remit around the governance of the *risk* that financial institutions could be engaged in corruption rather than around prosecuting *actual* corruption in finance. These corruption risks are defined as 'the risk of a firm, or anyone acting on the firm's behalf, engaging in corruption' (FCA, 2016: 58). The focus is on overseeing firms' internal systems and controls to prevent bribery, whilst the prosecution of *actual* bribery is left to the SFO's agenda. For example, the Authority has conveyed statements that, 'while we do not prosecute breaches of the Bribery Act, we have a strong interest in the anticorruption systems and controls of firms we supervise' (FCA, 2016: 57; see also Cole, 2009). Any blame for supervisory failures can be managed since the FCA can target its monitoring and enforcement resources in systems and controls oversight where it can claim success due to its expertise, as for example, also in prosecuting insider dealing cases (Jordanoska, 2017). This claim of 'ownership' is a simultaneous avoidance of blame for not taking actions of detecting, and sanctioning *actual* corruption, which is notoriously difficult to prove (Lord, 2014). The blame is further diffused through cooperating with the SFO in *actual* bribery matters, for example, the FSA passed its investigation findings into the ABC regulatory breaches by the insurer Willis[10] to the SFO.

## 2.1 Regulating bribery and corruption risks: rules and enforcement

ABC compliance in finance is governed through the FCA Handbook Principles and rules that cover the prevention of financial crime in general – there are no specific rules on ABC compliance. The FCA is a principles-based regulator as there are 11 short Principles at the basis of its regulatory architecture.[11] Principles-based regulation relies on a broad and abstract set of standards, rather than on more detailed or specific rules (Black, 2008). Their application means that though some of the rules and guidance in the Handbook might further specify the implementation of a Principle, these should not be viewed as exhaustive and the FCA can bring an enforcement action on the basis of a breach of a Principle alone. Four Principles are directly relevant for the governance of corruption *by* financial institutions: Principle 1 (conducting business with integrity), Principle 2 (conducting business with skill, care and diligence), Principle 3 (management and control) and Principle 11 (open and cooperative relations with regulators). Principle 3 is the most directly ABC-relevant provision since it imposes requirements of maintaining appropriate internal systems and controls to conduct an

---

10  Willis Ltd. FN 21/07/2011.
11  Prin 1.1.2 FCA Handbook.

FCA-authorised activity. It is also further specified by the two 'financial crime prevention' rules (SYSC 3.2.6R and SYSC 6.1.1R) that impose direct obligations upon regulatees to establish, implement and maintain adequate policies and procedures to prevent the risk that they might be used to further financial crime. The content of these obligations, however, is not defined in any detail in the FCA Handbook but, as seen later, is contained mostly in regulatory guidance.

The rules' requirements are, in many respects, comparable to the requirements of section 7 of the Bribery Act ('the corporate culture' offence or having adequate internal procedures to prevent the giving/receiving of bribery). However, the regulatory regime goes beyond the criminal justice one as Section 7 still requires that *actual* corruption to have occurred due to flawed corporate compliance structures. This exposes financial institutions to regulatory noncompliance risks even if compliant with the Bribery Act, since they are placed under the double requirements of assessing the adequacy of their ABC procedures. For example, the sanctioned commercial insurer JLTS had its due diligence procedures on introducer/facilitator relationships confirmed by an external legal counsel as 'comprehensive and broadly in line with the Bribery Act'.[12] Yet, the regulator took the view that the review was not "holistic" as it did not review the firm's compliance systems with the Authority's ABC requirements, so it fell under the expected standards. The wider FCA reach enables the punishing of *potential* corporate crime, unavailable to criminal prosecutors yet favoured by some commentators (Gobert and Punch, 2003), as the existence of opportunities and conditions for serious crime can sometimes tell us more about the corporate ethos than an *actual* crime. The additional FCA requirements also contribute to a more comprehensive criminal justice control; if these are implemented effectively, financial institutions are likely to have a higher level of compliance with the Bribery Act than other industries (BBA, 2014). In terms of which of the two regimes drives corporate behaviour, however, there is some evidence, on the basis of the Authority's own review of the market (FSA, 2010), that firms had worked on improving their compliance procedures mostly prompted by the introduction of the Bribery Act, rather than by the preceding FSA actions. The complimentary duality of the regulatory and criminal justice systems is therefore necessary to control industry malfeasance in this area. Though the regulatory regime is wider as it can control and penalise criminogenic opportunities and conditions, thus preventing corporate offending, the moral messages sent through criminalising bribery can achieve a greater general deterrence effect.

To some extent, the FCA regime has a similarly extra-territorial reach as the criminal justice control under Section 12 of the Bribery Act. Though the FCA's supervisory jurisdiction is solely national, in practice, its enforcement actions have captured the risk of transnational noncompliance by UK firms as insurers have been fined for suspicious payments to overseas third parties to win business. The FCA justified these actions on the basis that the lack of robust procedures

12 JLTS FN 19/12/2013.

exposed UK firms conducting business internationally to a risk of contravening UK and/or overseas anti-bribery laws.[13] The involvement of UK firms in corrupt or potentially corrupt practices overseas is also considered a risk to the FCA's domestic operational objective of protecting the integrity of the UK financial markets.

Despite the comprehensiveness of the regime, and the FCA's own findings on faulty systems in the industry (FSA, 2010, 2012; thereafter, FCA, 2013, 2014), its enforcement docket is relatively modest. Thus far, there have been only four enforcement actions on the basis of breaches of Principle 3 (Aon, JLTS and Besso Limited), and also the SYSC rules (Willis), all in the insurance industry. In none of these cases had *actual* bribery occurred, but the firms were sanctioned for not taking reasonable care to establish and maintain effective systems and controls. Comparatively, the US Securities and Exchange Commission (SEC) has recently been significantly more active in enforcing the US anti-bribery regime in finance. Enforcement under the Foreign Corrupt Practices Act (FCPA) has long been a high priority area for the SEC, and the agency has a dedicated FCPA enforcement unit. In finance, the SEC has settled FCPA charges for corrupt behaviour with prominent financial institutions such as JPMorgan, BNY Mellon, Aon and Och-Ziff for winning business by giving jobs to persons associated with foreign public officials, or paying bribes to third parties.[14]

The FCA's modest docket can be explained by several organisational behaviour reasons which may co-exist: the FCA oversees the provision of services by a large number of financial institutions, so the ability to undertake numerous enforcement actions within a modest budget is fairly limited; the enforcement work is fairly thematically driven at points in time (the FCA's financial crime focus is commonly announced in its Annual Business Plan, for example, in 2017/2018, its enforcement efforts centre on AML and fraud [FCA, 2017b]); and there might be a regulatory perception that the message on installing adequate ABC systems has been broadly transmitted to the industry. However, the value of its enforcement actions should not be underestimated. At the time of imposition, both the fines against Aon (£5.25) and Willis (£7m) were the highest penalties for financial crime ever issued by the FSA. Further, Aon, Willis and JLTS are all market leaders, indicating that the FCA is minded towards imposing penalties against big market players. Finally, as in the case of Willis, where the SFO declined to act upon the FSA findings (Macalister, 2011), the regulatory approach was the only social control response to the misconduct.

The absence of a larger number of enforcement actions means that the FCA response in this area is oriented predominately towards preventative and supervisory rather than towards reactive work against noncompliance. This brings the regime closer to a *compliance-oriented* enforcement model (on this see Black, 2008; Gray, 2006) in which the regulator prefers to rely on negotiation, advice

13 E.g. AON FN 06/01/09.
14 SEC docket. www.sec.gov/spotlight/fcpa/fcpa-cases.shtml.

and persuasion than through mobilising the formal legal process. The negotiation of non-contention is also the default position of the criminal justice response to foreign bribery (Lord and King, this volume). Yet the FCA has the advantage that its supervision is postulated on a particular mode of governance, inaccessible to the SFO: a risk-based and, to an extent, meta-regulation monitoring framework that relies on firms' own internal risk-based compliance programmes.

### 2.2 The surveillance of the markets: risk-based supervision

Risk-based considerations permeate the control of corruption *by* financial institutions, on both sides of the regulatory relationship. A risk-based regulatory approach is necessary since the size of the regulated community makes it too extensive for on-going supervision. The risk-based regulatory framework links the FCA's risk evaluation (risk scoring) with the allocation of ABC supervisory, inspection and enforcement resources. The types of supervisory activities undertaken by the FSA/FCA, as well as the messages distributed through speeches by its enforcement officials (e.g. McDermott, 2012), show that the sectors assessed as posing the highest noncompliance risks are: the commercial insurance sector (wholesale insurance intermediaries have been subjected to enhanced supervision through a follow-up thematic review), investment banking, and asset management platforms. Within these sectors, the practices evaluated at the highest-risk level are two-fold: (1) using third parties to win or retain business (the trading part of the business); and (2) using corporate hospitality, gifts and charity donations (the non-trading part of the business). These 'hotspots' are all within the wholesale and commercial sectors of finance, i.e. the providers of services mostly for corporate clients or of services that require more sophisticated expertise.

In practice, the FSA/FCA targeted ABC monitoring has significantly consisted of devising specialist inspection programmes – thematic reviews of ABC systems and controls within the 'hotspots' industries (FSA 2010, 2012; thereafter FCA, 2013, 2014). These are aimed at assessing the level of threat to the FSA/FCA's objectives by a *theme* that connects several firms within a sector or market. Thematic reviews are mostly used to evaluate the state of rule-abiding and the level of standards in an area (FCA, 2015), enabling a macro-level perspective of potential financial misconduct. Methodologically, on average, 10–15 firms were visited during a period of 6–9 months. The firm sizes varied, from large global banks and insurance intermediaries to smaller niche providers of banking and insurance services. The inspections commonly consisted of on-site visits, information-gathering on corporate ABC decision-making and policies, and sampling of files on due diligence to ascertain whether the firm fully understood the business case for using third parties, and whether it appropriately assessed and documented the associated risks.

Thematic reviews are an important basis for designing regulatory expectations of proper compliance systems, particularly through the identification of 'good'/'poor' corporate practices 'on the ground' that are then fed into the Authority's guidance on ABC compliance. However, aside from their function as a diagnostic and supervisory tool, thematic reviews serve also a deterrence function as they single out particular industries or activities for added scrutiny. Such efforts are attempts to increase firms' expectations that their violations will be discovered, thereby motivating greater compliance (Short and Toffel, 2008). The conduct of thematic reviews remains a prominent supervisory tool since, after the crisis, risk-based supervision shifted from mostly firm-specific to enhanced sector and cross-sector analysis, and thematic work (FCA, 2015). The focus on the key drivers of risk is in line with the post-crisis FCA judgment-oriented and intrusive supervisory style, and its credible deterrence enforcement philosophy (Wheatley, 2013).

## 2.3 'Meta-regulation' framework: a hybrid regime

Principle 3, and the demands that firms devise internal ABC systems and controls, continuously measure their performance and improve the systems and controls in consequence, contributes towards a type of a meta-regulatory governance of corruption *by* financial institutions. In meta-regulation systems (Parker, 2002), regulators command firms to analyse the risks that their operations pose to regulatory objectives, and to design internal plans, controls and regulations to mitigate these risks. The FCA ABC exhibits salient meta-regulatory traits, though it should still be considered a hybrid regime as there are some detours from a full meta-regulation system.

As in a true meta-regulatory regime, the FCA places a significant amount of responsibility on regulatees for interpreting the rules, devising compliance systems and achieving outcomes that are aligned with Principle 3. Coupled with this, it considerably relies on ABC commitment and actions by senior management of financial institutions, and regulations with management-based commands are commonly the most salient forms of meta-regulation (Coglianese and Mendelson, 2010). Thus the FCA's ABC monitoring also has traits of 'regulating at a distance' (Parker, 2002), in which regulatory oversight focuses on the quality of regulatees' self-assessment of the alignment between their compliance systems and regulatory outcomes and on the actions that they take in response (Gilad, 2010: 488). The FCA's Financial Crime Guide (FCA, 2016), a regulatory document without a binding legal power, asks firms to conduct such activities. It asks firms to self-evaluate their operations and corporate culture against the FCA financial crime prevention duty, set up appropriate risk-based systems and controls of ABC threats, continuously measure their performance, and provide evidence that the solutions that they were implementing resulted in relevant outcomes. The Guide leaves space for different responses by firms that will lead to compliance, and it does not replace the need for firms to still rely principally on interpreting the rules (FCA, 2016). Both of these requirements encourage the need for active firm 'thinking' of how to achieve the desired regulatory outcomes in practice, and can lead to what Gilad (2010) terms 'double-loop' or 'systemic' learning in which the continuous self-assessment can lead to readjustment to improve performance.

However, the hybridity of the regime lies in the prescriptive SYSC rules which impose more command-oriented expectations, and the monitoring and enforcement is also based on assessing (non)compliance with them. In addition, the ways in which the FCA treats the Guide and other regulatory documents with no legally binding powers, brings them closer to prescribed commands, complicating further the nature of the regime. A firm cannot be held in breach of the rules solely on the basis of not following an FCA guide, yet there are significant expectations that regulatees must familiarise themselves not only with the 'hard' law requirements of FSMA and the Handbook, but also with any 'soft' law such as guides and with purely policy papers (e.g. 'Dear CEO' letters, officials' speeches). If the FCA has published guidance or other materials on the misconduct, or has publicly called for an improvement in standards, these may escalate the enforcement response (i.e. dealing with the noncompliance through sanctions rather than through negotiations) and can also aggravate any penalty. The same is the case with past FCA enforcement actions on the same type of misconduct. For example, the FCA has expressed 'disappointment' that some of the visited insurers were not aware of its past enforcement actions (FCA, 2014), and the misconduct by Willis and JLTS was assessed as more serious because the FSA had already undertaken previous enforcement actions in the area. This means that the FCA considers previous enforcement as a type of public call for an improvement in standards. Although as an administrative agency the FCA is not bound by precedent (Black, 2008), it uses 'precedents' as signalling cases that should have been intercepted by the industry. Previous regulatory messages of all kinds are therefore frequently emphasised as an aggravating factor when imposing a penalty, so this is an important mechanism through which the Authority increases their impact, and the impact of formal enforcement actions on general deterrence. These more command- and control-oriented messages might also contribute to the ability of firms and their management to interpret and apply the regulations within their internal self-assessment risk-based frameworks.

## 3 Risk-assessment frameworks (and their flaws) within corporations

On the regulatee side of the relationship, ABC risk-based activities broadly mirror certain central elements of risk-based frameworks of regulators (see Black and Baldwin, 2010: 184–185). Firms need to: (1) determine the bribery and corruption risks posed by their business; (2) determine the firm's own risk appetite and risk tolerance; (3) develop a system for assessing such risks; (4) score these along the continuum low-high risk; and (5) link the scoring mechanism, and the allocation of compliance and audit resources in a targeted manner.

In determining ABC risks (the first element), the FCA's wide definition requires that firms are aware of a range of internal and external risks: (1) internal business model risks: use of third parties to win business; (2) internal organisational structure and culture risks, which arise from non-trading parts of the business and might downplay the extent of risks: claims of staff expenses, gifts, hospitality, donations, recruitment, training and remuneration; (3) external business risks: the characteristics of the third parties, jurisdictions and extent of exposure to public officials; and (4) external regulatory criticism risks: evolving legal and regulatory requirements. However, despite the comprehensive definition, a common problem in practice is limited self-diagnostic work. For example, firms may focus on understanding risks from individual relationships with third parties but not on understanding business-wide risks. Further common failures are limited attempts to understand the risks posed by other participants in the insurance chain (solicitors, introducers, etc.), beyond the immediate business relationship (FCA, 2014). The narrow focus prevents an appropriate identification of the firm's risk appetite (the second element). Also, as with any risk-based framework (Black and Baldwin, 2010), the proper scoring of extant and the prediction of emerging corruption risks, depends on having an adequate understanding of where the risks lie. Aon, for example, had adequate due diligence policies regarding UK-based introducers, but it did not have matching procedures for introducers based overseas. This shows an adequate identification of the internal business risks behind using third parties, but a failure to identify the external risk of regulatory criticism for inadequately dealing with third parties based overseas.

Problems also exist in the systems that firms develop to assess and score the level of corruption risks once they have been identified (the third and fourth element). Imperfect risk assessment is often the problem with risk-based models – a prominent example of this in finance was the failure to adequately assess the packaging, sale and acquisition of complex securitised products before the credit crisis. In the ABC area, imperfect risk assessments occur in the guise of inadequate due diligence of the political links of recipients of corporate hospitality and, more commonly, of third parties (e.g. FCA, 2014). This might entail superficial risk ratings (e.g. on the basis of jurisdiction), but without factoring in any connections to Politically Exposed Persons (FSA, 2010). Inadequate risk assessments of third parties represent a persistent problem in the insurance industry as the FCA found significant due diligence weaknesses in almost half of the individual relationships it examined in its follow-up review (FCA, 2014).

Any flaws in the risk assessment have significant 'blinding' effects for the fourth (scoring) and fifth (targeting compliance resources) elements of the framework. There are particular expectations that firms will use a risk-based approach to approving, monitoring and reviewing their individual business relationships (FCA, 2016). The identification of higher-risk situations should attract more extensive due diligence, and involvement by compliance staff and senior managers. However, though most intermediaries undertake some risk assessment, common failures occur with regard to linking their systems and on-going monitoring to the level of the identified risk (FCA, 2014), and in the employing of the same due diligence and sign off, regardless of the risk classification (FSA, 2012). The industry has been slow in internalising the extensive regulatory expectations on targeting compliance resources towards comprehensive, continuous and responsive third parties' risk assessment.

There is a developing trend of the FCA placing expectations that firms will employ their compliance resources to act as 'regulators' in their own right and use their business channels to enforce compliant behaviour beyond the firm's immediate reach. Firms are encouraged to extend their governance function beyond their employees, and beyond the immediate third-party contact towards other parties in the insurance chain (FCA, 2014). The expectation is to monitor the third parties that the firm conducts business with also regarding their own ABC compliance potential, and to the extent that the firm is satisfied that the intermediary has adequate controls to detect and prevent bribery to generate business (FCA, 2014). Good practices were identified where the firm included specific ABC clauses in contracts with third parties, and where it provided ABC training to third parties. This extension of private governance over other private businesses is an addition to a growing trend of expanding expectations placed on companies to monitor their supply chain. Comparative examples can be found in the use of some corporate social responsibility (CSR) programmes by multi-national corporations that focus on monitoring compliance with workers' rights, health and safety, and environmental regulations by third-party contractors in foreign jurisdictions. For example, after severe criticisms of grave breaches of workers' rights in some of its China-based third-party factories, Apple adopted a policy of regularly monitoring the workplace conditions with a threat of severing business relationships with noncompliant factories (Cedillo Torres et al., 2012). This use of CSR as a form of private transnational governance (Vogel, 2008) by multinational corporations, and the monitoring of third parties due to FCA regulatory expectations, have an equal effect of placing firms in the position of 'regulators' of compliant practices and cultures in other companies. At the threat of severing business relationships, these might be motivated towards compliant behaviour themselves. This provides a welcome addition to the complex network of public-private approaches to governing corruption *by* financial institutions.

### 3.1 The involvement of senior management

In line with true meta-regulatory regimes (Parker, 2002: 57–60), the FCA relies on top management commitment to proper ABC compliance systems. Senior management is considered 'responsible for ensuring that the firm conducts its business with integrity and tackles the risk that the firm, or anyone acting on its behalf, engages in bribery and corruption' (FSA, 2012: 8). Senior managers may suffer regulatory penalties for both their own misconduct and for supervisory failings.[15] However, the established challenges in pinpointing the extent of knowledge and levels of implication of individual managers (Coffee, 1981), have also been an obstacle to bringing successful FSA/FCA actions against managers for organisational noncompliance.[16] Therefore, an important regulatory development is the expectation that there is a clear charting of the organisational ABC decision-making tree so that the persons with ultimate

---

15  COCON (individual and senior managers' rules in the banking industry) and APER (Statements of Principle in the non-banking sector) chapters of the FCA Handbook.
16  E.g. Pottage v FSA 2010/33.

responsibility for ABC compliance are clearly documented. This mirrors the current enhanced requirements of firms through the Senior Managers Regime (SMR) in the banking and insurance industries to certify the actual extent of internal responsibilities in managerial decision-making rather than to rely on the formal job title of the individual (e.g. Head of Risk).[17]

Management commitment is promoted through the regulatory expectations that managers should be actively engaged with the firm's ABC: (1) *procedures*, and (2) *culture*. The procedural expectations concern demands of active engagement with the design, implementation, review and fixing of ABC controls (e.g. FCA, 2013). Such attitudes are expected also with regard to spotting and remedying flawed ABC controls. The fact that JLTS and its senior management had demonstrated to the FCA that they treated the matter 'with the utmost seriousness' represented a mitigating factor to the amount of the fine.[18] These assessments of management determination and compliance attitudes can have a significant impact in the risk-scoring systems of the FCA, since they can lower the 'net risk' of the firm where the regulator has general confidence in the team's ability to control relevant risks (Baldwin et al., 2012).

The thematic reviews, however, found significant deficiencies in management oversight and a poor understanding of the bribery risks threating the firm (FSA, 2012; thereafter FCA, 2013). In the firms who underperformed in this area, the poor understanding was due to an inadequate information relay, for example, there would be little or no information sent to the Board about higher-risk third-party relationships, or on new legislation (FSA, 2010). This negatively affects addressing corruption risks through managerial oversight; for example, the JLTS senior management did not recognise that the company's third-party assessment framework was not implemented properly so took no steps to address the noncompliance. Much of the FCA guidance concerns the relay of quality management information on ABC matters.

The FCA expectations of senior management regarding *culture* show the potentially deep reach of regulatory actions into changing profit-oriented towards ethical organisational environments. These concern the setting of an ethical 'tone from the top'; designing business models with ABC goals in mind, and close 'management' of the firm's human resources. Senior management is expected to 'foster a culture that promotes an ethical environment and requires employees to adhere to high standards of integrity' (FSA, 2012: 12). The FSA/FCA finds good governance examples where management demonstrated leadership on financial crime issues through leading by example in personal ABC compliance (FSA, 2012), and clearly displaying to staff their interest in monitoring corruption risks (FSA, 2010). 'Tones from the top' have consistently been emphasised as crucial for ethical corporate cultures (Clinard, 1983), though the net should be cast wider since much behaviour in finance is shaped by interactions with significant others, i.e. middle managers and peers.

17  SYSC 4.7R.
18  JLTS FN 19/12/2013.

The greater FCA intervention into dismantling criminogenic organisational cultures is further exemplified by the expectations that managers ensure the firm considers compliance with ABC legislation when discussing business opportunities, and designing new products and services, and to avoid an 'ask no questions' culture to generating business (FCA, 2016). Finally, managers are expected to engage with the remuneration and quality of staff. Incentives, or income-tied bonus programmes, are an important contributing factor to noncompliance with financial regulation (see, e.g. on retail finance, Moloney, 2012), as they entice staff to focus on generating profit and undue risk-taking at the cost of compliance. The FSA/FCA intervention in this area has caused palpable changes, in particular in wholesale insurance – its follow-up review found that most intermediaries had implemented remuneration and bonus structures that did not depend solely on the amount of generated business, and in some cases, they also took account of good compliance behaviour (FCA, 2014). The binding of staff payment with compliance is welcomed as it can incentivise positive sales behaviour.

In its first thematic review, the FSA identified the lack of adequate human resources in firms (poor staff vetting and training) as a key ABC governance problem (FSA, 2010). This prompted expectations that firms conduct their own gatekeeping of below the Board, sales and front-office staff, in addition to the FCA's own extensive SMR and APER approval processes aimed at managerial and top compliance roles. This concerns: vetting new staff and operating a private disciplinary regime for ABC breaches; ensuring that the individuals responsible for ABC compliance have the appropriate seniority, experience, credibility and independence from the Board; and providing ABC training (FCA, 2016). The focus on instilling an ethical culture through hiring individuals with matching values and sanctioning and firing noncompliant ones contributes towards eliminating the process of 'assortative matting' (Apel and Paternoster, 2009) in which companies with lax ethical cultures might attract those who already have less demanding personal ethical systems and/or knowledge of how to act upon criminal opportunities (also Babiak and Hare, 2006). Ultimately, this will result in a self-selection gatekeeping function of companies in financial markets. As of yet, the provision of ABC staff training has been the most significant improvement in industry compliance (FCA, 2014). The problems of 'cosmetic compliance', however, with respect to the quality and depth of training programmes challenges the extent of industry commitment to such programmes.

### 3.2 Implementation challenges

A significant challenge for meta-regulation is the fact that it depends upon business motivations, commitment to values that support compliance (Gunningham, 2011) and a broad business understanding of regulatory expectations. The absence of these factors has in practice led to inadequate implementation of existing risk-assessment frameworks, 'cosmetic compliance' with regulation and a mismatch between regulatory requirements and corporate understanding of them.

The potential hazards of dissonance between risk-assessment policies and their implementation in practice were evidenced in the case of JLTS. The firm had in place an elaborate system of scoring the risks behind overseas introducers through assigning them a certain number of alarm bells (the '7 Alarm Bells' policy). The number of alarm bells assigned to an overseas introducer was linked to a higher/lower audit level of sign-off required to authorise the business relationship. For example, if an overseas introducer was assigned six or more alarm bells, the relationship had to be approved by the JLTS Board. However, in practice, the staff incorrectly assessed high-risk jurisdictions (e.g. Argentina) as low risk in some cases, and in other cases, it did not assign an alarm bell to specific risks that existed in the relationship. This meant that the correct number of alarm bells was not assigned to an overseas introducer, preventing the adequate level of scrutiny by senior management. The ABC policy, therefore, represented a well-conceptualised risk assessment mechanism with targeted audit resources. Yet in the implementation of the scoring system in practice, JLTS staff did not follow the policy for a number of years and were not monitored or challenged during this period.

The potential for a discrepancy between internal firm policies and their implementation in practice raises further problems along the lines of 'cosmetic compliance' (Krawiec, 2003), in which firms' internal risk management systems are simply cosmetic in essence, with proper form but not substance. 'Cosmetic compliance' was, for example, identified where: firms designed ABC policies but did not make them easily accessible to staff; firms had in place approvers of third-party relationships but these were working within the broking department; and staff asked third parties to fill out irrelevant forms (e.g. individuals filling in forms aimed at corporate entities). These show that there is little engagement with the substance of regulation since the systems implementation is partial and on occasion symbolic. The expansion of the expectations of, and reliance on, senior management can mitigate some of these problems, though it remains to be seen whether this will lead to a more receptive corporate culture and more compliance-oriented business motives.

Even if there is business commitment towards ABC compliance, the meta-regulatory traits of the regime may impair the ability of regulatees to adequately interpret regulatory expectations. There may be a mismatch between compliance outcomes and what the firm thinks it should be doing to achieve them. For example, some firms in the reviews prohibited improper payments in their compliance codes, but had no other controls; other firms neglected appropriate staff training in the belief that robust payment controls are sufficient for achieving ABC compliance (FCA, 2014). Some of these challenges have been mitigated by an overall regulatory expectation that firms need to employ proactive thinking and design a continuous, responsive and adaptive risk assessment process, capable of identifying new or emerging risks and modifying the extant procedures in response (FCA, 2016). However, some ABC expectations, even with provided guidance, could leave firms at risk of enforcement actions since they impose a significant interpretative onus on them. This is further complicated by the overall principles-based nature of the regime: in a true PBR, firms always need more guidance, and where 'the balance should be struck between firms thinking for themselves and the regulators providing guidance is endlessly contested, and each thinks the other should be doing more' (Black, 2008: 443). JLTS was visited three times by FSA supervisors, who negotiated with the firm to comply with the ABC requirements, yet despite the fact that the firm undertook improvement work and strengthened its policies, the lack of implementation ultimately landed the firm in enforcement. This challenge cannot be easily resolved as the provision of more guidance depends on further FCA market reviews, which are risk-based, resource-intensive and protracted.

## 4 Conclusion

Corruption *by* financial institutions significantly threatens the integrity of the UK and comparative financial markets. This has led the UK regulator to prioritise bribery and corruption as risks to its regulatory objectives, in a bid to also avoid regulatory blame for untoward financial behaviour and in line with the expanding criminal justice control of (transnational) bribery. Yet the size of the market poses special challenges for an effective oversight through a command and control approach, resulting in the development of a range of innovative modes of governance. The reliance on a comprehensive guide on expected ABC corporate behaviour, on the basis of thematic diagnostic work, is coupled with a parallel development of a type of meta-regulatory regime in which firms are enlisted to think proactively about how to achieve ABC outcomes. The regulator's 'governance at a distance' is maintained via extensive expectations (though not rules) of responsive corporate procedures of ABC risk-assessment, and of senior management activism. The governance is expanded via expectations of ABC-infused corporate business models, and especially through enlisting firms as 'governors' of further participants in the supply chain. Though the regime can be assessed as comprehensive and increasing, issues such as 'creative compliance', mismatches between risk-assessment polices and implementation 'on the ground', and ultimately, the reliance on business compliance commitment and proper understanding of regulatory expectations, question whether it represents the public-private regulatory panacea on tackling bribery in industries in general.

## Bibliography

Alldridge P (2012) The UK Bribery Act: 'The Caffeinated Younger Sibling of the FCPA'. *Ohio State Journal* 73(5): 1181–1216.

Apel R and Paternoster R (2009) Understanding 'Criminogenic' Corporate Culture: What White-Collar Crime Researchers Can Learn from Studies of the Adolescent Employment–Crime Relationship, in S Simpson and D Weisburd (eds.), *The Criminology of White-Collar Crime*, 15–34. New York: Springer.

Babiak P and Hare RD (2006) *Snakes in Suits: When Psychopaths Go to Work*. New York: Regan Books.

Baldwin R, Martin C and Martin L (2012) *Understanding Regulation: Theory, Strategy, and Practice.* Oxford, UK: Oxford University Press.

BBA (2014) *Anti-Bribery and Corruption Guidance,* www.bba.org.uk/policy/financial-crime/anti-bribery-and-corruption/anti-bribery-and-corruption-guidance/ [accessed 31.10.2017].

Black J (2005) The Emergence of Risk-based Regulation and the New Public Management in the UK. *Public Law* (Autumn), 512–549.

Black J (2008) Forms and Paradoxes of Principles-based Regulation. *Capital Markets Law Journal* 3(4): 425–457.

Black J and Baldwin R (2010) Really Responsive Risk-based Regulation. *Law and Policy* 32(2): 181–213.

Cedillo Torres C, Garcia-French M, Hordijk R, Nguyen K and Olup L (2012) Four Case Studies on Corporate Social Responsibility: Do Conflicts Affect a Company's Corporate Social Responsibility Policy? *Utrecht Law Review* 8(3): 51–73.

Clinard BM (1983), *Corporate Ethics and Crime: The Role of Middle Management.* Beverley Hills, CA: Sage.

Coffee JC, Jr (1981) No Soul to Damn: No Body to Kick – An Unscandalized Inquiry into the Problem of Corporate Punishment. *Michigan Law Review* 79(3): 386–459.

Coglianese C and Mendelson E (2010) Meta-Regulation and Self-Regulation, in Baldwin R, Cave M and Lodge M (eds.), *The Oxford Handbook of Regulation.* New York: Oxford University Press.

Cole M (2009) *The FSA's Agenda for Fighting Financial Crime (Speech).* www.fsa.gov.uk/pages/Library/Communication/Speeches/2009/1119_mc.shtml [accessed 31.07.17].

FCA (2013) *Anti-Money Laundering and Anti-Bribery and Corruption Systems and Controls: Asset Management and Platform Firms,* TR13/9, www.fca.org.uk/publication/thematic-reviews/tr13-09.pdf [accessed 15.07.2017].

FCA (2014) *Managing Bribery and Corruption Risk in Commercial Insurance Broking (Update),* TR14/17, www.fca.org.uk/publication/thematic-reviews/tr14–17.pdf [accessed 16.07.2017].

FCA (2015) *The FCA's Approach to Advancing Its Objectives.* www.fca.org.uk/publication/corporate/fca-approach-advancing-objectives-2015.pdf [accessed 01/08/17].

FCA (2016) *Financial Crime: A Guide for Firms.* http://fshandbook.info/FS/html/FCA/FC/link/PDF [accessed 08.08.2017].

FCA (2017a) *Risk Management.* www.fca.org.uk/about/supervision/risk-management [accessed 30.09.2017].

FCA (2017b) *Annual Business Plan 2017/18,* www.fca.org.uk/publication/business-plans/business-plan-2017–18.pdf [accessed 01.10.2017].

FSA (2010) *Anti-Bribery and Corruption in Commercial Insurance Broking: Reducing the Risk of Illicit Payments or Inducements to Third Parties,* www.riskavert.com/wp-content/uploads/2011/10/UK-Bribery-Act-Financial-Services.pdf [accessed 13.08.2017].

FSA (2012) *Anti-Bribery and Corruption Systems and Controls in Investment Banks,* www.fca.org.uk/publication/corporate/fsa-anti-bribery-investment-banks.pdf [accessed 19.08.2017]

Gilad S (2010) It Runs in the Family: Meta-regulation and Its Siblings. *Regulation & Governance* 4: 485–506.

Gobert J and Punch M (2003) *Corporate Crime.* London: Butterworths/LexisNexis.

Gray G (2006) The Regulation of Corporate Violations: Punishment, Compliance, and the Blurring of Responsibility. *British Journal of Criminology* 46(5): 875–892.

Gunningham N (2011) Strategizing Compliance and Enforcement: Responsive Regulation and Beyond, in Parker C and Nielsen VL (eds.), *Explaining Compliance: Business Responses to Regulation*. Cheltenham, UK: Edward Elgar, 199–221.

Helleiner E and Pagliari S (2010) The End of Self-Regulation? Hedge Funds and Derivatives in Global Financial Governance, in Helleiner E, Pagliari S and Zimmermann H (eds.), *Global Finance in Crisis: The Politics of International Regulatory Change*. London: Routledge.

Hood C (2007) What Happens When Transparency Meets Blame-Avoidance? *Public Management Review* 9(2): 191–210.

House of Commons (2017) *Financial Services: Contribution to the Economy (briefing paper)*, Number 6193. London: House of Commons.

Jordanoska A (2017) Case Management in Complex Fraud Trials: Actors and Strategies in Achieving Procedural Efficiency. *International Journal of the Law in Context* 13(3): 336–355.

Krawiec KD (2003) Cosmetic Compliance and the Failure of Negotiated Governance. *Washington University Law Quarterly* 81(2): 487–544.

Lessig L (2013) Institutional Corruptions, *Edmond J. Safra Ctr. For Ethics, Working Papers*, No. 1, http://papers.ssrn.com/sol3/papers.cfm?abstract_id=2233582 [accessed 20.05.2017].

Levi M (2010) Policing Financial Crimes, in Pontell HN and Geis G (eds.), *International Handbook of White-collar and Corporate Crime*. Dordrecht, The Netherlands: Kluwer, 588–606.

Lord N (2014) *Regulating Corporate Bribery in International Business: Anti-Corruption in the UK and Germany*. London: Routledge.

Lord N and Levi M (2017) Organizing the Finances For and the Finances From Transnational Corporate Bribery. *European Journal of Criminology* 14(3): 365–389.

Macalister T (2011) Insurance Broker Willis Fined £7m by FSA, *The Guardian*, www.theguardian.com/business/2011/jul/21/willis-limited-fined-by-fsa [accessed 31.07.2017].

McDermott T (2012) Strengthening Defences: Tackling Financial Crime from the Regulator's Perspective (speech). www.fsa.gov.uk/library/communication/speeches/2012/0926-tm.shtml [accessed 31/07/17].

Moloney N (2012) The Investor Model Underlying the EU's Investor Protection Regime: Consumers or Investors? *European Business Organization Law Review* 13: 169–193.

O'Brien J (2013) Culture Wars: Rate Manipulation, Institutional Corruption, and the Lost Underpinnings of Market Conduct Regulation. *Edmond J. Safra Working Papers*, No. 14, https://ssrn.com/abstract=2277172 [accessed 25.05.2017].

Parker C (2002) *The Open Corporation*. Cambridge, UK: Cambridge University Press.

Pontell HN, Black WK and Geis G (2014) Too Big to Fail, Too Powerful to Jail? On the Absence of Criminal Prosecutions after the 2008 Financial Meltdown. *Crime, Law and Social Change* 61(1): 1–13.

Rose-Ackerman S and Palifka BJ (2016) *Corruption and Government: Causes, Consequences, And Reform*, (2nd ed.). Cambridge, UK: Cambridge University Press.

Salter MS (2010) *Lawful but Corrupt: Gaming and the Problem of Institutional Corruption in the Private Sector* (Harvard Business School Working Paper 11–060), www.hbs.edu/faculty/Publication%20Files/11–060.pdf [accessed 04.09.2017].

Salter MS (2013) *Short-Termism at Its Worst: How Short-Termism Invites Corruption and What to Do About It* (Edmond J. Safra Ctr. For Ethics, Working Paper No. 5, 2013), available at http://papers.ssrn.com/sol3/papers.cfm?abstract_id=2247545 [accessed 17.09.2017].

Short JL and Toffel MW (2008) Coerced Confessions: Self-Policing in the Shadow of the Regulator. *Journal of Law, Economics, & Organization* 24(1): 45–71.

Thompson DF (1995) *Ethics in Congress: From Individual to Institutional Corruption.* Washington, DC: The Brookings Institution.

Transparency International (2017) *How Do You Define Corruption?* www.transparency. org/what-is-corruption#define [accessed 07.07.2017].

Vogel D (2008) Private Global Business Regulation. *Annual Review of Political Science* 11(1): 261–282.

Wheatley M (2013) *The Changing Face of Financial Crime (Speech).* www.fca.org.uk/ news/speeches/the-changing-face-of-financial-crime [accessed 31.07.17].

# 10 Banks assessing corruption risk

## A risky undertaking

*Liliya Gelemerova, Jackie Harvey and Petrus C. van Duyne*

## 1 Introduction

The authorities have increasingly imposed tasks on business to lend support in the fight against acquisitive crime, including corruption. Business is expected to risk-categorise partners and clients to know where to invest the most anti-corruption effort. Regulators' focus on country risk, as opposed to case-specific risk, means businesses' primary driver in risk-categorising partners and clients is their country rather than their conduct. This creates unhelpful bias. The situation is exacerbated by the lack of constructive guidance from legislators and regulators on risk assessment and mitigation. As a result, banks, sitting on the frontline of the corruption-related anti-money laundering (AML) fight, may choose to take a blanket approach by de-risking, i.e. deeming clients linked to a specific country as being outside risk appetite. This chapter will examine: (i) how banks approach risk; and (ii) challenges banks face in the context of UK and US anti-corruption and related AML legislation, particularly the relativity of country risk and the intricacy of the Politically Exposed Person (PEP) definition, a category introduced to purportedly help the finance industry fight corruption. This chapter argues that while country risk should be considered, the key deciding factor in risk-categorising should be client-specific risk, i.e. the client's conduct in the context of the respective industry, combined with product risk.

## 2 Country risk: a moveable feast

### 2.1 Banks under fire

Having been castigated for reckless behaviour during the financial crisis, banks continue to find themselves in the regulator's spotlight. In 2017, the UK's Financial Conduct Authority (FCA) fined Deutsche Bank (DB) £163 million for failing to maintain adequate AML controls from 2012 to 2015. According to the FCA (2017, January 30), DB was unable to assess and manage its money laundering risk and engaged in suspicious transactions enabling customers to transfer US$10 billion from Russia to overseas, via DB in the UK, "without detection".

The transactions were mirror trades: a customer in Moscow bought liquid securities in roubles; the same amount of these securities was sold to DB in London for dollars by a related company.

FCA's finding was that DB failed to categorise Russian customers as 'high risk'. As a result, they were not subject to adequate checks.[1] This indicates that regulators expect banks to have country risk assessment factored into a customer's risk assessment and that Russia should be treated as high risk.[2] As to the goal of DB's transactions, it could have been a number of possibilities, including capital flight, tax evasion or concealment of corruption proceeds (or some combination). However, it remains unclear[3] whether they entailed crime proceeds. Caesar (2016) noted:

> To inspect the trades . . . was like standing too close to an Impressionist painting – you saw the brushstrokes and missed the lilies. These transactions had nothing to do with pursuing profit. They were a way to expatriate money . . . Mirror trades are not inherently illegal . . . A client might want to benefit . . . from the difference between the local and the foreign price of a stock . . . because the individual transactions involved in mirror trades did not directly contravene any regulations, some employees . . . [at DB Russia] at the time den[ied] that such activity was improper.

DB's case illustrates a bank can be fined even in the absence of proven crime proceeds, if the regulator decides the bank has failed to demonstrate it had assessed the risk.

There are many complex issues that banks need to consider in customer relationships, such as: does the rationale behind a transaction make sense; does a customer pose sanctions-related risks;[4] is a customer involved in corruption or other acquisitive crime, or in money laundering? Sometimes these

---

1  DB was also fined US$425 million by the New York State Department of Financial Services (DFS) and agreed to install a monitor. The DFS too noted Russia was high risk and stated that "greed and corruption motivated the DB Moscow traders" (DFS, 2017, January 30). This appears to generalise even though not all traders in Moscow were corrupt and many raised concerns, but their supervisor was dismissive and showed "hostility". He was central to the scheme and, allegedly, took a bribe to facilitate it. According to Caesar (2017), the supervisor was an American. Further, according to the DFS, the suspicious transactions, including transactions involving a counterparty referred to in Russian mainstream media as having its licence suspended by Russia's authorities for similar mirror trades, were cleared through DB in New York. This means that staff in the USA failed to see the red flags. It remains a question to what degree banks, in clearing transactions, can identify red flags and how consistent the approach is across the industry.

2  This period coincided partly with the introduction of international economic sanctions in relation to Russia over its conflict with Ukraine.

3  At the time of writing this chapter – mid-2017.

4  The risk of breaching economic restrictions such as the international sanctions imposed in relation to Iran and Russia.

risks are connected. The legal concept of money laundering has been defined so broadly that any handling of corruption proceeds, even the mere transfer, would count as laundering. These interconnected issues place banks in a difficult position. If a customer has used the bank's infrastructure to pay or receive a bribe and the bank has failed to identify and report the transaction to the authorities, the bank may face penalties for AML deficiencies.[5]

## 2.2 Placing focus on geography

How does the bank recognise the risk of laundering corruption proceeds when facing a similar scenario to that of DB?

### 2.2.1 Transparency International's CPI

The approach taken to identify risks varies, but geography is often a key driver behind client risk scoring. Most banks use Transparency International's (TI) Corruption Perception Index (CPI), among other information sources.[6] Countries that score well are deemed low risk.

But placing emphasis on geography in assessing risk is "risky" in itself, as risky transactions in "low-risk" countries may be overlooked. Based on the 2016 CPI, if we divide countries into three groups – low (score between 100 and 67), medium (66 to 33) and high risk (32 to 0)[7] – which is how banks usually classify clients (sometimes with sub-categories[8]) – the USA, Germany, Norway, France and the UK would be low risk. Russia, Ukraine and Kazakhstan would be high risk. The UAE, Qatar, Greece, Italy, Saudi Arabia, Oman, Bahrain, Kuwait, Malaysia, Cuba, Turkey, Belarus, Brazil, India and China would be medium. If we are to divide the countries into two groups – highly corrupt and less corrupt – these medium countries (apart from the UAE and Qatar), being under the median score of 50, will fall into the highly corrupt group.

The relativity of the CPI or any perception-based index is evident. Respondents in some societies may not feel they can freely form and express an opinion on governance processes or they simply do not question the status quo.

---

5 In addition to violating AML laws for handling corruption proceeds, banks need to be wary of breaching anti-corruption laws by generating corruption proceeds themselves (for instance, by hiring politicians' children for leverage in gaining business).
6 TI is a global non-government anti-corruption organisation.
7 TI (2017b) defines corruption as "the abuse of entrusted power for private gain" (www.transparency.org/what-is-corruption/). The CPI currently ranks 176 countries on a scale from 100 (very clean) to 0 (highly corrupt) (TI, 2017d). In 2016 Norway was 85, Germany – 81, the UK – 81, USA – 74, France – 69; the UAE – 66, Qatar – 61, Malaysia – 49, Cuba – 47, Italy – 47, Saudi Arabia – 46, Oman – 45, Greece – 44, Bahrain – 43, Kuwait – 41, Turkey – 41. Belarus, Brazil, China and India were 40, which was a better score than in 2015: 32, 38, 37 and 38 respectively. Russia, Ukraine and Kazakhstan scored 29.
8 For instance, the high-risk category can be divided into: high-one, high-two and high-three, followed by "outside risk appetite".

Consequently, perception indices do not necessarily objectively measure corruption or how closely business and government are intertwined: they represent opinions.[9] One would expect that in forming their country risk appetite, banks would take the CPI as a starting point rather than as the sole deciding factor.[10]

### 2.2.2 FCPA investigations

The relativity of corruption perception is also evident in FCPA[11] statistics. In the West, foreign bribery appears to have had greater resonance than domestic bribery. The USA pioneered the fight against foreign bribery by introducing the FCPA in 1977.[12] As the FCPA 2012 guide highlights, the US Congress enacted the FCPA in response to revelations, in the wake of the Watergate scandal, of widespread bribery of foreign officials[13] by US companies. Four decades later, it is clear that companies from the industrialised world – there is a long list of these – have not stopped offending, even though TI's index suggests these countries are low risk. Therefore, banks must consider their clients' international operations and the industry risk, and aim at having global standards.

FCPA enforcement actions launched by the SEC from 2010 to 2015 also shows that China features most on this list as a destination of corrupt payments. Other destinations include Saudi Arabia, Qatar, Bahrain, Greece, Russia and Italy. However, if we are to consider TI's index (as discussed earlier), these countries (apart from Russia) are "medium risk" (in the three risk-groups scenario).

### 2.2.3 FATF's reports

As the international AML-standard setting body and the issuer of Mutual Evaluation Reports (MERs) on countries' AML systems, the Financial Action

---

9  According to TI's methodology, countries must be assessed by at least three sources (e.g. the Economist Intelligence Unit, the World Bank) to appear in the CPI. These sources draw their data from surveys of the opinions of business people and experts (TI, 2017a, 2017c). The methodology has been criticised, including for the relativity of perception. Campbell (2013) pointed out: "A growing body of literature suggests that biases which influence corruption perception statistics prevent them from forming a valid basis for comparison between countries or over time. In spite of the limited validity of these corruption perception statistics, many lawyers in the United States advise their clients to use them to help calibrate FCPA compliance programs in their international operations" (see also Cobham, 2013; Hough, 2016).

10  One should also consider how serious a country is in investigating domestic corruption (as opposed to foreign bribery). One has to also assess how independent a country's judiciary, law enforcement bodies and prosecution are from the ruling elite.

11  The Foreign Corrupt Practices Act prohibits the payment of bribes to foreign officials to assist in obtaining or retaining business, and has extra-territorial jurisdiction. It also requires maintaining accurate records.

12  With important amendments in 1988.

13  Cassin, 2012, noted, bribery scandals involving Lockheed in Holland, Japan and Italy helped push US Congress to enact the FCPA. One of the revelations was that Prince Bernhard of the Netherlands had accepted a bribe to influence a deal with the Dutch government to Lockheed's benefit.

Task Force (FATF)[14] provides a source of country risk assessment material. However, the MERs of jurisdictions that score poorly on TI or feature in FCPA cases show insufficient analysis of money laundering statistics, in particular, to reveal a correlation between corruption and Suspicious Activity Reports (SARs). If there is so much corruption in Russia and China, it remains a question why the FATF has not provided any analysis of the suspicious activity reporting on bribes laundering?[15] When evaluating the US, the FATF does not appear to have paid attention to the fact that many US companies have been fined for corruption. One may wonder whether any of the FCPA enforcement actions have been based on SARs,[16] and if not, why the FATF has not investigated such omission.[17]

### 2.2.4 Simplified due diligence

To assess risk adequately, a bank is required by law to identify a company's ultimate beneficial owner(s) (UBO). However, there is scope for interpretations. EU policy makers have defined 'beneficial owner' as holding more than 25%[18] of the shares (see also Campbell, this volume, Chapter 5), and, at the same time, have allowed banks to apply simplified due diligence (SDD) in cases of listed companies (in jurisdictions where disclosure requirements ensure transparency). The third EU AML directive[19] allowed an automatic application of SDD, while the fourth directive[20] seeks to rectify this and explicitly requires risk analysis before SDD is applied. However, the fourth directive also allows customers resident in low-risk areas and public sector entities to be treated as potentially low risk from an AML perspective.

---

14  And FATF-style bodies, e.g. Moneyval.

15  Countries not part of TI's CPI are an interesting case. For instance, Equatorial Guinea, which is a member of an FATF-style organisation, is not part of TI's CPI (but was in 2013) as there is not enough data (a country must be in at least three CPI's data sources to appear in the CPI). One may wonder about banks' risk rating of Equatorial Guinea and the international companies that drill oil there.

16  In theory, one would expect that if a US company is serviced by an overseas branch of a US bank, that branch should apply the same standards as in the headquarters.

17  It is also notable that the FATF's typology reports on corruption fail to provide meaningful analysis of patterns and red flags relating to corruption proceeds management.

18  In the US, for AML purposes, a UBO is an individual who, directly or indirectly, owns 25% or more or a single individual who has significant responsibility to control, manage or direct a legal entity (FinCEN, 2016). For tax purposes, see comments on FATCA below.

19  Directive 2005/60/EC of the European Parliament and of the Council of 26 October 2005 on the prevention of the use of the financial system for the purpose of money laundering and terrorist financing.

20  Directive (EU) 2015/849 of the European Parliament and of the Council of 20 May 2015 on the prevention of the use of the financial system for the purposes of money laundering or terrorist financing, amending Regulation (EU) No 648/2012 of the European Parliament and of the Council, and repealing Directive 2005/60/EC of the European Parliament and of the Council and Commission Directive 2006/70/EC (Text with EEA relevance).

SDD has been commonly understood in the industry as providing a *carte blanche* for not investigating who is behind a company. A bank may not analyse ownership if no shareholder owns over 25% regardless of their jurisdiction (some banks have decreased this to 10% due to the US extraterritorial tax law FATCA[21] requirement to identify US persons holding an interest of 10% or greater). However, if five crime families or five controversial PEPs each own a 20% stake, this may be overlooked unless, in legislation and a bank's policies, it is explicitly stated that ownership has to be understood fully, regardless of jurisdiction. Although 20% is a considerable stake to have, sometimes a stake as low as 10% or even 5% can ensure both influence and considerable financial benefits.

The other problem is that neither EU nor domestic legislators have made clear exactly what SDD means – does it mean no need to:

(i)   identify the owner;
(ii)  document one's understanding of ownership;
(iii) obtain documentary evidence of identity (e.g. copies of passports, proof of address of owners, directors);
(iv)  run searches for adverse news;
(v)   or all in combination (or other)?
(See Gelemerova, 2009, for related issues, and Section 3.1.1)

How do you decide whether risk is low if you do not undertake sufficient research to understand a client's profile fully? By way of example, for a mirror trade involving companies from low-risk jurisdictions or companies in high-risk jurisdictions but with a first layer of shareholders holding each less than 25%, a bank might not investigate who is behind those companies, even though smaller shareholders may be controlled by a high-risk owner. In the era of globalisation of capital, boundaries become increasingly blurred.

## 3 Banks as guardians

The FCPA and UK Bribery Act have extraterritorial jurisdiction.[22] As a result, multinational companies – many have a US and a UK touchpoint – can find themselves liable under both the FCPA and UK Bribery Act. Banks providing financial management facilities to multinational companies are required to be watchful with respect to corrupt payments.

Regulators expect banks' programmes to include clear escalation lines, due diligence procedures, risk assessment processes, monitoring and training. A bank will likely seek to introduce compliance-related, including anti-corruption, clauses

---

21  The Foreign Account Tax Compliance Act.
22  For instance, under the FCPA, wiring US dollars or sending an email through a US-hosted server in furtherance of a corrupt payment will potentially suffice to make a foreign company liable. The UK Bribery Act's bribery offences are based on more conventional principles of jurisdiction. However, its offence of failure to prevent bribery has a broad reach.

in its contracts with clients and obtain their code of ethics and anti-corruption policy (ideally covering, inter alia, hospitality, gifts and entertainment).

However, in the first instance, banks should have clear policies and definitions as the basis for identifying risk. Banks have to understand whether they are facing an immediate corruption risk, i.e. a public sector entity or a company heavily depending on interaction with the state, or, if an individual, a public sector servant (or connected to a public sector servant) or someone who earns substantial income through public sector contracts. In this regard, policy makers have created the PEP concept (discussed later).

### 3.1 Categories of clients

### 3.1.1 Corporates

A bank has to assess the product risk in the context of the client's business and type of entity. When it comes to corruption in the public sector[23], high-risk clients can broadly be:

- companies which depend on state contracts (in terms of sales or supply chain) or on a high level of interaction with government agencies/officials (for instance, companies in such industries as public infrastructure maintenance and construction, and mining that are dependent on the above);
- state entities.

A bank can face a wide range of public sector entities, e.g. government agencies, intergovernmental bodies, municipalities, courts, hospitals, schools, state companies including utilities. It includes any type of entity funded by state money (the taxpayer or money coming from state-controlled sources).

Although entirely possible where corruption is endemic, a state entity itself is unlikely to be the direct recipient of a bribe. Typically, the recipient would be an individual working for that entity. However, a bank can be accused of laundering by processing a state entity's payments to a company under a corruptly assigned contract. Second, where a state entity is not assigning contracts but is granting licences or permits – situations in which a company could receive preferential treatment – a bank has to be wary of dealing with a state entity that has a reputation for systematically engaging in unfair practices. Third, banks have to watch out for outgoing payments that may be part of an embezzlement scheme. Access to state funds can be tempting where governance is weak.

Although the fourth EU directive allows public entities to be subject to SDD (if risk analysis justifies SDD), this does not necessarily mean low risk. Although unclear from legislation, presumably SDD on this occasion should mean no need to obtain documentary evidence of the identity of the individuals who run the entity.

---

23  The UK Bribery Act also criminalises private sector bribery, although it is expected to occur less frequently.

SDD should not be interpreted as negating the need to understand the client's activities and to monitor the client's transactions.

The degree of risk varies depending on the type of organisation and the nature of what they do and what product the bank will offer them.[24] State companies and public sector entities heavily involved in public procurement (e.g. municipalities, hospitals, utilities, commercial companies) are most exposed to risk. If banks start avoiding this risk, instead of managing it, the impact will fall on a range of law-abiding entities, affecting the livelihood of ordinary people.

Definitions of "state company" can vary. Generally, it is a legal entity conducting business on behalf of the government. It can be fully or partially owned by the state. Some banks consider only entities 50% or more owned by the state to be state companies. However, it may be more appropriate for the definition to include the *influence* element, i.e. whether the state has the directing mind by holding a controlling stake. The FCPA guide (2012) talks about the state's degree of control over the entity, including whether key officers and directors of the entity are, or are appointed by, government officials.[25] This should be considered together with ownership of the remainder of the company's shares. In principle, even shareholders holding as little as 5–10% ownership can exert influence in a publicly quoted company, without necessarily meaning significant or critical influence. So the question we would need to ask is whether a company is state-run as opposed to just state-(co)owned.

Some banks can choose to categorise as high risk any entity which has as little as 5% (or less) held by a state. This could be broadly defined as a government-linked entity as opposed to a government-controlled or a government-run entity. Such approach, though, may soon run into difficulty as it will place into the same category both types: companies controlled by the state and companies in which the state is merely an investor that, on balance, does not have more influence than any other stakeholder. Where the state's representatives are not the key decision makers and there is minimal involvement of state money, corruption and embezzlement risk may be lower or non-existent.

How do bona fide companies compare to obscure entities, i.e. companies of unclear track record, lacking transparent ownership and of unknown attitude towards compliance?[26] The risk arising from dealing with a bona fide company operating in a high-risk industry and/or in a high-risk jurisdiction can be mitigated (the one relating to obscure entities can hardly be). A bank may gain comfort from the fact that a client has a robust anti-corruption compliance programme, a transparent ownership that gives rise to no concerns, and is gaining state contracts through transparent tenders.

Ultimately, in either case where a bank's client is either a legitimate company interacting with state entities or a state company, what matters most is the nature of a bank's relationship with the company – what products/services a bank offers to its client. A business banking relationship, i.e. a current account

---

24  Political risk should also be considered.
25  The FCA guidance (July 2017) talks about state ownership over 50% and state control over the company activities.
26  For instance, such entities may be set up by intermediaries to facilitate corruption schemes.

enabling the client to make and receive third-party payments, would typically pose a heightened risk. A bank would need first to document the anticipated account activity and subsequently: (i) ensure it understands the rationale behind each payment, (ii) check whether the client's counterparties are bona fide, and (iii) analyse inconsistencies and red flags (e.g. the lack of a sensible rationale; payments to obscure entities). It is sensible that banks understand the rationale behind a transaction and look into who is behind their client, regardless of jurisdiction, for AML purposes, fraud prevention and credit risk management. For example, a mirror trade occurring between France and the UK – two countries perceived as low risk – may be facilitating tax evasion or may be conducted on behalf of French and UK companies controlled by individuals from the very same jurisdictions that banks consider high risk.

If a bona fide company has gained one contract corruptly but its other contracts have been fairly obtained, a bank would not want to find itself facilitating the funds management relating to that one corrupt contract. What about the rest of the company's activities? Are they safe to handle? One can argue that legislators have defined money laundering so broadly that even indirect exposure to corruption proceeds can be problematic, as corruption proceeds cannot necessarily be isolated from clean proceeds: thus, any funds would be tainted by association. One can only hope that the money laundering interpretation will not be so unreasonably overstretched by regulators to the extent that it becomes prohibitive to bona fide business.

### 3.1.2 Dealing with individuals

PEP DEFINITION

AML legislation requires banks to determine whether their client is a PEP. Originally, the definition focused on foreign PEPs. In 2012, the FATF expanded the requirements[27] to domestic PEPs and PEPs of international organisations, in line with Article 52 of the UNCAC,[28] adopted in 2003. The latter does not specifically refer to the term "PEP" but requires that financial institutions within its jurisdiction verify the identity of customers. This involves taking reasonable steps to determine the identity of beneficial owners of funds deposited into high-value accounts and conduct enhanced scrutiny of accounts sought or maintained by or on behalf of "individuals who are, or have been, entrusted with prominent public functions and their family members and close associates".

Similarly, according to the EU directives, a PEP means a natural person who is or who has been entrusted with a prominent public function.[29] Notably, this should *not* be understood as covering middle-ranking or junior officials.

---

27  It first issued requirements covering PEPs in 2003.
28  United Nations Convention against Corruption.
29  It includes: (i) heads of State, heads of government, ministers and deputy or assistant ministers; (ii) members of parliament or similar legislative bodies; (iii) members of the governing

According to the definition, "family members" includes the PEP's: (i) spouse (or equivalent); (ii) children and their spouses (or equivalent); and (iii) parents. The definition also includes "close associates". This means: (i) natural persons who are known to have joint beneficial ownership of legal entities or legal arrangements, or any other close business relations, with a PEP; and (ii) natural persons who have sole beneficial ownership of a legal entity or legal arrangement which is known to have been set up for the de facto benefit of a PEP.[30] In terms of close associates, while (ii) is rather limited, (i) is broad as "close business relations" can be interpreted in many ways.

The question is why the convention and, similarly, the FATF, focused on the element of prominence and, originally, *foreign* PEPs.

FOCUS ON FOREIGN PEPS

The FCPA, which preceded the convention, FATF's Recommendations and the EU directives, focuses on the bribery of *foreign* officials as it was the result of revelations that US companies were involved in foreign bribery. However, the FCPA covers corrupt payments irrespective of rank.[31] It also includes a wide range of entities, from government and government agencies to municipalities, state companies and public organisations. Arguably, employees of organisations that have been bailed out (e.g. amidst a crisis) by the state could also fall into this category (see Gelemerova, 2010). Consequently, the broad FCPA definition can give rise to practical difficulties.

The fourth EU Directive removed the distinction between foreign and domestic PEPs. However, the focus on country risk,[32] prominence and seniority remained.

---

bodies of political parties; (iv) members of supreme courts, constitutional courts, other high-level judicial bodies, the decisions of which are not subject to further appeal, except in exceptional circumstances; (v) members of courts of auditors or the boards of central banks; (vi) ambassadors, chargés d'affaires and high-ranking officers in the armed forces; (vii) members of the administrative, management or supervisory bodies of State-owned enterprises; (viii) directors, deputy directors and members of the board or equivalent function of an international organisation.

30  UK legislation reflects the definition in the EU directives.

31  Unlike the US Patriot Act, introduced in the aftermath of 9/11, which focuses on senior political figures, but aims to obstruct terrorism.

32  FCA's guidance on PEPs (2017, July) appears to contradict the spirit of the fourth directive by allowing PEPs in the UK and other "low-risk" jurisdictions to be deemed low risk. Also, in 2017, the media reported on a whistle-blower exposing a conflict of interest at the heart of a £170 million high speed contract awarded by the UK's government to US firm CH2M in 2017, out-competing Bechtel and a joint venture between Mace and Turner & Townsend. Notably, Transport Secretary Chris Grayling said the onus was "first and foremost" on the firms bidding to conform to the rules, rather than on the Department for Transport or the state company organising the tender to look for possible concerns (see Smith reporting for the City AM, 2017). It does not sound reassuring if the authorities of a "low-risk" country do not look for concerns.

FOCUS ON PROMINENCE AND SENIORITY

The elements of prominence and seniority are important in understanding how the compliance landscape has been affected. Banks have begun (almost indiscriminately) categorising as high risk those individuals holding senior positions with state institutions. However, if the PEP definition is meant to help banks fight corruption, why is it limited to people of prominence and seniority? Prominent people are indeed associated with a higher level of political exposure, which means that if the political tide turns against them, they will be exposed to criticism and, possibly, investigations and media attention. Interestingly, imposing an obligation on financial institutions to watch for funds linked to such individuals enables the authorities in the industrialised world to exercise global financial control. Quite understandably, where there is suspicion that a head of state is looting national funds, the international community should strive to stop that. However, shouldn't banks be on the alert about corrupt money in any event, whether or not it has been looted by a prominent figure or a low-profile public servant? Prominence is too subjective a term for selection purposes.

One can argue that the PEP definition is strictly for customers in the financial industry while foreign bribery legislation targets all industries. One can also argue that the PEP definition was designed to target grand corruption.[33] However, in banking this distinction is artificial and, potentially, misleading because the risk of corruption (and embezzlement) is associated with access to state funds (or some sort of business-related decision making, e.g. the issue of permits, licences, visas, customs clearance) rather than *political* exposure. Councillors and employees of a municipality, as well as those of council housing associations and low-ranking customs officials, for instance, may have access to funds and may be involved in assigning contracts or taking decisions. Renovation works, plumbing and other maintenance on council blocks of flats sometimes run into millions. Opportunities for corrupt enrichment abound irrespective of the decision-making level in the administration and does not need to imply political exposure (some public servants are politically neutral).

SUBJECTIVITY OF ASSESSMENT

The fourth EU money laundering directive states:

> The [PEP] requirements . . . are of a preventive and not criminal nature, and should not be interpreted as stigmatising [PEPs] as being involved in criminal activity. Refusing a business relationship with a person simply on the basis of the determination that he or she is a [PEP] is contrary to the letter and spirit of this Directive and of the revised FATF Recommendations.

---

33  The PEP concept originated in the context of the investigation into Nigeria's Sani Abacha in the late 1990s-early 2000s in Switzerland (French Senate, 2004).

However, by focusing on geography and prominence, and without providing adequate guidance on mitigation and how to factor in product risk, the authorities in the US and the UK have made it difficult for banks to service PEPs.[34]

The subjective element of deciding whether the wealth of a prominent political figure has been gained corruptly can be considerable (see Gelemerova, 2009). Banks also face perception challenges. For instance, the former Soviet Republics are usually viewed in the West as high risk. There is no clear-cut indication as to why. To some, they are not democratic enough; to others, TI's poor score means corruption risk is high. There is also a view that they are not AML-equivalent jurisdictions. FCA's finding against DB – that Russia should have been categorised as high risk – appears indicative of this latter view. There is also the argument that those countries went through a turbulent transition to a market economy when many became wealthy if not illegally, then unethically, and this has to be considered.

The nexus between the business elite and the ruling regime, whether a royal family or an elected, possibly authoritarian-style, ruler, must also be considered. In this sense, there are similarities between the Middle East and some former Soviet Republics.[35] However, the so-called non-democratic countries seem to fare worse than Arab kingdoms/sultanates, in terms of perception challenges. Somehow being a monarchy seems to make it acceptable, in the eyes of some, that business and government are closely intertwined. This way of looking at it can be misleading: banks should be careful in their considerations as Arab leaders can be the target of discontent (e.g. about corruption), and this is where political exposure matters. The higher up someone is in the hierarchy, the more likely it is for that person to have enemies. Where there is opposition and political rivalry, there are allegations and smear campaigns.

THE FAMILY CONNECTION

The other important element of the PEP definition is the family connection. As discussed, the definition "includes" close immediate family members. Some interpret this as 'limited to'. However, 'includes' means that a bank can exercise discretion and include the extended family, where appropriate (see Wolfsberg

---

34 FCA's financial crime handbook (2015) and the UK Joint Money Laundering Steering Group (JMLSG) (it issues industry guidance with Treasury Ministerial approval) provide high-level interpretation of the law with little practical contextual detail and they even contradict each other. For instance, the JMLSG states: "A specialist PEP database may be an adequate risk mitigation tool" (2017), while the FCA says "Relying exclusively on commercially available PEP databases" is poor practice.

35 For instance, Herb (2014) noted: "As in the rest of the Gulf, the Omani economy is dominated by a small group of families (including the ruling family) and access to state resources helps to determine business success and failure". He quoted a leaked US diplomatic cable describing Oman as follows: "Oman's business landscape remains dominated by a handful of local families who work either in tandem with, or in the shadow of, government-run enterprises . . . Oman's private sector is best described as an oligopoly".

Group, 2017). Financial institutions with an international client base should consider the cultural element of the markets they are targeting. In many regions of the world, including the Middle East, extended family connections are important. A public servant may entrust his business interests with a cousin, not an immediate family member. Equally, there may be no commercial or financial connection between two relatives. Due diligence is critical in determining the extent of a relationship and the related level of risk. Taking a risk-based approach that allows for resources to be allocated commensurate to the risk, one could argue that if there is financial independence, a financial institution should deem the PEP status of that relative as posing limited or no risk, hence non-material. Based on its risk assessment, a financial institution should have the discretion to decide whether a specific PEP is posing a real risk and what controls and measures to put in place and hope that a regulator will concur.

ASSOCIATES

As to close associates, again we see unavoidable stigma, given that policy makers have been focusing for years on *country risk* rather than the need to look at risk and mitigation cumulatively. For instance, in the context of Russia or Kazakhstan, the PEP definition can be so overstretched that it becomes prohibitive to business. If a bank is working with a company owned by someone described in the media as close to the Kremlin, but that company works with major Western partners and there is no evidence of improper conduct, a regulator may still argue a bank's mitigation is insufficient.

Further, a businessman or woman entering politics has to entrust the management of his/her assets with an associate. Equally, a politician who has never run a business but is earning money through bona fide engagements or is a well-paid public servant (e.g. a minister in the UAE) would naturally need a trusted person to manage his/her finances. How much economic power is vested in an associate by a PEP and whether any of this power is funded by corruption is to be determined through due diligence, to the extent possible, and not by a priori judgement. After all, we see similarities between the industrialised world and the developing markets: in the industrialised world, business tycoons control media and carve their influence in parliament through powerful lobby groups. It is the human factor that counts, regardless of culture, country or system. Due diligence must not only aim at identifying risk but also at providing contextual analysis and mitigation. What is adequate mitigation remains an open question, in the absence of clear guidance from regulators and policy makers. Banks are having to adjust through trial and error. Consequently, there is a danger of attrition: in the end, compliance fatigue may result in blanket de-risking.

TIMING OF PEP ROLE

Timing must also be considered. Some financial institutions take the approach that once a PEP is always a PEP. There is a valid argument behind this approach and that is, that an influential figure in politics today may be able to sustain this influence for years ahead. However, this approach runs into practical difficulties. Any retired supreme court judge, for instance, will be regarded as a high-risk client even though there may be no more risk associated with such relationships (provided he/she has a clean track record) than with any other customer.

Under EU legislation, where a PEP is no longer entrusted with a prominent public function, obliged entities shall, for at least 12 months, be required to consider the continuing risk and to apply risk-sensitive measures until such time as that person is deemed to pose no further risk.

This may be reasonable, but some interpret this as individuals who have held a public post in the preceding one year only, which is incorrect. However, where a bank assesses that an individual who has ceased to hold a public post in the past one year poses no further risk, it is uncertain whether regulators will concur – there is insufficient practical guidance. If a business owned by a former public servant, with a clean track record, does not depend on interaction with state agencies and the nature of it does not allow any scope for the individual to improperly benefit from her/his (potential) public sector/political connections, then why should this individual be deemed high risk? However, policy makers and regulators do not provide enough guidance on this matter and on how to mitigate risk in different scenarios (other than by referring to low country risk as a default mitigant[36]). Regulators' and policy makers' emphasis on country risk could mean that former public servants from high-risk jurisdictions should always be considered PEPs, i.e. high risk. Financial institutions have the discretion to decide, based on due diligence and risk assessment, hoping that a regulator will understand their reasoning.

### 3.2 Inherent risks versus conduct-specific risks

#### 3.2.1 Inherent sector- and country-risk

Banks will likely have a risk matrix of sectors and jurisdictions. As discussed, they will likely define as high risk: extractive industries (e.g. oil and gas, precious stones), construction and infrastructure, telecommunications, defence, pharmaceuticals, and other sectors with high interaction with government.

Size matters as well. The larger the company and its business, the more subsidiaries it has, the higher the need for public procurement, especially in some sectors (for instance, a company involved in building infrastructure, e.g. roads and bridges). However, banks will also tend to base their decisions on the country of affiliation of their customers. Country risk includes considering a country's history, culture, political context, economy, legislation. Is the country known for its wine and dine culture? Are business and politics closely intertwined? What is the perceived level of corruption? Evidently de-risking solely based on country risk connectivity will create more problems than it will solve.

36 See above comments on FCA's guidance paper.

*3.2.2 Conduct-specific risks*

Risk arising from a client's specific conduct and practices is important: what is the track record of a client? Is it known for systematic involvement in questionable deals or are controversies a matter of the past; is its public procurement process transparent; does it gain business through open tenders? As discussed, products can carry different risk, which must be considered in the context of the client's business. Pension fund management may be inherently less risky than a transactional account. A bank would not only need to examine the company's track record prior to on-boarding but also continuously monitor the company and learn the rationale behind every transaction. For instance, are outgoing funds a payment to a contractor in a genuine public procurement deal and is the contractor a bona fide business, or are the funds being channelled to an offshore entity with no clear corporate history for a service that appears inconsistent with this entity's profile?

It is also sensible to consider the source of wealth, funds and seed capital. For instance, a company's practices can change with ownership. Examining the new UBO's background can give a fuller risk picture. AML legislation requires examining the UBO's source of wealth – which is typically her or his background (in some instances, inheritance or other source) – only when the client is high risk, particularly if the UBO is a PEP. How to determine the risk without knowing the UBO's background? If a client is in a low-risk country, banks will tend to overlook the background, even though, as discussed, a UK company's UBO may turn out to be from a high-risk country. Likewise, the seed capital is important as the UBO may have criminal backers (e.g. a young UBO of a newly established business funded by corrupt PEPs).

Some might argue it is not the banks' job to police business. Others might argue that banks must play a role in fighting corruption and other crimes. Broadly cast money laundering laws, plus regulators who do not attempt to narrow down interpretation and in fact may even be driving over-compliance, leave banks with no choice. However, excessive risk uncertainty drives de-risking. In the longer run, de-risking may prove non-viable economically. Instead, banks must focus on conduct-specific risk, i.e. arising from the client's specific conduct and culture, in combination with product risk.

## 4 Conclusion

According to the FATF, by applying its recommendations, banks protect the financial system's integrity (FATF, 2014). But placing so much focus on country risk instead of highlighting the need for cumulative analysis with a particular focus on conduct-specific risks may have diverted attention from resolving the real issues. Developing countries and emerging markets need investment to fight poverty and root out corruption. Economic sanctions and focus on country risk potentially result in certain countries' economic and political isolation and to a blanket "no" approach in regard to clients from those countries. This is counterproductive, even if it serves an international policy agenda of undermining certain jurisdictions.

AML risk-scoring methodology has become a science of its own. Consultants are paid well to design risk-scoring formulas and software developers to provide the tools. Yet, compliance specialists are "scratching their heads" over how to risk-score a client when characteristics are on the border between two categories. A bank may end up spending more resources determining a risk rating than on actual "financial crime" prevention. Things must be kept simple: assessment should be prior to on-boarding and then continuously but consistent across clients at its foundation. This means seeking to find out, regardless of country and industry: who is behind a company; the background, conduct and occupation (and the revenue it brings) of the owner(s) (historically and current); the culture of the client's business (any adverse news?); and then, to analyse it all in the context of what product will be offered. On that basis, risk scoring can be simply "acceptable" or "unacceptable" risk. Where risk is seen as acceptable, monitor all transactions for inconsistencies. Any client on the border between "acceptable" and "unacceptable" should go through a governance committee process through which senior management takes responsibility and makes a decision.

Risk assessment is critical. However, with much focus on country risk and without adequate guidance on risk mitigation, regulators waving the stick will result in ships cruising near the shoreline without attempting to cross the ocean for what may be a world-saving journey.

## Bibliography

Caesar, Ed, (2016) "Deutsche Bank's $10-Billion Scandal", *The New Yorker*, 29 August 2016, www.newyorker.com/magazine/2016/08/29/deutsche-banks-10-billion-scandal (accessed 9 March 2017).

Caesar, Ed, (2017) "A Big Fine, and New Questions, on Deutsche Bank's 'Mirror Trades'", *The New Yorker*, 31 January 2017, www.newyorker.com/business/currency/a-big-fine-and-new-questions-on-deutsche-banks-mirror-trades (accessed 9 March 2017).

Campbell, Stuart Vincent, (2013) "Perception is Not Reality: The FCPA, Brazil, and the Mismeasurement of Corruption", *Minnesota Journal of International Law*, vol. 22, no. 1, p. 247–281.

Cassin, Richard L., (2012) "Dutch Won't Open Old Lockheed Wound", 10 February 2012, www.fcpablog.com/blog/2012/2/10/dutch-wont-open-old-lockheed-wound.html (accessed 28 April 2017).

Cobham, Alex, (2013) "Corrupting Perceptions. Why Transparency International's Flagship Corruption Index Falls Short", *Foreign Policy*, 22 July 2013, http://foreignpolicy.com/2013/07/22/corrupting-perceptions/ (accessed 15 April 2017).

FCPA, (2012) *A Resource Guide to the U.S. Foreign Corrupt Practices Act.* Washington, DC: Department of Justice and Securities and Exchange Commission, 14 November 2012.

Financial Conduct Authority, (2015, April) *Financial Crime: A Guide for Firms. Part 2: Financial Crime Thematic Reviews.* London: FCA.

Financial Conduct Authority, (2017, January 30) *Final Notice: Deutsche Bank AG.* London: FCA.

Financial Conduct Authority, (2017, July) *Finalised Guidance. The Treatment of Politically Exposed Persons for Anti-Money Laundering Purposes.* London: FCA.

Financial Action Task Force, (FATF), (2014) *Risk-based Approach Guidance for the Banking Sector*. Paris: FATF.

FinCEN, (2016) *Customer Due Diligence Requirements for Financial Institutions; Final Rule*. Washington, DC: FinCEN.

French Senate, Justice et Affaires Intérieures, (2004) *Proposition de directive du Parlement européen et du Conseil relative à la prévention de l'utilisation du système financier aux fins du blanchiment de capitaux, y compris le financement du terrorisme*, 30 June, www.senat.fr/ue/pac/E2734.html (accessed 28 April 2017).

Gelemerova, Liliya, (2009) "On the frontline against money-laundering: the regulatory minefield", *Crime, Law and Social Change*, vol. 52, no. 1, pp. 33–55.

Gelemerova, Liliya, (2010) "Fighting corruption of foreign officials or wielding the stick instead of better using the carrot", in P. C. van Duyne, G. Antonopoulos, J. Harvey, A. Maljevic, T. vander Beken and K. von Lampe (eds.), *Cross-Border Crime Inroads on Integrity in Europe*. Nijmegen, The Netherlands: Wolf Legal Publishers.

Herb, Michael, (2014) *The Wages of Oil: Parliaments and Economic Development in Kuwait and the UAE*. Ithaca, NY: Cornell University.

Hough, Dan, (2016) "Here's this year's (flawed) Corruption Perception Index. Those flaws are useful", *The Washington Post*, 27 January 2016, www.washingtonpost.com/news/monkey-cage/wp/2016/01/27/how-do-you-measure-corruption-transparency-international-does-its-best-and-thats-useful/ (accessed 15 April 2017).

Joint Money Laundering Steering Group, (2017) *Prevention of Money Laundering/ Combating Terrorist Financing. Guidance for the UK Financial Sector, Part I, UK*, June 2017. London: JMLSG.

Securities and Exchange Commission, (n.d.) *SEC Enforcement Actions: FCPA Cases*, www.sec.gov/spotlight/fcpa/fcpa-cases.shtml (accessed 15 April 2017).

Smith, Rebecca, (2017) "Asleep at the wheel: MPs and campaigners blast transport top dogs over botched HS2 contract", *City AM*, 20 April 2017, www.cityam.com/263204/asleep-wheel-mps-and-campaigners-blast-transport-top-dogs (accessed 28 April 2017).

The New York State Department of Financial Services, (2017, January 30) "In the Matter of Deutsche Bank AG and Deutsche Bank AG New York branch", *Consent Order under New York banking law §§ 39, 44 and 44-a*.

The Wolfsberg Group, (2017) *Wolfsberg Guidance on Politically Exposed Persons*. The Wolfsberg Group.

Transparency International, (2017a) *Corruption Perceptions Index 2016: Full Source Description*, www.transparency.org/news/feature/corruption_perceptions_index_2016 (accessed 15 April 2017).

Transparency International, (2017b) *What is Corruption?* www.transparency.org/what-is-corruption/ (accessed 15 April 2017).

Transparency International, (2017c) *Corruption Perceptions Index 2016: Short Methodology Note*, www.transparency.org/news/feature/corruption_perceptions_index_2016 (accessed 28 March 2017).

Transparency International, (2017d) "Corruption Perceptions Index 2016", 25 January 2017, www.transparency.org/whatwedo/publication/corruption_perceptions_index_2016 (accessed 15 April 2017).

# 11 The duty to disclose

## Implications for corruption in commercial enterprise

*Calum Darling*

Over two millennia ago, Roman law provided for "interdiction of fire and water", for crimes including corruption. Such a decree involved banishment, coupled with an order that no person should supply the exile with these two necessities of life (Kelly, 2006: 39–42). The result was to render the realm inhospitable. In recent times the laws of the United Kingdom have been adapted to deprive criminals of essential services upon which their prosperity depends. Such individuals and groups rely on and thrive through their access to facilitators, complicit or otherwise. Loss of facilities such as legal and financial services creates barriers to the acquisition and laundering of criminal wealth. New laws weaken the ties between crime and those who facilitate it. Lawyers, accountants, bankers and others now must report their clients to the authorities or else face significant punitive sanctions. This obligation is enforced through an expanding genus of offences which criminalise failure to report crime. The legal requirement to report knowledge or suspicion of criminality, once narrow and obscure, has broadened to encompass great swathes of professional practice and even private life. In modern times, the growth in reporting requirements in Scotland has exceeded that in England and Wales.

Though the parliaments at Westminster and Holyrood have yet to turn such measures into explicit terms against the facilitators of corruption, existing enactments nonetheless provide a means to counter corruption in commercial enterprise. The modern array of reporting obligations applies to treason, terrorism and terrorist finance, money laundering serious and organised crime. Of the modern measures, most directly applicable are those which target money laundering and organised crime. Corruption often relies on a network of facilitators whose services must be withheld and whose knowledge or suspicions disclosed. The proceeds of all crimes may be laundered and those of corruption are no exception. Organised criminals and their illicit enterprises frequently coexist in the same commercial environments as legitimate business, inhabited and serviced by lawyers, accountants and intermediaries whose intimacy with the intricacies of transactions can offer a rich source from which to glean reports and evidence of criminality. Most reporting obligations extend beyond such "facilitators" and apply to employees and associates of firms who are required to report on the activities of their employers, employees, colleagues and clients. Though some facilitators may be oblivious, through negligence or otherwise, as to the corruption they enable, without doubt there are some who engage knowingly. For them, disclosure offences offer avenues for prosecution other than for complicity in predicate offences.

The earlier of the extant reporting obligations are relevant primarily for different reasons. The ancient yet enduring duty to report treason is relevant because it marks the origin of the concept in Scots law. It thus gives context to the many modern and more relevant offences. The duties in respect of terrorism and terrorist finance are relevant primarily for similar reasons.

This chapter will chart and assess the rise of reporting offences in Scots law and explain its relevance for and value in countering corruption in commercial enterprise. Legislation targeting treason and terrorism are examined primarily for the purposes of context and comparison and as a secondary purpose for any utility they might hold in the fight against corruption. The offences concerned with money laundering and organised crime are then considered in turn as offering a valuable means of targeting those who engage in or facilitate corrupt activities. The aim is to map the obligation to report crime as it exists today, to serve as a guide to an emerging landscape and trace an expanding body of offences which are of increasing importance in countering corruption.

## Origins of the duty to report crime

The requirement to report crime is not indigenous to Scots law. Since the duty to report treason was imported in the eighteenth century, the obligation to inform on others lay unchanged, augmented only in the late twentieth century when the concept was extended to other categories of crime, gradually enveloping terrorism, money laundering and serious organised crime.

The common law of Scotland knows no general crime of failing to report the criminality of another person. Yet the idea that a failure to report a crime may itself be a crime is not a new concept. For centuries Scots law has recognised the crime of "misprision of treason", that is, the deliberate concealment of knowledge of treason. The offence lies in the failure to disclose known acts of treachery committed by others (Walker, 2011: 111), or to disclose information which might lead to the arrest of a traitor (Gordon, 2001: 565). Misprision of treason developed in the common law of England and Wales, and was imported into Scots law in the early eighteenth century. The earlier history of the crime in England was delineated briefly by Lord Denning in *Sykes v DPP [1962] AC 528, 551*. Prior to 1555, concealment of treason was itself treason, and treason was punishable by death. If a person knew that another was guilty of, or incriminated in treason, he was bound to report this to the King or to a member of the King's immediate circle, or else he too could be indicted for treason. Treason, like felony, could also be charged as a *misprision*, a word which Lord Denning notes was almost synonymous with a misdemeanour and which did not carry the death penalty. In cases of treason in which a man was deemed not to deserve to die, the King would take advantage of this rule for the sake of mercy.

Following the Act of Union, the *Treason Act 1708* brought the obligation into Scots law, where it has remained. Of the many forms of treason known to Scots law, some are now archaic whilst others, such as plotting or levying war against the Sovereign in her realm, giving aid and comfort to her enemies or killing certain public officials all remain, at least conceivably, relevant to modern times. Knowledge of any such act must be reported to authorities. The penalty for failure to do so may be life imprisonment (Gordon, 2001: 565). Despite now languishing in relative obscurity, misprision of treason endures as a reserved matter in terms of the *Scotland Act 1998, sch 5, para 10*, in which it is recognised expressly. For centuries, treason stood alone as the sole crime in Scots law in respect of which a person was obliged to report criminality to authorities on pain of punishment. Elsewhere in the United Kingdom, however, such offences gained greater traction far earlier than in Scots law.

Misprision of felony endured in England and Wales from medieval times until 1967, though it was never a crime in Scotland. The continuing existence of that crime was confirmed by the House of Lords in the 1962 case of *Sykes*. The crime comprised knowledge of a felony committed by someone else and a failure to report that felony to the authorities. The duty articulated by the House seemed without exception and thus lawyers were to inform upon clients and doctors upon patients (Williams, 1961: 142–143). Lords Goddard (*Sykes*, p. 569) and Morton (*Sykes*, p. 571) each called upon prosecutorial discretion, not law, as the appropriate limitation on the crime. Lord Denning noted that the crime had, like misprision of treason, been used historically as a means to avoid the death penalty carried by felony (*Sykes*, p. 554). Lord Denning, though, defended the currency of the crime on the basis that:

> [t]he arm of the law would be too short if it was powerless to reach those who are "contact" men for thieves or assist them to gather in the fruits of their crime; or those who indulge in gang warfare and refuse to help in its suppression.
>
> (*Sykes*, p. 564)

These observations illustrate the shifting justifications for the crime. Where once kings had used misprisions as a means of restricting punishment of those not deemed to deserve death, misprisions were by the twentieth century justified by their utility in extending punishment to those who might otherwise evade it. In any event, the *Criminal Law Act 1967, s 1* abolished the distinction between misdemeanour and felony and thus extinguished the crime of misprision of felony (Walker, 2011: 111).

In the same year in which the crime was abolished in England and Wales, in Northern Ireland the *Criminal Law Act (Northern Ireland) 1967, s 5(1)* imposed a duty to report the crimes of others, under pain of imprisonment. The *s 5(1)* duty is engaged where a number of conditions were met. First, is that a relevant offence has been committed. A relevant offence is one for which the sentence is fixed in law, such as murder, or one for which a first-time offender over the age of 21 could be sentenced to a period of five years' imprisonment. Second, is that a person knows or believes this to be the case. Third, is that the person knows or believes that he or she has information which is likely to secure, or to be of material assistance in securing, the apprehension, prosecution or conviction of any person for that offence. In such circumstances, the person is required to provide that information to a constable within a reasonable time. The penalty for failing to do so increases incrementally, in step with the original offence. Where, for example, the crime not reported is one for which the maximum sentence is one of fourteen years' imprisonment, the failure to report carries a sentence of not more than seven years' imprisonment. An exception from the duty is provided for the victim of a crime upon the making good of the loss or injury, providing that no further payment is made in order to prevent disclosure. The *s 5(1)* offence applies only in Northern Ireland and is far broader than the narrow duty to report treason left in Britain following the abolition of misprision of felony. Yet it was concern over Northern Ireland-related terrorism which led, less than a decade later, to the return of disclosure offences across the Irish sea.

## Duty to report terrorism

In 1976, some 268 years after the *Treason Act*, Parliament criminalised the failure to disclose information about acts of terrorism, an offence replaced in 1989 in near-identical terms. A few years later, Parliament focused on financial institutions (Walker, 2011: 111) and criminalised the failure to disclose that a person was providing financial assistance for terrorism. Since then, the requirements have been repealed, replicated and expanded by successive Acts of Parliament. The first of the current iteration of reporting offences dates from the early years of the new millennium. The relevance of these early terrorism offences for corruption and commercial enterprise lies in their contextual value. They offer early precedent for the later legislative move against launderers and others whose services more often enable corruption, and served as blueprints for those who drafted the later legislation (SC OR JC, 9 June 2009, col. 2066). It is relevant also, though, that terrorist groups engage in a host of activities, financial and logistical, which are enabled by corruption (Organisation for Economic Co-operation and Development, 2016: 2–4). Involvement in corruption, where connected with acts of terrorism or the financing thereof, may fall to be disclosed by those who know or suspect that it takes place.

### Acts of terrorism

The general duty to disclose information concerning acts of terrorism was introduced into UK law by the *Prevention of Terrorism (Temporary Provisions) Act 1976, s 11* (Walker, 2011: 110). Terrorism was then defined as the use of violence for political ends, and includes any use of violence for the purpose of putting the public or any section of the public in fear. This expansive early definition of terrorism was tempered by virtue of *ss 10(5)* and *11(a)* and *(b)* insofar as the obligation applied only to acts of terrorism connected with the affairs of Northern Ireland. The offence is no longer so confined. Recommended for repeal in 1996 (Lord Lloyd, 1996), the obligation was not at first included in the modern tranche of legislation. Change came, however, in the wake of the attacks in New York on 11 September 2001, when the general obligation was resurrected in the *Terrorism Act 2000, s 38B* as amended by the *Anti-Terrorism, Crime and Security Act 2001, s 117*, now in connection with all forms of terrorism (Walker, 2011: 117). Though in this sense far broader, with no requirement for a connection with Northern Ireland, the new legislation adopts a more nuanced definition of terrorism.

The provisions of *s 38(B)* apply to any information which might be of assistance in preventing the commission by another person of an act of terrorism or in securing the apprehension, prosecution or conviction of another person, in the United Kingdom, for an offence involving the commission, preparation or instigation of an act of terrorism. The obligation, in contrast with those in respect of terrorist property offences explored later, extends beyond professional life and is incumbent on the population at large. The offence may be committed through total inactivity and without any personal benefit from the concealment (Walker, 2011: 113). The information to be disclosed must be, or be believed to be, of material assistance, either in preventing an act of terrorism or in securing the apprehension, prosecution or conviction of another person for such an act, complete or inchoate. In common with earlier incarnations, the mental element of the modern offence comprises either knowledge or belief in this fact. Both impute a level of certainty exceeding that required by the terrorist property obligations, both of which include suspicion as a lesser degree of certainty. The distinction between knowledge and belief is relevant only as to the assistance which the information could provide (Walker, 2011: 133). Accuracy and materiality are irrelevant, providing that it is genuinely believed by the accused (Walker, 2011: 113). It is not sufficient, however, that the accused believed in the existence of an act of terrorism, and there must be an act of terrorism for which another is to be apprehended, prosecuted or convicted (Walker, 2011: 114). There is no requirement for the belief to be reasonable and neither does the offence include a provision to capture the accused who *ought reasonably* to have known. The Act provides for a single defence of reasonable excuse. In contrast with other modern disclosure obligations, *s 38B* does not provide an exception or defence for legal advisers in respect of information subject to professional privilege. Likewise, the Act does not articulate the implications for the right against self-incrimination, such as where an individual may be obligated to disclose the offences of another in which he or she is also implicated. In these two respects, the full implications of the legislation for two commonly understood rights are yet to be settled (Walker, 2011: 116–120).

The obligation to report terrorism joins misprision of treason in demanding the aid of the citizenry in pursuing crimes of a particular character. Common to both is the public characteristic of the offences which must be reported. Treason applies to crimes against the monarch and the state, while terrorism is intended to influence the government or to intimidate some portion of the public for, inter alia, a political or ideological cause.

### Terrorist finance

A narrower species of offences has developed in recent decades, designed to assist in the detection of criminal and terrorist financial activities. Though in some senses narrower than the disclosure offences so far outlined – yet in part overlapping – the obligations delve beyond the narrow core of "offences against the state" and into the complex world of financial criminality. With mandatory reporting requirements becoming commonplace throughout the world, two distinct approaches have been developed (Stessons, 2004: 161). The method initially adopted in the United States was to oblige institutions to disclose transactions valued in excess of a certain threshold, an approach characterised as imposing a huge administrative burden (Stessons, 2004: 161). The approach of the United Kingdom, to focus instead on suspicion-based reporting, carries an inherent tradeoff, lessening intrusion into the privacy of institutions and their customers whilst imposing greater levels of responsibility on those who must abide by the requirements (Stessons, 2004: 161). The earliest of the financial reporting requirements in the *Criminal Justice Act 1993* required the reporting of activities relating to terrorist finance and to drug money laundering. Though the two have since been separated, in their early incarnations the offences were substantively identical, beyond the nature of the activity which must be reported (Brown, 1996: 143).

The offence exists today as the *Terrorism Act 2000, s 19*. The obligation applies to a series of specific "terrorist property" offences which include, inter alia, financing of terrorist acts and terrorist groups. The obligation is triggered by knowledge or suspicion that another person has committed one of a number of offences, set out in *ss 15–18* of the Act, related to the handling of terrorist property. The offence of *s 16(1)* in particular is committed where a person uses money or other property for the purposes of terrorism, while *s 16(2)* provides that it is an offence to possess money or other property with reasonable cause to suspect that it may be used for the purposes of terrorism. The so-called "funding arrangements" offence of *s 17* meanwhile is committed where a person enters into or becomes in an arrangement as a result of which money or other property is made available, or is to be made available to another and where that person knows or has reasonable cause to suspect that it will, or may, be used for the purposes of terrorism. By virtue of *s 1(5)*, action taken for the purposes of terrorism includes a reference to action taken for the benefit of a proscribed organisation. Accordingly, offences under *s 16 may* be committed by a person funding bribery to support the aims of a terrorist group. Likewise, *s 17* may be committed by individuals and institutions whose financial services assist in the facilitation of such payments. Such conduct may therefore engage the *s 19* obligation.

Aimed at financial professionals (Walker, 2011: 403) and in common with the earlier offences, this obligation applies where the knowledge or suspicion arises from information obtained in the course of trade, profession, business or employment. In 2008 the provisions were amended by *s 77* of the *Counter Terrorism Act 2008* to include employment whether or not in the course of trade, business or profession. Accordingly, the offence is of concern in a far broader range of contexts than financial services alone (Walker, 2011: 403). As in earlier incarnations of the offence, a defence is provided for a person who has disclosed the matters in accordance with procedures maintained by his or her employer by virtue of *s 19(4)*. The legislation contains no provision to capture circumstances in which a person *ought reasonably* to know of or suspect criminality. Instead, the offence requires actual knowledge or belief. Conversely, and in common with earlier legislation, the provisions make no requirement for the knowledge or suspicion to be reasonable and thus impose a wholly subjective test (Walker, 2011: 403) without regard to the objective merit of the suspicion.

The *Anti-Terrorism, Crime and Security Act 2001, sch 2* inserted a narrower yet more onerous obligation into the *Terrorism Act 2000*, through *s 21A*. The offence applies, in tandem with the broader *s 19* offence, to those doing business in the regulated sector, an expression encompassing a broad range of financial services set out in *sch 3A, para 1* of the same Act. The obligation applies to the same set of terrorist property offences as does the *s 19* offence. In contrast with *s 19*, however, the *s 21A* offence applies not only to actual knowledge or belief, but in circumstances where a person has reasonable grounds to know of or suspect such offences, whether or not they do in fact form such an impression. This increased criminal liability is justified on the basis that the regulated sector, to which the offence is exclusive, is expected to maintain greater awareness and higher standards of reporting (Walker, 2011: 404). The corresponding growth in compliance practices in the sector – with the emergence of the distinct professional discipline concerned with adherence to the legislation – has been said to suggest a degree of success in ensuring that laundering should be taken seriously (Lord Carlile, 2004: 15).

## Money laundering

Alongside this terrorist finance reporting requirement, the *Criminal Justice Act 1993* introduced a duty on professionals in the United Kingdom to report knowledge or suspicion of drug money laundering, initially limited to drug trafficking. Since that time, the reporting requirements have been expanded to encompass proceeds of crime in all forms, so are of relevance far beyond corruption and commercial enterprise.

The current generation of money laundering offences was created by the *Proceeds of Crime Act 2002* (POCA). The reporting offences contained in *ss 330, 331* and *332* of the Act have been identified as forming the cornerstone of money laundering strategy in the United Kingdom (Brown, 2009: 74). No longer restricted to drugs money, the modern requirements extend to the money laundering offences set out in *ss 327, 328* and *329* of POCA. These criminalise a host of activities associated with criminal property, defined as property in any form which constitutes the benefit of criminal conduct in all forms. This expansive definition applies as much to the proceeds of corruption as to drug money. The *s 327* offence is concerned with concealment, disguise, conversion, transfer or removal from the United Kingdom or any part thereof. The *s 328* offence targets those who enter into or become concerned in arrangements to facilitate the acquisition, retention, use or control of criminal property by another. The *s 329* offence is addressed to those who themselves acquire, use or possess criminal property. Accordingly, the definition of money laundering far exceeds the traditional conception – which might entail the concealment of criminal profit – to include transfer and even possession of property derived from criminal conduct, such as corruption. The modern offence is therefore more expansive than the predecessors in the forms of laundering which must be reported. This broadening may be justified on the basis that it is impractical to expect individuals or institutions to identify the origins of funds sufficiently to differentiate between drugs money and funds derived from other forms of criminality (Stessons, 2004: 166).

The principal offence is that contained in *s 330* of the Act. The effect is to create a reporting obligation incumbent upon those employed in the regulated sector. Departing from its earlier iterations and in contrast with the *Terrorism Act 2000*, POCA imposes no equivalent obligation upon those engaged in wider forms of employment. The offence is committed when a set of three conditions are met, subject to certain defences.

The first condition is that a person knows or suspects, or has reasonable grounds for knowing or suspecting, that a person is engaged in money laundering, as defined by reference to the three statutory offences identified earlier. Suspicion requires a lesser degree of certainty than does knowledge. Paragraph 7.8 of the Joint Money Laundering Steering Group Guidance states that "knowledge means actually knowing something to be true". Suspicion, in terms of *R v da Silva [2007] 1 WLR 303*, "means to think that there is a possibility, which is more than fanciful, that the relevant facts exist. A vague feeling of unease would not suffice". Inclusion of suspicion thus has the effect of lowering the threshold at which the mental element of the offence may be triggered. The threshold is further reduced by *s 330(2)(b)*, which is instead satisfied where a person has reasonable cause to know or suspect that another person is engaged in money laundering. The condition may thus be satisfied in circumstances where a person *ought* to know or suspect, but does not. The *mens rea* therefore has both subjective and objective forms. This position echoes the approach taken in the *Terrorism Act 2000, s 21A* which, like *s 330*, applies only to business in the regulated sector.

This second condition of *s 330* – that the information or matter forming the basis for the knowledge or suspicion, or reasonable grounds therefore, arises in the course of business in the regulated sector – represents a narrowing in the ambit of the offence. Notably, the requirement applies to the context in which the information arises and not to the individual and thus no form of special capacity applies (Brown, 2009: 79). Accordingly, the *Criminal Procedure (Scotland) Act 1995, s 225* – which provides that where such a capacity is libelled, it need not, unless challenged by the accused, be proven by the prosecutor – is not engaged. The second condition remains, therefore, a matter to be proven by the prosecutor.

The third condition comprises one of two alternatives. The first is that the accused can identify the person engaged in money laundering. The second is that the accused believes, or it is reasonable to expect her or him to believe, that the information or matter will or may assist in identifying that person, or else the whereabouts of any of the laundered property. This provision, added by amendment in 2005, represents a further narrowing of the offence (Brown, 2009: 79). In either scenario, the condition is that the person does not make the required disclosure as soon as practicably possible after the information or other matter comes to her or him. Disclosures pursuant to the *s 330* obligation may be made either to the National Crime Agency or to a nominated officer.

There are a number of exceptions to the obligation imposed by *s 330*. Presented as limitations on the scope of, rather than defences to, the disclosure offence, the exceptions need only be negated when raised in evidence (Brown, 2009: 83). The first exception is where a person has reasonable excuse for not making the required disclosure. The second exception is made for professional advisers who receive information in privileged circumstances. The provisions apply both to professional legal advisers and to other professional advisers including accountants, auditors and tax advisers, though the latter only to the limited extent that they are carrying out functions analogous to legal advice (Brown, 2009: 84). Privileged circumstances, as defined in *s 330(10)*, are where information comes to a relevant adviser from a client or her or his representative in connection with the giving of advice, from a person or her or his representative seeking legal advice or by a person in connection with or contemplation of legal proceedings. This exception does not apply where the information is imparted in furtherance of criminal purpose, such as money laundering. The third exception is failure by an employer to discharge her or his duty to provide requisite training, the provision of which is obliged by the *Money Laundering Regulations 2007, reg 21*. This exception applies only to a person who has reasonable grounds to know of or suspect money laundering, but does not in fact do so. This exception to some extent makes fairer the application of the objective mental element, in effect limiting its application to those who are trained and thus may be expected to recognise the indicators of money laundering. The fourth and final exception is the dual criminality exemption for which *s 330(7A)* provides, by virtue of which a person is not guilty of an offence where he or she knows or reasonably believes that the money laundering is occurring in a country outside the United Kingdom and that it is legal in that country.

The obligation to report financial criminality has assumed growing prominence in the financial sector and in wider business, and has significant potential in addressing corruption in criminal enterprise. The number of reports made pursuant to the 2002 Act has risen annually, with 381,882 such reports between 2014 and 2015 (National Crime Agency, 2015: 6), rising from 354,186 in the previous year and from 316,527 in the year prior to that (National Crime

Agency, 2014: 7). This increase has been attributed to heightened awareness of the reporting obligations, rather than growth in financial criminality (National Crime Agency, 2014: 7). Of the many sectors caught by the requirements, banks represent the largest source of reports, representing 83.39% between 2014 and 2015; independent legal advisers, by contrast, accounted for only 1% of the total in the same year (National Crime Agency, 2015: 10). The effect of the reporting offences has been to effect a cultural change in sectors in which privacy has long been afforded a premium. Both terrorist finance and money laundering regimes provide exemptions from civil penalties for those who disclose information in accordance with the reporting regime. The effect is to pierce the cloak of privacy which had previously shrouded the relationship between banks and customers, including those involved in corrupt practices. This permeation of confidences in recent decades has represented a sea change in the previously secretive world of banking. The financial obligations, together with the more broadly based requirement to disclose information relating to terrorism, join the centuries-old misprision of treason in an obscure but expanding category of offences.

## Serious organised crime

Since 2010, Scots law has recognised a reporting obligation relating to "serious organised crime", the definition of which is broad enough to encompass corruption in criminal enterprise. The *Criminal Justice and Licensing (Scotland) Act 2010, s 31* creates an offence of failing to report knowledge or suspicion that a person is involved in, or is directing, serious organised crime, or has committed an offence aggravated by involvement in serious organised crime. Modelled upon similar provisions governing terrorism and the proceeds of crime (SC OR JC, 9 June 2009, col. 2066), the obligation applies to knowledge or suspicion arising in the course of the person's trade, profession, business or employment, or as a result of a close personal relationship between the accused and the other person, from which the accused has derived a material benefit. The language used to address the former category mirrors that of *s 19* of the 2000 Act prior to its amendment in 2008. Like the duty to report terrorism and unlike the financial reporting requirements, the *s 31* offence is not confined to the regulated sector and requires actual knowledge or suspicion. The obligation therefore applies to any person who, in the course of working life, encounters certain forms of illicit activity. The obligation applies also to information arising in the course of a close personal relationship from which material benefit is derived. In practice this creates an obligation to inform on clients, customers or business associates (as well as family members), who are known or suspected to be engaged in activities which fall within the sweeping category of conduct captured by the Act. Accountants, estate agents and even hauliers are designated as targets for the legislation (SC OR JC, 26 May 2009, col. 1909). Though there are exceptions for professional legal advisers in relation to information gleaned in privileged circumstances, this exception will not apply where the adviser has been involved in furthering criminality and the obligation will continue to apply.

In common with the financial reporting obligations, *s 31* is triggered by a fixed set of statutory offences known or suspected. Like the money laundering offence, these offences, whilst finite in number, are themselves so broadly defined as to render the reporting obligation sprawling in scope. The offences in question, created by *ss 28, 29* and *30* of the same Act, are those of directing, or involvement in, serious organised crime as defined within the Act, or any offences whatsoever, whether statutory or at common law, which by virtue of the 2010 Act are aggravated in connection with serious organised crime. The offence of involvement in serious organised crime is particularly broad in its breadth, requiring only that another person agrees to do something, knowing or suspecting that so doing will enable or further serious organised crime. The breadth of these offences is significantly exacerbated by the expansive definition given to "serious organised crime". The term is defined within the Act by *s 28(3)* as two or more persons acting together for the principal purpose of committing a serious offence, or series thereof, committed for the purpose of obtaining a material benefit for any person. A "serious offence" is defined as an indictable offence which is committed with the intention of obtaining a material benefit for any person, or which is an act of violence committed or a threat made with the intention of obtaining such a benefit in the future. The term "material benefit" is defined a right or interest of any description in any property, whether heritable or moveable and whether corporeal or incorporeal. Accordingly, the expansive definition afforded to the term "serious organised crime" will include two persons acting together in employing bribery to secure a commercial contract for a firm. This underlines the potential utility of the 2010 Act in terms of disrupting and prosecuting corruption in criminal enterprise.

This approach stands in contrast with that adopted in the United States, for instance. There the *Racketeer Influenced and Corrupt Organisations Act* and the *Continuing Criminal Enterprise Statute*, like *ss 28* and *30* of the 2010 Act, target those in positions of leadership within organised crime, yet confine their reach to defined predicate offences such as bribery and extortion commonly associated with organised crime and central to corruption in criminal enterprise. Whilst *s 31* on its face applies to a fixed list of offences, therefore, the broad definition accorded to "organised crime" renders the application potentially open-ended. The Scottish requirement may therefore be triggered where a solicitor comes across information which leads him or her to suspect that his or her client has engaged with others in bribery, insider dealing or any number of financial, regulatory or other offences from which material benefit may be derived. The *Criminal Justice and Licensing (Scotland) Act 2010* overlaps with – and exceeds – the reporting requirements of POCA 2002. Whereas the purchase of a house with the proceeds of crime may trigger both sets of provisions, *s 31* alone extends to the purchase of premises for use in cannabis cultivation, using funds of legitimate provenance (SC OR JC, 26 May 2009, col. 1909). Though solicitors or estate agent who carry out such business with knowledge of the criminal purpose might themselves be guilty of involvement in serious organised crime, it has been suggested that the same might not be said for senior staff members aware of, but not directly involved in, executing the transaction (SC OR JC, 26 May 2009, col. 1909). Such persons are obliged by virtue of *s 31* to report such conduct or else may be prosecuted and imprisoned.

The reporting protocol imposed by the *Criminal Justice and Licensing (Scotland) Act 2010* does not fit readily with those required by the *Terrorism Act 2000* and *POCA 2002*. By virtue of *s 31(3)* a report must be made to a constable. There are no provisions to permit reports to the National Crime Agency or a nominated officer, as might be made under POCA, which does not, in turn, provide for a report to a constable. That the overlapping obligations impose divergent reporting requirements raises practical questions for those upon whom the obligations are incumbent. Such is the overlap between money laundering and organised crime that a solicitor in Scotland might find him or herself in receipt of a single item of information which at once raises suspicions that a client is engaged in both. In such circumstances, the reporting requirements of the *2002 Act* and *2010 Act* are triggered simultaneously. With the two Acts imposing divergent requirements as to whom a report must be submitted, a single report cannot discharge both requirements. In such circumstances, that solicitor might resolve to report both to his or her firm's nominated officer pursuant to the requirements of the *2002 Act* and separately to a constable of the Police Service of Scotland to discharge his or her obligation under *s 31* of the *2010 Act*. The alternative course of action would be to submit a single report of the kind required by one or other of the two sets of provisions in the hope that he or she might avail him or herself of the defence of reasonable excuse, for which both Acts provide. The uncertainty of this situation places the solicitor in a somewhat unenviable position, to which the prospect of dual reporting may seem preferable. In the *2000 Act*, this conflict is avoided between *ss 19* and *21B*, both of which are triggered by the same set of offences but with the former requiring a report to a constable and the latter permitting disclosure to a nominated officer. This is by way of a provision to the effect that *s 31* does not apply in the regulated sector, whereas *s 21* applies exclusively so. No such distinction is made, however, in terms of *s 31*.

The duty in the *2010 Act* is, perhaps more so even than those of the *2002 Act*, most directly applicable to the business of corruption. The duty to disclose is no longer confined to laundering the proceeds of corruption and other crimes, as was the position under POCA alone. Bribery and corruption, where it is colluded in by two or more persons in order to obtain a material benefit, will meet the definition of serious organised crime in Scotland. Involvement in such activity is a crime, and such a crime must be reported to the authorities. It is not only those who facilitate such activities who must be on guard. Those who encounter corruption in the course of their working lives must disclose their knowledge or suspicions to the authorities. Any ties between corruption and commercial enterprise will be weakened or severed. Networks of facilitators are to be repelled and in their place a network of potential informers instated. The Scottish legislation creates a hostile environment for corruption as it does for other forms of serious organised criminality.

## Growth of the duty to report

The framework of reporting obligations in Scotland has grown in a piecemeal way from a time where such offences were not recognised. Terrorism and terrorist financing, money laundering and organised crime must all now be reported to authorities. The recent prevailing approach has been to specify certain statutory offences capable of triggering the obligation. A notable exception is *s 38B* of the *Terrorism Act 2000*, which refers to acts of terrorism rather than to specific statutory provisions. On the other hand, the greater specificity in the *Proceeds of Crime Act 2002* and the *Criminal Justice and Licensing (Scotland) Act 2010* is offset by the expansive definitions of the offences to which they apply.

The categories of persons to whom such obligations are of concern are equally sweeping. The broadest category is in *s 38B* of the *2000 Act*, which is concerned with the prevention and detection of acts of terrorism, imposing an obligation incumbent on "any person". Of narrower scope, but still broadly defined, are offences concerned with terrorist finance and serious organised crime. The former must be reported by any person encountering relevant information in the course of her or his trade, business or profession, or her or his employment whether or not in the course of trade, business or profession. The serious organised crime offence adopts the stricter formulation used in *s 19* of the *Terrorism Act 2000* in its unamended form, but adds an additional category for those who derive material benefit from a close personal relationship. More tightly defined – yet still sweeping – are those categories in the offences set out in *s 21B* of the *2000 Act* and *s 330* of POCA, which apply to those in the course of their business in the regulated sector. Finally, there are those offences contained in *ss 331* and *332* of POCA, which apply specifically to nominated officers.

The burden imposed on those carrying on business in the regulated sector is significant. Such persons, for whom the law demands specialist training, are held accountable not only for their failure to report knowledge or suspicion of crime, but also for their failure to recognise criminality. The remaining offences by contrast are less onerous, applying only in the case of actual knowledge or suspicion. The position is yet further complicated by the differing defences provided by the various Acts. The *s 38B* offence provides only for a defence of reasonable excuse, whilst others provide express exceptions for legal advisers. None replicate the Northern Irish provisions which except victims of crime from the obligation to report it, though such circumstances may fall within the scope of 'reasonable excuse'. The legislation as a whole is silent too on the position of investigative journalists, a matter of contention in relation to the duty to disclose information concerning acts of terrorism (Walker, 2011: 120–121) and relevant to all extant reporting obligations. This is a troubling lacuna, given the critical role played by investigative journalists in relation to exposés like the Russian Laundromat (see Campbell, this volume.)

The overlap between substantive offences creates opportunity for certain forms of conduct to trigger multiple reporting obligations. Such situations are made complex by the divergent forms of disclosure required by the various offences. An instance of suspected money laundering by a criminal group might be reported by a banker to her or his nominated officer and yet a report must still be made to a constable in terms of *s 31* of the *2010 Act*. Such interactions complicate an already complex and developed compliance regime which has grown up around the rise of reporting obligations.

### Future changes

Latterly, the tide of disclosure offences has continued to rise. Though the modern requirements overlap and entwine, the legal patchwork does not yet incorporate a general obligation to report crime and nor has it wholly enveloped the full spectrum of corrupt activities. Such a position remains some way off and indeed is not inevitable. New legislative strategies may yet gain greater currency. With the *Bribery Act 2010*, Parliament took aim directly at those engaged in bribery, but in doing so, omitted any form of disclosure offence from the legislation. Rather, in *s 7* of that Act, Parliament opted not to criminalise failure to report bribery, but instead created the corporate offence of failure to prevent bribery. The Act provides a defence where it is shown that the business had in place adequate procedures to prevent bribery. In the wake of the *2010 Act*, schemes operated by prosecutors north and south of the border encouraged businesses to voluntarily disclose past instances of wrongdoing, on the part of the company or its employees, in return for which it might forego prosecution in favour of financial settlement. In Scotland, a civil settlement regime was established, under which companies agreed to repay the proceeds of corruption. In England and Wales, Deferred Prosecution Agreements allow for similar remedies in cases of corruption (see Doig, and King and Lord, this volume). The *Criminal Finances Act 2017, ss 45* and *46* introduced two corporate offences modelled on *s 7* of the *2010 Act*. By virtue of *ss 45* and *46* of the *2017 Act*, a body corporate or partnership is guilty of an offence where a person associated with that body commits a tax evasion facilitation offence contrary to the laws of the United Kingdom or another country. As in the *2010 Act*, it is a defence to show that sufficient prevention measures were in place. The Acts of 2010 and 2017 may thus herald a new approach to tackling corruption, one which might exist as an alternative to (or else in future in parallel with) a statutory disclosure obligation. In contrast with "failure to report" offences, such "failure to prevent" offences – and associated voluntary reporting schemes – require businesses to take action against corruption and yet are without such severe consequences for individuals not themselves complicit in corruption.

Whether or not Scots law one day comes to recognise or include a general duty to disclose, there is little doubt that the reporting obligation has become a fixture of the Scottish legal system. From medieval origins and following a prolonged period of dormancy, the rapid expansion in the late twentieth and early twenty-first centuries has brought the concept to the fore. Once confined to treachery and terrorism, disclosure offences have spread across great tracts of criminality to become an accepted legislative tool. Such statutory duties to report figure prominently in legal strategies to tackle illicit financial activity. This expanding body of offences affords a new means by which to counter corruption, transforming the commercial environment into one hostile to corrupt practices. The recent tide of obligations compels a corporate culture of informing. Those who fail to do so risk capture through criminalisation. Facilitators of corruption, once caught, need no longer be shown to be complicit in the principal criminality. Their silence is sufficient and so the threshold at which corrupt facilitators may be prosecuted is lessened. Ultimately, the duty to disclose crime has become an accepted measure in the battle against corruption in commercial enterprise.

## Bibliography

Bribery Act 2010.

Brown, A. (1996) *Proceeds of Crime: Money Laundering, Confiscation and Forfeiture.* Edinburgh, UK: W. Green/Sweet & Maxwell.

Brown, A. (2009) *Money Laundering.* Edinburgh, UK: W. Green.

"Continuing Criminal Enterprise" 21 USC § 848.

Criminal Finances Act 2017.

Criminal Law Act 1967.

Criminal Law Act (Northern Ireland) 1967.

Gordon, G. (2001) *The Criminal Law of Scotland, vol. II.* Edinburgh, UK: W. Green.

Hume, D. (1819) *Commentaries on the Law of Scotland, Respecting Crimes, vol. I, 2nd edn.* Edinburgh, UK: Bell & Bradfute.

Kelly, G. (2006) *A History of Exile in the Roman Republic.* [ebook] Cambridge, UK: Cambridge University Press. Available from: https://play.google.com/books/reader?id=xVcg88VRu28C&printsec=frontcover&pg=GBS.PP1 [Accessed on 30 September 2017].

Lord Carlile of Berriew. (2004) *Report on the Operation in 2004 of the Terrorism Act 2000.* London: The Stationery Office Limited. Available from: http://tna.europarchive.org/20100419081706/http://security.homeoffice.gov.uk/news-publications/publication-search/legislation/terrorism-act-2000/independent-review-responses/lord-carlile-report-04?view=Binary [Accessed on 27 April 2017].

Lord Lloyd (1996) *Inquiry into Legislation against Terrorism* Cm 342. London: The Stationery Office.

National Crime Agency. (2014) *Suspicious Activity Reports (SARS) Annual Report.* Available from: www.nationalcrimeagency.gov.uk/publications/464–2014-sars-annual-report/file [Accessed on 27 April 2017].

National Crime Agency. (2015) *Suspicious Activity Reports (SARS) Annual Report.* Available from: www.nationalcrimeagency.gov.uk/publications/677-sars-annual-report2015/file [Accessed on 25 September 2017].

Organisation for Economic Co-operation and Development. (2016) *Terrorism, Corruption and the Criminal Exploitation of Natural Resources.* Paris: OECD.

Prevention of Terrorism (Temporary Provisions) Act 1976.

"Racketeer Influenced and Corrupt Organizations" 18 USC § 1961.

Scotland Act 1998.

Scottish Parliament Justice Committee Official Report, 26 May 2009.

Scottish Parliament Justice Committee Official Report, 9 June 2009.

Stessons, G. (2004) *Money Laundering: A New International Enforcement Model*. Cambridge, UK: Cambridge University Press.

*Sykes v DPP [1962] AC 528.*

Terrorism Act 2000.

Treason Act 1351.

Treason Act 1702.

Treason Act 1708.

Treason Act 1842.

Walker, C. (2011) *Terrorism and the Law*. Oxford, UK: Oxford University Press.

Williams, G. (1961) Criminal Law. Misprision of Felony. *Cambridge Law Journal*, 19(2), 142–144.

# 12 The fight against corruption in commercial enterprises

## A comparative overview in light of the Italian experience

*Maurizio Bellacosa*

## 1 Foreword

It is by now universally acknowledged how serious and damaging the phenomenon of corruption is. Corruptive behaviours not only offend the typical legal interests in the impartiality and good performance of Public Administration, but also distort competition and hinder the growth of an economic system (Severino, 2014: 4). From the same perspective, the Preamble to the Council of Europe Convention on Corruption signed in Strasbourg in 1999, points out that "corruption represents a major threat to the rule of law, democracy and human rights, fairness and social justice, hinders economic development and endangers the proper and fair functioning of market economies". In this context, the fight against corruption represents an increasing need precisely with regard to commercial enterprises, as the corruptive phenomenon also harms the freedom to conduct a business.

On the basis of said premise, in the debate regarding the countering of corruption, two fundamental requirements have arisen, in Italy as well as elsewhere: first of all, the need to pursue an anti-corruption policy that not only applies instruments of repression, but also resorts to prevention (Manacorda et al., 2014: 3; Mongillo, 2015: 14; Severino, 2014: 5); second, the need to take into account the international dimension of corruption, which makes it essential to introduce similar counter-measures among the different legal systems (Romano, 2013: 134).

Therefore, the aim of the present work is to analyse the Italian legal framework on the fight against corruption, with regard both to the repressive system, by examining the crimes of corruption in the public as in the private sector; and to the preventive measures, particularly as regards corporate criminal liability and the National Anti-Corruption Plan.

An analysis of the Italian counter-corruption system will be provided, by means of a comparative overview. This is valuable in order to better assess the efficiency of said measures; and second, in order to give a wider context in response to the perceived need for a homogeneous approach at the international level.

## 2 Corporate criminal liability in the field of counter-corruption: a comparative overview

In the Italian legal system, the first fundamental regulatory intervention for the prevention of corruption in commercial enterprises was Legislative Decree no. 231 of 8 June 2001, which introduced the liability of entities resulting from a large (and continually expanding) list of crimes. Decree 231, laying down "rules on the administrative liability of legal persons, companies and associations, including those without legal personality", implemented the OECD Convention on combatting bribery of foreign public officials in international business, as well as more articulated obligations set out in the Second Protocol to the PIF-Convention on fraud, corruption and money laundering (Di Giovine, 2010: 8).

It is a form of direct and autonomous[1] liability (Bellacosa, 2014a: 216; De Simone, 2012: 343), labelled by the lawmaker as "administrative" although the numerous points of contact with the parallel (and preliminary) criminal discipline have prompted doctrine and case law to recognize its essentially criminal nature (De Simone, 2012: 324; De Vero, 2008: 322; Guerrini, 2007: 105; Paliero, 2001: 845; Scaroina, 2006: 124; in case law, on the criminal nature of the penalties for legal persons, see Cass. Pen., Sez. II, n. 3615 of 20 December 2005, in *C.E.D.*, n. 232957; Cass. Pen., Sez. VI, n. 18941 of 3 March 2004, in *C.E.D.*, n. 228833).

Liability is criminal, deriving from a procedural viewpoint. Pursuant to articles 34 and following Decree 231, the assessment of the company's liability is deferred to the jurisdiction of the Criminal Judge and the provisions contained in the Code of Criminal Procedure are applied, insofar as compatible, to the related proceedings (Bassi, 2014: 869; Cimadomo, 2016: 117; Fidelbo, 2010: 435).

Moreover, also in the constitutive elements of the entity's offence, it is possible to identify some significant similarities with the typical structure of the crime. Indeed, in order to hold a company liable, it is necessary to assess both an objective and a subjective precondition.

As regards the objective requirement, first of all the alleged crime must have been committed by a person embedded within the company at a top management level (representatives, directors, top managers) or by a person subject to the direction and supervision of the former (employee; see De Vero, 2008: 150; Di Giovine, 2010: 56); second, the criminal offence must have been committed "in the interest or to the advantage" of the enterprise (as set forth by art. 5, Legislative Decree no. 231/2001; see De Vero, 2008: 150; Di Giovine, 2010: 69; Pecorella, 2002: 80).

In addition, the corporate criminal liability implies a particular form of culpability of the company, integrated by the omitted adoption, before the commission of the crime by the individuals, of business organizational models (so-called *modelli organizzativi*) providing for appropriate measures to prevent

---

1 The autonomy makes it possible to punish only the company even if the individual who committed the crime remains unknown.

crimes of the same type as that which has been committed. The entity may therefore avoid responsibility by proving it has adopted and successfully carried out an adequate business organizational model, which envisages, among others, the setting up of a supervisory board (*organismo di vigilanza*). The assessment of the entity's culpability changes depending on the category to which the individual who committed the crime belongs; indeed, if the crime has been committed by a top manager, it becomes significantly more complicated for the entity to be exempted from liability. In this case, it is also necessary to prove that the individual acted by "eluding fraudulently the organizational management models" (see art. 6, para. 1, lett. c. of the "Decree 231"; see Di Giovine, 2010: 75; Paliero, 2014: 186; Paliero and Piergallini, 2006: 177; Piergallini, 2010a: 153; Tripodi, 2004: 483).

As for sanctions, Decree 231 resorts to a very broad arsenal characterized by a marked "special-preventive" purpose (Piergallini, 2010b: 221). In addition to the more traditional pecuniary sanctions, a varied series of disqualification sanctions is available, to be applied in very serious cases and taking into account their specific suitability to prevent further illegal activities of the type committed (see art. 14, Decree 231). Moreover, pursuant to art. 16 Decree 231, the prohibition on conducting business activities may also be applied definitively to recidivist entities or to intrinsically criminal entities. In this perspective, in the Italian legal system there exists a real and proper "death penalty" for criminal enterprises, since in these cases there isn't any lawful business interest to protect, only the need to stop criminal activities.

The aforementioned distinction between top managers and employees, set forth by the international instruments which Decree 231 intended to implement, found an illustrious precedent precisely in English law.

As a matter of fact, as it is well known in the United Kingdom there are two main theories regarding the criterion for attributing liability to the entity: on the one hand, that of *vicarious liability* (founded on the principle *respondeat superior*), a form of objective and indirect liability, applying to the so-called *strict liability offences* (for which *mens rea* need not be proven) committed by employees or agents of the corporate entity. On the other hand, the *identification theory*, which applies to fault-based offences committed by an individual who represents its "directing mind and will" and thus acts as its *alter ego* (Bricola, 1970: 966; De Maglie, 2002: 148; De Vero, 2008: 71; Lottini, 2005: 5, 32; Wells, 2003: 111, 2014: 505).

In addition, in recent years, an important developmental step in UK corporate liability has occurred precisely in the fight against corruption, with the enactment of the Bribery Act (BA) 2010, in force since 1 July 2011. BA 2010 has defined from a regulatory point of view the preconditions of the accountability of the entities for corruptive facts, introducing in Section 7 a new and autonomous form of strict liability for failing to prevent bribery on behalf of commercial enterprises. In this chapter it will merely be pointed out that the resulting regulatory *corpus* has significant similarities with the above-mentioned Decree 231 in force in Italy. First of all, the discipline applies to the relevant commercial organizations. Therefore, as also happens in Italy, public entities and non-profit organizations are excluded.

Moreover, said responsibility is triggered in the presence of corruptive acts committed by an associated person (which means a person who performs services for or on behalf of the commercial organization – see Sec. 8, BA 2010), with the intention to "obtain or retain business" or "an advantage in the conduct of business" for said organization (as specified in Sec. 7, BA 2010). But it is in the provision under Section 7, para. 2, BA 2010 that the main *trait d'union* between the two disciplines can be identified. With a formula which indeed overlaps the one set out in art. 6 of Decree 231, the commercial organization is given the chance to set up a defence by proving that it had in place adequate procedures designed to prevent such conducts. By so doing, the aim is to spur commercial enterprises to adopt compliance programs (Wells, 2014: 507).

Going further in the analysis of the common law systems, also in the United States one may observe a growing web of forms of liability, further complicated by the binary distribution of jurisdictions between Federal and State Courts. However, it can be noted, in general terms, that the US concept of respon-sibility deriving from corporate crime is focused on a form of contamination among the paradigms of *vicarious responsibility* and *identification theory*. There arises a form of indirect responsibility, on the model of the *culpa in vigilando*, which extends in general to a broad list of crimes (Bertolini, 2003: 527; De Vero, 2008: 81; in general, on the experience of the United States, see De Maglie, 1995: 88). An important point of contact with the Italian discipline is represented by the undisputed central role of compliance programs. However, their proper implementation in the corporate fabric exerts for the most part just an attenuating effect on corporate liability (Bertolini, 2003: 532). On the other hand, compliance programs play a key role in allowing the entity to access specific procedural models characterized by a marked rewarding intent, such as deferred prosecution agreements and non-prosecution agreements (Sabia and Salvemme, 2016: 445; Thaman, 2014: 584).

Proceeding now with the analysis of civil law legal systems, and considering first the French legal system, the elements of distinction appear more evident when compared to the Italian one. The most significant one is the kind of liability which is also formally criminal: moreover, its discipline finds its place within the *Code Pénal*. Furthermore, the discipline at issue applies to a wider range of enti-ties: under art. 121–2 of the *Code Pénal*, all *personnes morales* excluding the State are equally criminally liable for the violations committed, on their behalf, by their bodies and representatives. In other words, with the sole exception of the State, even public entities, local authorities included, can be held criminally responsible (however, pursuant to par. 2 of art. 121–2 *Code Pénal*, the criminal liability of local authorities is restricted to offences committed "dans l'exercice d'activités susceptibles de faire l'objet de conventions de délégation de service public"; see Desportes and Le Gunehec, 2007: 532; Giavazzi, 2005: 876; Tricot, 2014: 477).

Another important element of distinction is the daring option, implemented by means of the *Loi Perben* II no. 204 of 9 March 2004, for a generalization of the entity's accountability which can potentially arise in relation to any type of crime (with the sole exclusion of press- and audiovisual communication-related crimes: see art. 121–3 *Code Pénal*). The applicability of the regulations at issue, however, is not automatic, but requires in any event a compatibility screening with the single incriminating type of crime. It must be observed, then, in matters of crimes of corruption that, if the entity is accountable for facts of *corruption active*, according to the *Code Pénal* the same may not occur in cases of *corruption passive*: being a proper crime (attributable only to those holding the offices of *dépositaire de l'autorité publique, chargées d'une mission de service public ou investie d'un mandat électif public*), it is claimed that the indictment cannot be extended to parties other than individuals (Pernazza, 2014: 548). Likewise, the crime of *abus de biens sociaux* is incompatible with the system of the responsibility of *personnes morales*, being a crime that, historically, was put in place to protect the entity, which structurally represents a victim and not a perpetrator (Pernazza, 2014: 555; in French case law, see Cass. Crim., 6 May 1985, no. 84-90.316 and Cass. Crim., 8 March 2006, no. 05-82.865). Moreover, it must be observed that, following the entry into force of Law 1691/2016 concerning "transparency, fight against corruption and modernization of the economy" (so called *Loi Sapin* II) – which provides for more stringent obligations of corruption prevention in the commercial sector, optionally through the adoption of codes of conduct, and the institution of an *Agence française anticorruption* with a leading and supervisory role – the French system came closer in many respects to the Italian anticorruption model (see "ANAC" in the Italian system in the next section).

Some similarities may also be found between the German system, introduced by the law on administrative offences (*Ordnungswidrigkeitengesetz* – OwiG), and the Italian one. An important point of contact is the choice for a sanctioning system that at least nominally appears to be administrative; moreover, also in Germany the entity's accountability is direct and autonomous, i.e. it is decoupled from the outcomes of possible proceedings against the individual. Instead, the structural requisites of the offence are only partially coincidental. In fact, rather than on the functional connection between the entity and the offence, the German discipline revolves around the violation of the obligations directly incumbent upon the entity (such a requisite, indeed, plays a key role both in the corporate liability following a misconduct of its representatives, as regulated by §§ 9 e 30 OWiG; and in the more generic offence as per § 130 OWiG. On this issue, see Bohnert, 2016: 122, 561; Dolcini and Paliero, 1980: 1141; Gandini, 2013; Hirsch, 1995: 285; Paliero, 1995: 129; Smacchi, 2014: 560; Tripodi, 2004: 483). Furthermore, with a curious reversal of perspective, while in the legal systems analysed so far the correct implementation of the models exerts an attenuating or liberating effect in respect of an offence that is structurally dependent on the individual's crime, in Germany it is precisely this omitted implementation of the models that becomes a structural requisite of the liability under consideration (reference is made to the more generic administrative offence as per § 130 OWiG).

However, there are certain more decisive differentiating elements. Indeed, unlike what occurs in France and Italy, the related proceedings are deferred to the administrative authority and not to the criminal judge (see art. 36 of Legislative Decree 231/2001). In addition, the sanctioning system is for the most part limited to measures of a patrimonial character (the seizure and the *Geldbusse*, a pecuniary sanction to be tailored to the seriousness of the fact and to the perpetrator's economic conditions). In this respect, the intent underlying the system at issue would seem to be more distinctly preventive and retributive, while the purposes of repair and compensation of the damaged interest remain secondary (Smacchi, 2014: 563).

## 3 The National Anti-Corruption Plan

Always with a view to the preventive instruments in the fight against corruption, it is important to recall the innovations introduced in Italy through Law no. 190 of 6 November 2012 (also named *legge Severino*, after the then Minister of Justice, Prof. Paola Severino), which lays out "provisions for the prevention and repression of corruption and unlawfulness in the Public Administration" (Bartoli, 2016: 1507; Guido, 2015: 280; Scaroina, 2017: 135). Such regulation has created in the context of the Public Administration an anti-corruption system, which shows some original aspects when compared to other countries.

In particular, Law 190/2012 established a National Anti-Corruption Authority (*Autorità Nazionale Anti-Corruzione* – ANAC), entrusted with controlling and preventing corruption and unlawfulness in the Public Administration. The provision of an Authority with specific competence for control and prevention of corruption represents an original and appropriate measure, having regard to the seriousness and complexity of the phenomenon to be countered.

The ANAC, in addition to exercising a general supervisory and control power on the implementation of the national anti-corruption instruments, adopts a National Anti-Corruption Plan on a three-year basis. The Plan provides a mapping, within the State's administrative machine, of the areas exposed to a higher risk of corruption and performs an important steering effect for the single Public Administrations, setting up the standards they must comply with. For every Public office, furthermore, there is an obligation to issue their own three-year Plan for corruption prevention, and to provide preventive models that are consistent with the peculiarities of the relevant administration, as occurs for business organizational models.

Law 190/2012 introduced for the public sector a type of administrative liability which revolves primarily around the adoption of an effective corruption prevention Plan. However, while in the system envisaged by Decree 231 liability is rooted in the entity, in the anti-corruption system it is instead focused on an individual – the so-called person "Responsible for the Prevention of Corruption" (RPC) – who is selected from inside the public entity to perform a supervisory function on the effectiveness of the Plan (therefore, pursuant to art. 1, co. 12 e 14, l. 190/2012, this person will have to prove that he or she had drawn up the Plan and that he or she had duly supervised its functioning.). Furthermore, if in the "231 system" liability emerges in connection with crimes committed in the interest of the entity, in the anti-corruption system the RPC's responsibility arises in relation to the corruption committed in the personal interest of the corrupted public official. The two disciplines take their inspiration from the same need for prevention, but their operating frameworks coincide only partially: while the anti-corruption Plans devote their attention to corruptive facts, the list of crimes that give rise to the entity's liability under Decree 231 is distinctly broader. In additon, while the adoption of the organizational model as per Decree 231 is optional, the failure to adopt a three-year prevention Plan is punishable by serious disciplinary sanctions imposed on the anti-corruption officer (see articles 1, paragraphs 12 and 13; in greater detail, on the similarities and differences between the two sectors under consideration, see Bartoli, 2016: 1510).

Furthermore, Decree 231 (aimed at business ventures) and the Anti-Corruption System (aimed at Public Administration) coincide in those corporate realities that are halfway between public and private, which perform their business activities under State control. Private law entities which are controlled or partially owned by the State, and economic public bodies are in fact subject to both disciplines (Scaroina, 2017: 148).

## 4 Public corruption

As regards the repression of the corruptive phenomenon, the current criminal regulation in Italy is characterized by the variety of types of crimes, the result of continuous revisions and reforms, which often take their inspiration from international and European sources.

The Italian criminal code provides a comprehensive regulatory system that was put in place for the protection of the impartiality and good performance of Public Administration. It is structured in several criminal provisions which embrace, each from a different angle, the same phenomenon: the commercialization of the public function.

In particular, a distinction must be drawn between "proper" corruption (i.e. 'against the rules'), when the activity required of the Public Official represents a violation of the tasks of his/her public office, and corruption "for the exercise of one's function" (i.e. 'according to the rules'), when the Public Official receives some money for the regular performance of his/her functions (Catenacci, 2016: 77; Fiandaca and Musco, 2012: 220; Palazzo, 2012: 228; Romano, 2013: 95).

Likewise, as also happens in other legal systems, a distinction must be made between antecedent corruption, i.e. when the corruptive agreement or receiving of a good is prior to the subservience of the public function to the private interest; and subsequent corruption, in the event that receiving or being promised a profit follows as a form of recognition that a favour has been done (Catenacci, 2016: 77; Dolcini, 2013: 543; Fiandaca and Musco, 2012: 220).

In general, the discipline's main focus is to be found in four principal types of crime: corruption for the exercise of one's function as per art. 318 of the Italian *codice penale* (c.p.); corruption for an act that is contrary to one's official duties as per art. 319 c.p. (corresponding to "proper", antecedent and subsequent corruption); corruption in judicial acts as per art. 319 *ter* c.p.; and the crime of instigation to corruption as per art. 322 c.p. Law no. 190/2012 has introduced two more types of crime comparable to the *genus* of corruption: the offence of "trafficking of unlawful influences" (art. 346 *bis* c.p.), a provision that was already present in numerous foreign legal systems (among which France, Spain and Portugal; for a comparative overview, see Bonini, 2012: 2 and Losappio, 2015: 1036) aiming to sanction third parties acting as intermediaries between private corruptor and corrupted public official (Fiandaca and Musco, 2013: 21; Grossi, 2016: 251; Scaroina, 2016: 811); and the "undue induction to give or promise a benefit" as per art. 319 *quater* c.p.

The ensemble of crimes committed by public officials is completed by the crime of *concussione* as per art. 317 c.p. It is a crime which is typical of the Italian legal tradition, which sanctions a sort of extortion committed by a public official through coercive abuse.

The choice of an autonomous provision, in addition to the crime of extortion, finds its traditional justification in the need to enhance – and consequently also to distinguish from the viewpoint of the sanctioning regime – the interests underlying the crime of *concussione*. While extortion is typically put in place to protect the victim's assets, *concussione* affects a plurality of legal interests and aims to protect impartiality and good performance of Public Administration as well as the victim's freedom of self-determination. In an international context, the crime of *concussione* has been at times considered an Italian "anomaly", because it would risk offering an *escamotage* (i.e. a gimmick to find an easy way out) to the private individual, who, even if he or she performed the illicit payment or the undue promise, declares him or herself as the victim of constraint, in order to be exempted from liability.

For this reason, Law 190/2012, in reforming the discipline with a view to adjusting to international standards, has split the crime of *concussione* (which beforehand comprised both the conducts of "coercion" and "induction"). On the one hand, it has maintained the crime of *concussion*, which nowadays only sanctions coercive abuses; on the other, it has introduced the offence of "undue induction to give or promise a benefit", and said offence sanctions both the public official abusing his or her power by means of induction, and (although with milder sanctions) the private individual who made the payment or the promise motivated by the prospect of an undue personal gain. In this way, the new crime of "undue induction" satisfies the request coming from international standards, while the *concussione* grants a stronger protection to the victims of coercive abuses of the Public Official.

The distinction between these two criminal offences has been outlined by the case law in the following terms: the *concussione* is characterized by the "coercive abuse of the Public Official, performed by means of violence or threat of a *contra jus* damage and which produces in the victim a serious restriction of his/her freedom of self-determination"; while the undue induction is characterized "by the inductive abuse" of the Public Agent, which means:

[b]y a conduct of persuasion, influence, deception, moral pressure, resulting for its addressee in a less effective conditioning of his/her freedom of self-determination; with the consequence that the addressee, maintaining his/her ability to decide, ends up accepting the request of the bribe, since motivated by the prospect of an undue personal gain.

(So stated by the "Sezioni Unite" of the Italian Court of Cassation, sent. no. 12228 of 2013, so called "sentenza Maldera"; on this issue, see Catenacci and Picardi, 2016: 110; Mongillo, 2013: 167; on the actual debate in Italy about the possible further reforms, see Viganò, 2014: 4.)

## 5 Corruption in the private sector

As regards corruption in the private sector, the Italian legal system endowed itself with a criminal provision in 2002, with the new art. 2635 of the civil code (c.c.); this same provision was modified twice, in 2012 and in 2017, in order to make it more similar to the European Union model.

In the doctrinal debate on this issue, critical voices have been raised on the decision to criminalize private corruption; as a matter of fact, it has been pointed out that the proposals for the introduction of a corruption offence in the private sector "were treading on the ground (rather slippery indeed) of the moralization of the private business activity" (Musco, 2004: 14) and that corruption in the private sector has no significant offensive action, but rather a "lack of morals", because of "that element of venality which is enough to make it despicable" (Spena, 2007: 834). A decisive boost for Italian lawmakers came from the international bodies (European and non-European) which have set a common goal of fighting corruptive phenomena in economic matters, considered as means to alter the fair competition among companies and as an obstacle to the development of socio-economic relationships (Bellacosa, 2006: 244; Huber, 2001: 467; Mongillo, 2012: 192). The United Nations Convention against Corruption, signed in Merida (Mexico) in December 2003 and which came into force on 14 December 2005, shares the basic approach of other international agreements as regards the wide and generalized incrimination of corruptive phenomenon in the private sector, in the performance of a business, financial or commercial activity. To this end, the relevant area for criminal law concerns those facts committed by any person working, in various capacities, for or with regard to a "private sector entity", including those entities which do not have a corporate structure, and the *pactum sceleris* recalls the broad notion of "in breach of his or her duties". The Framework Decision 2003/568/JHA, adopted by the Council of the European Union on 22 July 2003, is moving in the same direction.

In Italy, the crime introduced in 2002, called "disloyalty following an offer of money or a promise of a benefit" was an offence which sat in between corruption in the private sector and managerial disloyalty. It was a white collar crime – since the possible "corrupted" persons were directors, general managers, liquidators, managers tasked with the drawing up of the accounting documents, financial auditors and persons responsible for the auditing – and in order to constitute such crime, it was necessary not only for the action or omission of the action, which were the object of the unlawful dealing, to be actually performed, but also for an actual damage to be caused to the company (Musco, 2007: 237); in other words, the crime of corruption in the private sector as per art. 2635 c.c. used to imply the occurrence of an event (represented by the "damage"), and it was basically aimed at protecting the company's assets from a private-sector viewpoint, as it is also proven by the fact that the crime required there to be a complaint (*querela*) in order for it to be prosecuted (Bellacosa, 2006: 243; Foffani, 2003: 1981; Forti, 2003: 1115; Musco, 2007: 237).

The reform enacted by means of Law no. 190 of 2012 was the chance to reflect on the most suitable model of incrimination for corruption in the private sector, among the four paradigms which could reasonably be envisaged (Bellacosa, 2014b: 23; De la Cuesta Arzamendi and Blanco Cordero, 2003: 58; Foffani, 1997: 582; Forti, 2003: 1116; Militello, 200: 919; Nieto Martín 2003: 113).

The first paradigm is the "encompassing" one, characterized by the equalization between public and private corruption. It is the system adopted in Sweden (chapter 10, comma 5a and 5b, c.c.; in Sweden the legislation regarding the crimes of corruption has been reformed with Law n. 301 of 24 May 2012) and also in the United Kingdom, where corruption among private persons is disciplined (by Section 1 and 2 of the Bribery Act 2010) in the same way as corruption by public officials (Sullivan, 2011: 87).

A second intervention regime can be defined as "loyal-fiduciary", as it is based on the violation of the duties of loyalty and integrity binding the offender (employee) and his or her head or employer. In said context, the French legal system (articles 445–1 and 445–2 of the *Code pénal*, inserted by Law no. 2005-750 of 4 July 2005; see Segonds, 2012: 7), the Dutch one (see art. 328-ter of the Dutch Criminal Code, introduced by the Act on criminalization of bribery of others than public servants of 23 November 1967, and afterwards modified; Tak, 2003: 147), are to be found, as well as one of the two cases of private corruption set forth by the German legal system (section 299 StGB as modified by the "law for the fight against corruption", *Gesetz zur Bekämpfung der Korruption*, of 20 November 2015).

A third model of legislation centres on the protection of competition, since the corruptive phenomenon is classified as a factor of distortion. An example is given by the other corruption offence in the private sector envisaged in Germany by Section 299 StGB, integrated when the criminal agreement aims to favour (*bevorzugen*) someone "unfairly (*in unlauterer Weise*) in the purchase of assets or in professional performances subject to competition (*im Wettbewerb*)" (see Bannenberg, 2014: 700; Dannecker, 2013: 1305; Huber, 1999: 516; Krick, 2014: 1225; Tiedemann, 2008: 316; Vogel, 2003: 88). A similar model is followed by the Spanish legal system, where art. 286-*bis* of the criminal code, introduced in 2010 (by the *Ley Orgánica* no. 5 of 22 June 2010), sanctions the unlawful agreement "to favor oneself or another person before third parties, through the violation of their duties in the purchase or sale of assets or in the performance of professional services (*incumpliendo sus obligaciones en la adquisición o venta de mercancías o en la contratación de servicios profesionales*)" (Bañeres Santos, 2011: 1035; De la Cuesta Arzamendi, 2013; González Blesa, 2012; Navarro Frias and Melero Bosch, 2011: 1).

The model of competition, as explained in more detail later, is the one favoured by EU lawmakers. In general terms, the value of "competition" can be considered according to two different protection perspectives. First, reference can be made to a notion of competition in a micro-economic version, as an instrumental good aiming at safeguarding the additional interests pertaining to individuals or to groups of individuals, namely and basically to two groups of persons: competing entrepreneurs, whose economic initiative is guaranteed, seen as an opportunity to participate in a market and to take risks, fairly; and the consumers, whose freedom to choose the offer deemed the best is thus guaranteed (Spena, 2007: 828). Second, competition can occur in a macro-economic perspective, considered as the ultimate good of protection, deemed as general interest to market competition as such, as a condition of efficiency of the market itself and of growth of the national and EU economy (Spena, 2007: 831).

The fourth and final model of criminalization of corruption in the private sector is the "patrimonial" type, which punishes the manager who, following the *pactum sceleris*, violates the duties of loyalty towards his or her company or entity, endangering the latter's economic-patrimonial interest. The example is given by Austrian lawmakers who decided (in 1987) to strengthen the criminal law protection of the private patrimony by applying alongside it the offence of disloyalty (*Untreue*: para. 153 StGB), the offence of "acceptance of undue benefit on the part of the representative" (*Geschenkannahme durch Machthaber*: para. 153a StGB; see Foffani, 1997: 584).

In the reforms implemented over the last few years, the Italian legislator has been influenced by the Framework Decision 2003/568/JHA on combatting corruption in the private sector, adopted by the Council of the European Union on 22 July 2003 (published in the *OJEU*, L. no. 192 of 31 July 2003; see Bartoli, 2013: 438; Mongillo, 2012: 192, 480). Pursuant to art. 2, para. 3, Member States can make a statement through which they reserve the right to define the application scope of the crimes of corruption in the private sector "to such conduct which involves, or could involve, a distortion of competition in relation to the purchase of goods or commercial services". In the "preamble" of the Framework Decision, it is pointed out (at no. 9) that:

Member States attach particular importance to combating corruption in both the public and the private sector, in the belief that in both those sectors it poses a threat to a law-abiding society as well as distorting competition in relation to the purchase of goods or commercial services and impeding sound economic development.

(Bartoli, 2013: 438; Mongillo, 2012: 192, 480)

The Framework Decision thus aims at protecting an interest having a collective nature such as fair and free competition. In particular, there seems to be a reference to the protection of competition in its macro-economic meaning, given the reference (in the "preamble") to the fact that corruptive practices give rise to distortions of competition and hinder a "sound economic development" (Flick, 2010: 192; Mongillo, 2012: 200).

Art. 2, para. 1, of the Framework Decision sets the models of incrimination of active and passive corruption in the following terms:

> Member States shall take the necessary measures to ensure that the following intentional conduct constitutes a criminal offence, when it is carried out in the course of business activities: a) promising, offering or giving, directly or through an intermediary, to a person who in any capacity directs or works for a private-sector entity an undue advantage of any kind, for that person or for a third party, in order that that person should perform or refrain from performing any act, in breach of that person's duties; b) directly or through an intermediary, requesting or receiving an undue advantage of any kind, or accepting the promise of such an advantage, for oneself or for a third party, while in any capacity directing or working for a private-sector entity, in order to perform or refrain from performing any act, in breach of one's duties.

The conduct of the crime, in its form both active and passive, thus revolves around the notion of "breach of duty", which is defined (in art. 1 of the Framework Decision itself) referring to what "shall be understood in accordance with national law", but in any case, specifying that it:

> [s]hould cover as a minimum any disloyal behaviour constituting a breach of a statutory duty, or, as the case may be, a breach of professional regulations or instructions, which apply within the business of a person who in any capacity directs or works for a private sector entity.

It is a model of case with an early protection, in which the typical fact – whose extent depends on the meaning given to the vague concept of "private sector entity" – stands apart from the commission of the act which is the object of the unlawful agreement.

Art. 5 demands the liability of legal persons for facts of private corruption "committed for their benefit".

In Italy, the reform of 2012, besides modifying the *nomen iuris* in "corruption among private persons", maintained the structure of the crime with the event of "damage" for the company, but modified the provision regarding prosecution: "A complaint of the offended person is required, except for the case in which there is a distortion of competition in relation to the purchase of goods or commercial services". The resulting crime, characterized by two events (damage to the company and distortion in the competition for the purchase of goods or services; the first event being considered as an essential requirement for the crime, the second one as a possible further event) thus aimed to protect a double interest: first of all, the assets of the company, from a private and individual perspective, highlighted also by prosecution upon complaint; second, competition, with an offensive action outside the company, beyond individual interests and of a collective nature, so as to justify the passage to prosecution *ex officio* (Bellacosa, 2014b: 56; Severino, 2013: 11).

With the recent reform implemented by means of legislative decree no. 38 of 15 March 2017, the aim was to give a broader implementation in the Italian legal system to Framework Decision 2003/568/GAI related to the fight against corruption in the private sector (Bartoli, 2017: 5; La Rosa, 2016: 1; Seminara, 2017: 713). Nowadays the crime (art. 2635 c.c.) is described in the following terms:

1  Regardless of the fact that it constitutes a more serious crime, managers, general managers, and executives responsible for drawing up the company accounting documents, the statutory auditors and liquidators of companies and private entities who, also through an intermediary, solicit or receive, for him/herself or a third party, money or other undue benefit, or accepts the promise of such an advantage, in order to perform or refrain from performing any act, in breach of the duties deriving from their offices or of fidelity duties, are punished with imprisonment from one to three years.

2  The penalty is the imprisonment up to one year and six months if the fact is committed by someone who is under the direction or surveillance of one of the persons described in the first paragraph.

3  Whoever gives or promises money or other benefit to the persons described in the first and second paragraph is punished with the penalties provided in said paragraphs.

4  The penalties provided in the previous paragraphs are doubled for listed companies on . . .

5  A complaint of the offended person is required, except for the case in which there is a distortion of competition in relation to the purchase of goods or commercial services.

As can be seen, whereas beforehand the application scope was limited to the corporate context, now legislative decree 38/2017 has widened the application scope of the provision from commercial enterprises to any "private entity". The exact reach of the expression "private entity" is ambiguous; it is not clear, in fact, if reference is being made only to those having legal personality or also to those without it, in addition to de facto collective entities (La Rosa, 2016: 1). The lack of specifications in the expression "private entities" leads one to believe that it refers also to entities without legal personality, such as non-profit organizations and foundations; moreover, it seems that the provision may be applied to political parties and unions, too (Di Vizio, 2017: 5).

The reform implemented by means of legislative decree no. 38/17 marks a change in the punitive paradigm: from the "patrimonial" type of repression of corruption in the private sector to the so-called "loyalty" model, in which the offence hits, in the form of violation of duties, the fiduciary relationship binding the "corrupted" person and the company or entity in which he or she performs his or her activity (La Rosa, 2016: 3; Zannotti, 2017: 2).

In respect of the provision previously in force, by means of the reform implemented by legislative decree no. 38/17, the reference to causing a "damage to the company" has disappeared and it is no longer necessary for there to be an actual commission or omission of an act. The effect of said change is that of making the scheme typical of corruption among private persons more similar to that of proper antecedent corruption in the public sector (art. 319 c.p.). In addition, in the structure of the incriminated fact the actual commission or omission of an act is not necessary, but this latter element becomes the object of the specific intent (*dolo specifico*) to commit a crime (La Rosa, 2016: 2; Seminara, 2017: 722).

The reform of 2017 maintained prosecution upon complaint, unless "from the fact [there] derives a distortion of competition in the purchase of goods or services". The final result is a hybrid: the basic offence follows the "loyal" model, but when the illicit agreement causes a distortion of competition, the damaging effect increases to the point of determining the prosecution *ex officio* (Seminara, 2017: 725; Zannotti, 2017: 2).

The case *ex* art. 2635 c.c. seems to refer to competition in its micro-economic meaning, given that the single corruptive event in the private sector is not suitable, per se, to harm the structure or competitive stability of the market as such (Bartoli, 2013: 445). The event of "distortion of competition in the purchase of goods and services" occurs therefore every time the individual interests of the competitors or consumers are harmed by the alteration of the competitive rules that are already in the single and actual economic transaction which is the object of the corruption agreement. In this way, for instance, if enterprise A and enterprise B bring forth two offers to supply the same good or service, of the same quality, to the commercial company C, and this latter's director, being corrupted, chooses A's offer although at a higher purchasing price, enterprise B is the victim of a distortion of competition and has the legitimate right to report to the authorities the corruptive event, which, as such, can be prosecuted *ex officio*. The possibility that there may be a "distortion of competition" in a single economic transaction which is harmful for the competitors does not rule out, however, that the case in question may be used to offer a protection to competition in a macroeconomic sense. Indeed, it should not be ignored that a "serial" repetition of corruptive transactions may result in harm to the competitive structure of a whole market sector (Bellacosa, 2014b: 52).

## 6 Conclusions

In conclusion, the Italian system in terms of the fight against corruption has taken into account the indications arising at both European and international levels (as shown by the offence of trafficking of unlawful influences and by the changes made to the crime of private corruption). It has maintained some links with national tradition (as it is evident from the fact that the crime of *concussione* is still in force) and shows some aspects of indisputable originality (as it was highlighted by the provisions on ANAC and the national anti-corruption plan). After the *Mani Pulite* (i.e. clean hands) scandal, when, during the nineties, a series of judicial investigations brought out a well-established system of collusion between politics and entrepreneurship, a raft of profound reforms began in Italy, which today have been enhanced by the recent amendment of the statute of limitations (enacted with Law no. 103 of 2017, entered into force on 3 August 2017). These interventions give life to a complete and efficient system, with a large arsenal of both repressive and preventive measures.

Said regulatory interventions share the common intent of spreading a culture of legality, mostly in the world of commercial enterprise, to better protect fair competition and the freedom to conduct business.

As with all systemic reforms, only the coming years will show (by figures and statistics) how these measures work in practice.

## Bibliography

Bañeres Santos, F. (2011) El Delito de corrupción entre particulares, in *Rev. jur. de Catalunya*.

Bannenberg, B. (2014) Korruption, in H.B. Wabnitz, T. Janovsky (eds.), *Handbuch des Wirtschaftsund Steuerstrafrechts*. Monaco: C. H. Beck.

Bartoli, R. (2013) Corruzione tra privati, in B.G. Mattarella, M. Pelissero (eds.), *La legge anticorruzione. Prevenzione e repressione della corruzione*. Torino: Giappichelli: 435.

Bartoli, R. (2016) I piani e i modelli organizzativi anticorruzione nei settori pubblico e privato, in *Dir. pen. proc.*, n. 11: 1507.

Bartoli, R. (2017) Corruzione privata: verso una riforma di stampo europeo?, in *Dir. pen. proc.*, n. 1: 5.

Bassi, A. (2014) Disposizioni processuali applicabili, in M. Levis, A. Perini (eds.), *La responsabilità amministrativa delle società e degli enti*. Bologna: Zanichelli: 869.

Bellacosa, M. (2006) *Obblighi di fedeltà dell'amministratore di società e sanzioni penali.* Milano: Giuffré.

Bellacosa, M. (2014a) Autonomia delle responsabilità dell'ente, in M. Levis, A. Perini (eds.), *La responsabilità amministrativa delle società e degli enti.* Bologna: Zanichelli: 216.

Bellacosa, M. (2014b) La corruzione privata societaria, in A. Del Vecchio: Severino (eds.), *Il contrasto alla corruzione nel diritto interno e nel diritto internazionale.* Milano: Cedam: 11.

Bertolini, N. (2003) Brevi note sulla responsabilità degli enti e delle persone giuridiche negli Stati Uniti: in particolare, le federal sentencing guidelines, in *Il Foro Ambrosiano*: 527.

Bohnert, J. (2016) *Kommentar zum Ordnungswidrigkeitendgesetz OWiG.* Monaco: Beck.

Bonini, S. (2012) Traffico di influenze illecite, in *Giur. It.*, n. 12: 2694.

Bricola, F. (1970) Il costo del principio "societas delinquere non potest" nell'attuale dimensione del fenomeno societario, in *Riv. it. dir. proc. pen.*, n. 1: 951.

Catenacci, M. (2016) Caratteri Generali, in M. Catenacci (ed.), *Reati contro la pubblica amministrazione e contro la amministrazione della giustizia.* Torino: Giappichelli: 75.

Catenacci, M. and Picardi, A. (2016) Le diverse figure, in M. Catenacci (ed.), *Reati contro la pubblica amministrazione e contro la amministrazione della giustizia*. Torino: Giappichelli: 94.

Cimadomo, D. (2016) *Prova e giudizio di fatto nel processo penale a carico degli enti*. Milano: Cedam.

Dannecker, G. (2013) § 299 StGB, in U. Kindhäuser, U. Neumann, H.U. Paeffgen (eds.), *Strafgesetzbuch. Nomos Kommentar*, vol. III, IV ed. Baden Baden: Nomos: 1298.

De La Cuesta Arzamendi, J.L. (2013) *La corrupción ante el derecho y la justicia*. Available at: *www.penalecontemporaneo.it*. Accessed September 7, 2017.

De La Cuesta Arzamendi, J.L., Blanco Cordero, I. (2003) La criminalizzazione della corruzione nel settore privato: aspetti sovranazionali e di diritto comparato, in R. Acquaroli, L. Foffani (eds.), *La corruzione tra privati. Esperienze comparatistiche e prospettive di riforma*. Milano: Giuffrè: 43.

De Maglie, C. (1995) Sanzioni pecuniarie e tecniche di controllo dell'impresa. Crisi ed innovazioni nel diritto penale statunitense, in *Riv. it. dir. proc. pen.*: 88.

De Maglie, C. (2002) *L'etica e il mercato: la responsabilità penale delle società*. Milano: Giuffré.

De Simone, G. (2012) *Persone giuridiche e responsabilità da reato, Profili storici, dogmatici e comparatistici*. Pisa: ETS.

Desportes, F. and Le Gunehec, F (2007) *Droit Pénal Général*. Paris: Economica.

De Vero, G. (2008) *La responsabilità penale delle persone giuridiche*. Milano: Giuffrè.

Di Giovine, O. (2010) Lineamenti sostanziali del nuovo illecito punitivo, in. G. Lattanzi (ed.), *Reati e responsabilità degli enti*. Milano: Giuffrè: 3.

Di Vizio, F. (2017) *La riforma della corruzione tra privati*. Available at: www.*quotidiano giuridico.it*. Accessed September 7, 2017.

Dolcini, E. (2013) Appunti su corruzione e legge anti-corruzione, in *Riv. it. dir. proc. pen.*: 543.

Dolcini E. and Paliero, C.E. (1980) L'illecito amministrativo (Ordnungswidrigkeit) nell'ordinamento della Repubblica federale di Germania: disciplina, sfera di applicazione, linee di politica legislativa, in *Riv. it. dir. proc. pen.*: 1134.

Fiandaca, G. and Musco, E. (2012) *Diritto Penale, Parte Speciale*, Volume I. Bologna: Zanichelli.

Fiandaca, G. and Musco, E. (2013) *Diritto Penale, Parte speciale, I, Addenda. La recente riforma dei reati contro la pubblica amministrazione*. Bologna: Zanichelli.

Fidelbo, G. (2010) Le attribuzioni del giudice penale e la partecipazione dell'ente al processo, in G. Lattanzi (ed.), *Reati e responsabilità degli enti*. Milano: Giuffrè: 435.

Flick, G.M. (2010) A proposito della tutela della concorrenza: economia e diritto penale o economia di diritto penale? in C. Rabitti Bedogni: Barucci (eds.), *20 anni di antitrust. L'evoluzione dell'Autorità Garante della Concorrenza e del Mercato*. Torino: Giappichelli: 183.

Foffani, L. (1997) *Infedeltà patrimoniale e conflitto d'interessi nella gestione d'impresa. Profili penalistici*. Milano: Giuffrè.

Foffani, L. (2003) Società, in F.C. Palazzo, C.E. Paliero, *Commentario breve alle leggi penali complementari*. Padova: Cedam: 1793.

Forti, G. (2003) La corruzione tra privati nell'orbita di disciplina della corruzione pubblica: un contributo di tematizzazione, in *Riv. it. dir. proc. pen.*: 1115.

Gandini, F (2013) *Brevi cenni sulla responsabilità delle persone giuridiche in Germania*. Available at: www.rivista231.it. Accessed September 7, 2017.

Giavazzi, S. (2005) La responsabilità penale delle persone giuridiche: dieci anni di esperienza francese (parte seconda), in *Riv. trim. dir. pen. ec.*: 873.

González Blesa, F.J. (2012), Delito de corrupción entre particulares: comentarios y criticas al articulo 286 bis CP, in *Noticias Juridicas.*

Grossi, S. (2016) Il delitto di traffico di influenze illecite (art. 346-bis c.p.), in M. Catenacci (ed.), *Reati contro la pubblica amministrazione e contro la amministrazione della giustizia.* Torino: Giappichelli: 251.

Guerrini, R. (2007) *La responsabilità da reato degli enti.* Milano: Giuffrè.

Guido, E. (2015) Il valore della legalità nell'impresa a partire dalla normativa sulla responsabilità degli enti per l'illecito derivante da reato, in *Riv. It. Dir. Proc. Pen.*, n. 1: 280.

Hirsch, H.J. (1995) Strafrechtliche Verantwortlichkeit von Unternehmen, in *ZStW*, 107, vol. II: 285.

Huber, B. (1999) Il sistema tedesco di lotta alla corruzione: una comparazione con quelli di altri Paesi europei, in *Riv. trim. dir. pen. ec.*: 516.

Huber, B. (2001) La lotta alla corruzione in prospettiva sovranazionale, in *Riv. trim. dir. pen. ec.*: 467.

Krick, C. (2014) § 299 StGB, in *Münchener Kommentar zum Strafgesetzbuch, §§ 263–358*, vol. V, II ed. Monaco: C.H. Beck: 1207.

La Rosa, E. (2016) *Verso una nuova riforma della corruzione tra privati: dal modello "patrimonialistico" a quello "lealistico".* Available at: www.penalecontemporaneo.it. Accessed September 7, 2017.

Losappio, G. (2015) Millantato credito e traffico di influenze illecite. Rapporti diacronici e sincronici, in *Cass. Pen.*: 1036.

Lottini, R. (2005) *La responsabilità penale delle persone giuridiche nel diritto inglese.* Milano: Giuffrè.

Manacorda, S., Centonze, F., Forti, G. (2014) *Preventing Corporate Corruption.* Dordrecht, The Netherlands: Springer.

Militello, V. (2000) Infedeltà patrimoniale e corruzione nel futuro del diritto societario, in *Riv. trim. dir. pen. ec.*: 905.

Mongillo, V. (2012) *La corruzione tra sfera interna e dimensione internazionale.* Napoli: ESI.

Mongillo, V. (2013) L'incerta frontiera: il discrimine tra concussione e induzione indebita nel nuovo statuto penale della pubblica amministrazione, in *Dir. pen. cont.*, n. 3: 166.

Mongillo, V. (2015) Il "sacchetto d'oro" e la "spada inguainata": interazione pubblico-privato e il peso degli "incentivi", *in un recente modello di compliance anticorruzione.* Available at: www.penalecontemporaneo.it. Accessed September 7, 2017.

Musco, E. (2004) *L'illusione penalistica.* Milano: Giuffrè.

Musco, E. (2007) *I nuovi reati societari.* Milano: Giuffrè.

Navarro Frias, I. and Melero Bosch, L.V. (2011) Corrupción entre particulares y tutela del mercado, in *InDret*, 4: 1.

Nieto Martín, A. (2003) La corruzione nel settore privato: riflessioni sull'ordinamento spagnolo alla luce del diritto comparato, in R. Acquaroli, L. Foffani, (eds.), *La corruzione tra privati. Esperienze comparatistiche e prospettive di riforma.* Milano: Giuffrè: 111.

Palazzo, F. (2012) Corruzione, concussione e dintorni, in *Diritto Penale Contemporaneo*, n. 1: 228.

Paliero, C.E. (1995) Ordnungswidrigkeiten, in *Dig. Disc. Pen.*, vol. IX. Torino: UTET: 129.

Paliero, C.E. (2001) Il D.Lgs. 8 giugno 2001, n. 231: da ora in poi societas delinquere (e puniri) potest, in *Corr. Giur.*: 845.

Paliero, C.E. (2014) Soggetti sottoposti all'altrui direzione e modelli di organizzazione dell'ente, in M. Levis, A. Perini (eds.), *La responsabilità amministrativa delle società e degli enti.* Bologna: Zanichelli: 186.

Paliero, C.E. and Piergallini, C. (2006) La colpa di organizzazione, in *Resp. amm. Soc. enti*: 169.

Pecorella, C. (2002), Principi generali e criteri di attribuzione della responsabilità, in A. Alessandri et al. (eds.), *La responsabilità amministrativa degli enti. D. Lgs. 8 giugno 2001, n. 231.* Milano: IPSOA: 65.

Pernazza, F. (2014) Responsabilità penale delle società e corruzione in Francia, in A. Del Vecchio: Severino (eds.), *Il contrasto alla corruzione nel diritto interno e nel diritto internazionale.* Milano: Cedam: 535.

Piergallini, C. (2010a) La struttura del modello di organizzazione, gestione e controllo del rischio-reato, in G. Lattanzi (ed.), *Reati e responsabilità degli enti.* Milano: Giuffrè: 153.

Piergallini, C. (2010b) I reati presupposto della responsabilità dell'ente e l'apparato sanzionatorio, in G. Lattanzi (ed.), *Reati e responsabilità degli enti.* Milano: Giuffrè: 211.

Romano, M. (2013) *I delitti contro la pubblica amministrazione. I delitti dei pubblici ufficiali*, III ed. Milano: Giuffrè.

Sabia, R. and Salvemme, I. (2016) Costi e funzioni dei modelli di organizzazione e gestione ai sensi del d.lgs. n. 231/2001, in A. Del Vecchio: Severino (eds.), *Tutela degli investimenti tra integrazione dei mercati e concorrezza di ordinamenti.* Bari: Cacucci: 445

Scaroina, E. (2006) *Societas delinquere potest. Il problema del gruppo di imprese.* Milano: Giuffrè.

Scaroina, E. (2016) Lobbying e rischio penale, in *Dir. pen. proc.*, n. 6: 811.

Scaroina, E. (2017) Le specialità del modello organizzativo per la prevenzione dei reati nelle società a partecipazione pubblica, in F. Auletta (ed.), *I controlli nelle società pubbliche.* Bologna: Zanichelli: 135.

Segonds, M. (2012) Corruption active et passive de persone n'exerçant pas une fonction publique, in *JurisClasseur Pénal Code*: 7.

Seminara, S. (2017) Il gioco infinito: la riforma del reato di corruzione tra privati, in *Dir. pen. proc.*: 713.

Severino, P. (2013) La nuova legge anticorruzione, in *Dir. pen. proc.*: 11.

Severino, P. (2014) Il problema del contrasto alla corruzione, in A. Del Vecchio: Severino (eds.), *Il contrasto alla corruzione nel diritto interno e nel diritto internazionale.* Milano: Cedam: 3.

Smacchi, M., (2014) La responsabilità penale delle società nel diritto tedesco, in A. Del Vecchio: Severino (eds.), *Il contrasto alla corruzione nel diritto interno e nel diritto internazionale.* Milano: Cedam, 559.

Spena, A. (2007) Punire la corruzione privata? Un inventario di perplessità politico-criminali, in *Riv. trim. dir. pen. ec.*: 834.

Sullivan, G.R. (2011) The Bribery Act 2010: An Overview, in *Crim. Law Rev.*, n. 2: 87.

Tak, P. (2003) Il reato di corruzione privata in Olanda, in R. Acquaroli, L. Foffani (eds.), *La corruzione tra privati. Esperienze comparatistiche e prospettive di riforma.* Milano: Giuffrè: 144.

Thaman, S.C. (2014), L'esperienza statunitense nella lotta alla corruzione, in A. Del Vecchio, P. Severino (eds.), *Il contrasto alla corruzione nel diritto interno e nel diritto internazionale.* Milano: Cedam, 577.

Tiedemann, K. (2008), § 299 StGB, in H. W. Laufhütte, R. Rissing-van Saan, K. Tiedemann (eds.), *Strafgesetzbuch. Leipziger Kommentar*, X vol. Berlin: De Gruyter: 316.

Tricot, J. (2014) Corporate liability and compliance programs in France, in S. Manacorda, F. Centonze, G. Forti (eds.), *Preventing Corporate Corruption*. Dordrecht, The Netherlands: Springer: 477.

Tripodi, A.F. (2004) "Situazione organizzativa" e "colpa di organizzazione": alcune riflessioni sulle nuove specificità del diritto penale dell'economia, in *Riv. trim. dir. pen. ec.*: 483.

Viganò, F. (2014) I delitti di corruzione nell'ordinamento italiano: qualche considerazione sulle riforme già fatte, e su quel che resta da fare, in *Dir. pen. cont.*, n. 3–4: 4.

Vogel, J. (2003) La tutela penale contro la corruzione nel settore privato: l'esperienza tedesca, in R. Acquaroli, L. Foffani (eds.), *La corruzione tra privati. Esperienze comparatistiche e prospettive di riforma*. Milano: Giuffrè: 75.

Wells, C. (2003) Corporate criminal liability in England and Wales, in F. Palazzo (ed.), *Societas puniri potest: la responsabilità da reato degli enti collettivi*. Padova: Cedam: 111.

Wells, C. (2014) Corporate responsibility and compliance programs in the United Kingdom, in S. Manacorda, F. Centonze, G. Forti (eds.), *Preventing Corporate Corruption*. Dordrecht, The Netherlands: Springer: 505.

Zannotti, R. (2017) *Finalmente una nuova disciplina per la corruzione privata*. Available at: www.ilpenalista.it. Accessed September 7, 2017.

# 13 Negotiating non-contention

## Civil recovery and deferred prosecution in response to transnational corporate bribery

*Nicholas Lord and Colin King*

## Introduction

This chapter is about how state authorities negotiate non-contentious outcomes to criminal cases with corporations implicated in transnational corporate bribery. By 'negotiated non-contention' we mean the mutually beneficial agreement of sanctions (i.e. negotiation) that circumvent criminal prosecution and its associated adversarial contestation in the criminal courts (i.e. non-contention). These agreements are made between public prosecutors and implicated corporations, now with some form of judicial oversight, although this was not always the case. While in some circumstances full criminal prosecution may not be the desired outcome, we must recognise that governments criminalise behaviours, such as corporate bribery, on the basis that they are in some way immoral or inherently bad, and not just as a means for reducing crime. Given that *criminal* behaviours are reflective of societal moral boundaries, we need to explore why state authorities would avoid prosecution. In these terms, it is our aim in this chapter to inform a discussion of the nature and purpose of negotiated non-contention.

Corporate bribery in international business involves illicit transactions and relations, usually between commercial enterprises and foreign public officials,[1] whereby business is maintained or obtained through the use of inducements, whether actively offered, solicited or extorted (see Lord and Doig, 2014). While corporate bribery of foreign public officials is a serious *crime* as indicated in UK law (see s.6 Bribery Act 2010) and international conventions (see the OECD Anti-Bribery Convention 1997 and the UN Convention against Corruption 2003), that seriousness is often not reflected in the state's *criminal* justice response: due to a variety of reasons, it remains rare that companies are prosecuted in the UK for bribery.[2] This reflects pragmatic and practical obstacles such as enforcement/informational asymmetries across jurisdictions when obtaining evidence and the difficulties of proving corporate criminal liability, but also ideological

---

1 We can distinguish between public (i.e. commercial organisations induce public officials) and commercial bribery (i.e. commercial organisations induce other commercial actors). Our focus here is on public bribery.
2 From January to March 2017, a consultation was held on corporate liability for economic crime: Ministry of Justice (2017). See also Law Commission (2010).

predilections of the executive to protect national economic interests[3] as well as the normative preferences of regulators to negotiate with corporates, rather than engage in an adversarial encounter in the criminal courts (see Lord, 2014). In the context of foreign corporate bribery, there is an evident shift away from what has been termed 'regulation by enforcement' (Pitt and Shapiro, 1990) in preference for 'regulation by settlement' (Bennett et al., 2013; Turk, 2017). Indeed, Wells (2015) notes how corporate offenders in the UK are treated with a hands-off, or kid-glove, protective approach. This is a theme common in the response of specialist business regulation bodies more widely as criminal prosecution is overwhelmingly the road not taken (Levi and Lord, 2017: 734). Thus, rather than 'crime control' (i.e. pursuit of punitive punishments and prosecution of corporate offenders to ensure public justice and moral condemnation), we see the 'regulation' of corporate criminal behaviour through negotiation (see Croall, 2003).

The Serious Fraud Office (SFO) is the responsible enforcement authority in England and Wales (E+W), and Northern Ireland. The SFO has the dual responsibility of investigation and prosecution, and although formally a criminal law enforcement authority, its approach to 'policing' has better reflected practices associated with regulation (see Lord, 2013). As Croall (2003) notes, 'regulation' uses strategies of persuasion and cooperation (where forthcoming) to encourage and negotiate compliant behaviours with established standards, whereby private remedies or self-regulation are the desired outcomes. Persuasion is considered to be the more effective approach due to the inherent complexity of offences associated with transnational corporate bribery, for example, but low prosecution rates[4] raise questions about the deterrence impact and the closeness of the regulatory relationship (e.g. regulatory capture). Where such offences are committed on behalf of a commercial enterprise (i.e. organisational, corporate crime rather than individual, occupational crime), such regulatory control is the more likely response. In essence, such regulatory strategies avoid conflict and contention, and assume implicated actors are willing to comply with state intervention.

But embedded within such processes of negotiation are power dynamics, both in terms of the availability of knowledge to the regulator on the nature and extent of the bribery within business (i.e. how does the SFO find out about and understand bribery within closed business environments?), but also its ability to do something about such criminal behaviour (i.e. how it changes behaviour within business). Furthermore, this enforcement and regulatory scenario is further hindered, as those corporates and actors implicated in bribery are 'conscious opponents' (see Sparrow, 2008). The activities of these conscious opponents are driven by informed and intelligent actors, who are able to conceal and hide illicit transactions behind otherwise 'normal' business processes, making them difficult to detect, and if detected, they are well positioned and (cap)able of gaming

---

3 The case of BAE Systems is the most pertinent example of state protection, where then-PM Tony Blair intervened to have an investigation stopped. D. Leigh and R. Evans, 'How Blair put pressure on Goldsmith to end BAE investigation', *The Guardian*, 21 December 2017.

4 Though conversely this may also reflect 'successful' persuasion.

legal gaps, asymmetries and procedures, in turn hindering enforcement and regulatory intentions. Corporates are well placed in terms of resource (financially and personnel) and expertise (internal and external legal counsel) to be able to counter pervasive and punitive enforcement intentions, ensuring they retain a position of 'power' in any negotiation. In addition to this conscious opposition, corporate criminal liability laws underpinned by the identification principle in the UK make prosecuting large corporations improbable. Thus, it is difficult for UK enforcement authorities to pursue criminal justice responses. It is in this context that we have seen a shift towards the negotiation of non-contentious outcomes, due to both pragmatic and normative reasons as outlined earlier, in the domain of transnational corporate bribery. Most notably, we have seen this emerge since 2008 in the form of two main policy responses that reflect a strategic preference for negotiation, rather than contention, and a sanctioning preference characterised by deferred or non-prosecution. These responses – namely civil recovery orders (CROs) and deferred prosecution agreements (DPAs) – are the focus of this chapter.

We begin with an analysis of the negotiation of a non-contentious outcome in the form of civil recovery. Here we consider the SFO's early preference for civil settlement without also pursuing criminal prosecution – a policy that was heavily criticised. We go on to consider the cloak of secrecy that enveloped earlier CROs in particular – another practice of the SFO that attracted criticism. The lack of transparency in such deals was criticised by those in favour of negotiated settlements, on the grounds that it made the negotiation process more difficult, and also by those against such deal-making, on the basis that it allowed corporates to 'buy' their way out of criminal sanction and to avoid being labelled 'criminal'. Next, we consider the SFO's apparent shift to being more transparent and open about CROs, with reference to the case of Oxford Publishing Ltd. After this discussion of CROs, we then analyse the negotiation of non-contentious outcomes through DPAs, which are likely to supplant the use of CROs in the context of transnational corporate bribery. Here we analyse the nature and rationale of DPAs, considering the advantages and disadvantages to their implementation before analysing the case of Rolls Royce and the terms of that DPA. We identify several issues with the use of DPAs in England and Wales, including underlying concerns with policy transfer and the nature of corporate criminal liability. We conclude by arguing that – contrary to discourse emanating from the SFO – negotiated non-contentious outcomes are emerging as the 'new normal' and that the emphasis is on 'accommodation' of negotiated justice.

## Negotiating non-contention through civil recovery orders

Civil recovery powers have been in place in the UK since 2003,[5] enabling an enforcement authority to bring a proprietary action to target the proceeds of criminal activity. Civil recovery does not require criminal conviction; indeed, for

---

5  The civil recovery provisions came into force on 24 February 2003: SI 2003/120 The Proceeds of Crime Act 2002 (Commencement No.4, Transitional Provisions and Savings) Order 2003.

some that is its most pressing attraction (for consideration of arguments in favour of civil recovery, see Kennedy, 2004. See also Nicholls et al., 2011: 255 *et seq*). Others, however, have been critical, particularly in relation to undermining procedural protections of the criminal process (Campbell, 2010; Lea, 2004). Hendry and King (2015: 407) argue that 'the use of a civil process to target criminal assets in the absence of criminal conviction is an affront to legitimacy'.

In the context of corporate wrongdoing, civil recovery has been available to the SFO since 2008, and has been used on a number of occasions. With the advent of DPAs, it is to be expected that civil recovery actions will not be as prevalent in responding to corporate crime, yet it is worthwhile considering the use of such orders not least as that experience reinforces the emphasis on negotiation and non-contention since the late 2000s. As Alldridge (2018) notes about civil recovery powers, 'It was not the objective to litigate every case. As with any other civil case, a settlement will often be the preferred outcome'. Indeed, up until 2012, the SFO had an explicit policy of settling self-reported foreign bribery cases 'civilly wherever possible' without also pursing criminal prosecution (SFO, 2009).[6] The preference for civil settlements has, however, been criticised (see OECD, 2012: 33). Thomas LJ was particularly scathing in the *Innospec* case:

> Those who commit such serious crimes as corruption of senior foreign government officials must not be viewed or treated in any different way to other criminals. It will therefore rarely be appropriate for criminal conduct by a company to be dealt with by means of a civil recovery order . . . It is of the greatest public interest that the serious criminality of any, including companies, who engage in the corruption of foreign governments, is made patent for all to see by the imposition of criminal and not civil sanctions. It would be inconsistent with basic principles of justice for the criminality of corporations to be glossed over by a civil as opposed to a criminal sanction.[7]

## Civil recovery, corporate bribery and the cloak of secrecy

Following the disbanding of the Assets Recovery Agency, civil recovery powers were vested in, *inter alia*, the Director of the SFO on 1 April 2008.[8] Up until 2012, there was a noticeable cloak of secrecy surrounding CRO agreements entered into by the SFO. Change only came about following significant criticism, including in an OECD report (March 2012) and an HMCPSI report (November 2012). The lack of transparency was highlighted by the OECD (2012: 22): 'A principal concern is the paucity of publicly available information on the foreign

---

6 The explicit emphasis on settling such self-report cases 'civilly wherever possible' was removed in 2012. See Debevoise and Plimpton LLP (2012).

7 *R v Innospec Limited*, Sentencing Remarks, Crown Court at Southwark, 26 March 2010, Thomas LJ, para. 38.

8 Serious Crime Act 2007 (Commencement No.2 and Transitional and Transitory Provisions and Savings) Order 2008. Factors that might influence the use of non-conviction based powers are set out in Attorney General, Guidance for prosecutors and investigators on their asset recovery powers under Section 2A of the Proceeds of Crime Act 2002 (29 November 2012).

bribery cases conducted by the SFO that have been settled through civil recovery orders'. The use of consent CROs[9] facilitates behind-the-scenes negotiations/ agreements between the SFO and corporates with limited scrutiny:

> Unlike a criminal plea agreement, there is no court hearing. A Judge does not assess the factual basis of the order, or determine the amount that the defendant should pay. The judges and the SFO at the on-site visit described the procedure as 'a paper process'. The SFO and the defendant can thus dictate the terms of the settlement. Defendants therefore have the certainty in the outcome of settlement negotiations that is unavailable in the criminal plea negotiation process.
>
> (OECD, 2012: 23. See also Transparency
> International (UK), 2012: 64)

The HMCPSI report was also critical in this area, including one recommendation as follows: 'The SFO needs to design and document a transparent process for deciding to pursue civil recovery, and negotiating/agreeing any consent order' (HMCPSI, 2012: 3). Indeed, the team preparing that HMCPSI report were not given access to earlier CRO cases:

> Civil recovery consent orders in cases settled before April 2012 are not disclosable, due to a provision in the orders themselves. Inspectors have not been allowed access to them, and we are therefore unable to comment on them.
>
> (HMCPSI, 2012: 35)

This reinforces the cloak-and-dagger nature of such negotiations/agreements. Before proceeding further, it is worth setting out the use of CROs by the SFO. Table 13.1 outlines the details of such cases.[10]

As already mentioned, the lack of transparency surrounding CRO 'deals' in earlier cases has been criticised – albeit for different reasons. Some stakeholders have voiced concern that the use of such deals has allowed corporates and their directors 'to escape criminal justice on acceptance of a financial penalty' (HMCPSI, 2012: 35). Often the SFO seemed at pains to avoid labelling the

---

9  Section 276(1) of POCA states: 'The court may make an order staying . . . any proceedings for a recovery order on terms agreed by the parties for the disposal of the proceedings if each person to whose property the proceedings, or the agreement, relates is a party both to the proceedings and the agreement'.

10  Our discussion is confined to CROs obtained by the SFO. In Scotland, the Civil Recovery Unit (CRU) has been granted CROs against Abbot Group Ltd (2012), International Tubular Services Ltd (2014), Brand-Rex Ltd (2015) and Braid Group (Holdings) Ltd. See, respectively, BBC News, 'Aberdeen "corruption case" oil firm Abbot Group to pay £5.6m' (23 November 2012); BBC News, 'Aberdeen firm iTS pays £172,000 over Kazakhstan corruption' (17 December 2014); 'Fife company makes bribery civil settlement with Crown', *The Journal of the Law Society of Scotland* (25 September 2015); BBC News, 'Braid Group pays £2m bribery penalty' (4 April 2016). For published guidance in Scotland, see COPFS (2017).

Table 13.1 Civil Recovery Orders obtained by the SFO

| Date | Business | Nature of case | Unlawful conduct | Self-report | Business advantage gained | Nature of order |
|---|---|---|---|---|---|---|
| October 2008 | Balfour Beatty | Payment irregularities within a subsidiary company during a construction project in Egypt, which had been completed in 2001. | These payments did not comply with requirements of accurate business records under section 221 of the Companies Act 1985. | Yes | Linked to a $130 UNESCO construction joint venture. | £2.25 million CRO, plus a contribution towards the costs of the proceedings. |
| October 2009 | AMEC plc | Receipt of irregular payments associated with a project of which AMEC was a shareholder. | Failure to comply with the requirements of section 221 of the Companies Act 1985. | Yes | Unspecified | £4,943,648 CRO plus the costs incurred. |
| February 2011 | MW Kellogg Ltd | Criminal activity by third parties (i.e. MWKL's parent company and others). | The SFO acknowledged 'that MWKL was used by the parent company and was not a willing participant in the corruption'.[1] | Yes | Not specified. The amount in question related to share dividends from profits/revenues generated as a result of bribery and corruption by the third parties. | £7,028,077 CRO. |
| April 2011 | DePuy International Ltd | A DPA had been concluded with the US DoJ in relation to the same unlawful conduct, and the SFO were of the view that a criminal prosecution in the UK was precluded due to double jeopardy. | Payments to intermediaries for the purpose of making corrupt payments to Greek medical officials. | No (referral came via US authorities). | Estimated to be approx. £14.8 million. Retention and enhancement of market position. | £4.829 million CRO, plus prosecution costs. This figure took account of 'a global resolution' (including disgorgement and recovery in other jurisdictions). |

(continued)

*Table 13.1 (continued)*

| Date | Business | Nature of case | Unlawful conduct | Self-report | Business advantage gained | Nature of order |
|---|---|---|---|---|---|---|
| July 2011 | Macmillan Publishers Ltd | Allegations of bribery and corruption in relation to the supply of educational materials. | Not specified beyond general allegations of bribery and corruption. | No (referral came via World Bank). | Contracts to supply products (educational materials) valued at approximately £11.2m. | £11,263,852.28 CRO, plus SFO costs of £27,000. |
| January 2012 | Mabey Engineering (Holdings) Ltd | Share dividends derived from contracts that had been won as a result of unlawful conduct. The contracts in question had been won by Mabey and Johnson, a subsidiary company. | Included corruption and breaches of UN sanctions. | Yes. | Not specified. The amount in question related to share dividends from contracts that had been won as a result of unlawful conduct by a subsidiary company. | £131,201 CRO, plus costs of £2,440. The subsidiary company had previously been convicted, and this CRO was said to represent 'the conclusion of all matters related to the self-referral'.[2] |
| July 2012 | Oxford Publishing Ltd | OPL subsidiaries had offered and made payments, directly and through agents, intended to induce recipients to award competitive tenders and/or publishing contracts for schoolbooks. | Bribery and/or corruption. | Yes. | Unspecified. The amount in question related to money received by wholly owned OPL subsidiaries as a result of unlawful conduct. | £1,895,435 CRO, plus SFO costs of £12,500. |

Notes

1 Cited in the Stolen Asset Recovery Initiative (StAR) Initiative Corruption Database 'Bonny Island Liquefied Natural Gas Bribe Scheme (TSKJ Consortium) / KBR – M.W. Kellogg Ltd' available at: https://star.worldbank.org/corruption-cases/node/20226 (last accessed 28 July 2017).

2 See the Stolen Asset Recovery Initiative (StAR) Initiative Corruption Database 'Mabey Engineering (Holdings) Ltd', available at: http://star.worldbank.org/corruption-cases/node/20233 (last accessed 28 July 2017).

underlying conduct as 'criminal' (Transparency International (TI) (UK), 2012: 63–64). Moreover, at least in earlier years, there was no apparent basis as to how the monetary amounts were decided upon. This latter criticism has been emphasised by TI-UK (2012: 65):

> In the Balfour Beatty case it is noteworthy that the civil settlement amount of £2.25 million is far less than what could have been imposed under POCA as, arguably, the entire proceeds of the contract could be said to have been derived from the improper conduct. However, there is no public explanation as to the basis of the civil settlement amount. There was more explanation by the SFO as to the recovery order imposed on DePuy, but again the basis of the calculation is not clear.

Contrariwise, others have complained that the lack of transparency impacts on 'the negotiation process' – both for the SFO and corporates:

> [t]he lack of a set, transparent process for handling self-referral makes the negotiation process harder to navigate for the SFO and those making the referral. Further, there are few accessible records of the negotiation and decision-making process.
>
> (HMCPSI, 2012: 35)

A further point of criticism was the lack of engagement with the case investigation teams.[11] There was emphasis on 'the considerable risk that exclusion of the case team from the process, and inclusion of others who are less acquainted with the case, could lead to disadvantageous resolution' (HMCPSI, 2012: 36).

Even before the HMCPSI report was published, the SFO did recognise the need for a transparent process in CRO cases, and published details of the Oxford Publishing Ltd (OPL) case in July 2012.[12] In a follow-up HMCPSI report two years later, the SFO was deemed to have 'made good progress in setting out the basis on which it will make decisions regarding alternative resolutions and civil recovery orders in particular' (HMCPSI, 2014: 31). However, it was also emphasised that there is still a lack of clarity as to the actual process. We now move on to consider the OPL case in more detail, where the SFO responded to criticism as to a lack of transparency and made the CRO public.

## Civil recovery in practice

In announcing the OPL CRO, the SFO acknowledged previous criticism about a lack of transparency in civil recovery matters. This case, then, was

---

11  Often the case investigation teams found out about CRO agreements from staff at the corporate, rather than other staff within the SFO.
12  SFO Press Release (3 July 2012), 'Oxford Publishing Ltd to pay almost £1.9 million as settlement after admitting unlawful conduct in its East African operations'.

the first time that the CRO and Claim were made public.[13] The CRO was for the amount of £1,895,435 (plus costs), relating to money received by OPL subsidiaries[14] as a result of unlawful conduct, namely bribery and/or corruption. The SFO investigation came about following a self-referral from Oxford University Press (OUP),[15] and the costs of that investigation were met by OUP. The investigation concluded 'that OUPEA and OUPT had offered and made payments, directly and through agents, intended to induce the recipients to award competitive tenders and/or publishing contracts for schoolbooks to OUPEA and OUPT'.[16] As these are wholly owned subsidiaries, OPL would have received money derived from the unlawful conduct. Thus, the SFO conducted an accounting examination to determine the benefit from the tainted contracts and to determine the appropriate amount to be recovered. It is worth mentioning that no allowance was made for the bribes or inducement payments.

The SFO press release detailed a number of reasons as to why a CRO was sought instead of criminal prosecution. These reasons include:

1    The test under the Code for Crown Prosecutors was not met, and there was no likelihood that it would be met in future. This view was based on factors including (i) key material was not in an evidentially admissible format for criminal prosecution and (ii) witnesses for a prosecution were based overseas and were considered unlikely to assist or cooperate with a UK criminal investigation.
2    Difficulties in relation to obtaining evidence from the jurisdictions involved and potential risks to affected persons.
3    OUP satisfied the criteria set out in the SFO guidance on self-reporting matters of overseas corruption.
4    There was no evidence of Board level knowledge or connivance within OUP in relation to the conduct at issue.
5    The products supplied were of a good standard and were provided at open market values.
6    The resources needed to facilitate an investigation were considerable. It was thought that civil recovery would be 'a better strategic deployment of resources to other investigations which have a higher probability of leading to a criminal prosecution'.
7    All gross profit from tainted contracts will be disgorged.
8    The subsidiaries will be subject to parallel World Bank procedures, and will be debarred from future World Bank tenders for a number of years.

13  SFO Press Release (3 July 2012), 'Oxford Publishing Ltd to pay almost £1.9 million as settlement after admitting unlawful conduct in its East African operations'.
14  Namely Oxford University Press East Africa (OUPEA) and Oxford University Press Tanzania (OUPT).
15  OUP made a separate self-referral to the World Bank, as two of the tenders in question were funded by the World Bank.
16  SFO Press Release (3 July 2012), 'Oxford Publishing Ltd to pay almost £1.9 million as settlement after admitting unlawful conduct in its East African operations'.

The SFO acknowledged that OUP unilaterally offered to contribute £2 million to not-for-profit organisations in sub-Saharan Africa.[17] However, the SFO decided that that offer should not be included in the terms of the CRO 'as the SFO considers it is not its function to become involved in voluntary payments of this kind'.[18] Commenting on the CRO, the SFO Director, David Green stated:

> This settlement demonstrates that there are, in appropriate cases, clear and sensible solutions available to those who self report issues of this kind to the authorities. The use of Civil Recovery powers has been exercised in accordance with the Attorney General's guidelines. The company will be adopting new business practices to prevent a recurrence of these issues and these new procedures will be subject to an extensive and detailed review.[19]

The money realised from this CRO was to be used in accordance with the Asset Recovery Incentivisation Scheme (ARIS), whereby those involved in investigations/prosecutions would get a share of any money realised. While there is nothing to indicate that the SFO was influenced by this monetary incentive, such incentivisation schemes have been heavily criticised on the grounds that they skew policing priorities and lead to 'policing for profit' (Blumenson and Nilsen, 1998; Carpenter et al., 2015). The SFO participated in the ARIS scheme up to 2013–14, after which the SFO instead received a fixed sum in lieu, which amounted to the cost of running the SFO Proceeds of Crime Unit.[20]

Not only does the OPL CRO demonstrate the use of civil recovery powers, it is also an example of how the SFO can target parent or subsidiary companies following unlawful conduct by other companies, demonstrating the reach of such powers. Other cases where the SFO has used civil recovery orders in this way include MW Kellogg Ltd[21] and Mabey Engineering (Holdings) Ltd.[22] The latter case is worth further mention, having been described as a 'landmark development in anti-corruption enforcement'.[23]

---

17 According to the press release, 'This was a reflection of the seriousness with which OUP views the course of events that were subject to the investigation and a wish to acknowledge that the conduct of OUPEA and OUPT fell short of that expected within its wider organisation'.

18 SFO Press Release (3 July 2012), 'Oxford Publishing Ltd to pay almost £1.9 million as settlement after admitting unlawful conduct in its East African operations.

19 SFO Press Release (3 July 2012), Oxford Publishing Ltd to pay almost £1.9 million as settlement after admitting unlawful conduct in its East African operations'.

20 Serious Fraud Office website, 'About Us', available at: www.sfo.gov.uk/about-us/ (last accessed 24 July 2017).

21 See the Stolen Asset Recovery Initiative (StAR) Initiative Corruption Database 'Bonny Island Liquefied Natural Gas Bribe Scheme (TSKJ Consortium) / KBR – M.W. Kellogg Ltd' available at: https://star.worldbank.org/corruption-cases/node/20226 (last accessed 28 July 2017).

22 See the Stolen Asset Recovery Initiative (StAR) Initiative Corruption Database 'Mabey Engineering (Holdings) Ltd', available at: http://star.worldbank.org/corruption-cases/node/20233 (last accessed 28 July 2017); J. Hurley, 'SFO targets "criminal" companies' dividends', *The Telegraph*, 12 January 2012.

23 J. Pickworth and C. Lee, 'Dechert on point: Special alert' (January 2012), available at: https://www.dechert.com/files/Publication/1d9cdaa5-638d-4c9b-b0f5-865899aa38b8/Presentation/PublicationAttachment/d203cec1-b012-4e93-90fb-8a552c9e58af/White_Collar_SA_01-12_SFO_Recovers.pdf (last accessed 24 July 2017).

The CRO was granted in recognition of sums received through share dividends derived from contracts that had been won as a result of unlawful conduct. The contracts in question had been won by Mabey and Johnson (a subsidiary of Mabey Engineering (Holdings) Ltd) that had been convicted of foreign bribery.[24] The CRO was said to represent 'the conclusion of all matters related to the self-referral' following the successful criminal prosecution of the company and former company officers.[25]

This CRO attracted extensive criticism for many reasons including: the parent company did not know about the subsidiary's unlawful conduct (which was acknowledged by the SFO); questions as to whether it is appropriate to target shareholders who may not have access to information indicating unlawful conduct; and whether it is possible for institutional shareholders to micromanage companies.[26] The SFO was unmoved by such criticisms, however. As the then-SFO Director, Richard Alderman, stated:

> [s]hareholders who receive the proceeds of crime can expect civil action against them to recover the money. The SFO will pursue this approach vigorously. In this particular case, however, the shareholder was totally unaware of any inappropriate behaviour. The company and the various stakeholders across the group have worked very constructively with the SFO to resolve the situation, and we are very happy to acknowledge this. The second, broader point is that shareholders and investors in companies are obliged to satisfy themselves with the business practices of the companies they invest in. This is very important and we cannot emphasise it enough. It is particularly so for institutional investors who have the knowledge and expertise to do it. The SFO intends to use the civil recovery process to pursue investors who have benefitted from illegal activity. Where issues arise, we will be much less sympathetic to institutional investors whose due diligence has clearly been lax in this respect.[27]

## Negotiating non-contention through Deferred Prosecution Agreements (DPAs)

In 2012, the Government recognised that 'the present justice system in England and Wales is inadequate for dealing effectively with criminal enforcement against

---

24  D. Leigh and R. Evans, 'British firm Mabey and Johnson convicted of bribing foreign politicians', *The Guardian*, 25 September 2009.

25  See the Stolen Asset Recovery Initiative (StAR) Initiative Corruption Database 'Mabey Engineering (Holdings) Ltd', available at: http://star.worldbank.org/corruption-cases/node/20233 (last accessed 28 July 2017).

26  See, for example, C. Binham and K. Burgess, 'Investors alarmed by SFO warning', *Financial Times*, 12 January 2012.

27  Cited in FCPA Compliance Report, 'The SFO speaks in the Mabey & Johnson case: Private equity – Are you listening?' Available at: http://fcpacompliancereport.com/2012/01/the-sfo-speaks-in-the-mabey-johnson-case-private-equity-are-you-listening/ (last accessed 28 July 2017).

commercial organisations in the field of complex and serious economic crime' (Ministry of Justice, 2012a: para. 23). It was further stated that 'it is in the interests of justice and of economic well-being that investigators and prosecutors should be equipped with the right tools to tackle economic crime' (Ministry of Justice, 2012a: para. 22). The outcome of this was the introduction of DPAs to the legal system as an additional response to the use of criminal prosecution and/or civil recovery, despite those remaining 'useful tools' (Ministry of Justice, 2012a: para. 29).

Interestingly, an explicit justification for the need for such enforcement mechanism was based on the perception that commercial organisations that could be prosecuted in England and Wales would instead choose to engage with US authorities, such as the Department of Justice (DOJ) and the Securities and Exchange Commission (SEC), where DPAs (and non-prosecution agreements (NPAs)) could be sought, in order to prevent action being taken in England and Wales (Ministry of Justice, 2012a: para 40). It was argued that the 'lack of equivalent enforcement tools for UK prosecutors makes *negotiations* between UK and US prosecutors, and ultimately resolution of the case, difficult' (Ministry of Justice, 2012a: para. 40, emphasis added). The DPA Code of Practice includes a section on the process for invitation to enter into negotiations (SFO/CPS, 2013). Thus, negotiating non-contention has been central throughout the process of introducing DPAs.

Before proceeding further, it is worth outlining what a DPA is. A DPA is a discretionary tool to be used by the prosecutor that enables a formal, voluntary agreement between a prosecutor and a corporation to be reached with judicial approval whereby a criminal prosecution for alleged criminal conduct can be deferred in exchange for the fulfilment of certain 'terms'. Possible terms of a DPA include: a financial penalty; compensation to victims; donations to charities/third parties; disgorgement of any profits made; implementation of a rigorous internal compliance/training programme; cooperation in any investigation; payment of reasonable costs to the prosecutor; prohibition from engaging in certain activities; financial reporting obligations; robust monitoring; cooperation with sector wide investigations. The prosecutor would only need to have 'reasonable suspicion' that the corporation has committed an offence and there would only need to be 'reasonable grounds for believing' that with further investigation the evidence collected would establish a realistic prospect of conviction in accordance with the Full Code Test[28] ((i) evidential stage, (ii) public interest stage) in a reasonable amount of time.

An indictment will be preferred, but suspended pending agreement of the DPA. At the expiry of the DPA, unless the terms have been breached, proceedings will be discontinued. Alternatively, if these terms are not met, the prosecutors maintain the right to prosecute. Any agreement reached between the prosecutor

---

28  For an explanation of the Full Code Test see 'The Code for Crown Prosecutors', available at: www.cps.gov.uk/publications/code_for_crown_prosecutors/ (last accessed 8 August 2017).

and the corporation is subject to court approval where it must be demonstrated at a preliminary and final hearing that the agreement is in the 'interests of justice' (and the public), and that the proposed terms are 'fair, reasonable and proportionate' (SFO/CPS, 2013: para. 9.4). The DPA Code of Practice indicates that the SFO expects a high level of cooperation, honesty and proactive engagement (i.e. a self-report[29]) from the corporation in order for a DPA to be suitable. The commercial organisation and prosecutor would also agree to a *negotiated* 'statement of facts', detailing the nature of the wrongdoing. The DPA consultation explicitly stated that the statement of facts would be *negotiated* (Ministry of Justice, 2012a: para. 87). How a 'statement of facts' can be negotiated is an interesting insight into the construction of social realities.

## DPAs in England and Wales

In February 2014, DPAs became available to the Director of the SFO following their legal establishment through the Crime and Courts Act 2013. The decision to introduce DPAs was based on their perceived 'success' in the US where they are now widely used (following the 'disastrous' prosecution and initial conviction of Arthur Andersen) by the DOJ and by the SEC as an opportunity to restore equilibrium in the prosecution of corporations (Ridge and Baird, 2008: 197; see also Spivack and Raman, 2008). However, there have been concerns in the US about the use of DPAs, for example on the basis that they 'limit the punitive and deterrent value of the government's law enforcement efforts and extinguish the societal condemnation that should accompany criminal prosecution' (Uhlmann, 2013: 1302), and that their use has increased the quantity of cases dealt with, but has lowered the quality[30] of FCPA enforcement (Koehler, 2015). Table 13.2 identifies several purported advantages and disadvantages of the use of DPAs.

Critique in the US has indicated abuses of prosecutorial discretion due to a lack of judicial oversight (Ridge and Baird, 2008: 203), raising concerns that prosecutors' use of DPAs is inconsistent with the rule of law (Arlen, 2016). It has also been argued that 'although DPAs . . . may offer some short-term benefits, such as quicker resolution, long-term reliance on DPAs . . . as primary enforcement mechanisms in corporate law imposes significant costs, both to the market and federal law' (Brooks, 2010: 155). For example, DPAs hinder the development of case law and precedent that are used to establish the boundaries of permissible behaviour; this in turn creates regulatory uncertainties that can increase the

---

29  While the first two DPAs with Standard Bank and the Anonymous SME involved 'self-reports', this was not the case with Rolls Royce as the SFO became aware of the corruption via whistleblowers. This is an important issue, which is discussed further later.

30  In the words of Koehler (2015: 544) 'Instances in which the DOJ brings actual criminal charges against a business organization or otherwise insists in the resolution that the legal entity pleads guilty to FCPA violations represent a higher-quality FCPA enforcement action (in the eyes of the DOJ) and is thus more likely to result in related FCPA criminal charges against company employees'. In contrast, where the result is a DPA or NPA that, according to Koehler, represents a 'lower-quality' enforcement action.

*Table 13.2* Purported advantages and disadvantages of DPAs

| Advantages | Disadvantages |
| --- | --- |
| • An opportunity to restore equilibrium in the prosecution of corporations?<br>• Enables a corporation to make full reparation for criminal behaviour without the collateral damage of a conviction, i.e. the 'spill-over' effects<br>• Concluded in the UK under the supervision of a judge, who must be convinced that the DPA is 'in the interests of justice' and that the terms are 'fair, reasonable and proportionate'<br>• Avoids lengthy and costly trials, but allows transparency<br>• Provides scope for a variety of large financial penalties such as reparation and compensation, where appropriate<br>• Foregrounds structural and cultural reform | • Limits the punitive and deterrent value of the government's law enforcement efforts, i.e. 'out of court, out of mind'<br>• Extinguishes the societal condemnation that should accompany criminal prosecution<br>• Increases the quantity of cases dealt with but has lowered the quality of enforcement<br>• Abuses of prosecutorial discretion due to a lack of judicial oversight (in US, not UK)<br>• DPAs inconsistent with the rule of law<br>• Does UK corporate criminal liability and sanction severity generate motivation to agree like in the US?<br>• Hinders the development of case law and precedent<br>• Overreliance on a company's internal investigations? |

costs to corporates investing abroad as they attempt to determine efficient and optimal legal frameworks (i.e. what is legally permissible) (Brooks, 2010: 156). Notwithstanding these criticisms, it is recognised that notable differences exist in the system in England and Wales, such as the requirement of early judicial oversight and court approval (see Bisgrove and Weekes, 2014; Grasso, 2016). However, a core theory failure in the policy transfer to E+W was the failure to acknowledge that difficulties of corporate criminal liability (in E+W) – though mitigated somewhat because of the Bribery Act 2010 – mean prosecution is rare and that the severity of sanctions in the US generates a motivation (in the US) to agree to a DPA that is largely lacking in E+W.

In E+W, there is no requirement for formal admissions of guilt – corporations must only 'admit the contents and meaning of key documents referred to in the statement of facts' (Paragraph 6.3, DPA Code). The reader may ask themselves why it is that a corporation would agree to the terms of a DPA (e.g. substantial fine, monitoring) to settle a case if it is not admitting to any wrongdoing. Cynically, it might be argued that corporations may prefer the route of a DPA as with no formal admissions of guilt, the corporate will be less liable to class actions (e.g. from disgruntled shareholders or investors) and lateral litigation (e.g. from competitors), and closure and certainty (key for audience legitimacy) will be provided following the completion of the DPA. There is also anecdotal evidence that share prices of companies agreeing DPAs increase following public notification.[31]

---

31  P. Hollinger and C. Belton, 'Rolls-Royce shares climb on back of bribery settlement', *Financial Times*, 17 January 2017.

The SFO Director David Green suggested other benefits of DPAs are that they avoid a prosecution and the stigma of a possible conviction, they can be in private until the final declaration, they speed up the investigative process and save on the costs and paralysis attendant on a full criminal investigation, they permit at least some influence and control by the corporate, they improve the company's culture of compliance and prevention, and they may avoid disqualification from tendering for EU public contracts following a conviction.[32]

It might also be argued, however, that DPAs reflect normative preferences for the principal role of corporate criminal enforcement to be about the structural reform of corrupt corporate cultures rather than indictment, prosecution and punishment (Spivack and Raman, 2008: 161). At the same time as DPAs have been introduced into E+W law, 'there is increasing scrutiny of these agreements in the US and a larger debate about the appropriate use of such enforcement tools by regulators' (Raphael, 2016: 166). The inclination to resort to DPAs reflects prosecutors' willingness to compromise when corporations are 'too big to jail' (Arlen, 2016; Garrett, 2014). Thus, the fledgling use of DPAs in the UK coincides with increased scrutiny and criticism in the US.

There are several concerns over the use of DPAs in E+W. For instance, in the US, where DPAs have been deemed a 'success', the principle of vicarious liability applies – this means a corporation can be held criminally liable for the acts or omissions of its individual employees as the criminal intent and the performance of the legally prohibited act are automatically attributed to the corporation (Nanda, 2011: 65). In contrast, establishing whether a corporation can be criminally liable for the acts or omissions of individual employees in the UK is much more difficult, for example due to issues related to 'the corporate mind' and the 'identification principle' (see Gobert and Punch, 2003: 38; Wells, 2011).[33] In other words, corporations have been and are more likely to be prosecuted and convicted in the US, which makes DPAs a credible and legitimate alternative. There is a clear issue of policy transfer across jurisdictions here – decisive in the success and impact of such transfers are the cultural, socio-political and institutional contexts at the receiving end (Karstedt, 2007: 145) – the absence of a credible threat of corporate prosecution in the UK potentially undermines the tool. Notwithstanding, DPAs *have* been agreed with corporations implicated in corporate bribery. A DPA gives clarity and certainty to corporations and financial markets by drawing a line under criminal behaviour and previous criminal conduct, and this is preferable to corporations and financial markets. The real test of the regime will emerge when a corporation rejects a DPA to contest a prosecution or when the terms of a DPA are breached, as prosecution should follow.

32  See David Green speech on 'Ethical business conduct: An enforcement perspective' at PricewaterhouseCoopers, March 2014, available at: www.sfo.gov.uk/2014/03/06/ethical-business-conduct-enforcement-perspective/, accessed 7 August 2017.

33  Although Section 7 of the Bribery Act has a strict liability dimension, this is for the offence of 'failure to prevent bribery' as opposed to bribery itself.

The Director of the SFO, David Green, has also indicated that DPAs avoid 'severe collateral damage to those (like employees, shareholders or pensioners) who had no part in the criminality prosecuted' and the route to a DPA will 'also be cheaper, quicker and more certain for all parties'.[34] There are some concerns here, however. The SFO must be wary of replacing the principles of the rule of law and criminal justice with what is cheap or quick. Furthermore, the issue of corporate criminal liability implies that small and medium enterprises are more likely to be criminally convicted; it is more straightforward to establish that the 'controlling mind' knew of offending behaviour in smaller organisations. This may result in the differential sanctioning of large and small business, which raises questions of equality, and therefore legitimacy, before the law, as larger organisations will be better positioned to negotiate DPAs or civil settlements. A final point to mention here is that increased cooperation between large corporations and the state may have 'unintended' or 'collateral' consequences, such as the turning of corporations into agents of the state (i.e. self-investigation and provision of evidence) with resulting corporate governance and constitutional implications (Bohrer and Trencher, 2007: 1481), though given the knowledge and power problems facing the state, as outlined earlier, this may be beneficial in some cases.

## DPAs in practice

At the time of writing, DPAs have been agreed and approved for three companies involved in transnational bribery: Standard Bank, an Anonymous SME and Rolls Royce.[35] Table 13.3 outlines the details of these cases. Common features of the DPAs include financial penalties such as standalone financial orders, disgorgement of profits (essentially a blend of a confiscation order and a recovery order), payment of prosecution costs and, in the case of Standard Bank, the payment of compensation. All cases also involved a requirement of cooperation and the implementation of improved compliance procedures in an attempt to secure the maintenance of anti-bribery standards.

Of the three cases concluded, the DPA with Rolls Royce has been the most notable, both in terms of the size and significance of the company, but also in terms of the issues that have been raised. We analyse this case in more detail in order to provide concrete insight into the dynamics associated with the negotiation of deferred prosecution, and non-contention.

### *Case study: the Rolls Royce DPA*

In January 2017, the SFO secured approval from Lord Justice Leveson for its third DPA, with Rolls Royce PLC, involving 12 counts of conspiracy to corrupt, false accounting and failure to prevent bribery. The company, specifically

---

34  See n.35.

35  A fourth DPA has also been agreed with Tesco for accounting irregularities. Our focus here is on DPAs and bribery specifically.

*Table 13.3* Bribery-related DPAs in E+W (adapted from Lord and Levi, 2017)

| Sanctioned business (criminal and civil) – lead agency/year | Nature of case | Sanctioned offence | Business advantage obtained | Nature of DPA |
|---|---|---|---|---|
| Standard Bank SFO – 2015 | Failure to prevent bribery by its sister company, Stanbic Bank Tanzania, to a local partner in Tanzania, Enterprise Growth Market Advisors (EGMA) to induce members of the Government of Tanzania. | Failure of a commercial organisation to prevent bribery contrary to section 7 of the Bribery Act 2010. | Gained favour for a proposal for a US$600m [£398.8m] private placement to be carried out on behalf of the Government of Tanzania. The placement generated transaction fees of US$8.4m [£5.6m], shared by Stanbic Tanzania and Standard Bank. | DPA[1] with compensation of US$6m plus interest of US$1,046,196.58; disgorgement of profit of US$8.4m; payment of a financial penalty of US$16.8m; and payment of costs incurred by the SFO (£330,000). |
| Anonymous SME SFO – 2016 | Company's employees and agents involved in the systematic offer and/or payment of bribes to secure contracts in foreign jurisdictions. | Conspiracy to corrupt, contrary to section 1 of the Criminal Law Act 1977, conspiracy to bribe, contrary to section 1 of the same Act, and failure to prevent bribery, contrary to section 7 of the Bribery Act 2010. | The total gross profit from the implicated contracts amounted to £6,553,085. | DPA with financial orders of £6,553,085: comprising £6,201,085 disgorgement of gross profits and a £352,000 financial penalty. (The SFO agreed not to seek costs.) |
| Rolls Royce PLC SFO – 2017 | 12 counts of conspiracy to corrupt, false accounting and failure to prevent bribery. The company, and its associated persons, used a network of agents to bribe officials in at least seven different countries. | Six offences of conspiracy to corrupt, contrary to section 1 of the Criminal Law Act 1977; five offences of failure of a commercial organisation to prevent bribery contrary to section 7(1)(b) of the Bribery Act 2010; and one offence of false accounting contrary to section 17(1)(a) of the Theft Act 1968. | Profit gained equated to £258,170,000. | DPA with disgorgement of profit of £258,170,000, a financial penalty of £239,082,645, and payment of costs of £12,960,754. |

Note
1 The SFO recorded the figures in US Dollars. The exchange rate on the day of the announcement (November 30, 2015) was US1$: £ 0.6646439742.

its Civil Aerospace and Defence Aerospace businesses and its former Energy business, used a network of agents to bribe officials in at least seven different countries[36] to win lucrative contracts over a period spanning three decades – the profit gained was evaluated to be £258,170,000.[37] Consequently, the company agreed a financial settlement of £497.25m (comprising disgorgement of the profit gained plus a financial penalty of £239,082,645 in addition to almost £13m of prosecution costs) with the SFO in addition agreeing to a number of terms such as cooperation in the prosecution of individuals.[38] The DPA spans a five-year term (2017–2021/22) and also involves an agreement to cooperate with and assist the SFO with the prosecution of individual company actors as well as the implementation of a compliance programme that is to be supervised by Lord Gold.

When the details of the case were presented for judicial oversight and approval, the presiding judge, Lord Justice Leveson, stated:

> My reaction when first considering these papers was that *if Rolls-Royce were not to be prosecuted in the context of such egregious criminality over decades,* involving countries around the world, making truly vast corrupt payments and, consequentially, even greater profits, *then it was difficult to see when any company would be prosecuted*[39].

(Emphasis added)

With this comment in mind, how then was Rolls Royce able to negotiate a non-contentious outcome with the SFO? According to the judicial remarks, the DPA was agreed following 'full and extensive cooperation' (albeit with no self-report) and recognition that the personnel (i.e. board of executives) and culture of the company had since changed. This outcome raises several issues over the ability of Rolls Royce to have negotiated a DPA despite the extensive criminal behaviour.

In response to the DPA, UK NGO Corruption Watch labelled the outcome a 'failure of nerve' on the part of the SFO on the basis of several arguments.[40] First, the DPA represented a shift away from the necessity of a 'self-report', and this represents the setting of a dangerous precedent as corporations can await detection rather than proactively notifying the authorities and still retain

---

36 Indonesia, Thailand, India, Russia, Nigeria, China and Malaysia.

37 SFO Press Release (17 January 2017), 'SFO completes £497.25m Deferred Prosecution Agreement with Rolls-Royce PLC'.

38 Rolls-Royce also reached agreements with the US Department of Justice and Brazil's Ministério Público Federal. These agreements resulted in the payment of approximately US$170m to the US and $25m to Brazil.

39 *SFO v Rolls Royce Plc*, Approved DPA Judgment, Royal Courts of Justice, 17 January 2017, Leveson LJ, para. 61.

40 Corruption Watch, 'A failure of nerve: The SFO's settlement with Rolls Royce'. Available at: www.cw-uk.org/2017/01/19/a-failure-of-nerve-the-sfos-settlement-with-rolls-royce/ (last accessed 10 August 2017).

the possibility of negotiating non-prosecution. In these terms, what are the incentives for corporations to self-report internally detected criminal behaviour given they no longer need to anticipate the potential for a criminal sanction? Second, Rolls Royce received a reduction of 50% in the financial penalties levied, which represented a deliberate shift away from the permitted 30% reduction in the Crime and Courts Act 2013. Alongside this, the repayment terms were generous as Rolls Royce can pay the fine over the term of the DPA, creating an image of such fines as the 'cost of business'. Third, assurances were given that Rolls Royce would not be investigated or prosecuted for conduct that pre-dates the DPA despite other on-going investigations involving UNAOIL and Airbus where Rolls Royce may be implicated. Fourth, arguments against prosecution included the removal of the threat of debarment from public procurement contracts, but there is insufficient evidence that debarment actually has adverse consequences. Finally, questions remain over the role of judicial scrutiny, as DPAs cannot currently be judicially reviewed or challenged. All DPAs have so far been approved by a single judge, Lord Justice Leveson. While this practice may ensure consistency, there is a danger that DPAs will become the normalised response for the SFO, thus the only question will be whether the presiding judge is disposed towards approving DPAs.

## Concluding thoughts: negotiated non-contention as the 'new' accommodation

In its response to the consultation on DPAs, the UK Government stated that 'although prosecution will continue to be prioritised, prosecutors need new tools to enable them to take quicker and more effective action against organisations that commit wrongdoing' (Ministry of Justice, 2012b: para. 6). Given the small number of transnational bribery cases concluded in England and Wales to date, it is not possible to infer enforcement trends or patterns, but in absolute terms we can see that most cases do not involve criminal prosecution. While civil recovery orders were initially the preferred tool, it can be expected that they will be supplanted by DPAs as the predominant enforcement response; however, the preference for negotiating non-contentious outcomes in cases of transnational bribery remains.

Central principles to the DPA regime are transparency and consistency of the enforcement process. As the UK Government stated:

> [t]he public need to have the confidence that a prosecutor is not entering into a 'cosy deal' with an organisation behind closed doors, and parties entering into a DPA need to know what to expect of the DPA process and the likely outcome.
>
> (Ministry of Justice, 2012b: para. 16)

To some extent, the increased availability of the decision-making process, judicial sentencing remarks and case specific details have been a welcome improvement.

However, the very nature of the negotiations themselves remain elusive and hidden. This might be expected given the (commercially) sensitive nature of the discussions, but it makes these fundamental interactions between regulators and their conscious opponents, and the associated power dynamics, difficult to understand. While CROs are likely to be used less often going forward, we still see similar concerns there – while the SFO has argued that civil approaches are by their very nature private disputes, the underlying foreign bribery makes such issues criminal matters about which the public has an interest and right to be fully informed (OECD, 2012: 24).

The SFO Director, David Green, has suggested that DPAs should not be seen as the 'new normal'.[41] However, we consider it unlikely that this will not be the case. The use of DPAs is likely to become the default response to transnational corporate bribery, and this represents continued 'accommodation' of foreign bribery (see Lord, 2014). Rather than going down the criminal law route, the phenomenon of foreign bribery and associated enforcement difficulties are instead 'accommodated' through negotiated justice.

## Bibliography

Alldridge, P. 2018. Civil Recovery in England and Wales: An Appraisal, in C. King, C. Walker, and J. Gurulé (eds.), *The Handbook of Criminal and Terrorism Financing Law*. Basingstoke, UK: Palgrave.

Arlen, J. 2016. Prosecuting Beyond the Rule of Law: Corporate Mandates Imposed Through Deferred Prosecution Agreements. *Journal of Legal Analysis*, 8(1), pp.191–234.

Bennett, R.S., LoCivero, H.L., & Hanner, B.M. 2013. From Regulation to Prosecution to Cooperation: Trends in Corporate White Collar Crime Enforcement and the Evolving Role of the White Collar Crime Defense Attorney. *The Business Lawyer*, 68(2), pp.411–438.

Bisgrove, M., & Weekes, M. 2014. Deferred Prosecution Agreements: A Practical Consideration. *Criminal Law Review*, 6, pp.416–438.

Blumenson, E., & Nilsen, E. 1998. Policing for Profit: The Drug War's Hidden Economic Agenda. *University of Chicago Law Review*, 65(1), pp.35–114.

Bohrer, B.A., & Trencher, B.L. 2007. Prosecution Deferred: Exploring the Unintended Consequences and Future of Corporate Cooperation. *American Criminal Law Review*, 44(1481, pp.1481–1502.

Brooks, A.R. 2010. A Corporate Catch-22: How Deferred and Non-Prosecution Agreements Impede the Full Development of the Foreign Corrupt Practices Act. *Journal of Law, Economics and Policy*, 7, pp.137–162.

Campbell, L. 2010. The Recovery of "Criminal" Assets in New Zealand, Ireland and England: Fighting Organised and Serious Crime in the "Civil" Realm. *Victoria University Wellington Law Review*, 41, pp.15–36.

---

41  See G. Ruddick, 'Serious Fraud Office boss warns big names to play ball – or else', *The Observer*, 2 April 2017.

Carpenter, D.M., Knepper, L., Erickson, A.C., & McDonald, J. 2015. *Policing for Profit: The Abuse of Civil Asset Forfeiture* (2nd ed.). Arlington, VA: Institute for Justice.

COPFS, 2017. *Guidance on the Approach of the Crown Office and Procurator Fiscal Service to Reporting by Businesses of Bribery Offences (June)*. Available at: http://www.copfs. gov.uk/images/Documents/Prosecution_Policy_Guidance/Guidelines_and_Policy/ Guidance%20on%20the%20approach%20of%20COPFS%20to%20reporting%20by%20 businesses%20of%20bribery%20offences%20JUNE%202017.pdf (accessed 28 July 2017).

Croall, H. 2003. Combating Financial Crime: Regulatory Versus Crime Control Approaches. *Journal of Financial Crime*, 11(1), pp.45–55.

Debevoise and Plimpton LLP. 2012. *Serious Fraud Offices Issues New Policies on Self-Reporting, Facilitation Payments and Business Expenditures (October 12)*. Available at: http://www.debevoise.com/~/media/files/insights/publications/2012/10/serious %20fraud%20office%20issues%20new%20policies%20on%20self__/files/view%20 client%20update/fileattachment/serious%20fraud%20office%20issues%20new%20 policies%20on%20self__.pdf (accessed 27 July 2017).

Garrett, B. 2014. *Too Big To Jail: How Prosecutors Compromise with Corporations*. Cambridge, MA: Harvard University Press.

Gobert, J., & Punch, M. 2003. *Rethinking Corporate Crime*. London: Butterworths.

Grasso, C. 2016. Peaks and Troughs of the English Deferred Prosecution Agreement: The Lesson Learned from the DPA Between the SFO and ICBCSB Plc. *Journal of Business Law*, 5, pp.388–408.

Hendry, J., & King, C. 2015. How Far Is Too Far? Theorising Non-Conviction-Based Asset Forfeiture. *International Journal of Law in Context*, 11, pp.398–411.

HM Crown Prosecution Service Inspectorate (HMCPSI). 2012. *Report to the Attorney General on the Inspection of the Serious Fraud Office (November)*.

HM Crown Prosecution Service Inspectorate (HMCPSI). 2014. *Follow-up Inspection of the Serious Fraud Office (November)*.

Karstedt, S. 2007. Creating Institutions: Linking the 'Local' and the 'Global' in the Travel of Crime Policies. *Police Practice and Research*, 8(2), pp.145–158.

Kennedy, A. 2004. Justifying the Civil Recovery of Criminal Proceeds. *Journal of Financial Crime*, 12(1), pp.8–23.

Koehler, M. 2015. Measuring the Impact of Non-Prosecution and Deferred Prosecution Agreements on Foreign Corrupt Practices Act Enforcement. 49 *University of California, Davis Law Review*, p.497.

Law Commission. 2010. *Criminal Liability in Regulatory Contexts: A Consultation Paper* (CP no.195).

Lea, J. 2004. Hitting Criminals Where It Hurts: Organised Crime and the Erosion of Due Process. *Cambrian Law Review*, 35, pp.81–96.

Levi, M., & Lord, N. 2017. White-Collar and Corporate Crimes, in A. Liebling, S. Maruna and L. McAra (eds.), *Oxford Handbook of Criminology*, 6th ed. Oxford, UK: Oxford University Press.

Lord, N. 2013. Regulating Transnational Corporate Bribery: Anti-Bribery and Corruption in the UK and Germany. *Crime, Law and Social Change*, 60(2), pp.127–145.

Lord, N. 2014. *Regulating Corporate Bribery in International Business: Anti-corruption in the UK and Germany*. Abingdon, UK: Routledge.

Lord, N., & Doig, A. 2014. Transnational Corporate Bribery, in G. Bruinsma and D. Weisburd (eds.), *Encyclopedia of Criminology and Criminal Justice*. New York: Springer, pp.5289–5302.

Lord, N., & Levi, M. 2017. In Pursuit of the Proceeds of Transnational Corporate Bribery: The UK Experience to Date, in C. King, C. Walker and J. Gurule (eds.), *The Handbook of Criminal and Terrorist Financing Law*. Basingstoke, UK: Palgrave Macmillan.

Ministry of Justice. 2012a. *Consultation on a New Enforcement Tool to Deal with Economic Crime Committed by Commercial Organisations: Deferred Prosecution Agreements. CP9/2012 (Cm 8348) (May)*.

Ministry of Justice. 2012b. *Deferred Prosecution Agreements. Government Response to the Consultation on a New Enforcement Tool to Deal with Economic Crime Committed by Commercial Organisations. Response to Consultation CP(R)18/2012 (Cm 8463) (October)*.

Ministry of Justice. 2017. *Corporate Liability for Economic Crime: Call for Evidence (Cm 9370) (January)*.

Nanda, V. 2011. Corporate Criminal Liability in the United States: Is a New Approach Warranted? in M. Pieth & R. Ivory, eds. *Corporate Criminal Liability. Emergence, Convergence and Risk*. London: Springer.

Nicholls, C., Daniel, T., Bacarese, A., and Hatchard, J. 2011. *Corruption and Misuse of Public Office*, 2nd ed. Oxford, UK: Oxford University Press.

OECD. 2012. *Phase 3 Report on Implementing the OECD Anti-Bribery Convention in the United Kingdom (March 2012)*.

OECD Anti-Bribery Convention. 1997. www.oecd.org/daf/anti-bribery/ConvCombatBribery_ENG.pdf. (accessed 20 December 2017).

Pitt, H.L., & Shapiro, K.L. 1990. Securities Regulation by Enforcement: A Look Ahead at the Next Decade. *Yale Journal on Regulation*, 7, pp.149–304.

Raphael, M. 2016. *Bribery: Law and Practice*. Oxford, UK: Oxford University Press.

Ridge, R.J., & Baird, M.A. 2008. The Pendulum Swings Back: Revisiting Corporate Criminality and the Rise of Deferred Prosecution Agreements. *University of Dayton Law Review*, 33(2), pp.187–204.

SFO Press Release. 2009. July. *Approach of the Serious Fraud Office to Dealing with Overseas Corruption*, available at: www.pwc.co.uk/fraud-academy/insights/sfo-guidance-approach-of-the-serious-fraud-office-to-dealing-with-overseas-corruption.html (accessed 27 July 2017).

SFO Press Release. 2012. July 3. www.sfo.gov.uk/2012/07/03/oxford-publishing-ltd-pay-almost-1-9-million-settlement-admitting-unlawful-conduct-east-african-operations/ (accessed 20 December 2017).

SFO Press Release. 2017. January 17. www.sfo.gov.uk/2017/01/17/sfo-completes-497-25m-deferred-prosecution-agreement-rolls-royce-plc/ (accessed 20 December 2017).

SFO/CPS. 2013. *Deferred Prosecution Agreements Code of Practice. Crime and Courts Act 2013*.

Sparrow, M. 2008. *The Character of Harms: Operational Challenges in Control*. Cambridge, UK: Cambridge University Press.

Spivack, P., & Raman, S. 2008. Regulating the 'New Regulators': Current Trends in Deferred Proseuction Agreements. *American Criminal Law Review*, 45, pp.159–193.

Transparency International (UK). 2012. *Deterring and Punishing Corporate Bribery: An Evaluation of UK Corporate Plea Agreements and Civil Recovery in Overseas Bribery Cases*. London: Transparency International (UK).

Turk, M. 2017. Regulation by Settlement. University of Kansas Law Review, 66, pp. 259–324.

Uhlmann, D.M. 2013. Deferred Prosecution and Non-Prosecution Agreements and the Erosion of Corporate Criminal Liability. *Maryland Law Review*, 72(4), pp.1295–1344.

Wells, C. 2011. Corporate Criminal Liability in England and Wales: Past, Present, and Future, in M. Pieth and R. Ivory (eds.), *Corporate Criminal Liability. Emergence, Convergence and Risk*. London: Springer.

Wells, C. 2015. Enforcing Anti Bribery Laws Against Transnational Corporations: A UK Perspective, in P. Hardi, P. Heywood, and D. Torsello (eds.), *Debates of Corruption and Integrity: Perspectives from Europe and the US*. Basingstoke, UK: Palgrave Macmillan, pp. 59–80.

# 14 Non-conviction financial sanctions, corporate anti-bribery reparation and their potential role in delivering effective anti-corruption pay-back

The emerging UK context[1]

*Alan Doig*

## Introduction

This chapter addresses two topics. It notes the increasing use of pre-prosecution settlements, non-prosecution agreements (NPA) or deferred prosecution agreements (DPAs) in various jurisdictions for corporate entities involved in bribery (non-conviction settlements and sanctions (NCSS) will be used in this chapter for the terms[2]). Second it asks if, given the financial aspects of many such settlements and sanctions where overseas bribery[3] is involved, should the monies be used as far as possible to recompense victims, address country circumstances that gave rise to the bribery or more generally be used to promote anti-corruption work? Each could be considered as reflecting some of the themes of the United Nations Convention Against Corruption (UNCAC) and providing an improved focus from the experience of the limited number of such arrangements nationally and internationally.

The argument is that, rather than return funds to national Exchequers, all or part of funds secured through settlements and sanctions in terms of disgorgements (profits obtained as a consequence of, for example, winning a contract corruptly), fines, reimbursements, compensation, voluntary payments and so on

---

1 This chapter is based on a desk review, primary and secondary documentation (some of the former is paraphrased and not referenced because of its confidential nature). It is also based on interviews with Matthew Wagstaff (Serious Fraud Office – SFO), Phil Mason (Department for International Development – DFID), David Kirk, partner at MaguireWoods and former director of the Fraud Prosecution Service, and Gemma Aiolfi, Basel Institute of Governance.

2 The chapter will in the UK context look at pre-trial voluntary settlements and DPAs; NPAs as a formal mechanism don't exist in the UK in the same way as in the US or Germany.

3 The terms 'corruption' and 'bribery' are often used interchangeably. Corruption is essentially about the 'corruption' of public office or its use for private, personal or partisan interests. This may take a number of criminalised forms, such as bribery or embezzlement, or ethical issues, such as conflict of interest or nepotism. The chapter focuses primarily on corporate bribery as the source of the funding, reflecting the main focus of legislation in the UK, US and elsewhere that has led to settlements and sanctions, and the availability of reparations.

(collectively termed reparations for the purposes of this chapter), the funds may be better used as an additional resource in what is a highly competitive funding environment for anti-corruption resources.

Access to more resources could not only extend the opportunity for but also allow for diversity and innovation in new or expanded anti-corruption initiatives. It could also better emphasise the relationship between the offending corporate conduct and their funds being used for remedial or restorative consequences concerning the circumstances or location of the misconduct. This chapter explores the development of non-conviction settlements and sanctions and the scope for reparations, with a focus on the UK context.

## What are the precedents and approaches that would facilitate reparations against corporate offenders?

### *Why reparation?*

The idea of reparation or financial settlements and sanctions to be used for accepted remedial or restorative purposes, rather being returned to a country's general funds, is not significantly at variance with domestic legal approaches in other areas. Financial sanctions – fines, confiscation, and so on – and restitutions or compensation to identified victims are standard aspects of developed countries' criminal justice systems. These exist in both criminal and civil cases for material loss, as well as non-material harm and damages (although somewhat more difficult to quantify in monetary terms). The possibilities of confiscation, recovery, and return of the proceeds of corruption, as well as reparations to countries where corruption by international business has occurred, can be inferred from international conventions, with compensation/restitutions helping to repair the developmental damage caused by anti-corruption; it certainly has been a requirement imposed by international institutions.

The 1997 OECD Convention, which establishes legally binding standards to criminalise bribery of foreign public officials in international business transactions, talks of 'the identification, freezing, seizure, confiscation and recovery of the proceeds of bribery of foreign public officials'. UNCAC Article 57 includes provision for the return of confiscated assets such as embezzled public funds; 57(c) allows the return of such property to its prior legitimate owners or compensating the victims of the crime. While not directly associated with reparations, UNCAC Article 62 (2c) stipulates that State Parties have the option to 'provide technical assistance to developing countries and countries with economies in transition to assist them in meeting their needs for the implementation of this Convention' through adequate and regular voluntary contributions to a UN account. This could in part be 'a percentage of the money or of the corresponding value of proceeds of crime or property confiscated in accordance with the provisions of this Convention'. Finally, international organisations, such as the World Bank with its settlement with Siemens, have indicated a willingness to, first, engage in negotiations on non-conviction settlements or sanctions at international levels or use convictions – or non-conviction settlements and sanctions – at national level as grounds for imposing similar sanctions at international level.

Using the funds from non-conviction settlements and sanctions for reparation or restorative purposes also draws on perspectives in international criminal justice:

> [t]he core principle on reparation under international law was formulated by the Permanent Court of International Justice (PCIJ) in the case concerning the Factory at Chorzow: 'reparation must, as far as possible, wipe out all consequences of the illegal act and re-establish the situation which would, in all probability have existed if that act had not been committed' … Reparation should be proportional to the injury caused by the wrongful act, the term 'injury' incorporating both material and moral damages.
>
> (Amezcua-Noriega, 2011: 2–3)

Reparations can benefit both specific individuals and also address wider loss or harm to groups as well as their environments. In the 2013 US case of two defendants convicted of exceeding South Africa rock lobster harvesting quotas, most of which were smuggled to the US, the South African government was party to a reparations agreement, reflecting either the cost of restoring the lobster fishery levels or the value of the illicitly harvested stock (although any reparation had to be based on conduct that breached US law).

In the case of reparation for more general harm or damage, the commitment of the offender to reverse the consequences of its actions is also recognised, including funding of research, development, education and training.[4] Indeed, the restoration 'of impaired environmental conditions through remediation measures or monetary compensation' is an approach to environmental damage which, in most OECD countries:

> [i]s understood not as a monetary penalty payable by the responsible party to the government but either as remediation measures undertaken by the responsible party or as the reimbursement by the responsible party of the costs of such measures borne by the government. The policy objective is not to punish the operator who caused the damage but to restore the environment, which is reflected in specific requirements imposed by the law on liable parties.
>
> (OECD, 2012: 13)

---

4  See *US v. Arnold Bengis et al.* (S 1 03 Crim. 0308 (LAK)) 2013 at www.justice.gov/. In the case of BP and spillage in the Gulf of Mexico, the US Department of Justice reported that the criminal resolution is structured such that more than half of the proceeds will directly benefit the Gulf region. These included acquiring, restoring, preserving and conserving – in consultation with appropriate state and other resource managers – the marine and coastal environments, ecosystems, and bird and wildlife habitat in the Gulf of Mexico and bordering states, and improved oil spill prevention and response efforts in the Gulf through research, development, education and training. Available at: www.justice.gov/opa/pr/bp-exploration-and-production-inc-agrees-plead-guilty-felony-manslaughter-environmental, accessed 15 November 2016.

## Legal frameworks

Domestic legal frameworks that would allow reparations in relation to corruption convictions exist, although they vary by country. Thus, the German Criminal Procedures Code (section 153a) allows the public prosecutor to negotiate a sanctions settlement in lieu of a trial whereby the defendant agrees to perform a specified service in order to make reparations for damage caused by the offence, pay a sum of money to a non-profit-making institution or to the Treasury, and to perform some other service of a non-profit-making nature. The Swiss Criminal Code also allows for no prosecution where the offender has made reparation for the loss, damage or injury or made every reasonable effort to right the wrong that he or she has caused (Article 53).

As the OECD reports:

> [i]n 69% of foreign bribery cases, sanctions were imposed by way of settlement, using procedures including corporate probation (Canada); section 153(a) of the Criminal Procedure Code (Germany); *Patteggiamento* (Italy); Penalty Notice (Norway); *Réparation* under article 53 of the Penal Code (Switzerland); Non-Prosecution Agreements (NPAs), Deferred Prosecution Agreements (DPAs) and Plea Agreements (US).
>
> (OECD, 2014a: 9; see also OECD, 2014b and Makinwa, 2015)

### Non-conviction settlements and sanctions

Particular attention has been given to the use of non-conviction settlements and sanctions as a significant approach adopted by the US against corporate offenders in Foreign Corrupt Practices Act (FCPA) cases since 2011. With its roots in pre-trial diversion programmes (which had the intention to avoid criminalising first-time offenders and the better use of law enforcement and prosecutorial resources), the gradual emergence as a formal corporate sanction reflected a wish to move away from corporate criminal prosecutions and trials, and facilitate non-criminal sanctions on the grounds of cooperation, access to corporate information, avoidance of third-party collateral damage and a means of shaping future conduct (see Uhlmann, 2013).

Non-conviction settlements and sanctions are thus 'a discretionary tool that enables a formal, voluntary agreement between a prosecutor and a corporation to be reached whereby a criminal prosecution for alleged criminal conduct can be deferred in exchange for the fulfilment of certain "terms"' (Lord and Levi, 2017: 14) and which offer a number of benefits (but, to some critics, a number of disadvantages) to enforcement of anti-bribery legislation – see Table 14.1.

Further, and although the approach to non-conviction settlements and sanctions has been ad hoc and incremental, a number of countries, like the UK, have increasingly formalised the approach as part of the criminal justice response to corporate corruption, because it also addresses pressures from the tensions between, for example, promotion of trade and policing of corruption where governments face:

Table 14.1 NCSSs

| Advantages | | Disadvantages |
|---|---|---|
| to prosecuting country | to business | |
| Efficient use of law enforcement resources | Smaller or no penalties | Inadequate or no judicial supervision |
| | Protects corporate viability and competitiveness abroad | NCSSs are more lenient than convictions |
| Convenient resolution of complex cases; saves on trials | Financial ability to pay | Sanctions, both monetary and nonmonetary, are too low |
| Promotes reporting, identification of offences | Less bad publicity | Not enough of a deterrent for individuals or corporate crime generally |
| Protects corporate viability | Financial ability to pay | Not transparent enough |
| Promotion of corporate reform | Reduced risk/more certain outcome | Absence of the victim in the settlement |

Source: Drawn from World Bank and UNODC/StAR, 2014; Corruption Watch, 2016.

[p]ressures from those advocating competing agendas, in particular from the business community, some of whom perceive far-reaching anti-bribery legislation and corresponding enforcement as being prohibitive to a nation's economic interests overseas and creating an unfair playing field. In establishing enforcement legitimacy, governments must satisfy proponents of anti-corruption conventions/standards by being seen to be acting against corrupt corporations while also protecting and facilitating international business in which its corporations are involved.

(Lord, 2016: 22; see also Lord, 2015 and Makinwa, 2015)

### Promoting NCSSs as sources for reparation?

As the 2014 StAR review pointed out, while reparations address a number of issues associated with settlements or sanctions that avoid criminal convictions, the development of the approach has not given too much thought about possible uses of the financial returns. Some:

395 settlements cases … took place between 1999 and mid-2012. These cases resulted in a total of $6.9 billion in monetary sanctions. Nearly $6 billion of this amount resulted from monetary sanctions imposed by a country different from the one that employed the bribed or allegedly bribed official. Most of the monetary sanctions were imposed by the countries where the corrupt companies (and related individual defendants) are headquartered or otherwise operate. Of the nearly $6 billion imposed, *only about $197 million, or 3.3 percent, has been returned or ordered returned* to the countries whose officials were bribed or allegedly bribed.

(World Bank and UNODC/StAR, 2014: 2; italics in original text).

Of course, the development of non-conviction settlements and sanctions was never predicated on clear guidance as to the use of any financial penalties or agreements, where the need was more to address the allegations or evidence of corporate misconduct. Further, some countries' legislation, sentencing guidelines or legal precedents, according to some national authorities, have precluded or inhibited the use of non-conviction settlements and sanctions to impose some form of directed reparation. In the case of the UK, however, the introduction of DPAs has triggered the potential for directed reparation to be incorporated into some non-conviction settlements and sanctions.

Before considering what this may mean in the UK context in terms of developing a coherent and coordinated policy and procedures as to what uses such funds could be put, there are, first, a number of other interesting questions. These include: is there money available, and how much; is there a need for new resourcing of anti-corruption initiatives or organisations; is the use of sanctions as a basis for reparations wholly accepted; are there emerging models for the allocation of funds; what issues do these models raise, including the purposes to which the funds are put; what would be the added benefits and how would these be assessed?

## Answering the questions: adding value through reparations

### *Who wants funding, and how much could be available?*

While it is as hard to find out how much is spent on anti-corruption work by multilateral and bilateral donors as it is to find out the real cost of corruption work, what data is available suggests current amounts are not significant. Thus, UNDP's 2014–2017 GAIN (Global Anti-Corruption Initiative) had a total budget of $16 million. Further, not only do donors *not* spend significant amounts on anti-corruption work, but they often make block grants to other development agencies, have favourite government or institutional recipients, or wrap anti-corruption expenditure within wider governance and other programmes (within UK DFID's six-year global Governance and Transparency $200 million project, only 12% was allocated to anti-corruption organisations).

On the other hand, the number of anti-corruption organisations, initiatives and research projects continues to grow. There are some 350 civil society organisations from over 100 countries who are members of the UNCAC Coalition,[5] there are 23 countries operating EITI agreements, over 8,000 companies involved in the

---

5  In February 2017 the UNCAC Civil Society Coalition issued a series of recommendations on the management and disposal of recovered and returned stolen assets. These included: return to the country of origin, transparency and accountability in the management and disposal, victims should be interpreted broadly, the use of alternative ways for management and disposal if the country's budgeting and accounting processes fail to offer effective oversight. Settlements should ensure that a full assessment of the harm caused by the corruption to which the settlement relates is made, and that compensation for that harm is specifically addressed.

UN's Global Compact, and organisations such as the Council of Europe or the US American Bar Association have been responsible for multi-million dollar projects from the Balkans and the MENA region to the Asia-Pacific region. ANTICORRP (Anti-corruption Policies Revisited: Global Trends and European Responses to the Challenge of Corruption) was a large-scale research project funded by the European Commission's Seventh Framework Programme. Running for five years, it cost over 10 million euros, including 8 million euros from the Commission.[6]

At the same time, anti-corruption organisations are not cheap to run and constantly seek funding from a variety of sources. For example, Transparency International, the South African-based Institute for Security Studies, U4, Global Integrity and Integrity Action have a collective annual budget of nearly $50 million. Some, like U4 and Transparency International, rely almost entirely on governmental or international organisation funding or, like the Open Society Foundation, are both sources of funding and run their own in-house initiatives; others, such as Integrity Action, secure funding from a range of sources, from the World Bank to the UK Comic Relief charity. For organisations such as the International Anti-Corruption Academy (IACA), which is reliant on a limited number of countries and corporate donors and the Austrian government, the lack of secured resourcing is a major inhibitor; the Chair of its Board of Governors recently noted that the 'last two general budgets never received 90% of the funding that was unanimously agreed upon' by signatory member states.[7]

On the other side, in terms of the availability of corporate funds from settlements, fines, confiscations and disgorgements and so on, the amounts could be considered significant; the US Securities and Exchange Commission (SEC) and Ministry of Justice have secured nearly $3 billion (£2.1 billion or 2.7 billion euros) from US and foreign companies in the past five years (see http://www. sec.gov/spotlight/fcpa/fcpa-cases.shtml). In the UK, the amounts that *could* – if all such funds are made available – be used for reparations relating to anti-bribery legislations over seven years would be nearly £700 million; this figure was nearly doubled with the 2017 Rolls Royce DPA.[8] More generally, the OECD's 2014 survey of signatory countries to the Anti-Bribery Convention noted that a 'total of USD 5.4 billion has been imposed in monetary sanctions (including fines, confiscation and compensation)' with settlements rather than convictions the basis of the sanctions (69% as opposed to 31%) (OECD, 2014a: 19–21; see also OECD, 2014b, 2015 and TRACE, 2015).

6  http://cordis.europa.eu/project/rcn/103252_en.html.
7  www.iaca.int/images/sub/governance/assembly_of_parties/Assembly_2015/Board_of_Governors_Report_2015.pdf.
8  Unlike the USA, many countries do not have accessible information on regulatory fines. For example, the UK Financial Conduct Authority and its predecessor, the Financial Services Authority, have fined financial firms nearly £10 million in the past five years for offences relating to anti-bribery legislation (although the offences may include inadequate procedures that leave a company vulnerable to the possibility of being involved in bribery as well as allegations of the company or its associates being involved with bribery).

When considered against national country budgets, however, these figures are not only episodic but also in relative terms small rather than significant. Even in terms of developmental budgets (the UK 2014 development budget was over £11 billion while the US Federal USAID's budget is over $22 billion), the funds from non-conviction settlements and sanctions are small. While having the money in the consolidated fund for Treasury spending in times of budgetary austerity and post-Brexit financial uncertainty may offer justification for retention by the government, a sum equivalent to 10% of the UK aid budget could also offer equally persuasive economic and moral arguments for the use of anti-corruption reparations for specific anti-corruption work.

### Reparations in practice: options and uses

The emergence of a coherent set of criteria for the basis for and application of some form of reparations has to be set against what has been, to date, ad hoc and uncoordinated approaches to the use of funds, whether settlements or sanctions. Nevertheless, they provide some guidance on practice to date. In relation to cases involving overseas bribery, the limited experience to date suggests four main options that have been attempted – see Table 14.2.

Further there is also the possibility of a varied approach within a domestic jurisdiction as to how the funds may be used. Thus a number of approaches have been adopted between the Swiss government and different countries; in the case of Nigeria it was on the basis of agreement for funding pro-poor projects, overseen by the World Bank as part of public financial reform programme, while the Peruvian government set up a board drawn from government ministries; the Philippines set up a special account for agrarian reform. All had problems in both management and delivery (Jimu, 2009), an issue also noted among the various models used in Table 14.2.

### Issues and themes from delivery

Of course, the experience to date does raise the question as to whether the ad hoc nature and the use of various approaches is as a consequence of some of the questions above, and does not necessarily imply these occurred because of the absence of a standardised model. On the other hand, and if the funds are to be used for specific purposes, then such a model may be necessary to shape the processes and decisions. In any case, either relying on current approaches or seeking a standardised approach will need to address a number of issues and themes involved with either option, as the starting point to consider a more coherent and effective approach to using corporate reparations. These include: who should be responsible for administering settlement funds; how would funds be allocated; how to assess any benefits; who monitors and evaluates expenditure, and so on.

Table 14.2 Main reparation models

| Model | Reparation to the victim country | Reparation to the victim country through a third party | Reparation through an independent agency | Reparation through a self-administered fund |
|---|---|---|---|---|
| Key feature | The settlement can require the corporation to make a direct payment of a fixed amount to the country where the offences took place, with no conditionality. | The funds transferred to the victim country, or to an NGO, and earmarked for specific purposes. | An international organisation can be put in charge of supervising the allocation of funds. | A settlement requires the offending company to set up and administer its own fund, handing out grants or awards either for specific projects or in response to an open bidding process. |
| Examples | The 2011 UK settlement in the Mabey and Johnson case (which was a post-conviction settlement), and the 2015 DPA in the ICBC Standard Bank case, involved these sorts of payments to various countries. | In 2011 Alstom paid $1 million to the International Committee of the Red Cross, to be split between projects in Tunisia, Latvia and Malaysia. In the BAE case, a £29.5 million voluntary agreement was paid to the Government of Tanzania for educational purposes (see later for more detail). | The 2007 Mercator/Giffen case involved the convicted parties relinquishing rights to Swiss accounts, which in turn provided a $115 million resource for a specifically created NGO – the BOTA Foundation – to deliver social welfare projects over five years in Kazakhstan, the 'victim' country, under the supervision of an existing US NGO (IREX) in partnership with the UK Save the Children charity and monitored by the World Bank on behalf of the three governments involved in agreeing the settlement. | The Siemens Integrity Initiative was set up as a consequence of a settlement agreement with the World Bank. Since 2009, the Initiative has spent some $100 million in two rounds of competitive bidding; most of the successful bidders have been civil society organisations, with the largest recipients the Basel Institute of Governance ($5.8 million), various Transparency International bodies ($7.5 million) and IACA ($7.4 million). |

*Who should be responsible?*

There have been no criteria as to the effective or cost-effective way of determining what should be spent, by whom and how. In the related area of repatriated assets under UNCAC, the same question pertains:

> [t]he selection of the appropriate management arrangements for returned assets is likely to be the subject of much debate, the more so the larger the amount of money concerned. Perceptions, expectations and opinions may diverge markedly between key stakeholders in the administration, civil society and the broader public.
>
> (World Bank/StAR, 2009a: xii)

Certainly there are management, costs, capacity and oversight implications for any approach, including any competitive bidding process for allocating funds and monitoring expenditure. Experience and expertise already resides with some international and NGO organisations; different experience and expertise may be required for specific initiatives. There would be pressure not to see any approach develop into a commercial activity residing with or competed for by a limited number of such organisations. On the other hand, re-inventing the wheel every time there are funds for reparation would be seen as an unnecessary cost when experience and expertise already exist. There may also be country-specific issues as to who is involved and why; there may be concerns about simply following current aid agency initiatives if the intention is to seek an innovative and independent initiative.

*To whom should the funds be directed?*

There is an issue as to whether the intention is to use reparations to further anti-corruption work in general, to remediate 'harm' or damage to citizens in the country where the bribery took place, or to strengthen anti-corruption capacity in that country. In relation to these, then the further question is whether the company or 'victim' country should be involved:

> [i]n the vast majority of settled cases, the jurisdictions whose officials were allegedly bribed have played little role in the settlement process, providing them limited opportunity to recover any of the proceeds of such settlements, and they have not often undertaken their own prosecutions of such offences following settlements outside their jurisdictions.
>
> (World Bank and UNODC/StAR, 2014: 3)

On the one hand it could be argued that in 'victim' countries the:

> [l]ack of technical capacity in critical areas, lack of political will to investigate and prosecute public officials, and weak flows of information between different jurisdictions emerge as critical factors preventing developing countries

from benefitting from FBL (foreign bribery legislation) enforcement in other jurisdictions. Another problematic factor in some cases is that the country enforcing its FBL may be reluctant to share information and monies recovered (e.g. fines or disgorgements) with the country where the bribe was paid.

(de Simone and Zagaris, 2014: 2)

Indeed, in many cases, foreign officials, often at senior level may have been involved in the alleged offences but no action has been taken, raising questions as to whether the country, as represented by the government, can claim to be a victim or reasonably expect to be party to any reparations when their officials could have been complicit in the circumstances that led to the settlement or sanctions. Interestingly, in a small number of cases involving return of funds, these have been declined because the government refused to acknowledge the involvement of their officials or the presence of corruption.

Further attention has to be given as to whether the involvement of the recipient country could itself be a cause for concern. The UK SFO has noted that:

[o]ne of the issues to be considered here though would be whether it is always appropriate for the money to be returned to the citizens of the other country, particularly in circumstances where it is not feasible for the payment to be distributed except through a Government which may not distribute the money or may not distribute it fairly. In such circumstances (and no doubt in others), it may be that there are alternatives such as requiring the money to be given to international causes such as anticorruption or to international institutions.

(House of Commons International
Development, 2011: Evidence, 36)

### Should there be a link to anti-corruption?

The identification of a victim or victim country as a consequence of bribery is contestable. It may be worthy to profess, as did the UK SFO in the BAE case, that 'it is clear that the society in the other country and the individual citizens in that country have suffered damage as a result of these offences' (House of Commons International Development, 2011: Evidence, 35) when the Tanzanian authorities had no complaint about the equipment purchased (other than later allegations that they were over-charged). For example, in a number of countries it is questionable as to how far any country can claim to be a victim as the consequence of the conduct of its senior officials. It is also not clear how far a country should be eligible to seek reparations from a DPA where it itself is not taking rigorous action to punish its officials or to seek recovery of the proceeds of corruption from their perspective.

Diversion of funds from social welfare projects, such as health and education, or delivery of irrelevant or sub-standard products and services mean recipients do suffer. Nevertheless, in terms of reparations, and aside from such specific projects, it would also be difficult to identify specific harm or damage that reparations could redress or reverse or do more than simply supplement governmental budgets for socially worthy causes (see Taylor, 2012 and Itad, 2013 for differing views on the BAE Tanzanian settlement). Such arguments may be more valid where evidence of corruption is evidence of more general harm or damage to the governance environment or developmental progress and where reparations could usefully be deployed to prevent bribery re-occurring.

### What is the impact or added benefit?

In terms of the various options above, a key question has been – how are the proposals and expenditures to be assessed in terms of added-value, relevance and effectiveness? Siemens, for example, asks its recipient organisations for evidence of 'impact evaluation' both at individual level (e.g. have those trained influenced the policy, law and behaviour in their own countries) and organisational level (e.g. has the work of the organisation been taken up and incorporated into the various procedures in the countries concerned). While not all organisations can necessarily demonstrate either, Siemens has been very keen that all recipient organisations publish reports that discuss activities and achievements, and full financial information, including external evaluation reports, budget and expenditure report and audit reports (and here Siemens proposes voluntary GRI reporting[9]).

In practice it is noteworthy just how little information recipient organisations provide on project delivery. In relation to specific projects, at one end there is the Mercator/Giffen case which led to the funds being subcontracted to IREX, a US-based NGO, to deliver the project which was supervised by the World Bank, supported with technical expertise from Save the Children NGO, and evaluated by a UK-based consultancy. After it ended after five years, a detailed final report was published with some financial information (including a note that nearly one-third of available funds was spent on programme costs, overheads, etc.). At the other, there are only two evaluations reports on the BAE Tanzanian settlement (one by a UK consultant and one by a Tanzanian consultancy) which described issues of physical delivery, but nothing on costs or effectiveness (see DataVision International Ltd, 2014, and Burchell, 2014).

Part of the problem is the general absence of any meaningful financial data, especially the costs of delivering the projects or initiatives. Those funded by the Siemens Integrity Initiative generally have failed to respond fully to Siemens proposals, while one – the IACA – has provided no public financial information on expenditure (although it now provides limited information on its income streams), despite being the biggest single recipient from both funding rounds. Part of the problem is the absence of means of assessing added-value in terms

9  GRI is an international independent organisation that helps businesses, governments and other organisations understand and communicate the impact of business on critical sustainability issues such as climate change, human rights, corruption and many others (https://www.global reporting.org).

of impact where there is often a reliance on in-house reports. These are often descriptions of activities rather than evidence of change as a consequence of the funding; BOTA reports, for example, are detailed but lack both the links to suitability, effectiveness and impact in anti-corruption terms (Pachaeco and Balasubramanian, 2015 and IREX, 2015). More importantly, many reports, whether the Mercator/Giffen or BAE cases, do not always provide evidence that the project, however worthy its intentions and outcomes, can demonstrably indicate that the overall impact will mitigate or diminish the circumstances that gave rise to the allegations of corruption whose proceeds then funded the work.

## The UK context

### The BAE case

Prior to 2014 the UK only had a very limited number of cases involving a corporate entity allegedly involved in overseas bribery and reparations; only one involved a voluntary settlement that involved more than financial sanctions.[10] The UK BAE case, at least from the perspective of the SFO, drew attention to determining the link between the types of offences that are to be the basis of any prosecution and the focus of any settlement, the identification of the victim and the harm or damage that they have demonstrably suffered:

> [t]he position is much more difficult in talking about corruption or the books and records offence to which BAE pleaded guilty. There are no identifiable individual victims in such circumstances who have some legal right to obtain restitution from the defendant in the proceedings.
> (House of Commons International Development,
> 2011: Evidence, 35)

The BAE case originally involved multi-jurisdictional allegations of bribery, one of which involved Saudi Arabia. The latter allegation led to the British government exerting pressure on the head of the SFO to end the investigations on the grounds of national security. Challenged in the courts by two NGOs as to the legality of the decision, the head of the SFO was then required to plead on appeal that he should be allowed to exercise his independent judgement as to whether or not to discontinue the investigation. He won the case and ended the investigation into the Saudi Arabian allegations. The resultant 'resolution' with the SFO in February 2010 not only ended all existing investigations but also exempted the company from any future investigation against any as-yet unreported allegations, or allegations arising from investigations into other companies.[11] In exchange, BAE pled guilty to one

---

10 In the Mabey and Johnson case, the largest return – to the UN Iraq fund – was that part of the contract costs that the company used to pay bribes. In the later ICBC Standard Bank case, the reparations concerned compensation for estimated losses made by the Tanzanian government.

11 See *R v BAE Systems PLC*; Southwark Crown Court, Case No: 5201056 21 December 2010.

offence under the Companies Act 1995 (which did not imply any dishonesty or corruption from either the SFO or BAE perspective), and an ex gratia payment – a voluntary contribution – for 'the benefit of the people of Tanzania in a manner to be agreed between the SFO and the Company'. The amount was capped at £30 million, with any court-imposed fine to be deducted from it. In November 2010 BAE pled guilty to the offence in court, resulting in a sentence of £500,000, plus an agreed sum of £250,000 representing the SFO's costs (BAE paid SFO's costs itself, allowing £29.5 million to be applied as the ex gratia payment).

The Tanzanian allegations arose from the purchase by the Tanzanian government of BAE radar and air traffic control systems. The offence related to the use (and recording in its accounts) of a local intermediary. The ex gratia payment was not linked to the cost of the system but negotiated with the Tanzanian government. The Settlement Agreement contained:

> [n]o deadline by which the funds have to be applied, no requirement that the funds be paid out for the benefit of any one class of beneficiary and no restrictions stipulating the payment of a single lump sum or multiple payments over time.
>
> (House of Commons International Development
> Committee 2011, Evidence 33, 4.1)

BAE set up an advisory board with the intention to negotiate with the Tanzanian government and spend the money through a charitable foundation to local NGOs. In turn the Tanzanian government wanted the money in a lump sum with no conditions attached because it believed that BAE had over-charged them. At the SFO's request, DFID became involved, negotiating through their local office with the government to convince it that it was in their best interests that the funds should be spent transparently and that it should accept guidance on how the funds could be spent. This was agreed, with the funds to be used to buy essential teaching materials and to improve classroom facilities and teachers' accommodation through the government's budget line for the Non-salary Education Block Grant; DFID would monitor the expenditure and £200,000 was to be set aside for an external audit.

Implementation involved PwC, the Crown Agents and DataVision International, and a local public opinion company; BAE were not, according to DFID, involved in the agreement or its implementation. Although the final monitoring reports raised issues to do with quality of the equipment and distribution of the funds, there was no financial breakdown and no evidence of the link between reparations and the circumstances that led to the settlement. On the other hand, the experience did initiate discussions among the agencies involved as to how future funds should be used, at the same time as DPAs being used for potential offences under the UK Bribery Act 2010.

### The UK Bribery Act

Enacted in 2010, the UK Bribery Act (UKBA) replaced the three Prevention of Corruption Acts (as well as the 2001 UK Anti-terrorism, Crime and Security Act which extended the jurisdictional reach of the Acts overseas) from July 2011. The UKBA applies to bribery at all levels in the UK as well as abroad. There are no de minimis amounts and only a very specific number of circumstances where payments may not be subject to the law. The Act has a number of key offences, one of which concerns 'relevant commercial organisations' where the focus is on the company alone and not on individuals (albeit, of course, individuals may be guilty of other applicable offences under the Act).

## Introducing DPAs

DPAs were introduced on 24 February 2014, under the provisions of Schedule 17 of the Crime and Courts Act 2013. They are available to the Crown Prosecution Service (CPS) and the SFO; a Code of Practice for Prosecutors was published jointly by the SFO and CPS in 2013.[12] A DPA has a range of time-limited permutations:

- pay to the prosecutor a financial penalty;
- compensate victims of the alleged offence;
- donate money to a charity or other third party;
- disgorge any profits from the alleged offence;
- implement a compliance programme or make changes to an existing compliance programme or to training;
- co-operate in any investigation related to the alleged offence; and
- pay any reasonable costs of the prosecutor in relation to the alleged offence or the DPA.

It should be noted that these are only examples; the precise terms of any DPA will vary from case to case, albeit certain features, such as payment of a financial penalty, will always appear. DPAs were considered for the UK context very much along the lines argued in the US: avoidance of a long, costly and potentially uncertain trial; encouraging self-reporting, including cases not likely to be uncovered by the UK's rather reactive approach to investigations; and avoiding collateral damage to third parties, whether investors, employees or customers (see Corruption Watch, 2016). On the other hand, the UK legislation added judicial oversight – a formal judicial review of the DPA before it can be accepted.

## DPAs in practice

In terms of the limited DPA agreements to early 2017, the initiation (certainly after the Rolls Royce case) now will usually, rather than always, come after company self-reporting of corruption concerns – the first step of demonstrating openness and cooperation – to the SFO. From the outset the SFO retains all options – and at this point the reporting company cannot request DPA discussions. The self-reporting

---

12 See www.cps.gov.uk/publications/directors_guidance/dpa_cop.pdf.

should be followed by a full internal investigation. Investigations will be commenced where the Director is satisfied that there is a suspected offence which appears to him or her on reasonable grounds to involve serious or complex fraud and where the case meets the SFO's Statement of Principle (publicly available on the SFO website).

The intelligence unit then reviews the information to the point of a formal investigation, to see if this provides sufficient evidence for a possible prosecution. This includes reviewing the company's investigation to ensure it was both comprehensive and accurate, as well as being cooperative within the terms of the DPA Code of Practice. The question of the disposal of alleged criminal conduct (the DPA) is then discussed internally. Factors influencing any decision, apart from openness, cooperation and a full disclosure of wrongdoing, is information on changes to a company's culture. This includes whether the company is putting things right in terms of changes to senior management and whether those in post when the alleged wrongdoing took place are no longer with the company.[13] At that point a letter from the case team may invite the company to 'the opportunity' to engage in DPA negotiations.

A DPA does not preclude criminal charges subsequently being brought against anyone employed by or associated with the company[14] (and evidence for this can form part of a DPA). A DPA is an agreement with the company not to prosecute it, although only where the investigation agency considers it has sufficient evidence on which to begin prosecution proceedings and that the interests of justice are best served by way of a DPA rather than a criminal trial. What follows is an agreed statement of facts, which is intended for publication, and the penalties. These cover: the financial penalty, and disgorgements, compensation and any ancillary matters such as required verifiable compliance or remediation arrangements. The financial penalties have to be 'broadly' comparable to the sentence the company would have been likely to receive had it been prosecuted for the offence(s) and pleaded guilty. They also have to reflect culpability and harm, based on the sentencing guideline multipliers, while also acknowledging the likely impact on company finances (both sides use accountants to verify the amounts involved).

The agreement is submitted to court, largely because of the US experience and the UK judicial dislike of having to rubberstamp prosecutorial decisions – as was evident in the judge's comments in the 2010 sentencing statement in *R v BAE Systems PLC*. Currently a single judge reviews all DPAs to build up a body of expertise and approach; the first hearing is for the judge to determine if the DPA is likely to be in the interests of justice and the second to confirm that the DPA is in fact in the interests of justice and that the terms of the DPA are fair, reasonable and proportionate (see Lord and King, this volume).

13  These were many of the elements of the mitigating circumstances in the earlier Mabey and Johnson case.

14  Interestingly the US DoJ's April 2016 FCPA guidance was proposing a pilot scheme intended to encourage companies to disclose FCPA misconduct to permit the prosecution of individuals whose criminal wrongdoing might otherwise never be uncovered by or disclosed to law enforcement. Such voluntary self-disclosures thus promote aggressive enforcement of the FCPA and the investigation and prosecution of culpable individuals.

### Following the money

Unless reparations are made part of the DPA, financial sanctions go to HM Treasury (which may in turn unilaterally agree a proportion for reparation arrangements in consultation with the FCO and DFID; the SFO will only be involved as an 'interested observer').

Compensation – or reparation as a formal part of any DPA – has not been a simple inclusion within DPAs. In an earlier SFO case (Smith and Ouzman 2014; the first contested prosecution of a corporate entity involving bribery of overseas public officials), the judge disallowed reparations because there was no:

> [i]nformation surrounding it. Secondly, the application was not a formalized one. If he did not know what was being asked for and by whom exactly, he could not make an award of compensation part of the process. Thirdly, the prosecution's reply to his query was that there had been nothing in writing from the Kenyan authorities on this subject matter and no corresponding claim for civil recovery being made in Kenya regarding the company's wrongful conduct.
>
> (see www.cw-uk.org/trial-monitoring)

In terms of any financial aspect of a DPA, and after the BAE experience, there has been extensive discussions between DFID, the SFO and other agencies. A set of general principles was issued by the SFO and CPS in June 2017 which is intended to ensure that overseas victims – affected states, organisations and individuals – of bribery, corruption and economic crime, are able to benefit from asset recovery proceedings and compensation orders made in the UK. Compensation will be considered in all relevant cases, including DPAs, with a range of agencies; the SFO, the Crown Prosecution Service, DFID, the FCO, the Home Office, HM Treasury and the National Crime Agency.[15] The cooperation is intended to work toward:

- identifying who should be regarded as potential victims overseas, including an affected state;
- assessing the case for compensation;
- obtaining evidence which may include statements in support of compensation claims;
- ensuring the process for the payment of compensation is transparent, accountable and fair; and identifying a suitable means by which compensation can be paid to avoid the risk of further corruption.

---

15   The National Crime Agency (NCA) is a UK law enforcement agency responsible for serious organised crime. In 2015 the City of London Police overseas anti-corruption unit, along with the Metropolitan Police's international proceeds of corruption unit, was transferred to the NCA's Economic Crime Command to become the International Corruption Unit, funded largely by DFID.

The UK DPA policy itself is a work in progress. As an additional approach to investigations and sanctions it encourages self-reporting that should provide more evidence of wrongdoing than reactive investigations, and encourages good corporate conduct. It is also seen as mitigating risks associated with reputation, financial returns (DPAs may also assist in avoiding criminal convictions that would trigger debarment from contract competition at EU and international levels) and cost-effective policing. On the other hand, it is considered as having a lesser benefit to the taxpayer and the victims. Further, it is arguable that, in contrast with some of the grounds for a DPA, it has to date not necessarily made the investigative process shorter or less thorough.

The issue of assessing whether a DPA, predicated in assumptions or expectations of organisational culture and senior management changes, achieves this has yet to be fully tested. Current UK reliance on self-reporting is in contrast to a more inquisitive process under US DPAs. The US approach is much more rigorous in terms of implementation. The arrangements would normally cover training, procedural reforms (for example, changing the business model to delete or reduce the use of agents or brokers) and internal compliance changes (including hotline and whistleblowing arrangements). They also involve regular meetings with and submission of quantitative data to Department of Justice officials. Further, DPAs are invariably overseen by external consultants rather than being done in-house; not only is their involvement often open-ended in terms of costs and time commitments but also the general presumption is that they are keen to demonstrate to the Department their independence, thoroughness and expertise, to the point where they may appear to be acting as surrogate enforcers for the Department of Justice.

Claims for the advantages and disadvantages of introducing the UK DPA approach as opposed to the US approach – judicial oversight, compensation, transparency for the former, and full disclosure, reliance on a company's internal investigations, weaker breach requirements and no requirement for an admission of guilt in terms of the latter (see Corruption Watch, 2016: 20–23) – are not, however, as clear-cut as was first thought. In practice the three DPAs to 2017 show aspects of both advantages and disadvantages. One case remains anonymous because of continuing legal proceedings elsewhere. One – the ICBC Standard Bank case– included reparations in the form of compensation to the country concerned in terms of the difference between what the Tanzanian government received when fund raising by way of a sovereign note private placement after the bank bribed an intermediary company to win the contract, and what it could have received if it had used a more cost-effective intermediary. The ICBC DPA also names those involved (although a libel suit is now pending) and includes an external compliance review. In the case of Rolls Royce, the SFO began its enquiry not because the company self-reported but because it had been alerted to allegations of wrongdoing by public postings on the internet. In the DPA no company personnel or overseas public officials were named, and the significant financial sanctions were all remitted to HM Treasury.

### The reparation approach in the UK context

The point about describing the UK approach to DPAs is to emphasise that they are likely to be a permanent aspect of enforcement against corporate corruption. One consequence is that the DPA is likely to involve the availability of funds that could be available for reparations. After the BAE agreement there is also appetite for using the funds for purposes other than a simple remittance to the national Exchequer. UK agencies have worked toward a standard policy on what to do with the funds in terms of directed reparations. That policy references UNCAC, albeit this is derived more from chapter five of the Convention, which is on asset recovery. Further, the principle of return is being balanced by a perceived 'right' of victim countries to receive funds without qualifications but also a concern that the funds could then be corruptly appropriated. Thus, there are a number of models that offer a portfolio framework for reparation as the basis for some common standards; see Table 14.3.

All still come with their own sets of advantages and disadvantages. These may be grouped into a number of issues to be addressed before a uniform or effective implementation; see Table 14.4.

*Table 14.3* Standards for reparation

| *G8 Asset recovery initiative principles* | *Vehicles for return: options* |
|---|---|
| Principle 1: Transparency<br>Principle 2: Presumption of transfer<br>Principle 3: Case-specific treatment<br>Principle 4: Remedial objectives<br>Principle 5: Consistency and coordination<br>Principle 6: Encourage use of an agreement<br>Principle 7: Preclusion of benefit to offenders | • Pure country system (no additional measures): return with no conditions or framework<br>• General budget: assess the quality of expenditure and the soundness of budget processes and institutions as a whole<br>• Earmarking or tagging of expenditures: allocate additional resources to specific sectors or programmes, in which overall spending levels would be monitored to ensure the desired shift in budget composition<br>• Virtual fund: uses the existing budget system to tag and track spending items without setting up a separate institutional arrangement<br>• Extra-budgetary funds (EBFs) and forfeiture funds<br>• Ring-fencing/case-by-case: resources are allocated to specific or preferred projects following a completely off-budget procedure<br>• Stand-alone assets fund: resources to multiple users, reporting to funder countries<br>• Enhancing existing funds: using existing funds with similar goals and established procedures, such as the Siemens Integrity Initiative or the Millennium Development Fund<br>• Multilateral third party: enhancing existing World Bank, UN or other developmental programmes |

Source: World Bank/StAR, 2009b and interview.

*Table 14.4* Implementation issues

| Principles | The balance of returning and receiving countries' expectations | Vehicles for delivery |
|---|---|---|
| • The clarity of objectives and management<br>• Direct connectivity between returned funds and ultimate use<br>• Difficulties of establishing gains or impact<br>• Identifying activities closest to original offences or corruption circumstances. | • A focus on own-country priorities or priorities of developmental agencies<br>• Involvement of other developed countries in shared funding vehicle choices<br>• Multiplicity of vehicles in a single recipient country<br>• Misuse by recipient countries<br>• An inability to identify added-value<br>• The role of civil society | • Heavy transaction costs required to set up and manage a new agency<br>• The costs of a transparent bidding and selection process for delivery of projects<br>• The importance of accounting and audit oversights<br>• Uncertainty over income streams; sustainability of funding initiatives<br>• Financial management processes (including the location of recipient account; type of corporate governance structure and arrangements; mechanism for disbursement; internal control mechanisms; accounting standards; financial reporting requirements; internal auditing mechanism; independent auditing arrangements; and access and dissemination of information) |

In particular is the question of reparation specifically to address anti-corruption work:

> [s]hould incremental resources be used to fight corruption? Should they be used as restoration to victims of human rights abuses – an issue that unfortunately is usually tied to grand corruption? Institutional arrangements and other political economy factors can certainly influence these decisions. Taking the argument a step further, if anticorruption efforts and law enforcement activities are identified as a corner stone against organised crime and grand corruption, why are these agencies so under-funded that they need earmarked resources or extra-budgetary funds to supplement their operations?
> (World Bank/StaR, 2009b: 5)

## Toward an effective anti-corruption resource

The debate on the most effective and cost-effective model for the disbursement of reparations from non-conviction settlements and sanctions is in its infancy, but a number of key points as to future direction may, in the light of the issues noted above, be made. The funds should not necessarily fall within the responsibility of agencies that lack the experience and expertise, but neither should they become the resource for a small group of anti-corruption NGOs. Funds should be used transparently and those responsible held accountable; the funds should be focused on anti-corruption work in those countries where the corporate misconduct was alleged to have taken place.

The funds should be used to promote anti-corruption capacity, commitment and competences for those in victim countries and internationally whose work and interests may be necessary to hold corporate activity to account – whether parliamentarians, government agencies, NGOs, journalists, etc. – in ways not traditionally supported by donor or recipient countries. A competitive process, with appropriate cost-effective financial management and audit capabilities, should be overseen by independent monitoring and evaluation arrangements.

There are existing UK not-for-profit bodies and educational institutions that could provide – singly or collectively – the necessary organisational components for such a framework or network; a number also have the necessary anti-corruption experience and expertise that would allow them to analyse existing research for suitable areas for support and have the in-house capacity to exercise an informed judgement and overview of bids, added benefit, innovation, implementation and evaluation.

The overall point about such an approach is that the funds may be better used as an additional resource in what is a highly competitive funding environment for anti-corruption resources, but that access to more resources should not only extend the opportunity but also allow for diversity and innovation in new or expanded anti-corruption initiatives. It could also better emphasise the relationship between the offending corporate conduct and their funds being used for remedial or restorative consequences concerning the circumstances or location of the misconduct.

## Conclusion

It can be argued that reparations funded by non-conviction settlements and sanctions could be made available for directed reparations promoting anti-corruption work and could be a useful source for the significant numbers of anti-corruption organisations and initiatives seeking support, particularly in terms of both innovation and sustainability. At present, however, the continuation of the various current ad hoc and uncoordinated approaches to corporate reparation have the potential to be more concerned with the integrity of recycling funds from bribery settlements to enhance corporate reputations, if there is corporate involvement, maintain donor income streams if developmental agencies are involved, or become a captive resource if NGOs are involved, than to address the circumstances that led to the bribery in the first place in the countries where it was alleged to have occurred.

The answer as to who should be responsible for any settlement funds, to what anti-corruption purpose and to what assessment criteria is clearly complicated by a number of qualifications. None of the delivery options to date are problem-free, and the absence of detailed independent evaluation and financial management information does not help decisions on what options have been the most effective for anti-corruption work in the countries concerned, the best value-for-money and had the greatest anti-corruption impact. Further, where evidence of successful delivery, if not impact, is available, it often applies to initiatives whose relation to anti-corruption is elastic, to say the least.

In terms of the emerging UK DPA-linked reparations approach, the UK framework is likely to recognise a number of key components. The approach has to be based on a partnership with the receiving country, initiated as soon as possible and managed by the governments concerned with quick agreement on single points of contact, expectations on what is being returned, why and for what purposes, assurances on avoiding any misuse of returned assets, and arrangements on transparency and accountability. The uses should be, as far as is practically possible, focused on anti-corruption work that will promote the capacity, commitment and competences of groups and individuals in 'victim' countries not necessarily supported by more orthodox developmental and donor sources. If that were to be the outcome of any debate on reparations, then corporate misconduct could have a pay-back impact that is already an established feature of the UK domestic criminal justice system and will also facilitate the work of international conventions such as UNCAC.

## Bibliography

Amezcua-Noriega, O. (2011). *Reparation Principles under International Law and their Possible Application by the International Criminal Court: Some Reflections. Briefing Paper No.1.* Colchester, UK: Essex Transitional Justice Network; Reparations Unit.

Burchell, K. (2014). *Primary Education Support Programme (PESP) Tanzania: Case Study Report.* www.heart-resources.org/wp-content/uploads/2015/01/PESP-Full-report-Final-for-web.pdf. Accessed 20 December 2017.

Corruption Watch. (2016). *Out of Court, Out of Mind: Do Deferred Prosecution Agreements and Corporate Settlements Fail to Deter Overseas Corruption?* London: Corruption Watch (www.cw-uk.org).

DataVision International Ltd. (2014). *BAE Radar Change Books Delivery Monitoring: Report and Analysis.* Dar-es-Salaam: DataVison International Ltd.

House of Commons International Development Committee. (2011). *Financial Crime and Development.* Eleventh Report of Session 2010–12. Volume I: *Report, together with formal minutes, oral and written evidence.* London: TSO.

IREX. (2015). *The BOTA Foundation: Final Summative Report.* Washington, DC: IREX.

Itad. (2013). *Joint Evaluation of Budget Support to Tanzania: Lessons Learned and Recommendations for the Future. Final Report: Volume 1.* Hove: Itad.

Jimu, I. (2009). *Managing Proceeds of Asset Recovery: The Case of Nigeria, Peru, the Philippines and Kazakhstan.* Working Paper Series No 6. Basel: International Centre for Asset Recovery.

Lord, N. (2015). *Deferred Prosecution Agreements (DPAs): A 'Legitimate' Enforcement Response?* Cambridge International Symposium for Economic Crime, September 2015.

Lord, N. (2016). Establishing enforcement legitimacy in the pursuit of rule-breaking 'global elites': The case of transnational corporate bribery. *Theoretical Criminology* 20(3): 376–399.

Lord, N. and Levi, M. (2017). In pursuit of the proceeds of transnational corporate bribery: The UK experience to date, in C. King, C. Walker and J. Gurule (eds), *The Handbook of Criminal and Terrorist Financing Law*. Basingstoke, UK: Palgrave Macmillan.

Makinwa, A. O. (ed.). (2015). *Negotiated Settlements for Corruption Offences*. The Hague: Eleven International Publishing.

OECD. (2012). *Liability for Environmental Damage In Eastern Europe, Caucasus and Central Asia (EECCA): Implementation of good international practices*. Paris: OECD.

OECD. (2014a). *OECD Foreign Bribery Report: An analysis of the crime of bribery of foreign public officials*. Paris: OECD.

OECD. (2014b). *OECD Working Group on Bribery. Annual Report*. Paris: OECD.

OECD. (2015). *Working Group on Bribery: 2014 Data on Enforcement of the Anti-Bribery Convention*. Paris: OECD.

Pachaeco, C. and Balasubramanian, S. (2015). *Achieving Development Impact with an Inclusive Asset-Return Model: The Case of the BOTA Foundation in Kazakhstan*. Washington: IREX.

de Simone, F. and Zagaris, B. (2014). *Impact of Foreign Bribery Legislation on Developing Countries and the Role of Donor Agencies*. Bergen, Norway: U4.

Taylor, B. (2012). *BAE Payment to Tanzania Undermines Justice and Accountability*. www.theguardian.com/global-development/poverty-matters/2012/mar/20/bae-payment-tanzania-justice-accountability. Accessed 20 December 2017.

Trace International. (2015). *Global Enforcement Report 2014*. Annapolis, MD: TRACE International

Uhlmann, D. M. (2013). Deferred prosecution and non-prosecution agreements and the erosion of corporate criminal liability. *Maryland Law Review* 72(4): 1295–1344.

World Bank/StAR. (2009a). *Stolen Asset Recovery. Management of Returned Assets: Policy Considerations*. Washington, DC: World Bank.

World Bank/StAR. (2009b). *Proceeds of Corruption: Frameworks for the Management of Returned Assets. Draft Concept Note*. Washington, DC: World Bank.

World Bank and UNODC/StAR. (2014). *Left out of the Bargain. Settlements in Foreign Bribery Cases and Implications for Asset Recovery*. Washington, DC: StAR.

# Index

Italicised and bold page numbers refer to figures and tables respectively. Page numbers referring to notes are followed by 'n' and note number.

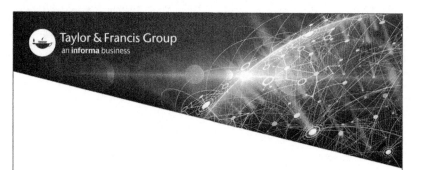